Surviving Schizophrenia:

A Manual for Families, Consumers, and Providers

Third Edition

E. Fuller Torrey, M.D.

HarperPerennial
A Division of HarperCollinsPublishers

This edition is dedicated to Pete and Nancy Domenici for their outstanding leadership and to Ted and Vada Stanley for their extraordinary generosity in supporting research. These four people have provided immeasurable hope to those who suffer from serious mental illness and to their families.

Permissions acknowledgments appear on pages 362–398.

HarperCollins books may be purchased for educational, business or sales promotional use. For information, please write: Special Markets Department, HarperCollins Publishers, Inc., 10 East 53rd Street, New York, NY 10022.

ISBN 0-06-095076-5

95 96 97 98 ❖/RRD 10 9 8 7 6 5

As for me, you must know that I shouldn't precisely have chosen madness if there had been any choice.

Vincent Van Gogh, 1889,
in a letter to his brother, written
while he was involuntarily
confined in the psychiatric
hospital at St.-Remy

I don't want nor need lachrymose pity,
Nor disguised papier mache contempt or religious piety,
Nor fear in most subtle forms;
No, no—let me rise independently
With pharmaceutical help
From the mat swollen with blood and sweat and rejection,
To do what I was born to do,
And with deep appreciation of those
Who, in the stands, outside necessarily,
The experiential epistemology, the agony,
Appreciate the strength, courage, *passion* of the combat.
I appreciate your appreciation of my
Guts, my gifts, feral courage, reddening rages,
In fighting this vortex of madness.

Bill Hensleigh, consumer, 1992,
from his poem "To Winifred, With Love"

CONTENTS

Illustrations   xii

Preface to the Third Edition   xiii

Preface to the First Edition   xv

Acknowledgments   xvii

1. DIMENSIONS OF THE DISASTER   1

   How Many People Have Schizophrenia in the United States?   6

   Where Are They?   8

   How Many People Have Schizophrenia Elsewhere in the World?   12

   Is Schizophrenia Increasing or Decreasing?   14

   What Is the Cost of Schizophrenia?   15

   Is Schizophrenia of Recent Origin?   18

   Deinstitutionalization: A Cradle for Catastrophe   21

2. THE INNER WORLD OF MADNESS:

   VIEW FROM THE INSIDE   27

   Alterations of the Senses   30

   Inability to Interpret and Respond   38

Delusions and Hallucinations   49

Altered Sense of Self   62

Changes in Emotions   64

Changes in Movements   69

Changes in Behavior   70

3. THE DIAGNOSIS OF SCHIZOPHRENIA:
   VIEW FROM THE OUTSIDE   83

Defining Schizophrenia   84

Schizophrenia Subtypes and Paranoid Disorders   87

Schizoaffective Disorder   89

Where Does Schizophrenia Begin? Schizotypal,
   Paranoid, and Schizoid Personality Disorders   90

Onset and Early Symptoms   93

Male-Female Differences   95

Childhood Schizophrenia   96

Late-Onset Schizophrenia   98

What Is the Ideal Diagnostic Workup?   98

4. WHAT SCHIZOPHRENIA IS NOT   104

A "Split Personality"   104

Mental Retardation   105

Manic-Depressive Psychosis   105

Borderline Personality Disorder   108

Brief Psychotic Disorder   109

Street Drug Psychosis   110

Prescription Drug Psychosis   111

Psychosis Due to Other Diseases   114

Psychosis Following Childbirth   117

Psychosis Following Trauma   118

Infantile Autism   119

Culturally Induced or Hysterical Psychosis 120

Creativity, Schizophrenia, and Famous People 121

5. PROGNOSIS AND POSSIBLE COURSES 125

Predictors of Outcome 125

Possible Courses: Ten Years Later 129

Possible Courses: Thirty Years Later 133

Why Do People with Schizophrenia Die at a Younger Age? 136

6. WHAT CAUSES SCHIZOPHRENIA? 139

What Is Known 141

Major Theories 154

Minor Theories 160

Obsolete Theories 164

Funding for Schizophrenia Research 171

7. THE TREATMENT OF SCHIZOPHRENIA 174

How to Find a Good Doctor 175

Hospitalization: Voluntary and Involuntary 179

Alternatives to Hospitalization 187

Antipsychotic Drug Treatment 189

Other Drugs Used to Treat Schizophrenia 210

Cost of Medications and Use of Generics 215

Nondrug Treatments of Schizophrenia 217

8. THE REHABILITATION OF SCHIZOPHRENIA 219

Medication and Counseling 220

Money, Food, and Housing 224

Employment 230

Friendship 234

Medical Care 236

Services for Children 237

Services in Rural Areas 238

Examples of Good Services   240

Quality of Life Measures   246

The Need for Asylum   247

9. SIX MAJOR PROBLEMS   250

Cigarettes and Coffee   250

Alcohol and Street Drugs   253

Sex, Pregnancy, and AIDS   256

Medication Noncompliance   261

Assaultive and Violent Behavior   268

Suicide   270

10. QUESTIONS ASKED BY CONSUMERS AND FAMILIES   274

Does Schizophrenia Change the Underlying Personality?   274

Are People with Schizophrenia Responsible for Their Behavior? 276

What Should Be the Right Attitude Toward the Disease?   279

How Can Relapses Be Reduced?   287

How Can Consumers Survive Schizophrenia?   290

How Can Families Survive Schizophrenia?   292

Is EE Expressed Emotion or Erudite Eructations?   301

What Is the Effect of Schizophrenia on Siblings, Children,

and Spouses?   303

Should People with Schizophrenia Drive Motor Vehicles?   306

What About Safety Issues?   307

How Do Religious Issues Affect People with Schizophrenia?   308

Why Is Confidentiality a Problem?   310

Should You Tell People That You Have Schizophrenia?   311

Genetic Counseling: What Are the Chances

of Getting Schizophrenia?   312

What Will Happen When the Parents Die?   314

11. HOW TO BE AN ADVOCATE   318

The Politics of Neglect   319

How to Decrease Stigma   321

How to Advocate for More Research   324

How to Improve Services   325

How to Organize for Advocacy   329

Appendix A: Readings on Schizophrenia:

  The 15 Best and the 15 Worst   331

Appendix B: Useful Videotapes   341

Appendix C: Useful Resources on Schizophrenia   347

Listing of the Best Journals to Read to Keep

  Up with What Is Going On   347

How to Get Information on Specific

  Interest Groups and Activities   348

Courses for Education on Schizophrenia   350

Addresses of Consumer Provider Training Programs   351

Addresses of Exemplary Clubhouses

  (Fountain House Model)   352

Addresses of Exemplary Continuous

  Treatment Teams (PACT Model)   353

Appendix D: Contacts for the Alliance

  for the Mentally Ill by State   356

Notes   362

Index   399

ILLUSTRATIONS

PHOTOGRAPHS
Works of art illustrating some symptoms of schizophrenia:
    Vincent van Gogh, "Starry Night" (1889)   78
    Joan Miró, "Head of a Catalan Peasant" (1924)   78
    Pablo Picasso, "Nude Woman" (1910)   79
    Marcel Duchamp, "Nude Descending a Staircase" (1912)   79
    Henri Rousseau, "The Dream" (1910)   80
    Edvard Munch, "The Scream" (1895)   80
MRIs from two sets of identical twins in which one has
    schizophrenia and the other is well   144
Identical microscopic sections from brains of normal control and
    person with schizophrenia showing impaired development of
    hippocampus   145

OTHER
Distribution of the 1.8 million persons with schizophrenia   10
Inpatients in public mental hospitals per 100,000 total population
    in the United States, 1830–1950.
The magnitude of deinstitutionalization: number of patients in
    public mental hospitals, 1950–1991   23
The course of schizophrenia   131
Location of the limbic system in the brain   141
Map showing location of some exemplary clubhouses, continuous
    treatment teams, and comprehensive treatment programs   243
Rex Morgan, M.D., educates the public about schizophrenia   325

PREFACE TO THE THIRD EDITION

Profound changes have taken place in schizophrenia research since the first edition of this book was published in 1982. Research on brain structure and function has conclusively demonstrated that it is a brain disease. Tantalizing clues to a definitive etiology emerge at an increasingly rapid rate from genetics, neurochemistry, virology, neuropathology, and epidemiology. Developmental studies have proven that some cases of schizophrenia begin early in life, perhaps even *in utero*. Research funds have increased sharply from the National Institute of Mental Health, and new research money has become available from the National Alliance for Research on Schizophrenia and Depression (NARSAD) and the Theodore and Vada Stanley Foundation. New drugs, such as clozapine and risperidone, have become available, public education has increased, and stigma has decreased. This is the good news.

The bad news is that services for individuals with schizophrenia continue to be mediocre on the best of days and disgraceful on the worst. The large number of individuals with schizophrenia who are homeless or in jails is appalling. The quality of most outpatient services, housing, and rehabilitation services is a national embarrassment. Clearly there is much work to be done. Improvements will come about through combined advocacy efforts of individuals who are afflicted and their families under the National Alliance for the Mentally Ill (NAMI).

This edition of *Surviving Schizophrenia* summarizes these changes. The new subtitle—*A Manual for Families, Consumers, and Providers*—reflects the increasingly important roles that are being played by individuals who are afflicted with this disease and by those who treat it. I use the word "consumer" because it is preferred in the United States by many of those who have schizophrenia. Personally I do not like the term and think that "sufferer," the term used in England, more accurately conveys the cruelty of this disease.

Most important, there is now more hope than there has ever been—hope for research breakthroughs, hope for better treatments, hope for better lives. Such hope will drive us forward until it is realized.

PREFACE TO THE FIRST EDITION

"Your daughter has schizophrenia," I told the woman.

"Oh, my god, anything but that," she replied. "Why couldn't she have leukemia or some other disease instead?"

"But if she had leukemia she might die," I pointed out. "Schizophrenia is a much more treatable disease."

The woman looked sadly at me, then down at the floor. She spoke softly. "I would still prefer that my daughter had leukemia."

This book is a product of a thousand such conversations. Conceived in the darkness of despair, it was fathered by education and mothered by hope. It is written for families whose lives are currently touched by schizophrenia. My sister is afflicted; perhaps your brother, aunt, or son is also. The book provides a scientific framework for understanding its symptoms, causes, and treatment and suggests how families can come to terms with the disease. Above all, the book tries to dispel the multitude of myths and alleviate the millstone of guilt which families have been condemned to carry by mental health professionals; surely this has been Original Psychiatric Sin.

Schizophrenia is a cruel disease. The lives of those affected are often chronicles of constricted experiences, muted emotions, missed opportunities, unfulfilled expectations. It leads to a twilight existence, a twentieth-century underground man. The fate of these patients has been worsened by our propensity to misunderstand, our failure to provide adequate treatment and rehabilitation, our meager research efforts. A disease which should be found, in the phrase of T. S. Eliot, in the "frigid purgatorial fires" has become through our ignorance and neglect a living hell.

Perhaps it is a disease whose time has come. There are rays of hope—research, treatment, the organizations of families and friends. If this book contributes just a little toward bringing schizophrenia out of the Slough of Despond and into the mainstream of American medicine then it will have accomplished its purpose.

ACKNOWLEDGMENTS

I continue to be indebted to many people for this book. Lou AvRutick originally found it a home at HarperCollins where Carol Cohen nurtured it to maturity. The library staffs at the NIMH Neuroscience Center and St. Elizabeths Hospital have assisted with the research, and Laurie Flynn and the staff of the National Alliance for the Mentally Ill have been unfailingly helpful. Portions of this edition were reviewed by Drs. Faith Dickerson, Frederick Frese, David Shore, and Mr. Edward Francell and I am grateful for their suggestions. Judy Miller typed this edition, substantially improving the manuscript in the process. Above all I continue to be indebted to my wife, Barbara, for the essential but ineffable ingredients that make writing a book possible.

I am also grateful to the following:

Joseph H. Berke for permission to reprint excerpts from *Mary Barnes: Two Accounts of a Journey Through Madness.*

Malcolm B. Bowers and Science Press for permission to reprint excerpts from *Retreat from Sanity: The Structure of Emerging Psychosis.*

Eliot T. O. Slater for permission to reprint excerpts from *Clinical Psychiatry.*

Andrew McGhie and The British Psychological Society for permission to reprint excerpts from an article in the *British Journal of Medical Psychology.*

British Journal of Psychiatry for permission to reprint excerpts from an article by James Chapman.

Journal of Abnormal and Social Psychology for permission to reprint excerpts from an article by Anonymous.

Anchor Press and Doubleday for permission to reprint excerpts from *These Are My Sisters,* by Lara Jefferson.

Presses Universitaires de France for permission to reprint excerpts from *Autobiography of a Schizophrenic Girl,* by Marguerite Sechehaye.

W. W. Norton and Company for permission to reprint excerpts from *In a Darkness,* by James A. Wechsler.

National Schizophrenia Fellowship for permission to reprint excerpts from *Coping with Schizophrenia,* by H. R. Rollin.

G. P. Putnam and Sons for permission to reprint excerpts from *This Stranger, My Son,* by Louise Wilson.

University Books for permission to reprint excerpts from *The Witnesses,* by Thomas Hennell.

J. G. Hall and *Lancet* for permission to quote from an article.

Nancy J. Hermon and Colin M. Smith for permission to quote from a presentation at the 1986 Alberta Schizophrenia Conference.

Psychological Bulletin and *Schizophrenia Bulletin* for permission to quote from articles.

Mrs. Gilda Nelson for permission to quote from poems by her deceased son, Robert L. Nelson.

Dr. Bernhard Bogerts for permission to utilize photographs of the brain.

North America Syndicate for permission to reprint the 1990 comic strip of Rex Morgan, M.D.

Bill Hensleigh for permission to quote from his poem "To Winifred, With Love," 1992.

Surviving Schizophrenia

The purpose of this book is to make you aware of the progress of schizophrenia and the possible ways in which it may develop. The assessment of symptoms requires an expert. For proper diagnosis and therapy of all symptoms, real or apparent, connected with schizophrenia, please consult your doctor. In my discussion of cases, I have changed all names and identifying details while preserving the integrity of the research findings.

1

DIMENSIONS OF THE DISASTER

Schizophrenia is to psychiatry what cancer is to medicine: a sentence as well as a diagnosis.

W. Hall, G. Andrews, and G. Goldstein,
Australian and New Zealand Journal of Psychiatry, 1985

Schizophrenia, I said. The word itself is ominous. It has been called "one of the most sinister words in the language." It has a bite to it, a harsh grating sound that evokes visions of madness and asylums. It is not fluid like *demence,* the word from which "dementia" comes. Nor is it a visual word like *ecrasse,* the origin of "cracked," meaning that the person was like a cracked pot. Nor is it romantic like "lunatic," meaning fallen under the influence of the moon (which in Latin is *luna*). "Schizophrenia" is a discordant and cruel term, just like the disease it signifies.

Our treatment of individuals with this disease has, all too often, also been discordant and cruel. It is in fact the single biggest blemish on the face of contemporary American medicine and social services; when the social history of our era is written, the plight of persons with schizophrenia will be recorded as having been a national scandal. Consider the current dimensions of the disaster.

1. *There are as many individuals with schizophrenia homeless and living on the streets as there are in all hospitals.* Studies of homeless individuals in the United States have estimated their total number to be between 250,000 and 550,000. A median estimate of 400,000 would be consistent with the data from most of the studies. Studies have also reported that approximately one-third of homeless individuals are seriously mentally ill, the vast

majority of them with schizophrenia. It is likely, therefore, that on any given day approximately 100,000 persons with schizophrenia are living in public shelters and on the streets. As will be described below, there are only approximately 100,000 people with schizophrenia in all hospitals at any given time.

2. *There are as many individuals with schizophrenia in jails and prisons as there are in all hospitals.* A 1992 survey of American jails reported that 7.2 percent of the inmates were overtly and seriously mentally ill. A shocking 29 percent of the jails acknowledged holding such individuals *with no charges* against them whatsoever, often awaiting a bed in a psychiatric hospital. The vast majority of those who do have charges have been charged with misdemeanors such as trespassing. The Los Angeles County Jail is now *de facto* the largest mental institution in the country. A study of American prisons concluded that 10 to 15 percent of the inmates have "thought disorder or mood disorder and need the services usually associated with severe and chronic mental illness." In 1991 there were a total of approximately 1.2 million individuals in jails and prisons in the United States. If patients with more covert symptoms of schizophrenia are also included, it would seem reasonable to estimate that approximately eight percent of all inmates have schizophrenia, which would mean that at any given time 100,000 individuals with schizophrenia are in jails and prisons.

3. *There are increasing episodes of violence committed by individuals with schizophrenia who are not being treated.* Individuals with schizophrenia who take medications are not more violent than the general population. Recent studies have shown, however, that some individuals with schizophrenia who are not taking medication *are* more violent. In one study nine percent of individuals with schizophrenia who were living in the community had used a weapon in a fight in the preceding year. In another study "27 percent of released male and female patients report at least one violent act within a mean of four months after [hospital] discharge." Assaults against family members by individuals with schizophrenia have also risen sharply. Drug and alcohol abuse and noncompliance with medications both appear to be important factors in increasing violent behavior in this population.

4. *There are increasing episodes of violence committed against individuals with schizophrenia.* Most crimes against individuals with schizophrenia are not reported; in those instances in which they are reported they are often ignored by officials. Purse snatchings and the stealing of disability checks are common, but rapes and even murders are not rare. In Massachusetts, when two mentally ill homeless individuals were savagely beaten to death by three teenagers, the newspaper editorialized: "The street people, among the most helpless of adult human beings ... are rabbits forced to live in company with dogs." In California, a boarding home operator was accused of killing nine tenants, some of whom had schizophrenia, in order to cash their disability checks.

5. *Housing for many individuals with schizophrenia is often abysmal.* Because of pressure from state departments of mental health to discharge patients from state hospitals, seriously mentally ill individuals are frequently placed into housing that would not be considered fit for anyone else. For example, in 1979 the police removed 21 "ex-mental patients" living in New York City board-and-care homes "amid broken plumbing, rotting food and roaches ... The police found the decaying corpse of a former patient lying undisturbed in one home inhabited by six other residents." Similar reports continued throughout the 1980s, and in 1990 the *New York Times* headlined still another report: "Mental Homes Are Wretched, A Panel Says." In Mississippi "9 ex-patients" were found in a primitive shed with "no toilet or running water" and "guarded by two vicious dogs" to insure that they did not run away.

6. *Many individuals with schizophrenia revolve between hospitals, jails, and shelters.* Because of the failure of mental health professionals to provide medications and insure aftercare for discharged patients, many individuals with schizophrenia undergo a revolving door of admissions and readmissions to hospitals, jails, and public shelters. In Illinois 30 percent of patients discharged from state psychiatric hospitals are rehospitalized within 30 days. In New York 60 percent of discharged patients are rehospitalized with a year. A study of readmissions to state psychiatric hospitals found patients with schizophrenia who had been readmitted as many as 121 times. The jail survey referred

to above identified individuals with schizophrenia who had been jailed as many as 80 times. Between hospitalizations and jailings these individuals consume inordinate amounts of police and social service time and resources. For example, in Los Angeles a 1993 study found that policemen had to respond to a "mental health crisis" call equally as often as they had to respond to a robbery call. Hospital, jail, shelter, and back around again in random order—it is an endless revolving door odyssey.

7. *Schizophrenia is remarkably neglected by mental health professionals.* Despite an increase in total psychiatrists, psychologists, and psychiatric social workers from approximately 9,000 in 1940 to over 200,000 in 1993, schizophrenia has been remarkably neglected by these professionals. For example, a study published in 1994 reported that only *three percent* of all patients seen by psychiatrists in private office practice have a diagnosis of schizophrenia. One major reason for the failure of mental health professionals to treat patients with schizophrenia is the shockingly poor preparation they receive in their training programs. State psychiatric hospitals frequently must fill their positions with poorly trained and/or incompetent professionals; indeed, Wyoming State Hospital went for almost a year without a single psychiatrist on its staff. Many Community Mental Health Centers (CMHCs), originally conceived and funded to provide care for seriously mentally ill individuals being discharged from psychiatric hospitals, merely evolved into counseling centers to do personality polishing for the "worried well." Some CMHCs also built swimming pools with federal funds and paid their administrators handsomely. In 1989 three administrators at a Utah CMHC were charged with 117 counts of felony for paying themselves $3.6 million over five years. In 1990 the executive director of a CMHC in Fort Worth was indicted on four counts of felony theft. These stolen funds are but a fraction of the resources that were originally intended for individuals with serious mental illnesses such as schizophrenia but which have been diverted, legally or illegally, to other purposes.

8. *Half the individuals with schizophrenia are receiving no treatment at any given time.* A recent report for the National Institute of Mental Health Epidemiologic Catchment Area (ECA) survey

revealed that only 60 percent of individuals with schizophrenia receive any psychiatric or medical care within a one-year period. At any given time within that year some of that 60 percent are receiving no treatment. A community survey in Baltimore found that half of all persons with schizophrenia were receiving no treatment for their illness. A major reason for this remarkably low treatment rate has been changes in laws making involuntary hospitalization and treatment more difficult to effect for individuals who have no insight into their need for treatment. Sadly misguided civil rights lawyers and "patient advocates" regularly defend individuals' right to be psychotic; the thinking of the lawyers and advocates is more thought-disordered than the people they are defending. For example, in Wisconsin a public defender argued that an individual with schizophrenia who was mute and eating his feces was not a danger to himself; the judge accepted the defense and released the man.

The disastrous care and treatment of individuals with schizophrenia is not unique to the United States, although it is probably worse in this country than in most other developed nations. Many Canadian provinces are proceeding with deinstitutionalization along the same lines as pioneered by the United States, and conditions in Ontario have especially deteriorated. England has had a series of homicides by discharged patients who were not receiving treatment, and mentally ill homeless individuals have increased markedly in Australia and France. Italy passed a law in 1978 prohibiting new admissions to psychiatric hospitals and, except in Verona and Trieste where community treatment facilities are good, the "Italian experiment" as it is known has been a massive failure. Japan puts individuals with schizophrenia into private hospitals, which are often owned by the doctors themselves, and keeps them there so that the patients' families will not be embarrassed; this abuse was so widespread that an international commission investigated it in 1986. The former Soviet Union was notorious for labeling political dissidents as having schizophrenia and involuntarily hospitalizing them. Nowhere in the world has the treatment of schizophrenia been without major problems, although the Scandinavian nations in general probably come closest to achieving a reasonable level of care.

HOW MANY PEOPLE HAVE SCHIZOPHRENIA
IN THE UNITED STATES?

Of all the people alive in the United States today, approximately 3.7 million have suffered or will suffer from schizophrenia sometime during their lifetimes (1.5 percent lifetime prevalence). At any given time approximately 1.8 million Americans are affected with the disease, which is one percent of all adults age 18 and over; 1.8 million people is the same number as those who live in West Virginia, and *more* people than live in 16 other states. It is also approximately the same number of people as those who live in Miami, Cleveland, Denver, San Francisco, or Seattle. Imagine that today every single person in West Virginia, or in one of these cities, has schizophrenia and you begin to realize the magnitude of the tragedy.

It should be emphasized that the 1.8 million includes *only* people with schizophrenia. It does not include 1.1 million more people who have manic-depressive disorder, or an even larger number with severe depression or obsessive-compulsive disorder. It is now widely accepted that on any given day at least 4 to 5 million people in the United States have a serious mental illness, including schizophrenia. But these are just numbers, like the number of people killed in an earthquake in Turkey or a flood in Bangladesh. They fail to convey the human sufferings and personal tragedies that accompany the event both for those affected and for those around them.

Another way to express the prevalence of schizophrenia at any given time is the number of individuals affected per 1,000 total population. In the United States that figure is 7.2 per 1,000. This means that a town of 3,000 people has approximately 21 cases of schizophrenia, while a city of 3 million people will have over 21,000 cases. These are just averages, for it appears that there are considerable variations in the prevalence rates in different parts of the United States and among different population groups.

The study from which the 7.2 per 1,000 prevalence figure was derived was the five-site Epidemiologic Catchment Area (ECA) study carried out by the National Institute of Mental Health between 1980 and 1984. Considerable variation in the prevalence of schizophrenia was found in that study, with researchers in New Haven, Baltimore, and Durham and its surrounding counties reporting a schizophrenia prevalence rate twice as high as was reported in St. Louis or among non-Hispanic residents of Los Angeles. The prevalence of schizophrenia among Hispanic residents of Los Angeles was less than half that of non-Hispanic residents, confirming the comparatively low prevalence of schizophrenia found in a previous study of Mexican-American residents of Texas.

There are other groups in America that also appear to have a low prevalence of schizophrenia. An extensive study of the rural, communal-living Hutterites published in 1955 reported a schizophrenia prevalence of only 1.1 per 1,000; a recent preliminary follow-up suggested that the Hutterites have continued to have a very low rate of schizophrenia. Studies of the rural Amish have also reported few cases of schizophrenia but a higher rate of manic-depressive disorder. There have also been impressions reported for over a hundred years that American Indians have a comparatively low prevalence of schizophrenia but this has yet to be verified by careful study.

One of the most clearly established differences in schizophrenia prevalence in the United States is a higher prevalence in urban than in rural areas. This was evident in a census study as early as 1850 and has been found in virtually every study done since that time. A small part of this urban excess is owing to people who have schizophrenia moving from rural areas to the cities, but the majority of the excess cannot be explained in this way. A recent study in Stockholm, Sweden, for example, found that having been raised in the city, rather than moving there later, increased one's risk for developing schizophrenia. In the ECA study in North Carolina, the prevalence of schizophrenia in Durham was almost twice that of the rural surrounding counties; this 2 to 1 urban to rural ratio is consistent with other studies. It is also probably the main reason why more urbanized states have been repeatedly shown to have more schizophrenia in both census studies and hospitalization rate studies. Schizophrenia has also been shown to occur in higher prevalence among the poorest, lowest-socioeconomic people in urban areas, but this socioeconomic difference is less marked in more rural areas.

Since large numbers of African Americans live in the poorer sections of large cities, it is not surprising to find that African Americans as a whole have a higher rate of schizophrenia than whites. Five separate studies have confirmed this in highly urbanized states such as New York, Maryland, and Ohio. The higher rate of schizophrenia among African Americans holds up even when corrections are made for the age distribution of the population; thus in a very careful study in Rochester, New York, African Americans still had a schizophrenia rate one and one-half times that of whites.

When African Americans who live in rural areas are compared with whites who live in rural areas, however, the results are different. This was done in Texas and in Louisiana and no differences were found. This argues strongly against race as being the cause of the difference. Rather it suggests that it is because African Americans live in the inner city, and not because of their race, that they have a higher schizophrenia rate. Others have claimed that African Americans appear to have a higher rate of schizophrenia because most psychiatrists are white and unconsciously (or consciously) racist; such psychiatrists would more readily label an African American patient than a white patient as having schizophrenia. This may well be so and is impossible to measure. Even if it were so, however, it would explain only a small portion of the differences, and we are left with the fact that poor people in inner cities, whatever their race, have a disproportionately high schizophrenia rate.

WHERE ARE THEY?

If in fact there are 1.8 million Americans with schizophrenia, then why is the disease so invisible? It is invisible because we have become experts in hiding it. Schizophrenia lurks in the closets, hiding behind euphemisms like "nervous breakdown" or "bad case of nerves." It stands quietly behind lace curtains but nobody bothers to mention it. It is the aunt who used to live with them but then moved; what they don't add is that she moved to the state hospital. It is the son who got in trouble in late adolescence and is now said to be living in Pennsylvania; what they don't add is that he is committed to the state hospital there. It is the sister who tragically committed suicide over, it is rumored, a love affair; what they don't add is that she committed suicide because she was plagued by voices and chose not to live with her disease. We hide it, hoping nobody will tell, hoping nobody will find out. It is a stigma.

The stigma of schizophrenia makes it all the more tragic. Not only must persons affected and their families bear the disease itself, but they must bear the stigma of it as well. People with schizophrenia are the lepers of the twentieth century. The aunt, son, or sister hidden in the closet may be discovered at any minute, and then the word will be out. Disaster, Dishonor, Disgrace. The magnitude of schizophrenia as a national calamity is exceeded only by the magnitude of our ignorance in dealing with it.

There is remarkably little hard information on where many of the 1.8 million persons with schizophrenia in the United States are living or receiving care. The Director of the National Institute of Mental Health (NIMH), testifying before the Senate Committee on Appropriations in late 1986, said that NIMH could only account for 42 percent of such individuals; for the other 58 percent their living and care arrangements were unknown. This shocking admission, by the federal agency responsible for maintaining such information, marks one more indication of the neglect this disease has suffered.

If all current sources of information on persons with schizophrenia are synthesized, however, it is possible to construct a reasonably accurate picture of where they are living on any given day. The figure on the next page shows the whereabouts of the 1.8 million persons currently diagnosed with this disorder.

Institutionalized: 450,000. On any given day approximately 450,000 of the 1.8 million individuals with schizophrenia are living in various institutions or on the streets. These institutions include:

1. Hospitals: 100,000.

state psychiatric hospitals	55,000
private psychiatric hospitals	2,500
psychiatric wards of general hospitals	7,000
VA hospitals	5,500
inpatient units of mental health centers and similar institutions	2,000
"semihospitals" such as crisis beds, respite beds, institutions for mental disease, etc.	28,000
	100,000

The hospital estimates are based on a 1986 survey carried out by the National Institute of Mental Health. "Semihospitals" are a new and rapidly growing type of hospital in which seriously mentally ill individuals are maintained in a house or other structure in the

Distribution of the 1.8 Million Persons with Schizophrenia

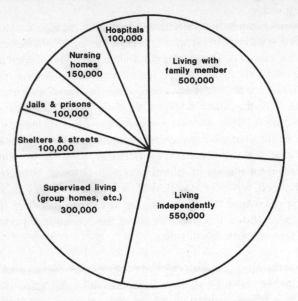

community with 24-hour nursing coverage. They function essentially as small psychiatric hospitals even though they are technically not classified as hospitals and have become popular because states can usually obtain partial federal reimbursement for patient costs, whereas they cannot do so if the same patients are in state psychiatric hospitals. The number of 28,000 "semihospital" beds for individuals with schizophrenia is an estimate.

2. *Nursing homes: 150,000.* There is estimated to be approximately 2.2 million individuals living in nursing homes in the United States. A 1988 survey of nursing homes in four cities reported that 5 percent of the residents had schizophrenia as a primary diagnosis. A 1993 random sampling of nursing home residents in Rochester, New York, found that 7.5 percent of them had a diagnosis of schizophrenia. These findings are consistent with older studies showing that approximately 8 percent of nursing home residents were "chronic mental patients, formerly residents of long-term psychiatric hospitals." Among nursing home residents under the age of 65 the percentage who have schizophrenia is approximately 33 percent.

3. Jails and prisons: 100,000. This is discussed above.

4. Public shelters and living on the streets: 100,000. This is discussed above.

Supervised living: 300,000. Supervised living arrangements for mentally ill individuals go by a variety of names including foster homes, family care homes, halfway houses, board-and-care homes, county homes, etc. The common denominator of them all is that the individual pays several hundred dollars a month (usually from their SSI or SSDI payments) and receives a room (often shared), three meals a day, and varying degrees of supervision for medication, keeping appointments, etc. As will be discussed in chapter 8 the quality of their facilities varies widely. Nobody knows precisely how many individuals with schizophrenia live in such facilities, but there are estimated to be approximately 600,000 individuals with all diagnoses living in such homes. Based on the rapidly increasing SSI and SSDI payments in recent years and on surveys of families with a seriously mentally ill relative, an estimate of 300,000 individuals with schizophrenia living in these facilities seems reasonable.

Living with family members: 500,000. A recent survey of members of the National Alliance for the Mentally Ill (NAMI) reported that 42 percent of the seriously mentally ill family members were living with a family member. It seems likely that NAMI members may be somewhat self-selected in having their ill family member live at home, and that the percentage of all individuals who live with family members is lower than this. An estimate of 500,000 seems reasonable.

Living independently: 550,000. The survey of NAMI members referred to above reported that 31 percent of the seriously mentally ill family members were living independently. It seems likely that NAMI members may include disproportionately few families of mentally ill individuals who are doing well and able to live independently, so an estimate of 550,000 such individuals seems reasonable. It should be added, however, that living "independently" may include a broad range of individuals, from those who are fully self-supporting and completely independent to individuals who live in their own apartment but whose family brings them food and provides care for them at least daily.

It should also be emphasized that this distribution of individuals with schizophrenia is a snapshot taken at a single point in time. Many of these individuals are almost constantly in motion from one venue to another. For example, it would not be unusual for an individual with schizophrenia, who had stopped taking his/her medicine and was therefore clinically deteriorating, to move from a supervised group home to the family home to a public shelter to jail to the psychiatric ward of a general hospital and back again to the group home all within a period of six months.

HOW MANY PEOPLE HAVE SCHIZOPHRENIA ELSEWHERE IN THE WORLD?

Studies comparing the prevalence of schizophrenia around the world have provided lively controversy among researchers. On one side are those who believe that most reported differences are methodological artifacts or of minor consequence; on the other side are those (including myself) who believe that the differences are real and may provide important clues regarding the causes of the disease. It should be pointed out, however, that all major diseases in which both genetic and nongenetic factors are thought to play a role show significant differences in geographic distribution. Heart disease varies approximately sixfold, rheumatoid arthritis tenfold, insulin-dependent diabetes thirtyfold, multiple sclerosis fiftyfold, and some cancers show even greater differences. Schizophrenia would be a unique disease if its prevalence was approximately the same everywhere in the world. The surprising finding, then, would be not that such differences exist, but rather that they did not exist.

By world standards the United States' schizophrenia prevalence rate of 7.2 per 1,000 is comparatively high. At the lower end of the spectrum are studies from countries such as Ghana, Botswana, Papua New Guinea, and Taiwan with prevalence rates of less than two per 1,000. Studies from Canada and from most European and Asian nations fall into the three to six per 1,000 prevalence range. In addition to the United States, countries that have reported schizophrenia prevalence rates higher than seven per 1,000 are Dominica, Ireland, Finland, and Sweden, with a study from northern Sweden reporting the highest rate (17 per 1,000).

Several studies of schizophrenia's prevalence have yielded especially interesting results. Careful studies in Croatia, for example, have shown that villages on the Istrian peninsula have a schizophrenia prevalence rate of 7.3 per 1,000 compared with villages 100 miles away that have a rate of only 2.9 per 1,000. In Micronesia two surveys found a fourfold difference among various islands from a low of 4.2 per 1,000 in the Marshall Islands to a high of 16.7 per 1,000 on Palau. In India nine separate studies have reported that the prevalence of schizophrenia is significantly higher among higher castes than among lower castes.

Ireland is another nation in which schizophrenia has been extensively studied because of reports dating to the last century of a high prevalence both among people who emigrated to other countries and among those who remained in Ireland. As early as 1808, it was claimed that in Ireland "insanity is a disease of as frequent occurrence as in any other country in Europe." Studies in the 1960s and 1970s established that Ireland had more hospitalized patients with schizophrenia than any country in the world and a three-county community case register reported a schizophrenia prevalence rate of 7.1 per 1,000 in one of the western counties. In 1982 I spent six months in western Ireland studying a small region thought to have an especially high prevalence of schizophrenia; its rate of 12.6 per 1,000 was more than twice that of the surrounding area. This 1982 study also indicated that the high schizophrenia rate in Ireland existed only in older people and not among younger people; subsequent studies have since confirmed that the Irish schizophrenia prevalence rate is lower for individuals born after 1940.

In recent years much interest has been generated by studies of schizophrenia among Caribbean immigrants to England. Such immigrants have been found to have a high schizophrenia prevalence rate that exists not only in the immigrants themselves but also in their offspring born in England. Studies in Jamaica, the country of origin of the largest number of Caribbean immigrants, suggest that the schizophrenia rate there is not especially high. However, a study of Dominica, which provides only a small percentage of the immigrants, did report a high schizophrenia prevalence on that island.

These are intriguing observations and, in my opinion, may offer important clues to the mystery of schizophrenia. If we can understand why the Caribbean immigrants or the western Irish or the Croatian villagers have more than their share of schizophrenia, or why the Hutterites have less than their share, then we may better understand its causes. Sadly, however, this research area has been relatively neglected, especially in the United States.

IS SCHIZOPHRENIA INCREASING OR DECREASING?

As noted above, there is evidence in Ireland that the prevalence rate of schizophrenia has decreased in recent decades. Since 1985 similar results have been published from studies in Scotland, England, Denmark, Australia, and New Zealand. The average decrease in schizophrenia in these studies is 35 percent over a 10- to 20-year period. Such studies have been criticized, however, because changing definitions and diagnostic standards make comparisons problematic. Therefore, at this time it can only be said that there is a *suggestion* of a decreasing prevalence of schizophrenia in those countries but that it remains to be confirmed by methodologically careful studies.

Studies in the United States suggest the possibility of a different story. Although no study comparable to the 1980–1984 five-site ECA study was done in the past, independent studies were done at two of the same sites. In Baltimore, a study in 1936 reported a one-year schizophrenia prevalence rate of 2.9 per 1,000. The ECA study, carried out in the same part of Baltimore in 1980–1984, found a six-month rate more than three times as high. Similarly, in New Haven the 1958 study by Hollingshead and Redlich found a six-month schizophrenia prevalence rate of 3.6 per 1,000, whereas the six-month rate for the ECA study was more than twice as high. Case-finding was more complete in the ECA study because a random sampling technique was used and this would tend to elevate the ECA prevalence rates. However, a narrower definition of schizophrenia was used in the ECA study that would tend to lower its prevalence rates compared to the two earlier studies. These methodological differences should at least partially cancel each other out.

One is left with the impression in the United States that the prevalence of schizophrenia has possibly increased in recent decades, at least in Baltimore and New Haven. This impression is further strengthened by the very high incidence of *new* cases of schizophrenia reported from the ECA study sites. In summary, in the United States schizophrenia may have recently increased, and may still be increasing in prevalence; this would stand in contrast to several other countries in which schizophrenia may be decreasing in prevalence.

WHAT IS THE COST OF SCHIZOPHRENIA?

To ask a question about the cost of schizophrenia is, in one sense, meaningless. Anyone who is familiar with schizophrenia knows that its magnitude and tragedy are light years beyond calculation in dollars and cents. At the same time we live in a society with finite resources and, whether we like it or not, cost-benefit thinking is part of the allocation of those resources. The decision-making process is a political one in which—either explicitly or implicitly—questions are asked such as the following: How much does the disease cost? How much money can be saved by finding better treatments? What is the cost-benefit ratio of spending more research funds on this disease? Because such questions arise it is important to understand the cost of schizophrenia.

The cost of schizophrenia, like any disease, can be calculated in a variety of ways. The economic cost for treating a single case of the disease can be assessed. Or the cost of treating all known cases can be added together. Lost wages because of the disease can be added, as well as the cost of social support (e.g., room and board, rehabilitation programs) needed to keep the person functioning over many years. The cost for treating schizophrenia can also be compared with the cost for treating other diseases, such as heart disease. Finally, but most difficult, the noneconomic cost of schizophrenia can be considered.

The cost for treating a case of schizophrenia in which the person recovers is not unreasonable compared with other serious diseases. The person usually requires hospitalization for a few weeks and then medication for several months. If the person is not among the fortunate one-quarter of patients who recover completely (see chapter 5), then the costs multiply rapidly.

Estimates have been made of the direct care cost for treating Sylvia Frumkin, the woman described in Susan Sheehan's *Is There No Place On Earth For Me?,* who over 18 years had 27 different admissions to hospitals for schizophrenia. The total cost of her care was estimated to be $636,000, which included only hospitalizations, halfway houses, and foster homes. It did not include outpatient medication costs, emergency room services, general health care, social services, law enforcement services needed to return her to the hospital, legal services, court costs, lost wages, or even the direct care costs incurred by Ms. Frumkin's family. I have made a similar approximation of direct care costs for my sister who has had schizophrenia for over 35 years and who required hospitalization for much of that time; the direct care costs for hospitalization in New York State mental hospitals alone during that time totals over $1.5 million. Such costs, I would submit, are not unusual for persons with severe schizophrenia.

Two recent studies have been done that attempted to calculate the direct costs (e.g., hospitalization costs, medication) as well as the indirect costs (e.g., lost wages) for everyone in the United States who has schizophrenia. One study, done by Drs. Dorothy Rice and Leonard Miller at the University of California, calculated the total cost of schizophrenia for 1990 at $32.5 billion. The other study, done by Dr. Richard Wyatt and colleagues at the National Institute of Mental Health, calculated the cost for 1991 at $65 billion. The two studies were similar in their estimates of direct costs ($19.5 and $18.6 billion, respectively) but differed substantially in estimates of indirect costs such as family caregiving, lost wages, and the losses due to suicides. Remarkably little hard data are available on which to make estimates of indirect costs.

Assuming for the moment that the current annual cost of schizophrenia lies halfway between the results of these two studies, it would then be approximately $50 billion. What *is* $50 billion, other than a long string of zeroes that most of us cannot comprehend? In relationship to other expenditures in 1990 by the United States government, $50 billion was 20 times the $2.5 billion spent on foreign aid under the Agency for International Development. It was more than six times the $7.4 billion spent on the space program or the $7.4 billion spent on all research funded by the National Institutes of Health. It was more than four times the $12.1 billion spent on the entire Veterans Administration medical care system and more than three times the $14.2 billion federal funds spent on highway programs. It was more than the $40.7 billion federal Medicaid expenditures. It was almost a quarter of the entire federal budget deficit of $220 billion. In short, $50 billion is a lot of money.

A major reason why schizophrenia is such an expensive disease is that it usually begins in early adulthood and often lasts until death 50 or more years later. People who get the disease have been raised and educated through childhood and adolescence, with all the costs associated, only to become disabled at precisely the moment they are supposed to become economically contributing members of society. Most of the 1.8 million persons with this disease continue to require services such as occasional hospitalization, foster homes, subsidized income, court costs, social services, outpatient psychiatric services, etc. People with schizophrenia are not beyond their economically most productive years when they become sick, such as patients with Alzheimer's disease. Nor do they die relatively quickly, such as happens to many patients with cancer. If a fiendish economist from another planet were trying to devise a disease that would force our society to incur the maximum costs, then he (or she) could not do better than schizophrenia. Schizophrenia is economically a three-time loser: Society must raise and educate the person destined to become afflicted, most people with the disease are unable to contribute economically to society, and at the same time many of them require costly services from society for the rest of their lives.

The cost of schizophrenia has also been compared with other diseases. In Australia, the direct and indirect costs for schizophrenia were compared with heart attacks. Despite the fact that heart attacks affect 12 times more people than schizophrenia does in Australia, the overall direct and indirect costs per case of schizophrenia are six times greater than those for heart attacks. These costs did not include pension or social security costs that, since persons with schizophrenia live much longer than persons with heart attacks, would make the disparity even greater.

The huge economic cost of schizophrenia leads directly to the question of economic benefits of research on this disease. As will be discussed in chapter 6, schizophrenia is one of the most under-researched diseases in the western world. In the Australian study referred to above, for example, it was found that research on schizophrenia received only one-fourteenth the funds spent on research on heart attacks. In terms of the relative cost of these diseases to society, this is a foolish allocation of research funds on economic grounds alone. In the United States, a calculation has been made that if research discoveries could reduce the cost of schizophrenia by only ten percent by 1998, the savings that would accrue over the following decade would total $180 billion.

From a public policy viewpoint, therefore, it would be wise to spend more research money on the causes and treatment of schizophrenia. The burden of schizophrenia to taxpayers is substantial; this was noted as early as 1855 by the Massachusetts Commission on Lunacy, which said:

> In whatever way we look at them, these lunatics are a burden upon the Commonwealth. The curable during their limited period of disease, and the incurable during the remainder of their lives, not only cease to produce, but they must eat the bread they do not earn, and consume the substance they do not create, receiving their sustenance from the treasury of the Commonwealth.

The greatest cost of schizophrenia, however, is the noneconomic costs to those who have it and their families. These costs are incalculable. They include the effects of growing up normally until early adulthood, then being diagnosed with a brain disease that may last for the rest of your life. Hopes, plans, expectations, and dreams are abruptly put on hold. Cerebral palsy and Down's syndrome are tragedies for families of newborns; cancer and Alzheimer's disease are tragedies for families of the elderly. There is no known disease, however, with noneconomic costs so great as for schizophrenia. It is the costliest disease of all.

IS SCHIZOPHRENIA OF RECENT ORIGIN?

The history of schizophrenia is a curious one that has provoked a lively debate among scholars. On one side are those who claim that "schizophrenia has existed throughout history. . . . There is definite evidence in support of the view that schizophrenia is an ancient illness." Advocates of this view cite early Sanskrit, Babylonian, and Biblical figures such as Nebuchadnezzar (who ate "grass as oxen" for seven years) and Ezekiel (who had visual and auditory hallucinations) to support their claims. They also argue that sick individuals were kept at home or were considered to be divinely inspired and so were not defined as sick. The other side (which includes myself) acknowledges that there were indeed occasional people who had brain damage (e.g., from birth injuries or fights) or brain diseases (e.g., epilepsy, syphilis, or viral encephalitis) that may have produced psychotic symptoms, but that schizophrenia with its hallmark auditory hallucinations and onset in early adulthood was virtually never described.

A stronger argument can be made for occasional cases of schizophrenia beginning in the late Middle Ages. A few small psychiatric hospitals were opened such as Bethlem Hospital (which gave birth to the term "bedlam") in London. King Henry VI, who lived from 1421 to 1471, appears to have had a schizophrenia-like disorder. William Shakespeare selected Henry VI as the subject for his first play in 1591. In *Hamlet* (1601) Shakespeare had Hamlet feign lunacy and Ophelia become insane when she discovered that her father had been killed by the man she loved. Nigel Bark makes a strong case that Poor Mad Tom in *King Lear* (1605) had schizophrenia but also concedes it is possible that he was merely feigning madness. One schizophrenia expert claims that the autobiography of George Trosse, an English minister who, as a young man in 1656, developed delusions, auditory hallucinations, and catatonic behavior, is a description of schizophrenia but another asserts that alcoholic psychosis was the more likely cause for Trosse's symptoms.

Sporadic cases of what may have been schizophrenia continued to appear in the 1700s but were remarkably few in number. Suddenly, at the turn of the century, schizophrenia appeared in unmistakable form. Simultaneously (and apparently independently) John Haslam in England and Philippe Pinel in France both described cases that were certainly schizophrenia. These were followed by a veritable outpouring of descriptions continuing throughout the nineteenth century and also by evidence that schizophrenia was increasing in frequency. It was a dramatic entrance for a disease. Haslam's publication in 1809 was an enlarged second edition of his 1798 book, *Observations on Insanity*. It is a remarkable book, with descriptions of delusions, hallucinations, disorders of thinking, and even autopsy accounts of abnormalities in the brains of some of the patients. His descriptions of patients leave no doubt that he was describing what we now call schizophrenia. In 1810 Haslam published an extended description of one patient with schizophrenia, entitling it "Illustrations of Madness: Exhibiting a Singular Case of Insanity," which implied that such cases were very unusual at that time.

From the observations of John Haslam and Philippe Pinel until the end of the nineteenth century there were continuing arguments in

Europe whether insanity was increasing and, if so, why. As early as 1829 Sir Andrew Halliday warned that "the numbers of the afflicted have more than tripled during the last twenty years" and in 1835 J.C. Prichard added that "the apparent increase is everywhere so striking ... cases of insanity are far more numerous than formerly." In 1856 in France, E. Renaudin published extensive data demonstrating an increase in insanity, especially among young adults and in urban areas, and the following year in England, John Hawkes wrote: "I doubt if ever the history of the world, or the experience of past ages, could show a larger amount of insanity than that of the present day." By 1873 Harrington Tuke warned that "a great wave of insanity is slowly advancing" and three years later R. Jamieson added that "the most remarkable phenomenon of our time has been the alarming increase of insanity."

Those who believed that the increase in insanity was real offered a variety of possible explanations, ranging from genetics (e.g., increasing consanguinous marriages) and the increasing complexity of civilization to increased masturbation, use of alcohol, or train travel. Those who argued that the increase was not real claimed that it was a statistical artifact due to increased life expectancy of individuals with mental illnesses, part of a social movement to confine troublesome persons to institutions, or the product of increasing industrialization whereby families left home to work and so could no longer maintain their sick relative at home. Dr. Edward Hare in England analyzed these arguments in detail and concluded that the nineteenth century increase in insanity was most probably real.

In the United States an awareness of a possible increase in insanity appears to have taken place somewhat later than in Europe. The first American hospital for mentally ill individuals opened in Williamsburg, Virginia, in 1773 with 24 beds, but it was not full for over 30 years. Not a single hospital was opened in the 43-year period between 1773 and 1816, but 22 hospitals were added between 1816 and 1846.

The accompanying graph illustrates the per capita increase in patients in public mental hospitals in the United States from 1830 to 1950. The initial alarm about increasing insanity in America was sounded in 1852 by Pliny Earle, one of the founders of the American Psychiatric Association, who warned that "insanity is an increasing disease." In 1854 Edward Jarvis undertook an extensive census of insane persons in Massachusetts and became convinced that their numbers were increasing; in 1871 Jarvis wrote that "the successive reports, upon whatever source or means of information procured, all tend to show an increasing number of the insane." In 1894 the superintendent of one Massachusetts state psychiatric hospital added that "the insane have increased twice as fast as the whole people. . . . We find this insane accumulation going on as fast as 50 years ago."

Inpatients in Public Mental Hospitals Per 100,000 Total Population in the United States, 1830 to 1950

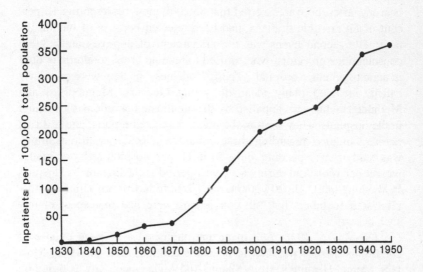

With the advent of World War I interest waned in the question of increasing insanity. Retrospective analyses by medical historians such as Gerald Grob (*Mental Institutions in America,* 1973) and David Rothman (*The Discovery of the Asylum,* 1971) have argued that the increase in insanity was not real but rather was caused by sociological factors. In fact we do not know whether the increase was real or not and a strong case can be made that it was. If so, it may offer important clues to the causes of schizophrenia.

DEINSTITUTIONALIZATION: A CRADLE FOR CATASTROPHE

During the first half of the twentieth century the number of patients in public psychiatric hospitals in the United States continued to increase three-and-one-half-fold, from 144,653 in 1903 to 512,501 in 1950. The per capita increase based on population was almost twofold. The largest single diagnostic group was patients with schizophrenia. The problem received remarkably little public attention, however, until World War II, when two events conspired to bring mental illness to center stage.

The first event was the extraordinarily high number of young men who were rejected for induction into military service because of mental illness. General Lewis B. Hershey, testifying before House and Senate hearings after the war, asserted that 856,000 men, representing 18 percent of all possible draftees, had been rejected because of mental illness. The second event was the assignment of approximately 3,000 conscientious objectors, who refused to take up arms, to alternate duty in state psychiatric hospitals. These "conchies," as they were popularly called, included many idealistic young Quakers, Mennonites, and Methodists who were appalled by the inhumane conditions they found in the hospitals. They went to the press, organized reports, and testified before Congress regarding these conditions. Kentucky, for example, was said to be spending only $146.11 per hospitalized psychiatric patient *per year.* And during a 12-year period at St. Elizabeths Hospital in Washington, D.C., 20 patients were said to have been killed by hospital staff members but "no convictions were had in respect of any such cases."

On May 6, 1946, *Life* magazine published a 13-page expose of conditions in state psychiatric hospitals entitled "Bedlam 1946: Most U.S. Mental Hospitals Are A Shame And A Disgrace." It was based on the reports of the conscientious objectors and included pictures of naked patients living in filthy conditions. That same month *Reader's Digest* included a condensation of a new novel by Mary Jane Ward entitled *The Snake Pit,* which detailed the terrifying experiences of a woman confined to a psychiatric hospital. In September 1946, Mike Gorman, a young reporter with *The Daily Oklahoman,* published a scathing series of articles about Oklahoma's state psychiatric hospitals (e.g., "the dining room made Dante's *Inferno* seem like a country club. . . ."), which was published as a book the following year. In 1948 Albert Deutsch published *The Shame of the States,* based on visits to psychiatric hospitals in 12 states. Deutsch claimed that "in some of the wards there were scenes that rivaled the horrors of the Nazi concentration camps—hundreds of naked mental patients herded into huge, barnlike, filth-infested wards. . . ." and included pictures to prove his points. The problem of the mentally ill in America had been etched into the nation's consciousness and conscience as nothing had previously done.

The stage was set for deinstitutionalization, and the introduction in the 1950s of chlorpromazine and reserpine, the first effective antipsychotic drugs, made it more feasible. The election of John F. Kennedy as president in 1960 provided the impetus and funds for emptying the hospitals. Kennedy's younger sister had been publicly identified as mentally retarded but in fact had also developed schizophrenia and undergone a lobotomy. Kennedy therefore championed the mentally retarded and the mentally ill and proposed a series of federally funded Community Mental Health Centers (CMHCs) that, it was said, would function as alternatives to state psychiatric hospitals. In his introduction of the CMHC proposal Kennedy specifically noted that "it has been demonstrated that two out of three schizophrenics—our largest category of mentally ill—can be treated and released within six months." It was to be the launching of a psychiatric Titanic, the largest failed social experiment of twentieth century America.

The magnitude of deinstitutionalization is difficult to comprehend.

The Magnitude of Deinstitutionalization: Number of Patients in Public Mental Hospitals, 1950–1991

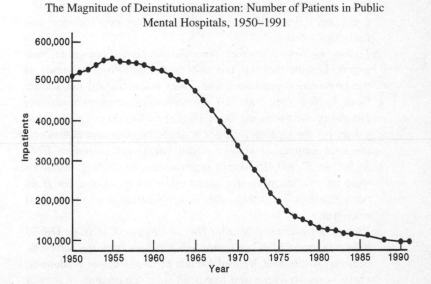

In 1955, there were 559,000 seriously mentally ill individuals in state psychiatric hospitals. Today there are less than 90,000. Based on the nation's population increase between 1955 and 1993 from 166 million to 258 million, if there were the same number of patients per capita in the hospitals today as there were in 1955, their total number today would be 869,000. This means that there are approximately 780,000 individuals—over three-quarters of a million—who would have been in state psychiatric hospitals in 1955 but who are in the community today. This also means that *90 percent of the people who would have been in the hospital 40 years ago are not in the hospital today.*

The vast majority of these individuals can live successfully outside the hospital *if* medication and aftercare services are provided. In that sense deinstitutionalization was and is a humane and reasonable idea. Why, then, has it been such a disaster? There are six major reasons:

1. *Misunderstanding about causes of serious mental illnesses.* When deinstitutionalization got under way in the early 1960s, Thomas Szasz' *Myth of Mental Illness* (1961) and Ken Kesey's *One Flew Over the Cuckoo's Nest* (1962) held sway. The belief became widespread that hospitalization *caused* mental illness; that as soon as you released the patients they would live happily ever after. It was a romantic view but in retrospect incorrect and remarkably naive.

2. *Failure to shift resources from hospitals to community programs.* Despite the massive shift of patients from hospitals to the community, personnel and fiscal resources did not follow them. In New York State, for example, the state hospital patients population was reduced from 93,000 to 24,000 over 25 years, yet during the same period not a single hospital was closed and the total number of state hospital employees *increased* from 23,800 to 37,000. The main impediments to shifting resources were unions and powerful members of state legislatures from rural districts in which the state hospital was the largest employer.

3. *Failure of Community Mental Health Centers (CMHCs).* The $3 billion federal CMHC program was a failure from the start. The National Institute of Mental Health provided vague guidelines, virtually no oversight, and bypassed state departments of mental health, thereby ensuring that there would be no cooperation

between state hospitals and the CMHCs. Approximately five percent of the 789 federally funded CMHCs took responsibility for the patients being discharged from the hospitals, whereas the remainder evolved into being counseling and psychotherapy centers for family and personal problems. Some CMHCs built swimming pools and tennis courts with the federal funds, and one Florida CMHC even hired swimming instructors with a federal staffing grant.

4. *Lawyers as destructive forces.* Between 1965 and 1990, when deinstitutionalization was taking place, the number of lawyers in America increased from 296,000 to 800,000, more than four times faster than the general population. Some of the lawyers read Szasz' *Myth of Mental Illness* and dedicated their careers to bringing lawsuits against states, getting mental patients released from hospitals, making it extremely difficult to involuntarily hospitalize or treat them, and passing state legislation to effectively hasten deinstitutionalization. Through organizations such as the American Civil Liberties Union and the Mental Health Law Project these lawyers have accomplished their goals. The numbers of mentally ill homeless persons, with freedom to be perpetually psychotic, are a testimony to their success.

5. *Mental health professionals as unavailable.* Federal subsidies for the training of psychiatrists, psychologists, and psychiatric social workers began in 1948 and 20 years later had reached $119 million per year. State subsidies were even more generous. The professionals, however, were trained to be mental *health,* not mental *illness* professionals. No service payback was required in exchange for their publicly subsidized training so the vast majority of them went immediately to the private practice of psychotherapy. A 1980 survey of private practitioners found that only six percent of patients seen by psychiatrists and three percent of patients seen by psychologists had ever been hospitalized for mental illness. For most deinstitutionalized individuals with schizophrenia and other serious mental illnesses the professionals were unavailable.

6. *Federal incentives to empty the hospitals.* Following passage of the federal CMHC legislation, seriously mentally ill individuals being discharged from the hospitals were made eligible for fed-

eral Medicaid, Medicare, Supplemental Security Income (SSI), Social Security Disability Insurance (SSDI), food stamps, special housing, and other programs. In effect this meant that as long as such individuals were in state mental hospitals they were the fiscal responsibility of the states; once discharged, however, the majority of the fiscal responsibility for their care was shifted to the federal government. The states had a large fiscal incentive to empty their hospitals but no incentive whatever to provide aftercare. It did not take the states long to learn how to game the system, and this has been a major contributor to the failure of deinstitutionalization.

Given these mistakes it is no wonder that deinstitutionalization has been a massive failure. Homelessness, jails, violence, victimization, abysmal housing, revolving doors, few professionals, minimal treatment—these consequences were entirely predictable. I could ask the most thought-disordered individual with schizophrenia to set up a scheme for deinstitutionalization and the product would be better than what we have.

Who should be blamed? Blaming conservative politicians, especially former President Reagan, has become the politically correct but factually incorrect answer that is frequently given by mental health professionals. In fact the debacle of deinstitutionalization has taken place under four Democratic (Kennedy, Johnson, Carter, and Clinton) and four Republican (Nixon, Ford, Reagan, and Bush) presidents. The *real* blame for the failure of deinstitutionalization rests squarely on the shoulders of the psychiatrists, psychologists, psychiatric social workers, lawyers, and federal and state officials who were responsible for it.

RECOMMENDED FURTHER READING

Baum, A. S., and D. W. Burnes. *A Nation in Denial: The Truth About Homelessness.* Boulder: Westview Press, 1993.

Hare, E. "Was Insanity on the Increase?" *British Journal of Psychiatry* 142 (1983):439–55.

Isaac, R. J., and V. C. Armat. *Madness in the Streets.* New York: Free Press, 1990.

Jeste, D. V., R. del Carmen, J. B. Lohr, and R. J. Wyatt. "Did Schizophrenia Exist Before the Eighteenth Century?" *Comprehensive Psychiatry* 26

(1985):493–503. This is the strongest case that has been made for the existence of schizophrenia in ancient medical texts.

Torrey, E. F. *Schizophrenia and Civilization*. New York: Jason Aronson, 1980.

Torrey, E. F. *Nowhere to Go: The Tragic Odyssey of the Homeless Mentally Ill*. New York: Harper and Row, 1988.

2

THE INNER WORLD OF MADNESS:
VIEW FROM THE INSIDE

What then does schizophrenia mean to me? It means fatigue and confusion, it means trying to separate every experience into the real and the unreal and not sometimes being aware of where the edges overlap. It means trying to think straight when there is a maze of experiences getting in the way, and when thoughts are continually being sucked out of your head so that you become embarrassed to speak at meetings. It means feeling sometimes that you are inside your head and visualising yourself walking over your brain, or watching another girl wearing your clothes and carrying out actions as you think them. It means knowing that you are continually "watched," that you can never succeed in life because the laws are all against you and knowing that your ultimate destruction is never far away.

Patient with schizophrenia, quoted in Henry R. Rollin,
Coping with Schizophrenia

When tragedy strikes, one of the things which make life bearable for people is the sympathy of friends and relatives. This can be seen, for example, in a natural disaster like a flood and with a chronic disease like cancer. Those closest to the person afflicted offer help, extend their sympathy, and generally provide important solace and support in the person's time of need. "Sympathy," said Emerson, "is a supporting atmosphere, and in it we unfold easily and well." A prerequisite for sympathy is an ability to put oneself in the place of the person afflicted. One must be able to imagine oneself in a flood or getting cancer. Without this ability to put oneself in the place of the person afflicted, there can be abstract pity but not true sympathy.

Sympathy for those afflicted with schizophrenia is sparse because it is difficult to put oneself in the place of the sufferer. The whole disease process is mysterious, foreign, and frightening to most people. It is not like a flood, where one can imagine all one's possessions being washed away. Nor like a cancer, where one can imagine a slowly growing tumor, relentlessly spreading from organ to organ and squeezing life from the body. No, schizophrenia is madness. Those who are afflicted act bizarrely, say strange things, withdraw from us, and may even try to hurt us. They are no longer the same person—they are *mad!* We don't understand why they say what they say and do what they do. We don't understand the disease process. Rather than a steadily growing tumor, which we can understand, it is as if the person has lost control of his/her brain. How can we sympathize with a person who is possessed by unknown and unseen forces? How can we sympathize with a madman or a madwoman?

The paucity of sympathy for those with schizophrenia makes it that much more of a disaster. Being afflicted with the disease is bad enough by itself. Those of us who have not had this disease should ask ourselves, for example, how we would feel if our brain began playing tricks on us, if unseen voices shouted at us, if we lost the capacity to feel emotions, and if we lost the ability to reason logically. This would certainly be burden enough for any human being to have to bear. But what if, in addition to this, those closest to us began to avoid us or ignore us, to pretend that they didn't hear our comments, to pretend that they didn't notice what we did? How would we feel if those we most cared about were embarrassed by our behavior each day?

Because there is little understanding of schizophrenia, so there is little sympathy. For this reason it is the obligation of everyone with a relative or close friend with schizophrenia to learn as much as possible about what the disease is and what the afflicted person is experiencing. This is not merely an intellectual exercise or a way to satisfy one's curiosity but rather to make it possible to sympathize with the person. For friends and relatives who want to be helpful, probably the most important thing to do is to learn about the inner workings of the schizophrenic brain. One mother wrote me after listening to her afflicted son's descriptions of his hallucinations: "I saw into the visual hallucinations that plagued him and frankly, at times, it raised the hair on my neck. It also helped me to get outside of *my* tragedy and to realize how horrible it is for the person who is afflicted. I thank God for that painful wisdom. I am able to cope easier with all of this."

With sympathy, schizophrenia is a personal tragedy. Without sympathy, it becomes a family calamity, for there is nothing to knit people together, no balm for the wounds. Understanding schizophrenia also helps demystify the disease and brings it from the realm of the occult to the daylight of reason. As we come to understand it, the face of madness slowly changes before us from one of terror to one of sadness. For the sufferer, this is a significant change.

The best way to learn what a person with schizophrenia experiences is to listen to someone with the disease. For this reason I have relied heavily upon patients' own accounts in describing the signs and symptoms. There are some excellent descriptions scattered throughout English literature; the best of these are listed at the end of this chapter. By contrast one of the most widely read books, Hannah Green's *I Never Promised You a Rose Garden,* is not at all helpful. It describes a patient who, according to a recent analysis, should not even be diagnosed with schizophrenia but rather with hysteria (now often referred to as somatization disorder).

When one listens to persons with schizophrenia describe what they are experiencing and observes their behavior, certain abnormalities can be noted:

1. Alterations of the senses
2. Inability to sort and interpret incoming sensations, and an inability therefore to respond appropriately
3. Delusions and hallucinations
4. Altered sense of self
5. Changes in emotions
6. Changes in movements
7. Changes in behavior

No one symptom or sign is found in all individuals; rather the final diagnosis rests upon the total symptom picture. Some people have much more of one kind of symptom, other people another. Conversely, there is no single symptom or sign of schizophrenia which is found exclusively in that disease. All symptoms and signs can be found at least occasionally in other diseases of the brain, such as brain tumors and temporal lobe epilepsy.

ALTERATIONS OF THE SENSES

In Edgar Allan Poe's "The Tell-Tale Heart" (1843), the main character, clearly lapsing into a schizophrenialike state, exclaims to the reader, "Have I not told you that what you mistake for madness is but overacuteness of the senses?" An expert on the dark recesses of the human mind, Poe put his finger directly on a central theme of madness. Alterations of the senses are especially prominent in the early stages of schizophrenic breakdown and can be found, according to one study, in almost two-thirds of all patients. As the authors of the study conclude: "Perceptual dysfunction is the most invariant feature of the early stage of schizophrenia." It can be elicited from patients most commonly when they have recovered from a psychotic episode; rarely can patients who are acutely or chronically psychotic describe these changes.

The alterations may be either enhancement (more common) or blunting; all sensory modalities may be affected. For example, Poe's protagonist was experiencing predominantly an increased acuteness of hearing:

> Truol   norvouu   vory, vory droudfully norvouu I hud boon und uul but why will you say that I am mad? The disease had sharpened my senses— not destroyed—not dulled them. Above all was the sense of hearing acute. I heard all things in the heaven and in the earth. I heard many things in hell. How, then, am I mad? Harken! and observe how healthily—how calmly—I can tell you the whole story.

Another described it this way:

> During the last while back I have noticed that noises all seem to be louder to me than they were before. It's as if someone had turned up the volume. . . . I notice it most with background noises—you know what I mean, noises that are always around but you don't notice them. Now they seem to be just as loud and sometimes louder than the main noises that are going on. . . . It's a bit alarming at times because it makes it difficult to keep your mind on something when there's so much going on that you can't help listening to.

Visual perceptual changes are even more common than auditory changes. Two patients described it as follows:

Colours seem to be brighter now, almost as if they are luminous painting. I'm not sure if things are solid until I touch them. I seem to be noticing colours more than before, although I am not artistically minded. The colours of things seem much clearer and yet at the same time there is something missing. The things I look at seem to be flatter as if you were looking just at a surface. Maybe it's because I notice so much more about things and find myself looking at them for a longer time. Not only the colour of things fascinates me but all sorts of little things, like markings in the surface, pick up my attention too.

And another noted both the sharpness of colors as well as the transformation of objects:

Everything looked vibrant, especially red; people took on a devilish look, with black outlines and white shining eyes; all sorts of objects—chairs, buildings, obstacles—took on a life of their own; they seemed to make threatening gestures, to have an animistic outlook.

In some instances the visual alterations improved the appearance:

Lots of things seemed psychedelic; they shone. I was working in a restaurant and it looked more first class than it really was.

In other cases the alterations made the object ugly or frightening:

People looked deformed, as if they had had plastic surgery, or were wearing makeup with different bone structure.

People were pulling hideous faces.

People were deformed, squarish, like in plaster.

Colors and textures may blend into each other:

I saw everything very bright and rich and pure like the thinnest line possible. Or a shiny smoothness like water but solid. After a while things got rough and shadowed again.

Sometimes both hearing *and* visual sensations are increased, as happened to this young woman.

These crises, far from abating, seemed rather to increase. One day, while I was in the principal's office, suddenly the room became enormous, illuminated by a dreadful electric light that cast false shadows. Everything was exact, smooth, artificial, extremely tense; the chairs and tables seemed models placed here and there. Pupils and teachers were puppets revolving without cause, without objective. I recognized nothing, nobody. It was as though reality, attenuated, had slipped away from all these things and these people. Profound dread overwhelmed me, and as though lost, I looked around desperately for help. I heard people talking, but I did not grasp the meaning of the words. The voices were metallic, without warmth or color. From time to time, a word detached itself from the rest. It repeated itself over and over in my head, absurd, as though cut off by a knife.

Closely related to the overacuteness of the senses is the flooding of the senses with stimuli. It is not only that the senses become more sharply attuned but that they see and hear everything. Normally our brain screens out most incoming sights and sounds, allowing us to concentrate on whatever we choose. This screening mechanism appears to become impaired in many persons with schizophrenia, releasing a veritable flood of sensory stimuli into the brain simultaneously.

This is one person's description of flooding of the senses with auditory stimuli:

Everything seems to grip my attention although I am not particularly interested in anything. I am speaking to you just now, but I can hear noises going on next door and in the corridor. I find it difficult to shut these out, and it makes it more difficult for me to concentrate on what I am saying to you. Often the silliest little things that are going on seem to interest me. That's not even true: they don't interest me, but I find myself attending to them and wasting a lot of time this way.

And with visual stimuli:

Occasionally during subsequent periods of disturbance there was some distortion of vision and some degree of hallucination. On several occasions my eyes became markedly oversensitive to light. Ordinary colors appeared to be much too bright, and sunlight seemed dazzling in intensity. When this happened, ordinary reading was impossible, and print seemed excessively black.

Frequently these two things happen together.

> I can probably tell you as much or more about what really went on those days than lots of people who were sane: the comings and goings of people, the weather, what was on the news, what we ate, what records were played, what was said. My focus was a bit bizarre. I could do portraits of people who were walking down the street. I remembered license numbers of cars we were following into Vancouver. We paid $3.57 for gas. The air machine made eighteen dings while we were there.

> An outsider may see only someone "out of touch with reality." In fact we are experiencing so many realities that it is often confusing and sometimes totally overwhelming.

As these examples make clear, it is difficult to concentrate or pay attention when so much sensory data is rushing through the brain. In one study more than half of people who had had schizophrenia recalled impairments in attention and in keeping track of time. One patient expressed it as follows:

> Sometimes when people speak to me my head is overloaded. It's too much to hold at once. It goes out as quick as it goes in. It makes you forget what you just heard because you can't get hearing it long enough. It's just words in the air unless you can figure it out from their faces.

Sensory modalities other than hearing and vision may also be affected in schizophrenia. Mary Barnes in her autobiographical account of "a journey through madness" recalled how "it was terrible to be touched. . . . Once a nurse tried to cut my nails. The touch was such that I tried to bite her." A medical student with schizophrenia remembered that "touching any patient made me feel that I was being electrocuted." Another patient described the horror of feeling a rat in his throat and tasting the "decay in my mouth as its body disintegrated inside me." Increased sensitivity of the genitalia is occasionally found, explained by one patient as "a genital sexual irritation from which there was no peace and no relief." I once took care of a young man with such a sensation who became convinced that his penis was turning black. He countered this delusional fear by insisting that doctors— or anyone within sight—examine him every five minutes to reassure him. His hospitalization was precipitated by his having gone into the local post office where a girlfriend worked and asking her to examine him in front of the customers.

Another aspect of the overacuteness of the senses is a flooding of the mind with thoughts. It is as if the brain is being bombarded both with external stimuli (e.g., sounds and sights) and with internal stimuli as well (thoughts, memories). One psychiatrist who has studied this area extensively claims that we have not been as aware of the internal stimuli in persons with schizophrenia as we should be.

> My trouble is that I've got too many thoughts. You might think about something, let's say that ashtray, and just think, oh! yes, that's for putting my cigarette in, but I would think of it and then I would think of a dozen different things connected with it at the same time.

> My concentration is very poor. I jump from one thing to another. If I am talking to someone they only need to cross their legs or scratch their heads and I am distracted and forget what I was saying. I think I could concentrate better with my eyes shut.

And this person describes the flooding of memories from the past:

> Childhood feelings began to come back as symbols, and bits from past conversations went through my head. . . . I began to think I was hypnotized so that I would remember what had happened in the first four and a half years of my life. . . . I thought that my parents had supplied information about the nursery school teacher and pediatrician to someone—perhaps my husband—with the hope that I would be able to straighten myself out by remembering the early years.

Perhaps it is this increased ability of some patients to recall childhood events which has mistakenly led psychoanalysts to assume that the recalled events were somehow causally related to the schizophrenia (as will be discussed in chapter 6). There is no scientific evidence to support such theories, however, and much evidence to support contrary theories.

A variation of flooding with thoughts occurs when the person feels that someone is inserting the flood of thoughts into his/her head. This is commonly referred to as thought insertion and when present is considered by many psychiatrists to be an almost certain symptom of schizophrenia.

All sorts of "thoughts" seem to come to me, as if someone is "speaking" them inside my head. When in any company it appears to be worse (probably some form of self-consciousness), I don't want the "thoughts" to come but I keep on "hearing" them (as it were) and it requires lots of will power sometimes to stop myself from "thinking" (in the form of "words") the most absurd and embarrassing things. These "thoughts" do not mean anything to me and cause "lack of concentration" in whatever I am doing at work, etc.

In college, I "knew" that everyone was thinking and talking about me and that a local pharmacist was tormenting me by inserting his thoughts into my head and inducing me to buy things I had no use for.

With this kind of activity going on in a person's head, it is not surprising that it would be difficult to concentrate.

I was invited to play checkers and started to do so, but I could not go on. I was too much absorbed in my own thoughts, particularly those regarding the approaching end of the world and those responsible for the use of force and for the charge of homicidal intent. By nightfall my head was all in a whirl. It seemed to be the Day of Judgment and all humanity came streaming in from four different directions.

Concentrating on even as simple a task as walking from one building to another may become impossible.

Fear made me ill; just the same I ran out to visit a friend who was staying at a nearby sanatorium. To get there, a way led through the woods, short and well marked. Becoming lost in the thick fog, I circled round and round the sanatorium without seeing it, my fear augmenting all the while. By and by I realized that the wind inspired this fear; the trees, too, large and black in the mist, but particularly the wind. At length I grasped the meaning of its message: the frozen wind from the North Pole wanted to crush the earth, to destroy it. Or perhaps it was an omen, a sign that the earth was about to be laid waste. This idea tormented me with growing intensity.

Esso Leete, who has written many useful articles from a consumer's point of view, describes a similar experience in the early stages of her illness:

It was evening and I was walking along the beach near my college in Florida. Suddenly my perceptions shifted. The intensifying wind became an omen of something terrible. I could feel it becoming stronger and stronger; I was sure it was going to capture me and sweep me away with it. Nearby trees bent threateningly toward me and tumbleweeds chased me. I became very frightened and began to run. However, though I knew I was running, I was making no progress. I seemed suspended in space and time.

When all aspects of overacuteness of the senses are taken together, the consequent cacophony in the brain must be frightening, and it is so described by most patients. In the very earliest stage of the disease, however, before this overacuteness becomes too severe, it may be a pleasant experience. Many descriptions of the initial days of developing schizophrenia are descriptions of heightened awareness, commonly called "peak experiences"; such experiences are also common in manic-depressive illness and in getting high on drugs. Here is one patient's description:

Suddenly my whole being was filled with light and loveliness and with an upsurge of deeply moving feeling from within myself to meet and reciprocate the influence that flowed into me. I was in a state of the most vivid awareness and illumination. What can I say of it? A cloudless, cerulean blue sky of the mind, shot through with shafts of exquisite, warm, dazzling sunlight.

Many patients interpret such experiences within a religious framework and believe they are being touched by God.

Before last week, I was quite closed about my emotions; then finally I owned up to them with another person. I began to speak without thinking beforehand and what came out showed an awareness of human beings and God. I could feel deeply about other people. We felt connected. The side which had been suppressing emotions did not seem to be the real one. I was in a higher and higher state of exhilaration and awareness. Things people said had hidden meaning. They said things that applied to life. Everything that was real seemed to make sense. I had a great awareness of life, truth, and God. I went to church and suddenly all parts of the service made sense. My senses were sharpened. I became fascinated by the little insignificant things around me. There was an additional awareness of the world that would do artists, architects, and painters good. I ended up being too emotional, but I felt very much at home with myself, very much at ease. It gave me a great feeling of power. It was not a case of seeing more broadly but deeper. I was losing touch with the outside world and lost my sense of time. There was a fog around me in some sense, and I felt asleep. I could see more deeply into problems that other people had and would go directly into a deeper subject with a person. I had the feeling I loved everybody in the world.

In view of such experiences it is hardly surprising to find excessive religious preoccupation listed as a common early sign of schizophrenia.

Sensations can be blunted, as well as enhanced, in schizophrenia. Such blunting is more commonly found late in the course of the disease whereas enhancement is often one of the earliest symptoms. The blunting is described "as if a heavy curtain were drawn over his mind; it resembled a thick deadening cloud that prevented the free use of his senses." One's own voice may sound muted or faraway, and vision may be wavy or blurred: "However hard I looked it was as if I was looking through a daydream and the mass of detail, such as the pattern on a carpet, became lost."

One sensation which may be blunted in schizophrenia is that of pain. Although it does not happen frequently, when such blunting does occur it may be dramatic and have practical consequences for those who are caring for the person. It is now in vogue to attribute such blunting to medication, but in fact it was clearly described twenty and thirty years before drugs for schizophrenia became widely available. There are many accounts in the older textbooks of surgeons, for example, being able to do appendectomies and similar procedures on some patients with schizophrenia with little or no anesthesia. One of my patients had a massive breast abscess which was unknown until the fluid from it seeped through her dress; although this is normally an exceedingly painful condition, she insisted she felt no pain whatsoever. Nurses who have cared for patients with schizophrenia over many years can recite stories of fractured bones, perforated ulcers, or ruptured appendixes which the patient said nothing about. Practically, it is important to be aware of this possibility so that medical help can be sought for persons if they look sick, even if they are not complaining of pain. It is also the reason that some people with schizophrenia burn their fingers when they smoke cigarettes too close to the end.

It may well be that there is a common denominator for all aspects of the alterations of the senses discussed thus far. All sensory input into the brain passes through the limbic area in the lower portion of the brain. It is this area that is most suspect as being involved in schizophrenia, as will be discussed in chapter 6. The limbic system filters this sensory input, and it is likely that disease of this system accounts for many or most symptoms. Norma MacDonald, a woman who published an account of her illness in 1960, foresaw this possibility in a particularly clear manner several years before psychiatrists and neurologists understood it, and she wrote about her conception of the breakdown in the filter system.

At first it was as if parts of my brain "awoke" which had been dormant, and I became interested in a wide assortment of people, events, places, and ideas which normally would make no impression on me. Not knowing that I was ill, I made no attempt to understand what was happening, but felt that there was some overwhelming significance in all this, produced either by God or Satan, and I felt that I was duty-bound to ponder on each of these new interests, and the more I pondered the worse it became. The walk of a stranger on the street could be a sign to me which I must interpret. Every face in the windows of a passing streetcar would be engraved on my mind, all of them concentrating on me and trying to pass me some sort of message. Now, many years later, I can appreciate what had happened. Each of us is capable of coping with a large number of stimuli, invading our being through any one of the senses. We could hear every sound within earshot and see every object, hue, and colour within the field of vision, and so on. It's obvious that we would be incapable of carrying on any of our daily activities if even one-hundredth of all these available stimuli invaded us at once. So the mind must have a filter which functions without our conscious thought, sorting stimuli and allowing only those which are relevant to the situation in hand to disturb consciousness. And this filter must be working at maximum efficiency at all times, particularly when we require a degree of concentration. What had happened to me in Toronto was a breakdown in the filter, and a hodge-podge of unrelated stimuli were distracting me from things which should have had my undivided attention.

INABILITY TO INTERPRET AND RESPOND

In normal people the brain functions in such a way that incoming stimuli are sorted and interpreted; then a correct response is selected and sent out. Most of the responses are learned, such as saying "thank you" when a gift is given to us. These responses also include logic, such as being able to predict what will happen to us if we do not arrive for work at the time we are supposed to. Our brains sort and interpret incoming stimuli and send out responses hundreds of thousands of times each day. The site of this function is also thought to be the limbic system, and it is intimately connected with the screening function referred to above.

A fundamental defect in schizophrenia is a frequent inability to sort, interpret, and respond. Textbooks of psychiatry describe this as a thought disorder, but it is more than just thoughts which are involved. Visual and auditory stimuli, emotions, and some actions are misarranged in exactly the same way as thoughts; the brain defect is probably similar for all.

We do not understand the human brain well enough to know precisely how the system works; but imagine a telephone operator sitting at an old plug-in type of switchboard in the middle of your limbic system. He or she receives all the sensory input, thoughts, ideas, memories and emotions coming in, sorts them, and determines those which go together. For example, normally our brain takes the words of a sentence and converts them automatically into a pattern of thought. We don't have to concentrate on the individual words but rather can focus on the meaning of the whole message.

Now what would happen if the switchboard operator decided not to do the job of sorting and interpreting? In terms of understanding auditory stimuli, two patients describe this kind of defect:

> When people are talking I have to think what the words mean. You see, there is an interval instead of a spontaneous response. I have to think about it and it takes time. I have to pay all my attention to people when they are speaking or I get all mixed up and don't understand them.

> I can concentrate quite well on what people are saying if they talk simply. It's when they go on into long sentences that I lose the meanings. It just becomes a lot of words that I would need to string together to make sense.

One pair of researchers described this defect as a receptive aphasia similar to that found in some patients who have had a stroke. The words are there but the person cannot synthesize them into sentences, as explained by this person with schizophrenia:

> I used to get the sudden thing that I couldn't understand what people said, like it was a foreign language.

Difficulties in comprehending visual stimuli are similar to those described for auditory stimuli.

> I have to put things together in my head. If I look at my watch I see the watchstrap, watch, face, hands and so on, then I have got to put them together to get it into one piece.

> Everything is in bits. You put the picture up bit by bit into your head. It's like a photograph that's torn in bits and put together again. If you move it's frightening. The picture you had in your head is still there but broken up. If I move there's a new picture that I have to put together again.

One patient had similar problems when she looked at her psychiatrist, seeing "the teeth, then the nose, then the cheeks, then one eye and the other. Perhaps it was this independence of each part that inspired such fear and prevented my recognizing her even though I knew who she was."

It is probably because of such impairments in visual interpretation that some persons with schizophrenia misidentify someone and say he or she looks like someone else. My sister with schizophrenia does this frequently, claiming to have seen many friends from childhood who I know in fact could not have been present. Another patient with schizophrenia added a grandiose flair to the visual misperception:

> This morning, when I was at Hillside [Hospital] I was making a movie. I was surrounded by movie stars. The X-ray technician was Peter Lawford. The security guard was Don Knotts . . .

In addition to difficulties in interpreting individual auditory and visual stimuli in coherent patterns, many persons with schizophrenia have difficulty putting the two kinds of stimuli together.

> I can't concentrate on television because I can't watch the screen and lis-

ten to what is being said at the same time. I can't seem to take in two things like this at the same time especially when one of them means watching and the other means listening. On the other hand I seem to be always taking in too much at the one time and then I can't handle it and can't make sense of it.

I tried sitting in my apartment and reading; the words looked perfectly familiar, like old friends whose faces I remembered perfectly well but whose names I couldn't recall; I read one paragraph ten times, could make no sense of it whatever, and shut the book. I tried listening to the radio, but the sounds went through my head like a buzz saw. I walked carefully through traffic to a movie theater and sat through a movie which seemed to consist of a lot of people wandering around slowly and talking a great deal about something or other. I decided, finally, to spend my days sitting in the park watching the birds on the lake.

These persons' difficulties in watching television or movies are very typical. In fact it is striking how few patients with schizophrenia on hospital wards watch television, contrary to what is popularly believed. Some may sit in front of it and watch the visual motion, as if it were a test pattern, but few of them can tell you what is going on. This includes patients of all levels of intelligence and education, among them college-educated persons who, given little else to do, might be expected to take advantage of the TV for much of the day. On the contrary, you are more likely to find them sitting quietly in another corner of the room, ignoring the TV; if you ask them why, they may tell you that they cannot follow what is going on, or they may try to cover up their defect by saying they are tired. One of my patients was an avid New York Yankees baseball fan prior to his illness, but he refuses to watch the game now even when the Yankees are on and he is in the room at the time, because he cannot understand what is happening. As a practical aside, the favorite TV programs and movies of many persons with schizophrenia are cartoons and travelogues; both are simple and can be followed visually without the necessity of integrating auditory input at the same time.

But the job of the switchboard operator in our brain does not end with sorting and interpreting the incoming stimuli. The job also includes hooking up the stimuli with proper responses to be sent back outside. For example, if somebody asks me, "Would you like to have lunch with me today?" my brain focuses immediately on the overall content of the question and starts calculating: Do I have time? Do I want to? What excuses do I have? What will other people think who see me with this person? What will be the effect on this person if I say no? Out of these calculations emerges a response which, in a normal brain, is appropriate to the situation. Similarly, news of a friend's death gets hooked up with grief, visual and auditory stimuli from a Woody Allen movie are hooked up with mirth, and a new idea regarding the creation of the universe is hooked up with logic and with previous knowledge in this area. It is an orderly, ongoing process, and the switchboard operator goes on, day after day, making relatively few mistakes.

The inability of patients with schizophrenia not only to sort and interpret stimuli but to select out appropriate responses is one of the hallmarks of the disease. It led Swiss psychiatrist Eugen Bleuler in 1911 to introduce the term "schizophrenia," meaning in German a splitting of the various parts of the thought process. Bleuler was impressed by the inappropriate responses frequently given by persons with this disease; for example, when told that a close friend has died, a person with schizophrenia may giggle. It is as if the switchboard operator not only gets bored and stops sorting and interpreting but becomes actively malicious and begins hooking the incoming stimuli up to random, usually inappropriate, responses.

The inability to interpret and respond appropriately is also at the core of patients' difficulties in relating to other people. Not being able to put the auditory and visual stimuli together makes it difficult to understand others; if in addition you cannot respond appropriately, then interpersonal relations become impossible. One patient described such difficulties:

> During the visit I tried to establish contact with her, to feel that she was actually there, alive and sensitive. But it was futile. Though I certainly recognized her, she became part of the unreal world. I knew her name and everything about her, yet she appeared strange, unreal, like a statue. I saw her eyes, her nose, her lips moving, heard her voice and understood what she said perfectly, yet I was in the presence of a stranger. To restore contact between us I made desperate efforts to break through the invisible dividing wall but the harder I tried, the less successful I was, and the uneasiness grew apace.

It is for this reason that many persons with schizophrenia prefer to spend time by themselves, withdrawn, communicating with others as little as possible. The process is too difficult and too painful to undertake except when absolutely necessary.

Just as auditory and visual stimuli may not be sorted or interpreted by the person's brain and may elicit inappropriate responses, so too may actions be fragmented and lead to inappropriate responses. This will be discussed in greater detail in a subsequent section, but it is worth noting that the same kind of brain deficit is probably involved. For example, compare the difficulties this patient has in the simple action of getting a drink of water with the difficulties in responding to auditory and visual stimuli described above:

> If I do something like going for a drink of water, I've got to go over each detail—find cup, walk over, turn tap, fill cup, turn tap off, drink it. I keep building up a picture. I have to change the picture each time. I've got to make the old picture move. I can't concentrate. I can't hold things. Something else comes in, various things. It's easier if I stay still.

It suggests that there may be relatively few underlying brain deficits leading to the broad range of symptoms which comprise the disease of schizophrenia.

When schizophrenia thought patterns are looked at from outside, as when they are being described by a psychiatrist, such terms as "disconnectedness," "loosening of associations," "concreteness," "impairment of logic," "thought blocking" and "ambivalence" are used. To begin with disconnectedness: one of my patients used to come into the office each morning and ask my secretary to write a sentence on paper for him. One request was "Write all kinds of black snakes looking like raw onion, high strung, deep down, long winded, all kinds of sizes." This patient had put together several apparently disconnected ideas which a normally functioning brain would not join. Another patient wrote:

> My thoughts get all jumbled up, I start thinking or talking about something but I never get there. Instead I wander off in the wrong direction and get caught up with all sorts of different things that may be connected with the things I want to say but in a way I can't explain. People listening to me get more lost than I do.

Sometimes there may be a vague connection between the jumbled thoughts in schizophrenia thinking; such instances are referred to as loose associations. For example, in the sentence about black snakes above, it may be that the patient juxtaposed onions to black snakes because of the onionlike pattern on the skin of some snakes. On another occasion I was drawing blood from a patient's arm and she said, "Look at my blue veins. I asked the Russian women to make them red," loosely connecting the color of blood with the "Reds" of the former Soviet Union. And the great Russian dancer Nijinsky wrote the following as he was developing schizophrenia, jumping from the round shape of a stage to his eye:

> I am not artificial. I am life. The theatre is not life. I know the customs of the theatre. The theatre becomes a habit. Life does not. I do not like the theatre with a square stage. I like a round stage. I will build a theatre which will have a round shape, like an eye. I like to look closely in the mirror and I see only one eye in my forehead.

Occasionally the loose association will rest not upon some tenuous logical connection between the words but merely upon their similar sound. For example, one young man presented me with a written poem:

> *I believe we will soon*
> *achieve world peace. But*
> *I'm still on the lamb.*

He had confused the lamb associated with peace with the expression "on the lam," the correct spelling of which he apparently did not know. There is no logical association between "lamb" and "lam" except for their similar sound; such associations are referred to as clang associations.

Another characteristic of schizophrenia thinking is concreteness. This can be tested by asking the person to give the meaning of proverbs, which require an ability to abstract, to move from the specific to the general. When most people are asked what "People who live in glass houses shouldn't throw stones" means, they will answer something like: "If you're not perfect yourself, don't criticize others." They move from the specific glass house and stones to the general concept without difficulty.

But the person with schizophrenia frequently loses this ability to abstract. I asked one hundred patients with schizophrenia to explain the proverb above; less than one-third were able to think abstractly about it. The majority answered simply something like "It might break the windows." In many instances the concrete answer also demonstrated some disconnected thinking.

> Well, it could mean exactly like it says 'cause the windows may well be broken. They do grow flowers in glass houses.

> Because if they did they'd break the environment.

> Because they might be put out for the winter.

A few patients personalized it:

> People should always keep their decency about their living arrangements. I remember living in a glass house but all I did was wave.

> Because it might bust the wall and people could see you.

Others responded with totally irrelevant answers that illustrated many facets of the schizophrenic thinking disorder.

> Don't hit until you go—coming or going.

> Some people are up in the air and some in society and some up in the air.

A few patients were able to think abstractly about the proverb, but in formulating their reply incorporated other aspects of schizophrenic thinking.

> People who live in glass houses shouldn't forget people who live in stone houses and shouldn't throw glass.

> If you suffer from complexities, don't talk about people. Don't be agile.

The most succinct answer came from a quiet, chronically ill young man who pondered it solemnly, looked up and said, "Caution."

Concrete thinking can also occur during the everyday life of some persons. For example, one day I was taking a picture of my sister who has schizophrenia. When I said, "Look at the birdie," she immediately looked up to the sky. Another patient, passing a newspaper stand, noticed a headline announcing that a star had fallen from a window. "How could a big thing like a star get into a window?" he wondered, until he realized it referred to a movie star.

An impairment of the ability to think logically is another facet of schizophrenic thinking, as illustrated in several of the previous examples. Another example was a patient under my care who, in psychological testing, was asked, "What would you do if you were lost in a forest?" He replied, "Go to the back of the forest, not the front." Similarly, many patients lose the ability to reason causally about events. One, for example, set his home on fire with his wheelchair-confined mother in it; when questioned carefully he did not seem to understand the fact that he was endangering her life.

In this kind of impaired thinking, opposites can coexist.

> I was extremely unhappy, I felt myself getting younger; the system wanted to reduce me to nothing. Even as I diminished in body and in age, I discovered that I was nine centuries old. For to be nine centuries old actually meant being not yet born. That is why the nine centuries did not make me feel at all old; quite the contrary.

Given this impairment of causal and logical thinking in many persons with this disease, it is not surprising that they frequently have difficulty with daily activities, such as taking a bus, following directions, or planning meals. It also explains the fantastic ideas that some patients offer as facts. One of my patients, for example, wrote me a note about "a spider that weighs over a ton" and "a bird which weighs 178 pounds and makes 200 tracks in the winter and has only one foot." The writer was college-educated.

In addition to disconnectedness, loosening of associations, concreteness, and impairment of logic, there are other features of schizophrenic thinking. Neologisms—made-up words—are occasionally heard. They may sound like gibberish to the listener, but to those saying them they are a response to their inability to find the words they want.

> The worst thing has been my face and my speech. The words wouldn't come out right. I know how to explain myself but the way it comes out of my mouth isn't right. My thoughts run too fast and I can't stop the train at

the right point to make them go the right way. Big magnified thoughts come into my head when I am speaking and put away words I wanted to say and make me stray away from what was in my mind. Things I am speaking just fade away and my head gets very heavy and I can't place what I wanted to say. I've got a lot to say but I can't focus the words to come out so they come out jumbled up. A barrier inside my head stops me from speaking properly and the mind goes blank. I try to concentrate but nothing comes out. Sometimes I find a word to replace what I wanted to say.

Another uncommon but dramatic form of schizophrenic thinking is called a word salad; the person just strings together a series of totally unrelated words and pronounces them as a sentence. One of my patients once turned to me solemnly and asked, "Bloodworm Baltimore frenchfry?" It's difficult to answer a question like that!

Generally it is not necessary to analyze the thought pattern in detail to know that something is wrong with it. The overall effect on the listener is both predictable and indicative. In its most common forms, it makes the listener feel that something is fuzzy about the thinking, as if the words have been slightly mixed up. John Bartlow Martin wrote a book about mental illness called *A Pane of Glass,* and Ingmar Bergman portrayed the onset of schizophrenia in his *Through a Glass Darkly.* Both were referring to this opaque quality in schizophrenic speech and thinking. The listener hears all the words, which may be almost correct, but at the end of the sentence or paragraph realizes that it doesn't "make sense." It is the feeling evoked when, puzzled by something, we squint our eyes, wrinkle our forehead, and smile slightly. Usually we exclaim "What?" as we do this. It is a reaction evoked often when we listen to people with a schizophrenic thinking disorder.

I feel that everything is sort of related to everybody and that some people are far more susceptible to this theory of relativity than others because of either having previous ancestors connected in some way or other with places or things, or because of believing, or by leaving a trail behind when you walk through a room you know. Some people might leave a different trail and all sorts of things go like that.

There can, of course, be all degrees of these thinking disorders in patients. Especially in the early stages of illness there may be only a vagueness or evasiveness that defies precise labeling, but in the full-blown illness the impairment usually is quite clear. It is an unusual patient who does not have some form of thinking disorder. Some psychiatrists even question whether schizophrenia is the correct diagnosis if the person's thinking pattern is completely normal: they would say that schizophrenia, by definition, must include some disordered thinking. Others claim that it is possible, though unusual, to have genuine schizophrenia with other symptoms but without a thinking disorder.

A totally different type of thinking disorder is also commonly found in persons with schizophrenia: blocking of thoughts. To return to the metaphor of the telephone operator at the switchboard, it is as if she suddenly dozes off for a few moments and the system goes dead. The person is thinking or starting to respond and then stops, often in mid-sentence, and looks blank for a brief period. John Perceval described this as long ago as 1840:

> For instance, I have been often desired to open my mouth, and to address persons in different manners, and I have begun without premeditation a very rational and consecutive speech . . . but in the midst of my sentence, the power had either left me, or words have been suggested contradictory of those that went before: and I have been deserted, gaping, speechless, or stuttering in great confusion.

Other people have given these accounts:

> I may be thinking quite clearly and telling someone something and suddenly I get stuck. You have seen me do this and you may think I am just lost for words or that I have gone into a trance, but that is not what happens. What happens is that I suddenly stick on a word or an idea in my head and I just can't move past it. It seems to fill my mind and there's no room for anything else. This might go on for a while and suddenly it's over.

> If I am reading I may suddenly get bogged down at a word. It may be any word, even a simple word that I know well. When this happens I can't get past it. It's as if I am being hypnotized by it. It's as if I am seeing the word for the first time and in a different way from anyone else. It's not so much that I absorb it, it's more like it is absorbing me.

Sometimes I commit brief disappearances—my mind pauses and closes down for a short while, like falling asleep suddenly.

Everyone who has spent time with persons with schizophrenia has observed this phenomenon. James Chapman claims it occurs in 95 percent of all patients. Some of the patients explain it by saying the thoughts are being taken out of their head. This symptom—called thought withdrawal—is considered by many psychiatrists to be strongly suggestive of a diagnosis of schizophrenia when it is present.

Ambivalence is another common symptom of schizophrenic thinking. Although now a fashionable term used very broadly, it was originally used in a narrower sense to describe schizophrenic patients who were unable to resolve contradictory thoughts or feelings, holding opposites in their minds simultaneously. A person with schizophrenia might think: "Yes, they are going to kill me and I love them." One woman described the contradictory thoughts as follows:

I am so ambivalent that my mind can divide on a subject, and those two parts subdivide over and over until my mind feels like it is in pieces and I am totally disorganized.

Sometimes the ambivalence gets translated into actions as well. For example, one of my patients frequently leaves the front door of the building, turns right, then stops, takes three steps back to the left and stops, turns back and starts right, and may continue in this way for a full five minutes. It is not found as dramatically in most patients, but is of sufficient frequency and severity for Bleuler to have named it as one of the cardinal symptoms of schizophrenia. It is as if the ability to make a decision has been impaired. Normally our brain assesses the incoming thoughts and stimuli, makes a decision and then initiates a response. The brains of some persons with schizophrenia are apparently impaired in this respect, initiating a response but then immediately countermanding it with its opposite, then repeating the process. It is a truly painful spectacle to observe.

DELUSIONS AND HALLUCINATIONS

Delusions and hallucinations are probably the best-known symptoms of schizophrenia. They are dramatic and are therefore the behaviors usually focused on when schizophrenia is being represented in popular literature or movies. The person observed talking to himself or to inanimate objects is almost a *sine qua non* for schizophrenia; it is the image evoked in our minds when the term "crazy" or "mad" is used.

And certainly delusions and hallucinations are very important and common symptoms of this disease. However, it should be remembered that they are not essential to it; indeed no *single* symptom is essential for the diagnosis of schizophrenia. There are many people with schizophrenia who have a combination of other symptoms, such as a thought disorder, disturbances of affect, and disturbances of behavior, who have never had delusions or hallucinations. It should also be remembered that delusions and hallucinations are found in brain diseases other than schizophrenia, so their presence does not automatically mean that schizophrenia is present. Finally, it is important to realize that most delusions and hallucinations, as well as distortions of the body boundaries, are a direct outgrowth of overacuteness of the senses and the brain's inability to interpret and respond appropriately to stimuli. In other words, most delusions and hallucinations are logical outgrowths of what the brain is experiencing. They are "crazy" only to the outsider, to the person experiencing them they form part of a logical and coherent pattern.

Delusions are simply false ideas believed by the patient but not by other people in his/her culture and which cannot be corrected by reason. They are usually based on some kind of sensory experience that the person misinterprets. This may be as simple as brief static on the radio or a flicker of the television screen that the person interprets as a signal. Family members often wonder where the delusional ideas in the affected person came from. Here is an example:

I went to the door of my small room and peered into the hall. Men and women with unstylish clothes and expressionless eyes paraded back and forth past my door.

"Where do I know you from?" I asked a hefty woman with a tiny face. The woman's short curly hair circled her pudgy face in ringlets. I thought I knew her.

"In a cottage by the sea," said the woman, squinting austerely at me, "I was you and you were me."

This enigmatic message must be a piece to the puzzle. I pondered it. Grandma, before she had died, had lived by the sea. Suddenly I knew the woman was my grandma.

One simple form of a delusion is the conviction that random events going on around the person all relate in a direct way to him or her. If you are walking down the street and a man on the opposite sidewalk coughs, you don't think anything of it and may not even consciously hear the cough. The person with schizophrenia, however, not only hears the cough but may immediately decide it must be a signal of some kind, perhaps directed to someone else down the street to warn him that the person is coming. The schizophrenia sufferer *knows* this is true with a certainty that few people experience. If you are walking with such a person and try to reason him/her past these delusions, your efforts will probably be futile. Even if you cross the street, and in the presence of the same person question the man about his cough, the individual will probably just decide that you are part of the plot. Reasoning with people about their delusions is like trying to bail out the ocean with a bucket. If, shortly after the cough incident, a helicopter flies overhead, the delusion may enlarge. Obviously the helicopter is watching the person, which further confirms suspicions about the cough. And if in addition to these happenings, the person arrives at the bus stop just too late to catch the bus, the delusional system is confirmed yet again; obviously the person who coughed or the helicopter pilot radioed the bus driver to leave. It all fits together into a logical, coherent whole.

Normal persons would experience these events and simply curse their bad luck at missing the bus. The person with schizophrenia, however, is experiencing different things so the events take on a different meaning. The cough and the helicopter noise may be very loud to him/her and even the sound of the bus may be perceived to be strange. While the normal person responds correctly to these as separate and unrelated events, similar to the stimuli and events of everyday life, the person with schizophrenia puts them together into a pattern. Thus both overacuteness of the senses and impaired ability to logically interpret incoming stimuli and thoughts may lie behind many of the delusions experienced by afflicted minds. To them the person who *cannot* put these special events together must be crazy, not the other way around.

There are many excellent examples of delusional thinking in literature. Chekhov, in his well-known "Ward No. 6," described it as follows:

A policeman walking slowly passed by the windows: that was not for nothing. Here were two men standing still and silent near the house. Why? Why were they silent? And agonizing days and nights followed for Ivan Dmitritch. Everyone who passed by the windows or came into the yard seemed to him a spy or a detective.

Another good example was written by a patient:

I got up at seven A.M., dressed and drove to the hospital. I felt my breathing trouble might be due to an old heart lesion. I had been told when I was young that I had a small ventricular septal defect. I decided that I was in heart failure and that people felt I wasn't strong enough to accept this, so they weren't telling me. I thought about all the things that had happened recently that could be interpreted in that light. I looked up heart failure in a textbook and found that the section had been removed, so I concluded someone had removed it to protect me. I remembered other comments. A friend had talked about a "walkie-talkie," and the thought occurred to me that I might be getting medicine without my knowledge, perhaps by radio. I remembered someone talking about a one-way plane ticket; to me that meant a trip to Houston and a heart operation. I remembered an unusual smell in the lab and thought that might be due to the medicine they were giving me in secret. I began to think I might have a machine inside me which secreted medicine into my bloodstream. Again I reasoned that I had a disease no one could tell me about and was getting medicine for it secretly. At this point, I panicked and tried to run away, but the attendant in the parking lot seemed to be making a sign to motion me back. I thought I caught brief glimpses of a friend and my wife so I decided to go back into the hospital. A custodian's eyes attracted my attention; they were especially large and piercing. He looked very powerful. He had to be "in on it," maybe he was giving medicine in some way. Then I began to have the feeling that other people were watching me. And, as periodically happened throughout the early stages, I said to myself that the whole thing was absurd, but when I looked again the people really were watching me.

A young man with paranoid schizophrenia expressed the anguish of his own delusions in a poem:

> Anxiety:
> like metal on metal in my brain

Paranoia: it is
making me run
away, away, away
and back again quickly
to see if I've been caught
Or lied to
Or laughed at
Ha ha ha. The ferris wheel
in Looney Land is not so funny.

In many cases the delusions become more complex and integrated. Rather than simply being watched, the person becomes convinced that he/she is being controlled by other persons, manipulated, or even hypnotized. Such persons are constantly on the alert for confirmatory evidence to support their beliefs; needless to say, they always find it from among the myriad visual and auditory stimuli perceived by all of us each day. A good example of this was a kind, elderly Irish lady who was a patient on my ward. She believed that she had been wired by some mysterious foreign agents in her sleep and that through the wires her thoughts and actions could be controlled. In particular she pointed to the ceiling as the place from which the control took place. One morning I was dismayed to come onto the ward and discover workmen installing a new fire alarm system; wires were hanging down in all colors and in all directions. The lady looked at me, pointed to the ceiling, and just smiled; her delusions had been confirmed forever!

Delusions of being wired or radio controlled are relatively common. Often it is the FBI or the CIA which is the suspected perpetrator of the scheme. One patient was convinced that a radio had been sewn into his skull when he had had a minor scalp wound sutured and had tried to bring legal suit against the FBI innumerable times. Another man, at one time a highly successful superintendent of schools, became convinced that a radio had been implanted in his nose. He went to dozens of major medical centers, even to Europe, seeking a surgeon who would remove it. He even had an X ray of his nose showing a tiny white speck which he was convinced was the radio.

Friends of the unfortunate people often try to reason them out of their delusions. Rarely is this successful. Questions about why the FBI would want to control them are deftly brushed aside as irrelevant; the important point is that they do, and the person is experiencing sensations (such as strange noises) which confirm the fact. Reasoning a person with schizophrenia out of a delusion is hampered by the distorted stimuli he/she is perceiving and also by the fact that the thinking processes may not be logical or connected. A further impediment is the fact that delusions frequently become self-fulfilling. Thus someone who believes others are spying on him/her finds it logical to act furtively, perhaps running from shelter to shelter and peering anxiously into the faces of passersby. Such behavior inevitably invites attention and leads to the delusional person's actually being watched by other people. As the saying goes, "I used to be paranoid but now people really *are* watching me."

Delusions in which the person is being watched, persecuted, or attacked are commonly called paranoid delusions. Paranoia is a relative concept; everybody experiences bits and pieces of it from time to time. In some places a little paranoia even has survival value; the fellow who works across the hall may really be stealing your memos, because he wants your job. Paranoid thinking by itself is not schizophrenia; it is only when it becomes a frank delusion (unaffected by reason) that it *may* be. Even then, however, it must be remembered that paranoid delusions can occur in brain diseases other than schizophrenia.

Paranoid delusions may on occasion be dangerous. "During the paranoid period I thought I was being persecuted for my beliefs, that my enemies were actively trying to interfere with my activities, were trying to harm me, and at times even to kill me." The paranoid person may try to strike first when the threat is perceived as too close. Facilities for the criminally insane in every state include among their inmates a large number of persons with schizophrenia who have committed a crime in what they believed to be self-defense. It is this subgroup that has produced the general belief that people with schizophrenia as a whole are dangerous. In fact, when we take into consideration all persons with schizophrenia, this subgroup is very small. Most persons with schizophrenia are not dangerous at all, and I would far rather walk the halls of any mental hospital than walk the streets of any inner city.

Delusions may be of many types other than paranoid; grandiose delusions are quite common: "I felt that I had power to determine the weather, which responded to my inner moods, and even to control the movement of the sun in relation to other astronomical bodies." This often leads to a belief by the person that he/she is Jesus Christ, the Virgin Mary, the President, or some other exalted or important person. One admission to our hospital believed himself to be Mao Zedong. We began him on medication and, by the next day, knew he was getting better because he had become only the brother of Mao Zedong. Other individuals with grandiose delusions may believe that they are starring in a movie:

> I once believed that I was in the process of making a gigantic film of which I was the star. Everywhere I went in London there was a hidden camera and microphone and everything that I said and did was being recorded.

Grandiose delusions can on occasion be dangerous. People who believe that they can fly, or stop bullets with their chest may place themselves in a position to demonstrate the truth of their belief with predictably tragic consequences.

There is one particular type of grandiose delusion which, although not seen commonly, is so distinctive that it has acquired its own name. It is the delusion that another person, usually famous, is deeply in love with the patient. Such cases, originally called *psychoses passionnelles* by Dr. de Clerembault, a French psychiatrist, now often bear the designation of de Clerembault syndrome, or erotomania. One of my patients, who believed that Senator Edward Kennedy was in love with her, spent all her time and money following him around but always staying at a distance; she produced a multitude of incredible reasons why he could not acknowledge her presence. Another patient believed she was engaged to a man whom she had met once casually several years before, and spent all day walking the city streets looking for him. Most patients with such delusions have schizophrenia, although a few may have bipolar disorder. These patients have a pathos to their lives which is unusually evocative.

A relatively common delusion is that a person can control other people's minds. One young woman I saw had spent five years at home because each time she went into the street she believed that her mind compelled other people to turn and look at her. She described the effect of her mind as "like a magnet—they have no choice but to turn and look." Another patient believed he could change people's moods by "telepathic force": "I eventually felt I could go into a crowded restaurant and while just sitting there quietly, I could change everyone's mood to happiness and laughter." Here is a variant on this delusion:

> I like talking to a person but not in audible words. I try to force my thoughts into someone. I concentrate on how they move. I think of a mes-

sage and concentrate in my head. It's thought you're passing over. I send
the messages by visual indication. Sometimes the shoulder, sometimes my
whole body.

Another variant is the delusional belief that one's thoughts are radiat-
ing out of one's head and being broadcast over radio or television; this
is called thought broadcasting and is considered to be an almost certain
indication of schizophrenia.

In evaluating delusions it is very important to keep in mind that
their content is culture-bound. It is not the belief *per se* that is delusional, but how far the belief differs from the beliefs shared by others
in the same culture or subculture. A man who believes he is being
influenced by others who have "worked roots" (put a hex) on him may
be completely normal if he grew up in lowland South Carolina where
"working roots" is a widespread cultural belief. If he grew up in
Scarsdale, on the other hand, his belief in being influenced by "worked
roots" is more likely to suggest schizophrenia. Minority groups in particular may have a culturally induced high level of paranoid belief, and
this belief may be based upon real discrimination and real persecution.
In other subcultural groups it may be difficult to assess the pathological nature of delusional thinking, for instance regarding grandiose
delusions among the deeply religious and paranoid delusions among
employees of the intelligence community. Imagine, for example, the
dilemma of a Mother Superior in evaluating a novitiate who claims to
have a special relationship with the Virgin Mary, or a supervisor at the
CIA who is told by one of his undercover employees that he is being
watched all the time. Beliefs of persons suspected of having schizophrenia must *always* be placed within a cultural context and regarded
as only one facet of the disease.

Occasionally individuals come to attention who have odd
thoughts, but it may be very difficult to decide whether these thoughts
constitute true delusions. Such an individual, apparently, is John
Hinckley, who in 1981 attempted to assassinate President Ronald
Reagan. According to court testimony, Hinckley had a fantasy relationship with Jodi Foster, a young movie actress, and spent much of his
time and energy trying to engage her attention; the assassination
attempt was said to be Hinckley's ultimate effort to prove his love for
Jodi Foster. At his trial, psychiatrists for the defense and the prosecu-
tion differed sharply on whether such thinking constituted a true delusion.

One other aspect of delusions is important to note. Delusions may be fixed and static in some individuals with schizophrenia, but in others the delusions may be labile and held with varying degrees of conviction. I recall one patient, for example, who believed that another patient was trying to kill him. On one day he would avoid the feared person completely, on the next day he would socialize with him pleasantly, and on the following day he would avoid him again. This lack of consistency in response to delusional thinking is difficult to understand for families of individuals with schizophrenia.

Hallucinations are very common in schizophrenia and are the end of that spectrum which begins with overacuteness of the senses. To take vision as an example: the spectrum has overacuteness of vision at one end of it, that is, lights are too bright, colors take on a more brilliant hue. In the middle of the spectrum are gross distortions of visual stimuli (also called illusions), such as a dog which takes on the appearance of a tiger. And at the far end of the spectrum are things which are seen by the person with schizophrenia when there is nothing there; this is a true hallucination. The experiences described by patients are usually a mixture of different points on the spectrum.

Gross distortions of visual or auditory stimuli are not uncommon experiences in schizophrenia.

I was sitting listening to another person and suddenly the other person became smaller and then larger and then he seemed to get smaller again. He did not become a complete miniature. Then today with another person, I felt he was getting taller and taller. There is brightness and clarity of outline of things around me. Last week I was with a girl and suddenly she seemed to get bigger and bigger, like a monster coming nearer and nearer. The situation becomes threatening and I shrink back and back.

This phenomenon can perhaps best be depicted by a description of the first time I experienced it. I was one of four men at a bridge table. On one of the deals, my partner bid three clubs. I looked at my hand: I had only one small club. Though my hand was weak, I had to bid to take him out. My bid won. When my partner laid down his cards, he showed only two small clubs in his hand. I immediately questioned why he had bid three clubs. He denied having made such a bid. The other two men at the table supported him. There was no opportunity and no reason for the three clubs despite the fact that I had distinctly heard him do so. Not only had the hallucination included a spatial component synchronized with the man's position, but it had also duplicated exactly the vocal tones of the man. Furthermore, the man had actually declared a different bid at the time I had heard him bidding three clubs. This bid I had not heard. Somewhere along the line of my nervous system the words which he had actually spoken were blocked and the hallucinatory words substituted.

In both instances there was a stimulus of some kind, but the person saw or heard it in a grossly distorted way. It is as if the person's brain is playing tricks.

Even worse tricks are played in forming true hallucinations, in which there is no initial stimulus at all. The brain makes up what it hears, sees, feels, smells, or tastes. Such experiences may be very real for the person. A person who hallucinates voices talking to him may hear the voices just as clearly as, or even more clearly than, the voices of real people talking to him and people with schizophrenia frequently talk back to the voices. There is a tendency for people close to patients to scoff at the "imaginary" voices, to minimize them and not believe the persons really hear them. But they do, and in the sense that the brain hears them, they are real. The voices are but an extreme example of the malfunctioning of the sufferer's sensory apparatus.

Auditory hallucinations are by far the most common form of hallucination in schizophrenia. They are so characteristic of the disease that a person with true auditory hallucinations should be assumed to have schizophrenia until proven otherwise. They may take a variety of forms. They may be a simple swishing or thumping sound, such as the beating of the heart in Poe's famous short story:

> No doubt I now grew very pale;—but I talked fluently, and with a heightened voice. Yet the sound increased and what could I do? It was a low, dull, quick sound—much such a sound as a watch makes when enveloped in cotton. I gasped for breath—and yet the officers heard it not. I talked more quickly—more vehemently; but the noise steadily increased. Why would they not be gone? I paced the floor to and fro with heavy strides, as if excited to fury by the observation of the men—but the noise steadily increased.

They may be a single voice: "Thus for years I have heard daily in hundredfold repetition incoherent words spoken into my nerves without any context, such as 'Why not?' 'Why, if,' 'Why, because I,' 'Be it,' 'With respect to him.'"

Or they may be multiple voices or even a choir:

There was music everywhere and rhythm and beauty. But the plans were always thwarted. I heard what seemed to be a choir of angels. I thought it the most beautiful music I had ever heard. Two of the airs I kept repeating over and over until the delirium ended. One of them I can remember imperfectly even now. This choir of angels kept hovering around the hospital and shortly afterward I heard something about a little lamb being born upstairs in the room just above mine.

The hallucinations may be heard only occasionally or they may be continuous. When occasional, the most common time for them, in my clinical experience, is at night when going to sleep.

For about almost seven years—except during sleep—I have never had a single moment in which I did not hear voices. They accompany me to every place and at all times; they continue to sound even when I am in conversation with other people, they persist undeterred even when I concentrate on other things, for instance read a book or a newspaper, play the piano, etc.; only when I am talking aloud to other people or to myself are they of course drowned by the stronger sound of the spoken word and therefore inaudible to me. But the well-known phrases recommence at once, sometimes in the middle of a sentence, which tells me that the conversation had continued during the interval, that is to say that those nervous stimuli or vibrations responsible for the weaker sounds of the voices continue even while I talk aloud.

I have taken care of people with similar manifestations. One unfortunate woman had heard voices continuously for twenty years. They became especially loud whenever she tried to watch television, so she couldn't watch it at all.

In the vast majority of cases, the voices are unpleasant. They are often accusatory, reviling the victims for past misdeeds, either real or imagined. Often they curse them, and I have had many people refuse to tell me what the voices say to them because they were embarrassed by it. In a minority of cases the voices may be pleasant, as in the example with lovely music cited above. Occasionally they are even helpful, as with a woman who announced to me one day that she was getting well: "I know I am, because my voices told me so."

The precise mechanism of auditory hallucinations is not well understood. The most plausible explanation is that the schizophrenic disease process selectively affects auditory centers in the brain, thereby producing auditory hallucinations. There are several different auditory centers in the brain, some of which are contiguous with temporal lobe and frontal lobe areas thought to be involved in schizophrenia. In one recent study an increase in blood flow to a major language area was demonstrated to occur in schizophrenia during auditory hallucinations. Another study showed that "auditory hallucinations involve language regions of the cortex in a pattern similar to that seen in normal subjects listening to their own voices," which may explain why auditory hallucinations sound so real to the person hearing them. Studies of brain structures in individuals with schizophrenia have also shown that auditory hallucinations are more common in patients who have larger third ventricles, one of the fluid-filled spaces in the brain. As technology improves for measuring brain structures, it is likely that additional correlations will be found between symptoms such as auditory hallucinations and specific abnormalities of brain structures. It is also of interest that individuals who are born deaf and who later develop schizophrenia can experience auditory hallucinations.

Visual hallucinations also occur but less frequently. One patient described the variety of these hallucinations:

> At an early stage the appearance of colored flashes of light was common. These took the form either of distant streaks or of near-by round glowing patches about a foot in diameter. Another type, which took place five or six times, was the appearance of words or symbols on blank surfaces. Closely connected with this was the occasional substitution of hallucinatory matter for the actual printed matter in books which I have been reading. On these occasions, the passage which I have been seeing has dissolved while I have been looking at it and another and sometimes wholly different passage has appeared in its place. . . . A further form of visual hallucinations that happened on two occasions was the appearance on a wall of the pictures of the heads of young women as though projected from a projection machine. These pictures were of women whom to the best of my knowledge I had never met.

Visual hallucinations usually appear in conjunction with auditory hallucinations. When only visual hallucinations appear, it is unlikely that schizophrenia is the cause. Many other brain diseases, notably drug intoxications and alcohol withdrawal, cause purely visual hallucinations and are the more likely diagnosis in such cases.

Like delusions, hallucinations must always be evaluated within their cultural context. In medieval times and today among some religious groups, visual hallucinations are not uncommon and do not necessarily suggest mental illness. Dr. Silvano Arieti has attempted to distinguish the hallucinations of the profoundly religious from those of schizophrenia by proposing the following criteria:

A. Religious hallucinations are usually visual, while those in schizophrenia are predominantly auditory.
B. Religious hallucinations usually involve benevolent guides or advisers who issue orders to the person.
C. Religious hallucinations are usually pleasant.

Hallucinations of smell or taste are very unusual but do occur. One patient gave this description of hallucinations of smell:

On a few occasions, I have experienced olfactory hallucinations. These have consisted of the seeming smelling of an odor as though originating from a source just outside the nose. Sometimes this odor has had a symbolical relationship with the thoughts-out-loud, as for instance, the appearance of an odor of sulphur in connection with a threat of damnation to hell by the thoughts-out-loud.

Another patient illustrated the same phenomenon of associating a smell with a thought:

During the time I was getting sick again, I began to think about the abortions I had before I was married. I was feeling guilty about them again. In those days you always tried to abort yourself first by taking quinine. When I was taking a shower and thinking about the past, I suddenly noticed the unmistakable smell of quinine. Soon after that, my mother and I were talking and she said something about oranges. I immediately began to smell oranges.

Hallucinations of taste usually consist of familiar food tasting differently. I have had two patients with paranoid schizophrenia, for example, who decided that they were being poisoned when their food began tasting "funny." Certainly if one's food suddenly starts changing in taste, it is logical to suspect that somebody is adding something to it.

Hallucinations of touch are also found among individuals with schizophrenia although not commonly. I have provided care for one woman who feels small insects crawling under the skin on her face; it is an understatement to say that this is very upsetting to her. Another patient experienced hallucinatory pain.

> To the person who experiences hallucinatory pains, the pains feel identical with actual pains. There is no difference between the sensation of hallucinatory and the sensation of actual pain. The person who experiences it can distinguish it only by its lack of normal cause and its interrelations with other hallucinatory phenomena. The person who feels it undergoes real suffering. . . . To give some specific data concerning hallucinatory pains that I have experienced, it may be stated that they have varied considerably in intensity, in duration, and in locus. In intensity, they have ranged from a fraction of a second up to ten minutes or so. In locus, they have ranged over all parts of the body. In type, they have included smarting, burning, aching.

ALTERED SENSE OF SELF

Closely allied with delusions and hallucinations is another complex of symptoms which is characteristic of many patients with schizophrenia. Normal individuals have a clear sense of self; they know where their bodies stop and where inanimate objects begin. They know that their hand, when they look at it, belongs to them. Even to make a statement like this strikes most normal persons as absurd because they cannot imagine its being otherwise.

But many persons with schizophrenia can imagine it, for alterations in their sense of self are not uncommon in this condition. Such alterations are frequently associated with alterations in bodily sensations, such as was described by one man with schizophrenia who wrote to me:

> My body has the same forms of distortions as my vision and these are manifested throughout my anatomy. My body feels like there are indentations, ridges, and agonizing disfigurements all over. Strands of hair falling

down on my forehead feel much larger, heavier, and more noticeable. My body feels dry like it is brittle. My skin and underlying fat feels deadish like when you get novocaine, except you still have sensation. Eyes feel hollow, like they extend further back in the skull. Appendages frequently feel different shapes, narrower or fuller or curved in opposite directions. Hands, arms, and legs sometimes feel an inch to the side of where they really are at. Fingers at times feel and look longer or shorter than usual. My face can feel twice as long as it is.

Alterations of the self may range from such somatic perceptual distortions to, on the other end of the spectrum, confusion in distinguishing oneself from another person, as described by Marguerite Sechehaye in her biography:

Sometimes I did not know clearly whether it was she or I who needed something. For instance if I asked for another cup of tea and Mamma answered teasingly, "But why do you want more tea; don't you see that I have just finished my cup and so you don't need any?" Then I replied, "Yes, that's true, I don't need any more," confusing her with myself. But at bottom I did desire a second cup of tea, and I said, "But I still want some more tea," and suddenly, in a flash, I realized the fact that Mamma's satiety did not make me sated too. And I was ashamed to let myself be thus trapped and to watch her laugh at my discomfiture.

Another patient described a similar experience in which

I saw myself in different bodies. . . . The night nurse came in and sat under the shaded lamp in the quiet ward. I recognized her as me, and I watched for some time quite fascinated; I had never had an outside view of myself before. In the morning several of the patients having breakfast were me. I recognized them by the way they held their knives and forks.

A patient's body parts may develop lives of their own, as if they have become disassociated and detached. One patient described this feeling:

I get shaky in the knees and my chest is like a mountain in front of me, and my body actions are different. The arms and legs are apart and away from me and they go on their own. That's when I feel I am the other person and copy their movements, or else stop and stand like a statue. I have to stop to find out whether my hand is in my pocket or not. I'm frightened to move or turn my head. Sometimes I let my arms roll to see where they will land. After I sit down my head clears again but I don't remember what happened when I was in the daze.

Sechehaye also describes confusion regarding where her body stopped and the rest of the world began: "This was equally true in body functions. When I urinated and it was raining torrents outside, I was not at all certain whether it was not my own urine bedewing the world, and I was gripped by fear."

Confusion about one's sexual characteristics is also not uncommonly found among people with schizophrenia, as in this man who believed his body was acquiring a feminine appearance:

My breast gives the impression of a pretty well-developed female bosom; this phenomenon can be *seen* by anybody who wants to observe me *with his own eyes.* . . . A brief glance would not suffice. The observer would have to go to the trouble of spending ten or fifteen minutes near me. In that way anybody would notice the periodic swelling and diminution of my bosom.

The altered sense of self may be further aggravated if hallucinations of touch or delusions about the body are also present. One possible example of this is Kafka's famous story "The Metamorphosis," in which Gregor awakens in the morning and slowly realizes that he has been transformed into a huge beetle. Such passages in Kafka have led some scholars to speculate that Kafka himself may have had schizophrenia at times.

The origin of this altered sense of self in persons with schizophrenia is unknown. Normally our sense of self is formed by a complex set of tactile and visual stimuli through which we can feel and see the limits of our body and by which we differentiate it from the objects around us. It is likely that the same disease process which alters the senses and the thinking process is also responsible for the altered sense of self.

CHANGES IN EMOTIONS

Changes in emotions—or affect, as it is often called by professionals—are one of the most common and characteristic changes in schizophrenia. In the early stages of the illness depression, guilt, fear, and rapidly fluctuating emotions may all be found. In the later stages flattening of emotions are more characteristic, often resulting in individuals who appear to be unable to feel emotions at all. This in turn makes it more difficult for us to relate to them so we tend to shun them even more.

Depression is a very common symptom early in the course of the disease but is often overlooked. In a 1994 study it was reported that "81 percent of the patients ... presented a well defined episode of depressive mood." In half the patients the symptoms of depression preceded the onset of delusions or hallucinations. Most such depression is biologically based, caused by neurochemical changes in the brain as part of the disease process, although some of it may also be a reaction of the person to the realization that he/she is becoming sick. One of the tragic and not uncommon sequelae of such depression is suicide, which is discussed in chapter 9.

Early in the course of illness the person with schizophrenia may also feel widely varying and rapidly fluctuating emotions. Exaggerated feelings of all kinds are not unusual, especially in connection with the peak experiences described previously.

> During the first two weeks of my psychosis, religious experience provided that dominant factor of the psychotic phenomena. The most important form of religious experience in that period was religious ecstasy. The attempts of the thoughts-out-loud to persuade myself to adopt a messianic fixation formed the hallucinary background. In affective aspects, a pervasive feeling of well-being dominated the complex. I felt as though all my worries were gone and all my problems solved. I had the assurance that all my needs would be satisfied. Connected with this euphoric state, I experienced a gentle sensation of warmth over my whole body, particularly on my back, and a sensation of my body having lost its weight and gently floating.

Guilt is another commonly felt emotion in these early stages:

> Later, considering them appropriate, I no longer felt guilty about these fantasies, nor did the guilt have an actual object. It was too pervasive, too enormous, to be founded on anything definite, and it demanded punishment. The punishment was indeed horrible, sadistic—it consisted, fittingly enough, of being guilty. For to feel oneself guilty is the worst that can happen, it is the punishment of punishments. Consequently, I could

never be relieved of it as though I had been truly punished. Quite the reverse, I felt more and more guilty, immeasurably guilty. Constantly, I sought to discover what was punishing me so dreadfully, what was making me so guilty.

And fear is frequently described by patients, often a pervasive and nameless fear that exists without any specific object. It is well described by a young man with schizophrenia:

> I sat in my basement with a fear that I could not control. I was totally afraid—just from watching my cat look out the window.

Exaggerated feelings usually are not found in patients beyond the early stages of the disease. If they are, they should raise questions as to whether schizophrenia is the correct diagnosis. It is the *retention* of such feelings and emotions which is the single sharpest dividing line between schizophrenia and manic-depressive illness (see chapter 4). If the person retains exaggerated feelings to a prominent degree beyond the early stages of the disease, it is much more likely that the correct diagnosis will turn out to be manic-depressive illness.

In addition to the exaggerated emotions that are experienced by individuals with schizophrenia, there is also evidence that some people affected with this disease have difficulties in assessing emotions in other people. A recent review of studies in this area asserted that "there has been a growing literature suggesting that schizophrenics differ substantially from controls in processing emotional communication." One research technique used to demonstrate this is to ask individuals with schizophrenia to describe the emotions of people in photographs, which is frequently a difficult task for them. This impaired ability to judge emotions in others is a major reason why many people with schizophrenia have trouble in social communications and forming friendships.

The most characteristic changes in emotions in schizophrenia are inappropriate emotions or flattened emotions. It is an unusual patient who does not have one or the other—and sometimes both—by the time the disease is full-blown.

Inappropriate emotions are to be expected in light of the previous analogy of the telephone operator at the switchboard. Just as he/she hooks up the wrong thoughts with incoming stimuli, so she also hooks up wrong emotions. The incoming call may carry sad news but she hooks it up with mirth and the patient laughs. In other instances a patient responds with an inappropriate emotion because of the other things going on in his/her head which cause laughter.

> Half the time I am talking about one thing and thinking about half a dozen other things at the same time. It must look queer to people when I laugh about something that has got nothing to do with what I am talking about, but they don't know what's going on inside and how much of it is running round in my head. You see I might be talking about something quite serious to you and other things come into my head at the same time that are funny and this makes me laugh. If I could only concentrate on the one thing at the one time I wouldn't look half so silly.

These inappropriate emotions produce one of the most dramatic aspects of the disease—the victim suddenly breaking out in cackling laughter for no apparent reason. It is a common sight in mental hospitals, and one familiar to those who have worked or lived with people with this disease.

The flattening of emotions may be subtle in the earlier stages of the disease. Chapman claims that "one of the earliest changes in schizophrenic experience involves impairment in the process of empathy with other people." The person with schizophrenia loses the ability to put him/herself in the other person's place or to feel what the other person is feeling. As the disease progresses this flattening or blunting of the emotions may become more prominent: "During my first illness I did not feel the emotions of anger, rage, or indignation to nearly as great an extent as I would have normally. Attitudes of dislike, estrangement, and fear predominated."

Emotions may become detached altogether from specific objects, leaving the victim with a void, as poignantly described by this patient:

> Instead of wishing to do things, they are done by something that seems mechanical and frightening, because it is able to do things and yet unable to want to or not to want to. All the constructive healing parts that could be used healthily and slowly to mend an aching torment have left, and the feeling that should dwell within a person is outside, longing to come back and yet having taken with it the power to return. Out and in are probably not good terms, though, for they are too black and white and it is more like gray. It is like a constant sliding and shifting that slips away in a jelly-like fashion, leaving nothing substantial and yet enough to be tasted.

And Michael Wechsler summarized it neatly in a statement to his father: "I wish I could wake up feeling really bad—it would be better than feeling nothing."

In the advanced stage of flattening of the emotions there appear to be none left at all. This does not happen frequently, but when it does it is an unforgettable experience for those who interact with the victims. I have had two such patients in whom I was unable to elicit *any* emotion whatsoever under any circumstances. They were polite, at times stubborn, but never happy or sad. It is uncannily like interacting with a robot. One of these patients set fire to his house, then sat down placidly to watch TV. When it was called to his attention that the house was on fire he got up calmly and went outside. Clearly the brain damage in these cases has seriously affected the centers mediating emotional response. Fortunately most persons with schizophrenia do not have such complete damage to this area of the brain.

One must be cautious, however, in assuming that a person with schizophrenia who apparently is experiencing no emotions *really* is experiencing no emotions. A 1993 study of individuals with schizophrenia who were videotaped while watching emotion-laden films found that the individuals "reported experiencing as much positive and negative emotion" despite the fact that they expressed much less of the emotion. Ms. Jean Bouricius, the mother of a young man with schizophrenia, published excerpts from her son's writings that demonstrated that he was experiencing intense, although unexpressed, emotions at the same time as mental health professionals were rating him as being emotionally very flat. His writings included: "Loneliness needs a song, a song of love and pain, sweet release and hope for the future," and "I close my eyes softly and become that part of midnight winds where emotion is choked and no cries can emerge." It is becoming increasingly apparent that some individuals with schizophrenia, who on the surface appear to be experiencing no emotions, are inwardly feeling intense emotions.

Often associated with a flattening of emotions are apathy, slowness of movement, underactivity, lack of drive, and a paucity (usually called poverty) of thought and speech. The composite picture is frequently seen in patients who have been sick for many years. They appear to be desireless, apathetic, seeking nothing, wanting nothing. It is as if their will had eroded: and indeed something like that probably does happen as part of the disease process.

It is fashionable nowadays to believe that much of the flattening of emotions and apathy common in patients with schizophrenia are side effects of the drugs used to treat the disease. In fact there is only a little truth to this. Many of the drugs used to treat schizophrenia do have a calming or sedative effect (see chapter 7). Most of the flattening of emotions and weakening of motivation, however, are products of the disease itself and not of the drug effects. This can easily be proved by reviewing descriptions of patients in the literature prior to the introduction of these drugs. Emotional flattening and apathy are just as prominent in those early descriptions as they are today.

CHANGES IN MOVEMENTS

In recent years changes in movements have been closely linked in people's minds with the side effects of drugs used to treat schizophrenia. And indeed the antipsychotic drugs and lithium may cause changes in movements, varying from a fine tremor of the fingers to gross jerky movements of the arms or trunk.

But it is important to keep in mind that the schizophrenic disease process can also cause changes in movements, and that these were clearly described in accounts of the disease for many years before modern drugs became available. One study of changes of movements in schizophrenia found that they occur "in virtually all cases of conservatively defined schizophrenia" and concluded that they were consequences of the disease process and not of the medication being taken by the patients. In another study half the patients in remission remembered changes in their movements. In some cases their movements appeared to speed up while in others they slowed down. A feeling of awkwardness or clumsiness is relatively common, and persons with this disease may spill things, or stumble while walking, much more commonly than before they became sick.

Another change in movement is decreased spontaneity and the person may be aware of this. One recalled: "I became the opposite of spontaneous, as a result of which I became very diffident, very labored." Some patients with schizophrenia have decreased spontaneous swinging of their arms when they walk, a finding which has led some researchers to theorize that the cerebellum or basal ganglia portions of the brain may be affected in this disease.

Repetitious movements such as tics, tremors, tongue movements and sucking movements are also seen. In the majority of patients in whom they occur they are side effects of the medication being given the patient, but in a minority they will not be due to the medication but rather to the schizophrenic disease process. Even subtle body movements like eye blinking may be affected in schizophrenia. Some patients with the disease blink much less often than normal people. Drugs can account for some of this decrease but not for all of it. Balzac noted it in a patient in the early years of the nineteenth century: "[He] stood, just as I now saw him, day and night, with fixed eyes, never raising or lowering the lids, as others do."

The most dramatic change of movements in schizophrenia, of course, is catatonic behavior. A patient may remain motionless for hours, and if the person's arm is passively moved the arm will often remain in its new position for an hour or longer. Catatonic forms of schizophrenia were seen more commonly in the earlier years of this century but have become much less common; the availability of antipsychotic medication may be one reason for this as catatonic symptoms usually respond promptly to medication.

CHANGES IN BEHAVIOR

Changes in behavior are usually secondary rather than primary symptoms of schizophrenia; that is, the behaviors shown by persons with this illness are most often a response to other things occurring in their brains. For example, if the person with schizophrenia is beset by overacuteness of the senses and an inability to synthesize incoming stimuli, it makes perfect sense for him/her to withdraw into a corner. Many of the other behaviors seen in this disease can be similarly and logically explained.

Withdrawing, remaining quietly in one place for long periods, and immobility are all common behaviors in this illness. The extreme versions of such behaviors are catatonia, where the person remains rigidly fixed in one position for long periods of time, and mutism, where the person does not speak at all. Catatonia and mutism are part of a continuum that includes the less blatant forms of withdrawal and immobility so commonly seen in the disease.

A person with schizophrenia may withdraw and remain silent for any one of a number of reasons. Sometimes this occurs when the person becomes lost in deep thought:

When I am walking along the street it comes on me. I start to think deeply and I start to go into a sort of trance. I think so deeply that I almost get out of this world. Then you get frightened that you are going to get into a jam and lose yourself. That's when I get worried and excited.

Or it may be adopted in order to slow down the incoming sensory stimuli so the brain can sort them out:

I don't like moving fast. I feel there would be a breakup if I went too quick. I can only stand that a short time and then I have to stop. If I carried on I wouldn't be aware of things as they really are. I would just be aware of the sound and noise and the movements. Everything would be a jumbled mass. I have found that I can stop this happening by going completely still and motionless. When I do that, things are easier to take in.

Unexpected sensory stimuli can also result in a slowing.

I get stuck, almost as if I am paralysed at times. It may only last for a minute or two but it's a bit frightening. It seems to happen even when something unexpected takes place, especially if there's a lot of noise that comes on suddenly. Say I am walking across the floor and someone suddenly switches on the wireless: the music seems to stop me in my tracks, and sometimes I freeze like that for a minute or two.

The movements may also be slowed so as to allow them to be integrated into a whole in exactly the same way that visual and auditory stimuli may need to be integrated.

I am not sure of my own movements any more. It's very hard to describe this but at times I am not sure about even simple actions like sitting down. It's not so much thinking out what to do, it's the doing of it that sticks me. . . . I found recently that I was thinking of myself doing things before I would do them. If I am going to sit down, for example, I have got to think of myself and almost see myself sitting down before I do it. It's the same with other things like washing, eating, and even dressing—things that I have done at one time without even bothering or thinking about at all. . . . All this makes me move much slower now. I take more time to do things because I am always conscious of what I am doing. If I could just stop noticing what I am doing, I would get things done a lot faster.

Other unusual behaviors are also found in persons with schizophrenia. Ritualistic behaviors are not uncommon. Some patients repeatedly walk in circles, and I have one who walks through all doors backwards. There are reasons why they do such things, as explained by this woman who felt compelled to beat eggs a certain way when making a cake:

> As the work progressed, a change came. The ingredients of the cake began to have a special meaning. The process became a ritual. At certain stages the stirring must be counter-clockwise; at another time it was necessary to stand up and beat the batter toward the east; the egg whites must be folded in from the left to the right; for each thing that had to be done there were complicated reasons. I recognized that these were new, unfamiliar, and unexpected, but did not question them. They carried a finality that was effective. Each compelling impulse was accompanied by an equally compelling explanation.

Another example of ritualistic behavior is the following:

> The state of indifference reigning until now was abruptly replaced by inner and outer agitation. At first I felt obliged to get up and walk; it was impossible to stay in bed. Singing a requiem without pause, I marched three steps forward and three steps back, an automatism that wearied me exceedingly and which I wished someone would help me break. I could not do it alone, for I felt forced to make these steps and if I stopped from exhaustion, even for a moment, I felt guilty again. Moreover, when any behavior became automatic, I felt guilty in interrupting it. But no one could believe that I wanted to stop, for as soon as they made me give up some stereotyped procedure, I began anew.

Certain gestures may be repeated often, for reasons which are quite logical to the person doing them but appear bizarre to the onlooker. One patient shook his head rhythmically from side to side to try and shake the excess thoughts out of his mind. Another massaged his head "to help to clear it" of unwanted thoughts. It is because of such ritualistic and repetitive behaviors that occasional patients with schizophrenia may be misdiagnosed with obsessive-compulsive disorder. Obsessions and compulsions are indeed frequently present in schizophrenia; however, a person with true obsessive-compulsive disorder will not have the thought disorder, delusions, hallucinations, or other symptoms that are also present in schizophrenia.

Specific postures may also be adopted by persons with schizophrenia. One of my patients marches endlessly up and down the sidewalk with his left hand placed awkwardly on his left shoulder. It appears to be uncomfortable but he invariably returns to it for reasons I have not been able to ascertain. Another posture was described by Perceval:

> There were two or three other delusions I laboured under of which I hardly recollect how I was cured—one in particular, that I was to lean on the back of my head and on my feet in bed, and twist my neck by throwing my body with a jerk from side to side. I fancy that I never attempted this with sincerity, because I feared to break my neck.

Occasionally a person with schizophrenia will repeat like a parrot whatever is said to him/her. In psychiatric language this is called echolalia. Chapman believes that repeating the words probably is useful to the patient because it allows time to absorb and synthesize what was said. Much rarer is the occurrence of behavior which is parroted, called echopraxia. When it occurs it may be the consequence of a dissolution of boundaries of the self so that the person does not know where his/her body leaves off and where the body of the other person begins.

Most worrisome to friends and relatives of individuals with schizophrenia, for obvious reasons, are socially inappropriate behaviors. Fortunately most patients who act inappropriately on hospital wards usually act quite appropriately when taken out of the hospital on trips. It is always impressive to see patients from even the most regressed hospital wards go to public places; they are usually more distinguishable by their dress (characteristically poorly fitting) than by their behavior. A small number of patients are so ill that they continue inappropriate behaviors (such as random urination, open masturbation, spitting on others) even in public, but such patients are comparatively rare. Some—but not all—of them can be improved by proper medication or conditioning techniques.

It should always be remembered that the behavior of persons with schizophrenia is internally logical and rational; they do things for reasons which, given their disordered senses and thinking, make sense *to them*. To the outside observer the behavior may appear irrational, "crazy," "mad," the very hallmark of the disease. To the ill person, however, there is nothing "crazy" or "mad" about it at all. Here, for example, is an account of a woman who broke two pairs of glasses worn by her nurses, an action which must have seemed inexplicable ("crazy") to those who observed it.

> My feelings about excessive light and truth were shown in ideas I had about glasses. I was afraid of people who wore glasses, and thought that I was being deliberately persecuted by doctors and nurses who refracted an excessive amount of light into my eyes by wearing glasses. At the same time glasses symbolized false or literary vision, a barrier between the individual and the direct apprehension of life. I myself normally wear glasses (slightly tinted, as my eyes are normally somewhat oversensitive to light). I grabbed and broke two pairs of glasses worn by nurses.

A woman with schizophrenia who believed that a pharmacist was controlling her mind decided "the only way I could escape his influence and radiation was to walk a circuit a mile in diameter around his drugstore."

Similarly Daniel P. Schreber, in the autobiographical account of his illness, describes sleeping with his feet out the window and clinging to icy trees with his hands until they were almost frozen in order to accomplish an important goal—such exposure to cold was the only way he could successfully divert the "rays" that afflicted him away from his head. Even bizarre behavior like taking one's clothes off in public may be done for logical reasons. One man with schizophrenia wrote me that he did so in an effort to be pure, like Adam and Eve when they first entered the Garden of Eden.

This same point can be made about everything a person with schizophrenia says and does. It is "crazy" only to the outsider who sits on the sidelines and observes from afar. To someone who will take the time to listen, a person with schizophrenia is not "crazy" at all if by "crazy" one means irrational. The "craziness" has its roots in the disordered brain function that produces erroneous sensory data and disordered thinking.

Schizophrenia, then, is a disorder of the brain. The distinguished neurologist C.S. Sherrington once referred to a normal brain as "an enchanted loom," taking the threads of experience and weaving them into the fabric of life. For persons whose brains are afflicted with schizophrenia the loom is broken, and in some cases appears to have been replaced by a Waring blender which produces jumbled thoughts and loose associations. Given the resulting cerebral cacophony, is it any wonder that patients with this disease often describe their life as like being in the Twilight Zone?

Some people with schizophrenia are aware of the misfunctioning of their brain; this is what is called insight. A few of them even tell those around them in the early stages of illness that something is going wrong with their head. One mother remembered her son holding his head and pleading: "Help me, Mom, something is wrong in my head." John Hinckley wrote a letter to his parents (but never sent it), in which he said: "I don't know what's the matter. Things are not going well. I think there's something wrong with my head." One of the most poignant stories I have ever heard concerned a very bright teenage boy who realized that something was going wrong with his brain in the earliest stages of the disease and then spent months in the local medical libraries researching the illness before his symptoms became too severe. In another instance a parent told me that her son "had diagnosed himself as having schizophrenia" before anyone in the family fully realized that he was sick.

Such insight is often lost as the disease becomes fully manifest. This is not surprising since it is the brain which is malfunctioning and it is also the brain which we use to think about ourselves. In fact I am always surprised at the many patients with schizophrenia who have insight. Even in the stage of chronic illness an occasional person with schizophrenia will exhibit surprising insight. One woman, afflicted by schizophrenia for many years, wrote me that she would gladly "sacrifice my right arm to make my brain work." Another woman who has had severe schizophrenia for seven years, when I asked her what she was asking for at Christmas, looked at me sadly, paused for a moment, and then replied: "A mind."

Imagine what it would be like to have the alterations of the senses, the inability to interpret incoming stimuli, the delusions and hallucinations, changes in bodily boundaries, emotions, and movements that are described above. Imagine what it would be like to no longer be able to trust your brain when it told you something. As one very articulate woman with schizophrenia explained to me, the problem is one of "a self-measuring ruler"—that is you must use your malfunctioning brain to assess the malfunction of your brain. Is it any wonder that people with this disease get depressed? Is it any wonder that they frequently feel humiliated by their own behavior? If a worse disease than schizophrenia exists, it has not come to light. One young man with the disease captured its essence in a poem entitled "Lost":

> *Gigantic tides have overwhelmed me*
> *I don't see anymore*
> *Swept to the bottom of the*
> *oceans floor.*
>
> *The great pull has drawn me beneath*
> *to the bottom*
> *I can't hear anymore*
> *What had he said?*
> *I may never see home again*
> *It feels that way*
> *down here*
> *Dead on the oceans floor*
>
> *I'm so sad*
> *I can't pull against the tow*
> *I'm trapped*
> *I'm gone*
> *I'll never relive again*
> *Somebody has pressed a pillow*
> *against my face and*
> *I can't breathe*

How can family and friends of persons with schizophrenia understand what they are going through? Taking mind-altering drugs will produce alterations of the senses and even delusions that may resemble schizophrenia briefly, but it is not recommended that families use these drugs. A better way to understand the experience of having schizophrenia is to take a walk by yourself through an art museum and pretend that you are inside some of the pictures. (It is better not to tell your friends that you are doing this; they may worry about *your* mental status.) Some of the works described below are reproduced on the following pages.

Begin with works by Vincent van Gogh painted in late 1888 and 1889 when he was undergoing a psychosis; "Starry Night" and "Olive Grove with White Cloud" especially illustrate van Gogh's distorted

Vincent van Gogh's "Starry Night," painted in 1889 while he was intermittently psychotic, shows distortions of textures, light, and color as perceived by some individuals with schizophrenia. (Collection, The Museum of Modern Art, New York. Acquired through the Lillie P. Bliss Bequest. Oil on canvas, 29" × 36¼".)

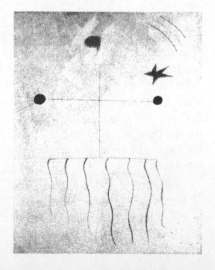

Joan Miró's "Head of a Catalan Peasant," painted in 1924, shows facial features grossly disjointed and distorted. (National Gallery of Art, Washington. Gift of the Collectors Committee, 1981.)

Marcel Duchamp's "Nude Descending a Staircase," painted in 1912, illustrates the disjointed perceptions and lack of coordination that often accompany schizophrenia. (Philadelphia Museum of Art. Louise and Walter Arensberg Collection. Oil on canvas, 58" × 35".)

Pablo Picasso's "Nude Woman," a work from 1910, presents the viewer with the perplexing task of synthesizing the pieces into a coherent whole; this is not unlike the task faced every day by some persons with schizophrenia. (National Gallery of Art, Washington. Ailsa Mellon Bruce Fund.)

Henri Rousseau's "The Dream," painted in 1910, evokes the dreamlike, otherworldly quality of life expressed by some patients, as well as the unnamed terrors of watching eyes described in paranoid schizophrenia. (Collection, The Museum of Modern Art, New York. Gift of Nelson A. Rockefeller. Oil on canvas, 6'8½" × 9'9½".)

Edward Munch's lithograph "The Scream" was created in 1895 as an expression of anxiety and fear. It also mirrors the despair, depression, and bewilderment of auditory hallucinations experienced so often in schizophrenia. (National Gallery of Art, Washington. Rosenwald Collection.)

perception of light, colors, and texture. Many other artists, although they themselves were not psychotic, included in their artistic creations elements that are reminiscent of the perceptions of people with schizophrenia. Joan Miró, for example, in paintings such as "Portrait IV, 1938," "Head of a Woman, 1938," and "Head of a Catalan Peasant," shows facial features as grossly distorted and disjointed. The viewer of a painting such as "Nude Woman" by Pablo Picasso is faced with the perplexing task of synthesizing the individual pieces into a whole, a task not unlike that faced every day by some individuals with schizophrenia. Marcel Duchamp's "Nude Descending a Staircase" suggests the jerky movements, lack of coordination, and clumsiness complained of frequently by persons with schizophrenia; this painting was specifically cited by one woman with schizophrenia symptoms from viral encephalitis to illustrate to the doctor how she felt.

Distorted emotions are evoked in several paintings of Henri Rousseau. Imagine yourself in "The Dream," for example, with eyes staring at you and unnamed terrors lurking behind every bush. Move on to lithographs or paintings by Edvard Munch, such as "The Scream," which mirrors the depression, despair, and loneliness of schizophrenia; the woman in the picture is covering her ears just as some patients do to try and shut out the auditory hallucinations. Finally end your tour of the art museum at Hieronymus Bosch's "Garden of Earthly Delights." Study the tortures designed by Bosch for the "Hell" portion of the triptych, and think about the fact that the experience of having schizophrenia is much worse than anything Bosch ever imagined.

In summary, schizophrenia is a disease in which the brain, the essence of being, plays cruel tricks on the person affected. Roy Porter, in *A Social History of Madness,* noted "that *strangeness* has typically been the key feature in the fractured dialogues that go on, or the silences that intrude, between the "mad" and the "sane." Madness is a foreign country." Kathy Bick, in the earliest stages of what was to become severe schizophrenia, poignantly captured that strangeness in her diary: "Something inside me is going thru this funny, alien state, a sense of being at the mercy of some strange force, and this pathetic scarecrow figure inside me at the mercy of other forces." Given the disordered brain function as a starting point, many persons with schizophrenia are heroic in their attempts to keep a mental equilibrium. And the proper response of those who care about the unfortunate persons with this disease is patience and understanding. Perhaps nowhere is this better illustrated than by Balzac's heroine in "Louis Lambert," a

young woman who married a man who developed schizophrenia. She
then dedicates her life to caring for him:

> "No doubt Louis appears to be 'insane,'" she said, "but he is not so, if the
> word insanity is applied only to those whose brain, from unknown causes,
> becomes vitiated, and who are, therefore, unable to give a reason for their
> acts. The equilibrium of my husband's mind is perfect. If he does not rec-
> ognize you corporeally, do not think that he has not seen you. He is able
> to disengage his body and to see us under another form, I know not of
> what nature. When he speaks, he says marvellous things. Only, in fact
> often, he completes in speech an idea begun in the silence of his mind, or
> else he begins a proposition in words and finishes it mentally. To other
> men he must appear insane; to me, who lives in his thought, all his ideas
> are lucid. I follow the path of his mind; and though I cannot understand
> many of its turnings and digressions, I nevertheless reach the end with
> him. Does it not often happen that while thinking of some trifling matter,
> we are drawn into serious thought by the gradual unfolding of ideas and
> recollections? Often, after speaking of some frivolous thing, the acciden-
> tal point of departure for rapid meditation, a thinker forgets, or neglects to
> mention the abstract links which have led him to his conclusions, and
> takes up in speech only the last rings in the chain of reflections. Common
> minds to whom this quickness of mental vision is unknown, and who are
> ignorant of the inward travail of the soul, laugh at dreamers and call them
> madmen if they are given to such forgetfulness of connecting thoughts.
> Louis is always so; he wings his way through the spaces of thought with
> the agility of a swallow; yet I can follow him in all his circlings. That is
> the history of his so-called madness."

Such dedication and understanding, unachievable except in fiction,
is a worthy ideal. It exists to some degree in many families and among
some professionals who must care for such individuals on the wards of
mental hospitals or in outpatient clinics. As Louis Lambert's wife illustrates, compassion follows understanding. It is therefore incumbent on
us to understand as best we can; the burden of disease will become
lighter for all.

RECOMMENDED FURTHER READING

Chapman, J. "The Early Symptoms of Schizophrenia." *British Journal of
Psychiatry* 112 (1966):225–51.

Cutting, J., and F. Dunne. "Subjective Experience of Schizophrenia." *Schizophrenia Bulletin* 15 (1989):217–31.

Kaplan, B., ed. *The Inner World of Mental Illness.* New York: Harper & Row, 1964.

McGhie, A., and J. Chapman. "Disorders of Attention and Perception in Early Schizophrenia." *British Journal of Medical Psychology* 34 (1961):103–16.

North, C. *Welcome Silence: My Triumph Over Schizophrenia.* New York: Simon and Schuster, 1987.

Sechehaye, M. *Autobiography of a Schizophrenic Girl.* New York: Grune & Stratton, 1951. Paperback by New American Library. Part 2 of the book, a psychoanalytic interpretation of the woman's symptoms, should be skipped.

3

THE DIAGNOSIS OF SCHIZOPHRENIA: VIEW FROM THE OUTSIDE

Insanity is a chronic disease of the brain, producing either derange-
ment of the intellectual faculties, or prolonged change of the feelings, affections and habits of an individual.

Dr. Amariah Brigham, 1845

The definition of most diseases of mankind has been accomplished. We
can define typhoid fever by the presence of the bacteria which cause it,
kidney failure by a rise in certain chemicals in the blood, and cancers
by the appearance of the cells under the microscope. In almost all diseases there is something which can be seen or measured, and this can
be used to define the disease and separate it from nondisease states.

Not so with schizophrenia! To date we have no single thing which
can be measured and from which we can then say: Yes, that is schizophrenia. Because of this, the definition of the disease is a source of
great confusion and debate. This confusion is exacerbated because of
the likelihood that schizophrenia is more than one disease entity.

Since we do not yet have anything which can be reliably measured
to help define schizophrenia, we are left only with its symptoms. These
may be misleading, however, for different diseases may cause the same
symptoms. For example, a pain in the abdomen is a symptom, but the
disease which may cause this symptom number well over one hundred.
Thus to use symptoms to define diseases is risky. Such is the state of
the art with schizophrenia; yet precise diagnosis is of utmost importance. It will both determine the appropriate treatment for the patient
and provide the patient and family with an informed prognosis. It also
makes research on the disease easier because it will allow researchers

to be certain that they are talking about the same thing.

DEFINING SCHIZOPHRENIA

Although there is no single symptom that is found only in schizophrenia, there are several that are found very uncommonly in diseases other than schizophrenia. When these are present they should elevate the index of suspicion considerably. Bleuler, for example, believed that loosening of associations in the thinking process was central to the disease. More recently, Kurt Schneider, a German psychiatrist, proposed a list of symptoms which he called "first rank" symptoms, meaning that when one or more of them are present they point strongly toward schizophrenia as the diagnosis. This is his list:

1. Auditory hallucinations in which the voices speak one's thoughts aloud
2. Auditory hallucinations with two voices arguing
3. Auditory hallucinations with the voices commenting on one's actions
4. Hallucinations of touch when the bodily sensation is imposed by some external agency
5. Withdrawal of thoughts from one's mind
6. Insertion of thoughts into one's mind by others
7. Believing one's thoughts are being broadcast to others, as by radio or television
8. Insertion by others of feelings into one's mind
9. Insertion by others of irresistible impulses into one's mind
10. Feeling that all one's actions are under the control of others, like an automaton
11. Delusions of perception, as when one is certain that a normal remark has a secret meaning for oneself

These symptoms are commonly used in European countries as grounds for the diagnosis of schizophrenia, although less so in the United States. Studies have shown that at least three-quarters of patients with schizophrenia have one or more of these symptoms. However, they cannot be considered as definitive for the disease because they are also found in at least one-quarter of patients with manic-depressive illness.

Until recently, the term "schizophrenia" was used much more loosely and broadly in the United States than in most European countries. In fact the only other country in the world where schizophrenia was diagnosed just as loosely was in the former Soviet Union, where it was abused as a label to discredit and stigmatize opponents of the government.

American psychiatry took a major step forward in 1980 when it adopted a revised system of diagnosis and nomenclature in the third edition of the *Diagnostic and Statistical Manual of Mental Disorders,* usually referred to as *DSM-III.* This was followed by revisions in 1987 (known as *DSM-III-R*) and then by further revisions in 1994 *(DSM-IV).* Under this system a diagnosis of schizophrenia should be made only when the following criteria have been fulfilled:

1. Symptoms of illness have been present for at least six months.
2. There has been some deterioration of functioning from previous levels in such areas as work skills, social relations, and self-care.
3. The disease symptoms do not suggest organic mental disorders or mental retardation.
4. The disease symptoms do not suggest manic-depressive illness.
5. Either a, b, or c must be present:
   a. Two of the following for a significant portion of time for at least a one-month period:
      delusions
      hallucinations
      disorganized speech (e.g., frequent loose associations or incoherence)
      grossly disorganized or catatonic behavior
      negative symptoms (e.g., emotional flattening, severe apathy), *or*

   b. Bizarre delusions which other people in the individual's sub-culture regard as totally implausible, e.g., the belief that your thoughts are being taken out of your head and broadcast over the radio, *or*
   c. Prominent auditory hallucinations consisting of voices keeping up a running commentary on the person's behavior, or two or more voices conversing with each other.

These criteria for diagnosing schizophrenia have achieved wide acceptance in the United States and may be utilized by families who are seeking a definition of the disease. If these criteria are not met, the diagnosis of schizophrenia should not be made.

Lists of symptoms such as the above give the impression that schizophrenia is relatively easy to diagnose. In its fully developed form it usually is, but in the earlier stages it may be difficult to diagnose with certainty. The symptoms may appear intermittently or be relatively mild, and the affected individual may be able to cover up some manifestations of the disease. It is therefore quite common for mental illness professionals to write "rule out schizophrenia" on their initial encounter with a patient, which simply means that their diagnosis is tentative until the clinical picture is clearer.

Requiring that symptoms be present for at least six months before schizophrenia can be diagnosed is a sharp departure from traditional American practice. It is a useful advance, however, for schizophrenia is a serious diagnosis and should not be applied indiscriminately to someone with any schizophrenialike symptom, however brief, as happened frequently in the past. For persons with schizophrenialike symptoms of less than six months' duration, the *DSM-IV* recommends the use of schizophreniform disorder as a diagnosis. If the duration is less than one month, the diagnosis of brief psychotic disorder should be used.

Although the *DSM IV* criteria have been valuable in clarifying the diagnosis of schizophrenia, problems persist. Diagnosis remains based on the psychiatrist's subjective evaluation of patients' behavior and what patients say they are experiencing. What is clearly needed, and may be available before many years, are objective measures for diagnosis, such as laboratory tests of blood and cerebrospinal fluid. Until that time the diagnosis of schizophrenia will remain a complicated matter requiring skilled clinical judgment.

A highly publicized experiment carried out by Dr. David L. Rosenhan, a psychologist at Stanford University, in 1973 illustrates some of the ongoing diagnostic problems. Rosenhan had volunteers go to psychiatric hospitals seeking admission and claiming to be hearing voices which had lasted for three weeks. Auditory hallucinations of any kind are unquestionably important and common symptoms of schizophrenia, with the majority of patients experiencing them at some point in the course of their illness. They are so important as symptoms that most psychiatrists take their presence as an indication of schizophrenia until proven otherwise. Thus it should not have been surprising that all the volunteers were admitted as genuine patients. Rosenhan used this study to mock psychiatrists and their ability to diagnose patients, but this is erroneous. It would have been much *more* disturbing if these volunteers, who said they were being greatly troubled by the voices, had *not* been admitted for further investigation. Auditory hallucinations are to schizophrenia what abdominal pain is to appendicitis or vomiting blood is to a peptic ulcer. They are all danger signs suggesting that more definitive studies need to be done. Dr. Seymour Kety illustrates the fallacy of the Rosenhan study nicely:

> If I were to drink a quart of blood and, concealing what I had done, come to the emergency room of any hospital vomiting blood, the behavior of the staff would be quite predictable. If they labeled and treated me as having a bleeding ulcer, I doubt that I could argue convincingly that medical science does not know how to diagnose that condition.

SCHIZOPHRENIA SUBTYPES AND PARANOID DISORDERS

During the last half of the nineteenth century different subtypes of what we now call schizophrenia were described as separate diseases. Thus paranoid psychosis was characterized in 1868, hebephrenia in 1871, and catatonia in 1874. These three were grouped together in 1896 by Emil Kraepelin and called dementia praecox (dementia of early life). Bleuler changed the name to schizophrenia in 1911 and added the simple schizophrenia subtype as well.

Since that time these subtypes of schizophrenia have continued to be widely used. Their differentiation is based exclusively on the symptoms of the illness. Thus paranoid schizophrenia is characterized by delusions and/or hallucinations with a predominantly persecutory or, less commonly, a grandiose content. Hebephrenic schizophrenia, called the "disorganized type" in the DSM-IV nomenclature, has as its predominant symptoms disorganized speech, disorganized behavior, and flat or inappropriate affect. Catatonic schizophrenia is diagnosed when the outstanding features of the disease are behavioral disturbances, such as posturing, rigidity, stupor, and often mutism. And simple schizophrenia, not included as a separate entity under *DSM-IV,* is characterized by an insidious loss of interest and initiative, withdrawal, blunting of emotions, and the absence of delusions or hallucinations.

The validity and utility of these subtypes are very questionable despite their widespread usage. Few patients fall cleanly into one subtype or another, with most having some mix of symptoms. Of greater concern is the fact that persons with schizophrenia often show a shift in their symptoms over time, so that initially the person may appear to be a catatonic subtype but a few years later may have symptoms of a hebephrenic nature. Even the old psychiatric axiom "Once a paranoid always a paranoid" has been found not to hold up; I have seen many patients who present initially classic paranoid schizophrenia symptoms and five years later may have a quite different constellation of symptoms. For these reasons there has been an increasing tendency among psychiatrists in recent years to diagnose most patients as having the "undifferentiated type," which simply means that their symptoms are mixed, and to rely less on the traditional four-part division.

Paranoid schizophrenia presents special diagnostic problems because it is one end of the spectrum of a common personality type. Paranoid personalities are found in all walks of life and are known for being suspicious, mistrusting, guarded, quick to take offense, and emotionally distant. The other end of the spectrum is the person with full-blown paranoid schizophrenia with delusions and hallucinations of persecution. Between these two poles, however, can be found a continuum of individuals with more or less disabling paranoid personality traits. The architects of *DSM-IV* chose to restrict the diagnosis of paranoid schizophrenia only to those individuals who had the fully developed disease and to classify less severely disabled paranoid individuals as a delusional disorder or a paranoid personality disorder. Thus a patient with fixed delusions of persecution or jealousy without other symptoms of schizophrenia should not technically be classified as having schizophrenia under the new criteria.

There is also a belief among some researchers that paranoid schizophrenia and its related disorders are a separate disease entity altogether and probably have causes different from the larger group of schizophrenias. Such researchers point to genetic studies suggesting that paranoid schizophrenics are more likely to occur within the same family than are other types of schizophrenias and to biochemical studies which found an increase in some brain chemicals in paranoid schizophrenia but not in other types. This research area remains completely unresolved, and for the time being paranoid schizophrenia should continue to be viewed as a legitimate variant of schizophrenia.

Another method of subtyping schizophrenia that has been used by researchers divides patients into those with predominantly "positive" symptoms and those with predominantly "negative" symptoms. Although the use of "positive" as an adjective for any symptoms seems like a contradiction of terms, it denotes those symptoms which are present but should be absent (e.g., delusions, hallucinations, thinking disorders such as loose associations). "Negative" symptoms, on the other hand, indicate symptoms which are absent but should be present (e.g., apathy, social withdrawal, poverty of thoughts, blunting of emotions, slowness of movement, lack of drive). This subtype has been elaborated into type I (those with predominantly "positive" symptoms) and type II (those with predominantly "negative" symptoms) by Dr. Timothy Crow and his colleagues in London who claim that these are separate diseases. Whether or not this is so remains to be ascertained.

SCHIZOAFFECTIVE DISORDER

As will be discussed in chapter 4, there is another brain disease called manic-depressive psychosis, which is distinct from schizophrenia and on which there is widespread agreement regarding symptoms. Textbooks of psychiatry and psychology usually imply that patients with psychosis fall neatly into either the schizophrenia or the manic-depressive category and that the two can be readily distinguished. Unfortunately that is not always the case, as a large percentage of patients have symptoms of both diseases. Futhermore it is not rare to find patients whose symptoms change over time, appearing initially as a textbook case of schizophrenia or manic-depressive psychosis, and a year or two later clearly exhibiting symptoms of the other disease. It has been facetiously suggested that either we need to insist that patients read the books and choose the disease they wish to have or we must become more flexible in our psychiatric thinking. I personally have seen patients with virtually every possible combination of schizophrenic and manic-depressive symptoms.

The resolution of the problem within the psychiatric establishment has been the creation of an intermediate disease category called schizoaffective disorder. Prior to *DSM-III* it was officially included as a subtype of schizophrenia. *DSM-III* classified it independently and noted that "at the present time there is no consensus on how this category should be defined." DSM-IV defines schizoaffective disorder as the occurrence of symptoms of major depression or mania concurrent with the symptoms of schizophrenia, but there must be at least a two-week period in which the symptoms of schizophrenia have been present without the depression or mania.

If this sounds like arguments among psychiatrists about how many angels can dance on the head of a pin, to a large extent it is. For patients and families, however, it is often confusing because they think that schizophrenia and schizoaffective disorder are different diagnoses. In fact they are two aspects of a diagnostic spectrum. Current research on patients with schizoaffective disorder suggest that most of them belong in the broad category of schizophrenia and that a minority are more closely related to manic-depressive disorder. At a practical level the diagnosis of schizoaffective disorder implies statistically a somewhat better prognosis than classical schizophrenia, although this may not be true for any given patient. Other than that, the treatment of schizoaffective disorder and schizophrenia is virtually identical with the same medication being used in both cases.

WHERE DOES SCHIZOPHRENIA BEGIN? SCHIZOTYPAL, PARANOID, AND SCHIZOID PERSONALITY DISORDERS

There are two questions that are guaranteed to stir up instant controversy whenever schizophrenia researchers meet. The first is the relationship of schizoaffective disorder to schizophrenia and manic-depressive illness. The second is the concept of the schizophrenia spectrum and the relationship of the schizotypal, paranoid, and schizoid personality disorders to schizophrenia itself. In brief the question is, where does schizophrenia end?

There are few murkier lands to enter in medicine than the shadowy terrain lying at the edge of schizophrenia; travelers to this region must have a high tolerance for ambiguity. Personality disorders are said to be collections of personality traits which "are inflexible and maladaptive and cause either significant impairment in social or occupational functioning or subjective distress." These personality disorders, then, are not categorized as diseases like schizophrenia and manic-depressive psychosis, but rather are considered to be maladaptive lifestyles. Let us consider each in turn and then discuss them as a group.

Schizotypal Personality Disorder

These individuals were in the past said to have such things as borderline schizophrenia, ambulatory schizophrenia, pseudoneurotic schizo-

phrenia, latent schizophrenia, subclinical schizophrenia, and schizophrenic character. They have oddities and eccentricities of perception,
thinking, speech, and behavior. To meet criteria for this diagnosis under
DSM-IV the individual should have at least five of the following:

A. ideas of reference, meaning that the person frequently thinks
   that other people are talking about him/her
B. odd beliefs or magical thinking that influence behavior and are
   inconsistent with subcultural norms (e.g., superstitiousness,
   belief in clairvoyance, telepathy, or "sixth sense"; in children
   and adolescents, bizarre fantasies or preoccupations)
C. unusual perceptual experiences, including bodily illusions
D. odd thinking and speech (e.g., vague, circumstantial, metaphori-
   cal, overelaborate, or stereotyped)
E. suspiciousness or paranoid ideation
F. inappropriate or constricted affect
G. behavior or appearance that is odd, eccentric, or peculiar
H. lacks close friends or confidants other than first-degree relatives
I. excessive social anxiety that does not diminish with familiarity
   and tends to be associated with paranoid fears rather than nega-
   tive judgments about self

Paranoid Personality Disorder

These individuals are known for their hypersensitivity, mistrust, and
suspiciousness of other people's motivations. They are always on
guard, easily slighted, and quick to take offense. They believe that others are trying to trick or harm them, and will go to great lengths to
prove it. They question the loyalty of others and often see plots where
nobody else can see them. They are often rigid, argumentative, and liti-
gious. Many are interested in electronics and mechanical devices that
can be used for spying. They appear to have few tender feelings, dis-
dain weak people, and lack any sense of humor.

Schizoid Personality Disorder

These individuals are loners and have virtually no friends. They avoid social situations and seek employment in which they do not have to interact with others (e.g., forest ranger, computer programmer). Schizoid men rarely marry. Such individuals appear incapable of experiencing feelings for others, either those of affection or those of hostility, and are relatively indifferent to praise or criticism. Some also appear to be detached from their enviornment as if in a perpetual fog.

Controversy has continued for many years regarding the validity of these personality disorders and their relationship to schizophrenia. It is widely acknowledged that the three personality disorders overlap and that many individuals have combinations of these traits. Studies of families of individuals with schizophrenia have found more relatives with schizotypal and paranoid personality disorders, suggesting that they may be genetically related to schizophrenia. They can, in a theoretical sense, be considered a mild form of the disease. This possibility, generally referred to as the "spectrum concept" of schizophrenia, implies that there may be individuals at all points on the spectrum between mild personality disorder and severe schizophrenia. The concept has received support from the finding that many individuals with schizotypal personality disorder feel better and function better on low doses of antipsychotic drugs.

At the same time it should be pointed out that the concept of "mild schizophrenia" without biological markers to clearly delineate the disease poses potential danger. This concept was used until recently in the Soviet Union, where political dissidents and other undesirables were so labeled and involuntarily hospitalized. Until we have clear biological and laboratory markers of "mild schizophrenia," it is preferable to maintain it as a personality disorder.

An example of a schizotypal personality disorder with schizoid features follows:

> Samuel had always been a shy, withdrawn child who avoided other people. As an adult he became a bookkeeper who was known to do good work as long as he was left alone. Colleagues at work regarded him as eccentric and strange, saying he misinterpreted their remarks in a paranoid fashion and remarking that his replies were sometimes off-target to their questions. On one occasion Samuel implied that he had known what they were going to say by means of mental telepathy.

In summary, where does schizophrenia end? At this time research studies suggest that many cases of schizotypal personality disorder and some cases of paranoid personality disorder are in fact mild cases of schizophrenia. The relationship of schizoid personality disorder to schizophrenia is less clear because large numbers of people have schizoid personality traits with no evidence of schizophrenia. It is likely that within a few years we will have biological markers that can be used to definitively diagnose schizophrenia. Until that time we should probably err on the conservative side in our attempts to determine where schizophrenia ends.

ONSET AND EARLY SYMPTOMS

One of the questions most frequently asked by families is how to identify the early symptoms of schizophrenia. This question is different from that of relapse of the disease, which is discussed in chapter 10. The question is asked by families who are raising difficult teenage children and are wondering if they might be developing schizophrenia. It is also asked by families in which an older child has been diagnosed with schizophrenia and the parents are worried about the younger children.

In thinking about the early symptoms of schizophrenia it is helpful to remember that this disease has a strikingly narrow age of onset. In the United States three-quarters of those who get schizophrenia do so between ages 17 and 25. Having an initial onset before age 14 or after age 30 is unusual; the former will be discussed below under childhood schizophrenia.

Why the onset of schizophrenia occurs in this particular age group is unknown. It should be pointed out, however, that other chronic brain diseases, such as multiple sclerosis and Alzheimer's disease, have particular age ranges of onset and we do not understand the reasons in these diseases either. There are also suggestions that the average age of onset of schizophrenia may be younger in the United States than it is in Europe, that the age of onset for paranoid schizophrenia is older than for the other subtypes, and other suggestions that the average age of onset in the United States is younger now than it was twenty years ago.

There are some patients for whom it is impossible to date the onset of the disease. The family says things like "She was always different from the other children" or "Throughout childhood his teachers noticed he was eccentric and told us to get him evaluated." The suggestion in such cases is that the schizophrenic disease process began early in life despite the fact that the full-blown thinking disorder, delusions, and hallucinations did not begin until the late teens or early twenties. Such individuals with an insidious onset probably comprise no more than a third of patients with schizophrenia; whether they represent a different causal group or not is unknown.

This raises the question of when families with an eccentric child should worry. It is known that the great majority of individuals who develop schizophrenia have normal childhoods and are not identifiable in their early years. And it is also known that the vast majority of eccentric children will not develop schizophrenia; many, in fact, grow up to be leaders. The problem of separating the eccentricities of normal childhood from the early symptoms of schizophrenia is especially difficult in adolescence, approximately ages 11 to 13, when the norms of behavior are very strange indeed. Overacuteness of the senses is a common symptom of schizophrenia, yet how many adolescents have not had some such experiences? Moodiness, withdrawal, apathy, loss of interest in personal appearance, perplexity, the belief that people are watching one, preoccupation with one's body, and vagueness in thoughts may all be harbingers of impending schizophrenia, but they may also be just normal manifestations of early adulthood and its accompanying problems. For this reason families should *not* worry about every quirk in their children, but rather should assume they are normal until proven otherwise. This can be particularly difficult for a parent who has already had one child diagnosed with schizophrenia and who is expecting the worst for the younger children, but it is important. A 15-year-old has enough to worry about without being told things like "Don't daydream. That's what your brother did and it got him sick and into the hospital."

At what point *should* parents begin to worry that something may be wrong? When do the normal psychological vicissitudes of early adulthood cross the line and enter the realm of early symptoms of schizophrenia?

Alterations of the senses or in body image are common early symptoms as might be surmised from the discussion in chapter 2. Often the patient will be aware of them but will not confide in others. Perhaps more common early complaints are somatic symptoms, especially weakness, pains, and bizarre bodily sensations. Researchers in Canada asked newly diagnosed patients how frequently such symptoms occur in the early stages of illness and found that 86 percent complained of weakness, 38 percent of bodily pains or aches, 23 percent of headaches, 22 percent of poor coordination, and 47 percent of "bizarre symptoms."

Changes in the sleep pattern occur very commonly in early schizophrenia. The person may sleep less, or more, or simply begin sleeping at unusual times (e.g., up all night, sleeps all day). The important thing to notice is that the pattern has changed, sometimes dramatically. I have also found this to be one of the most reliable harbingers of relapse in schizophrenia, and I routinely ask patients about it whenever I have reduced their medication.

Disorders of thinking, including delusions, are occasionally the earliest signs of schizophrenia. Patients may have ideas of reference in which they think everyone is talking about them. Or their thinking may take a bizarre turn, and they come out with off-the-wall ideas at the dinner table that startle everyone. Some patients simply begin talking in a vague way in the early stages of their illness, with tangential thoughts that sound almost, but not quite, logical.

Changes in behavior are one of the commonest signs of early schizophrenia. The patient's personal habits may slowly change: for example, they stop taking showers, or they may no longer straighten up their room when previously they had been compulsively neat. Another common behavior change is social withdrawal; previously outgoing and socially adroit young adults are noticed to withdraw and spend increasingly long periods in their room by themselves. The emphasis in evaluating all these symptoms is on *change* in a young adult. Parents may say things such as: "John has become a different person over the last six months," or "None of Jennifer's friends come around anymore, and she doesn't seem to want to see anyone." Such changes may of course be caused by things other than schizophrenia; the use of street drugs must always be considered as a possibility in this age group.

MALE-FEMALE DIFFERENCES

Although textbooks say that schizophrenia occurs equally in men and women, that generalization neglects some important gender differences in this disease. Most striking is the earlier age of onset for men, which in the United States occurs two to three years earlier than in women. An analysis of a group of 17- or 18-year-old individuals with schizophrenia will reveal four or five males for every female.

Schizophrenia is also a more serious disease in men than it is in women. Men do not respond as well to antipsychotic drugs, they require higher doses of the drugs, they have a higher relapse rate, and their long-term adjustment—measured by such indices as social life, marriage, work record, suicide rate, and level of function—is not nearly so good as women's. There are, of course, many women with schizophrenia who have had a severe course and many men who have done well, but statistics clearly establish that schizophrenia occurs earlier and in more severe form in the male.

The reasons for such gender differences, still unknown, provide one of the many questions about schizophrenia needing to be researched. It should be noted that both infantile autism and childhood schizophrenia also have a strong predominance for males, and that male fetuses generally are known to be more susceptible to environmentally caused problems such as infections. The fact that males get schizophrenia both younger and more severely, then, may simply be another reflection of Mother Nature's dictum that in many ways men are the weaker sex. Another speculation about why schizophrenia might be more severe in males is the possibility that female sex hormones (estrogens) may exert an antipsychotic effect and be protective. It is also possible, although unlikely, that schizophrenia resembles diabetes in having two major subgroups: an early-onset, more severe variety that affects mostly men, and a later-onset, less severe variety more apt to afflict women.

Another facet of male-female differences in schizophrenia is the effect of the menstrual cycle on the disease in some women. Although it has not been adequately studied, clinicians and families have noted for many years that some women with schizophrenia have a worsening of their symptoms in the days immediately preceding their menstrual period. This is almost certainly caused by the ebb and flow of hormones during the cycle, and lends further support to theories linking male-female differences in schizophrenia to hormonal differences.

CHILDHOOD SCHIZOPHRENIA

It is generally believed that childhood schizophrenia is simply an early version of the adult disease, although much rarer. Approximately two males are affected for every female. Only about 2 percent of individuals with schizophrenia have the onset of their disease in childhood although that percentage varies, depending on where one fixes the childhood-adult line. Schizophrenia beginning before age 5 is exceedingly rare (see section on infantile autism, chapter 5), and between ages 5 and 10 it increases slowly. From age 10, schizophrenia increases in incidence until age 15, when it begins its sharp upward peak as the adult disease.

The symptoms of childhood schizophrenia are very similar to those of adult schizophrenia with the predictable exception that their content is age-related. For example, one study of young children with schizophrenia reported that the source of auditory hallucinations was frequently believed to be pet animals or toys and that "monster themes were common. . . . As age increased, both hallucinations and delusions tended to be more complex and elaborate." The other distinguishing feature of childhood schizophrenia is that the affected child also often has one or more of the following: seizures, learning disabilities, mild mental retardation, neurological symptoms, hyperactivity, or other behavioral problems. In an attempt to resolve this confusion the American Psychiatric Association deleted "childhood schizophrenia" from its official nomenclature and suggested instead using schizophrenia with onset in childhood or "childhood-onset pervasive developmental disorder," a catchall term for many poorly defined brain disorders of childhood.

Like adult schizophrenia, childhood schizophrenia is thought to have some genetic roots, although their relative importance is unclear. It is also known that these children have an excess number of minor physical anomalies and mothers' history of having had excess pregnancy and birth complications. The fact that childhood schizophrenia is a brain disease has been demonstrated by the findings of EEG abnormalities on electroencephalographs and enlarged cerebral ventricles on MRI scans.

Childhood schizophrenia is treated with the same antipsychotic medication used for adult schizophrenia. A follow-up of ten children with this disease from fourteen to thirty-four years after its onset found them still diagnosed with schizophrenia but with relatively few delusions or hallucinations. Instead they tended to be quiet and withdrawn with poverty of thought and lack of drive. A minority of children with schizophrenia will recover and do quite well as adults, but what percentage this constitutes is uncertain. In general it is thought that the earlier the age of onset of schizophrenia, the worse the outcome is likely to be, but there are major exceptions to this rule. A good description of childhood schizophrenia is provided by Louise Wilson in *This Stranger, My Son.*

LATE-ONSET SCHIZOPHRENIA

Just as there is a form of schizophrenia that begins early in childhood, so there is also a form that begins later in life. Late-onset schizophrenia is variously defined as beginning after the age of 40 or 45. Its precise incidence is unclear but it is not rare. Almost all studies of it have been done by Europeans, with little interest having been shown by American researchers. That fact is especially pertinent since the mean age of onset of schizophrenia in general is almost invariably reported as being older in European studies compared to American studies. It seems possible, therefore, that late-onset schizophrenia is of more interest to European researchers because it occurs more commonly there for reasons that are unknown.

Clinically, late-onset schizophrenia is similar to the earlier-onset variety except for having a predominance of females affected; having more schizoid and paranoid personality traits in the person before he/she becomes sick; and having more paranoid delusions and more visual, tactile, and olfactory (smell) hallucinations. Neuropsychological tests and MRI scans show deficits similar to early-onset schizophrenia. The other way in which late-onset schizophrenia differs is in having a more chronic course and less favorable prognosis than would be expected given the general rule that the later the onset of the disease, the better the prognosis is likely to be.

WHAT IS THE IDEAL DIAGNOSTIC WORKUP?

In its full-blown stages, most cases of schizophrenia are not difficult to diagnose. Auditory hallucinations and/or delusional thinking are among the commonest and most prominent symptoms, and more than three-quarters of all patients will have one or the other. Various kinds of thinking disorders become evident on simple conversation (e.g., thought blocking) or on asking the patient to give the meaning of proverbs (e.g., inability to think abstractly). Emotions may be blunted or inappropriate, and the individual's behavior may vary from unusual to catatonic to bizarre.

For a person with the symptoms of schizophrenia who has become ill for the first time, what kind of diagnostic tests and procedures are appropriate? Most public psychiatric hospitals, and many private ones as well, offer cursory diagnostic workups, and there is no question that some patients are diagnosed with schizophrenia who have the diseases described in chapter 4. Given this fact, what should be done diagnostically to maximize the chances of uncovering all potentially reversible diseases masquerading as schizophrenia? Although I recognize that some of my psychiatric colleagues may disagree, the following diagnostic workup is what I would personally want to happen to me if I or a member of my family was admitted to a hospital with symptoms of schizophrenia for the first time.

History and Mental Status Examination

These are routinely done for all psychiatric admissions but often incompletely so. Visual hallucinations, headaches, and recent head injury should be specifically asked about. A general review of organ systems other than the central nervous system may turn up diseases masquerading as schizophrenia (e.g., abdominal pains suggesting acute intermittent porphyria, urinary incontinence suggesting normal pressure hydrocephalus). Perhaps the single most important question which the examining physician can ask is: "What drugs are you using?" It is a two-pronged question intended to elicit information about street drug use, which may be producing or exacerbating the psychiatric symptoms, as well as prescription drug use which may be producing psychiatric symptoms as a side effect (see chapter 4). Since acutely psychotic patients often cannot give a coherent history, family members and friends play an essential role in providing the needed information.

Physical and Neurological Examinations

These are also often done superficially with the consequence that many medical and neurological diseases are missed. A careful neurological examination of patients with schizophrenia will elicit abnormal findings in a significant number of them (see chapter 6). A useful part of the neurological exam, which can be taught to nonphysicians who must screen psychiatric patients, is a series of pencil-and-paper tests such as write-a-sentence and draw-a-clock; as Dr. Robert Taylor describes in *Mind or Body,* such tests can help identify patients with other brain diseases, such as brain tumors or Huntington's disease, who may initially present with schizophrenialike symptoms.

Basic Laboratory Work: Blood Count, Blood Chemical Screen, and Urinalysis

These are also routine everywhere, but abnormal results are sometimes not noticed or followed up. The blood count may elicit unexpected findings suggesting such diseases as pernicious anemia, AIDS, or lead intoxication. Blood chemical screens have become widespread and do many different tests on a single sample of blood. These normally include tests which may screen endocrine or metabolic imbalances. If a thyroid function test is not included in the routine blood chemical screen, it should be ordered separately. A routine test to screen for syphilis should also be included. Urinalysis should include screening tests to detect street drugs in the urine. A useful and cost-effective diagnostic algorithm for detecting physical disease in psychiatric patients has been developed by Dr. Harold Sox and colleagues.

Psychological Tests

The choice of psychological tests varies from hospital to hospital and depends on the psychologist. Such tests can be extremely useful in making the diagnosis of schizophrenia in early or borderline cases, and can also point the examiner away from schizophrenia and toward other brain diseases. Acutely agitated patients with the full-blown schizophrenic syndrome frequently are unable to concentrate long enough to do psychological tests.

MRI Scan

Magnetic resonance imaging (MRI) scans are now widely available and, with improving technology, should become less expensive.

Computerized tomography (CT) scans can also be used if MRI scans are not available but are much less sensitive for detecting most brain pathology. An MRI scan should be done on every individual who presents with psychosis for the first time. Diseases that mimic schizophrenia and that may be detected by MRI scans include brain tumors, Huntington's disease, Wilson's disease, metachromatic leukodystrophy, sarcoidosis, subdural hematomas, Kuf's disease, viral encephalitis, and aqueductal stenosis. For a person who has had symptoms of schizophrenia for many years, a scan probably is not justified diagnostically, for the diseases which the procedure is capable of detecting would have become evident over the years because of other signs or symptoms.

Lumbar Puncture

Despite the stereotype to the contrary, lumbar punctures are simple procedures producing little more discomfort than the drawing of blood. Cerebrospinal fluid is withdrawn by a needle from a sac in the lower back; since the sac is connected to fluid channels in the brain, examination of the cerebrospinal fluid often provides clues (e.g., antibodies to viruses) about events in the brain. They are routinely used in the diagnosis of brain diseases, such as multiple sclerosis, and probably will become routine for schizophrenia in the future. They are capable of detecting a variety of diseases, especially viral diseases of the central nervous system. Indications for their use in patients admitted for a first episode of schizophrenia include the following:

A. Patient complains of headache (20 percent do) or stiff neck with nausea or a fever
B. Rapid onset of psychotic symptoms
C. Fluctuations in patient's orientation (e.g., patient knows where he is one day but does not know the next day)
D. Visual or olfactory (smell) hallucinations
E. Neurological signs or symptoms suggesting central nervous system disease other than schizophrenia (e.g., nystagmus of the eyes in which the gaze moves rapidly from side to side)
F. Concurrent or recent history of flu or fever.

Lumbar punctures in patients with schizophrenia are relatively free of side effects, persons with schizophrenia being especially immune to getting post-lumbar-puncture headaches that occur in approximately one-third of people who do not have schizophrenia. The utility of routine diagnostic use of lumbar puncture and CT scans was illustrated by a recent German study of 130 newly admitted patients with symptoms of schizophrenia; 12 cases of neurological diseases were found among the 130 patients including three cases of AIDS encephalitis, two cases of encephalitis caused by other viruses, two cases of cerebral syphilis, one case of Lyme disease, and one case of multiple sclerosis.

Electroencephalogram (EEG)

The indications for an EEG are virtually identical to those for lumbar puncture, and in fact the two are often ordered together. I personally believe that both the lumbar puncture and EEG should be routinely included in the diagnostic workup of any young adult presenting with symptoms of psychosis for the first time. An EEG should always be ordered if there is a history of meningitis or encephalitis, birth complications, or severe head injury; it should be mandatory for any patient who has had episodic attacks of psychosis with a sudden onset. An EEG may detect temporal-lobe epilepsy, which sometimes mimics schizophrenia.

To be most useful an EEG should be done using nasopharyngeal leads (electrodes are put into the mouth as well as on the scalp) and be done after the person has been kept up all night (sleep-deprived); the diagnostic rewards for doing this more sophisticated type of EEG are appreciable. EEGs are completely harmless procedures which simply measure electrical impulses in the brain; there are no known side effects or harmful effects of any kind.

Other

Other diagnostic tests may be indicated by specific findings but are not routine. Newer brain scans can be done in a variety of ways (e.g., xenon scans, PET scans) but their use is still experimental. The dexamethasone suppression test (DST) was originally thought to be useful to differentiate certain kinds of patients, but it has not proven to be so. As technology improves, the ideal diagnostic workup of schizophrenia will become increasingly complex and sophisticated.

RECOMMENDED FURTHER READING

Cadet, J. L., K. C. Rickler, and D. R. Weinberger. "The Clinical Neurologic Examination in Schizophrenia." In *The Neurology of Schizophrenia,* edited by H. M. Nasrallah and D. R. Weinberger. Amsterdam: Elsevier, 1986.

Harris, M. J., and D. V. Jeste. "Late-Onset Schizophrenia: An Overview." *Schizophrenia Bulletin* 14 (1988):39–55.

Lewis, S. "Sex and Schizophrenia: Vive la Difference." *British Journal of Psychiatry* 161 (1992):445–450.

Peschel, E., R. Peschel, C. W. Howe, and J. W. Howe, eds. *Neurobiological Disorders in Children and Adolescents.* San Francisco: Jossey-Bass, 1992.

Schizophrenia Bulletin, vol. 16, no. 2, 1990. This entire issue is devoted to the effects of gender on schizophrenia.

Slater, E., and M. Roth. *Clinical Psychiatry.* Baltimore: Williams & Wilkins, 1969. This is the best textbook description of schizophrenia by a wide margin.

Taylor, R. L. *Mind or Body: Distinguishing Psychological from Organic Disorders.* New York: McGraw-Hill, 1982. This useful manual for distinguishing brain diseases which may mimic schizophrenia is especially recommended for mental health workers, psychologists, social workers, and psychiatric nurses.

Wilson, L. *This Stranger, My Son.* New York: Putnam, 1968. Paperback by New American Library.

4

WHAT SCHIZOPHRENIA IS NOT

> What consoles me is that I am beginning to consider madness as an illness like any other, and that I accept it as such.
>
> Vincent van Gogh, 1889, in a letter to his brother, Theo

One way to understand a disease is to describe what it is, which has been the task of the past two chapters. The alternative is to describe what it is not. In the case of schizophrenia this is especially important to do, for the term has been used very broadly and imprecisely in both popular culture and in medicine. If we hope to move forward in our understanding of this disease, then we must first be clear what we are talking about.

A "SPLIT PERSONALITY"

Schizophrenia is *not* a multiple or "split personality," although many people mistakenly believe that it is. A "split personality," like *Sybil* or *The Three Faces of Eve,* is officially called a dissociative disorder. It is much less common than schizophrenia, occurs almost exclusively in women, and is thought in most cases to be a reaction to sexual or physical abuse in childhood.

In recent years a dissociative disorder has become a trendy diagnosis among some psychiatrists and is being applied to individuals with a wide variety of symptoms. I am even aware of a few patients with clear signs and symptoms of schizophrenia who have been rediagnosed with dissociative disorder. This represents the ultimate confusion for patients and their families: We tell them that schizophrenia is *not* a "split personality," then turn around and tell them that some patients who appear to have schizophrenia really *do* have a "split personality."

MENTAL RETARDATION

Mental retardation is an impairment of cognitive functions measured by the intelligence quotient (IQ). Depending on the person's IQ, mental retardation is divided into mild (50 to 70), moderate (35 to 49), severe (20 to 34), and profound (below 20). It may be caused by chromosomal abnormalities (e.g., Down's syndrome), metabolic diseases (e.g., phenylketonuria), or brain damage from any cause either prior to or after birth. Most individuals with schizophrenia have a mild loss of IQ that is caused by their impaired functioning on tests of cognitive skills; their innate IQ is not necessarily impaired, but their ability to demonstrate their IQ is impaired.

Occasional individuals may have both schizophrenia and mental retardation. Each may arise independently and the combination merely occurs by chance, or both may be related to a common cause of brain damage. When this occurs it is virtually impossible to get adequate care for the person because treatment facilities are organized either for people with mental illness or mental retardation. In most states such individuals are passed back and forth from one agency to another, each agency disclaiming ultimate responsibility, with the individual made to feel like a leper's leper. Families of such individuals often achieve heroic heights providing services at home with little or no assistance from mental health officials.

MANIC-DEPRESSIVE PSYCHOSIS

The fundamental division of the psychoses into dementia praecox (now called schizophrenia) and manic-depressive psychosis was proposed by Emil Kraepelin in 1896 and has continued to be widely accepted in psychiatry. In 1980 the American Psychiatric Association under *DSM-III* proposed changing the name of manic-depressive psychosis to bipolar disorder, but the new term offers no significant advantages.

Manic-depressive psychosis is approximately one-half as prevalent as schizophrenia. It has a modest predilection for women over men and is thought to be disproportionately common in higher socioeconomic groups for unknown reasons. It usually begins before age 30 but, unlike schizophrenia, later onsets are not unusual. Research on the causes of the disease is proceeding along the same lines as that for schizophrenia. A genetic predisposition is clearly established, with some researchers arguing that it is an inherited disease. In 1987 a study of the Pennsylvania Amish reported that the transmission of manic-depressive psychosis was associated with a gene on chromosome number 11, but subsequent studies did not support this finding; other researchers claimed that the location of the putative gene was on other chromosomes. Biochemical dysfunction in the brain of individuals with manic-depressive psychosis is also suspected, with interest centered on serotonin and its metabolites rather than on dopamine. Most biological abnormalities found in schizophrenia (e.g., ventricular enlargement on MRI scans, neurological abnormalities) are also found in manic-depressive psychosis, although they are not as marked.

The major clinical characteristic of manic-depressive psychosis is episodes of mania, depression, or some combination thereof. Manic episodes consist of elevated (or occasionally irritated) mood, during which time the person is excessively cheerful, talkative, sociable, expansive, grandiose, energetic, and hypersexual, and apparently needs little sleep. The person's speech may be rapid (pressured), with ideas thrown out faster than the listener can sort through them (flights of ideas). Grandiosity may proceed to a delusional state (e.g., belief that one is the President), dress may turn flamboyant, and behavior may become dangerous and inappropriate (e.g., buying sprees, foolish investments). Depressive episodes consist of sad ("dysphoric") mood with hopelessness, poor appetite, sleep disturbances (either insomnia or excessive sleeping), loss of interest in usual activities, hyposexuality, loss of energy, slowed thinking, feelings of guilt or worthlessness, and often suicidal ideas. To qualify for these diagnoses under current *DSM-IV* diagnostic standards, a manic episode must last at least one week (or require hospitalization) and a depressive episode must last at least two weeks.

Although the public stereotype of manic-depressive illness is a person who swings from one extreme to the other and back again, this is found only rarely. Some affected persons have a series of manic episodes, some have a series of depressive episodes, while others have the two in every conceivable combination. Many months or even years may separate episodes; between episodes the person is characteristically normal. There are, of course, all gradations of mood swings in either direction within the general population; some people have great energy and cheerfulness as part of their personality, others are chronically self-deprecating and depressed. A person who falls just short of being fully manic is referred to as hypomanic. If a person has numerous mood swings that fail to meet the full criteria for manic-depressive psychosis, the psychiatric diagnosis used is cyclothymic disorder. Approximately 10 percent of persons with manic-depressive psychosis commit suicide, similar to the suicide rate in schizophrenia.

In its typical form, then, manic-depressive psychosis is easy to differentiate from schizophrenia. The onset of manic-depressive psychosis is not centered in the late teens and early twenties but spread over a much wider age range; males are not affected earlier or more severely; and the predominant clinical symptoms involve disorders of *mood* rather than disorders of *thought*. Patients with manic-depressive psychosis may have delusions or hallucinations, but when they occur they accompany and are congruent with the elevated or depressed mood. Most important, manic-depressive psychosis occurs in discrete episodes with a return to normal functioning between episodes being the rule; schizophrenia rarely occurs in such discrete episodes and residual disability is the rule. Because of their recovery, it is common to find people with manic-depressive psychosis holding important jobs in government, industry, and the entertainment field, and some traits of the hypomanic (e.g., high energy, inflated self-esteem, decreased need for sleep) lead to greater productivity and success in such fields.

The treatment of manic-depressive psychosis is hospitalization when necessary, until the episodes can be controlled. Manic episodes respond to antipsychotic medication, and depressive episodes respond to antidepressants and occasionally electroconvulsive therapy (ECT). Lithium has become an exceedingly useful drug in treating this condition, especially when used between episodes to reduce both the number of episodes and their severity.

John, a resident in psychiatry who came from a wealthy family, became gradually more energetic, talkative, and grandiose over one week's time. He then proceeded to buy three new cars in a 48-hour period, invest the remainder of his savings in a highly questionable venture, and begin new relationships with several women simultaneously. His family had him involuntarily hospitalized, where he was successfully treated with antipsychotics and lithium. He has remained on lithium for ten years with only modest mood swings and has become a successful practicing psychiatrist.

In recent years suggestions have been made increasingly that perhaps Kraepelin was wrong, with schizophrenia and manic-depressive psychosis simply being two ends of the spectrum of a single disease. Perhaps the specifically affected part of the brain determines symptoms, or the period in brain development when the damage occurs. The genetics of the two disorders suggests that schizophrenia and manic-depressive psychosis should occur in separate families (and this usually is the case), yet occasionally both are found in families predisposed to only one. Also of interest are examples such as a pair of identical twins, in which both became psychotic at age 20, one with classical schizophrenia and the other with manic-depressive psychosis, or a set of identical triplets, two of whom were diagnosed with schizophrenia and the third with manic-depressive psychosis. Despite the assumptions of textbooks and the utilization of Kraepelin's dichotomy for almost a century, in fact no conclusive evidence exists for dividing patients with psychosis into separate disease entities.

BORDERLINE PERSONALITY DISORDER

Borderline personality disorder is a most unfortunate term, since it is invariably confused with the older term borderline schizophrenia, now categorized as schizotypal personality disorder. Individuals with borderline personality disorder are unstable in their behavior, relationships, and moods. Their behavior is often impulsive and unpredictable in such areas as money management, sex, alcohol and drug abuse, gambling, shoplifting, fights, reckless driving, and suicide gestures. Their relationships are intense but shift markedly over short periods of time. Their mood also shifts unpredictably and often includes temper tantrums or outbursts.

There is no evidence that borderline personality disorder is related to schizophrenia. Studies of the family history of those with borderline personality disorder suggest that it may be related to major depression or manic-depressive disorder.

BRIEF PSYCHOTIC DISORDER

Brief episodes of schizophrenialike symptoms occur occasionally among individuals who are otherwise normal. Characteristically the illness begins suddenly, lasts a few days, and then remits suddenly. The causes of these illnesses are unknown but probably include brief viral infections of the brain (encephalitis), as well as other brain diseases which may mimic schizophrenia. Such illnesses may apparently also be precipitated by overwhelming stress and are seen in some soldiers undergoing enemy fire, inmates in prisons or concentration camps, and in individuals in extreme sensory deprivation situations (e.g., alone in a lifeboat for several days at sea.)

The symptoms displayed by such patients may mimic schizophrenia closely, with delusions and hallucinations being prominent; disorders of thinking are much less common. Here is an example of such a patient:

> Frank, a 21-year-old Peace Corps volunteer, had only been in Africa for a month. Assigned to a small village with two coworkers, he was having difficulty mastering the language and complained of feeling isolated. One evening he began complaining that the Africans were spying on him. Within twenty-four hours his illness had developed into a full-blown psychosis with delusions of persecution and hallucinations. When seen by a physician, he was hiding under the bed saying that he could hear the army marching down the road to take him and hang him.

At this stage of the illness, based on symptoms alone, it looked very much like schizophrenia. He was removed from his village and hospitalized, treated with drugs, and within one week he was completely well again. Such patients will usually recover whether they are treated with drugs or not and usually do not get sick again.

These patients should not be diagnosed with schizophrenia but rather with brief psychotic disorder. If the illness persists for longer than one month but less than six months, it should then be called a schizophreniform disorder. The more rapid the onset and the shorter the duration of illness, the more likely the person is to return to full normality and not experience recurrence. A minority of such individuals will later develop schizophrenia; a 1994 study in England reported that 28 percent of individuals with brief psychotic disorders had been diagnosed with schizophrenia three years later.

STREET DRUG PSYCHOSIS

It is a well-recognized fact that many drugs which are abused for their psychic effects may produce symptoms similar to schizophrenia. Even after ingesting a comparatively mild drug like marijuana the user may experience strange bodily sensations, loss of body boundaries, and paranoid delusions. There is even a subgroup of people who give up using marijuana because it leads to an unpleasant paranoid state after each usage. Stronger drugs, such as LSD and PCP, regularly produce hallucinations (although these are more likely to be visual than auditory), delusions, and disorders of thinking. Occasionally these symptoms become so severe that the person must be hospitalized and, if the history of drug abuse is not known, the person may be diagnosed with schizophrenia by mistake. Amphetamines (speed) in particular are well known for producing symptoms which may look identical to those of schizophrenia.

The question naturally arises whether drug abuse can *cause* schizophrenia. It is a question asked frequently by families and relatives of patients with this disease. There is now abundant evidence that chronic and repeated usage of many of the mind altering drugs can damage the brain, impairing intellectual functions and memory. There is virtually no evidence, however, that the use of these drugs can actually *cause* schizophrenia in a person who is not already in the process of getting it.

Why, then, is it so common to see schizophrenia begin after a person has used mind-altering drugs? The answer is probably twofold. First, both drug abuse and the onset of schizophrenia occur in the same age range of the late teens and early twenties. The percentage of people in this age range who have at least smoked a few "joints" is very high. Assuming there is no connection whatsoever between drug abuse and schizophrenia, it would still be expected that a considerable number of people developing schizophrenia would also have tried mind-altering drugs.

Second, and more important, is the common sequence of people developing the early symptoms of schizophrenia and then turning to mind-altering drugs to provide a rationalization for what they are experiencing. Hearing voices for the first time in your life, for example, is a very frightening experience; if you then begin using hashish, PCP, or some similar drug, it provides you with a persuasive reason for hearing the voices. Drug use can put off the uncomfortable confrontation with yourself that tells you something is going wrong—very wrong—with your mind. You are, quite literally, losing it. Drugs, and alcohol as well, may also partially relieve the symptoms. In these cases persons can be said to be medicating themselves.

The families of persons who are developing schizophrenia are often not aware of the earliest symptoms of the disease. Not knowing what their relative is experiencing, all they see is him/her turning to increasingly heavy drug abuse. Three to six months later the person is diagnosed with schizophrenia and the family immediately concludes that it was caused by the drug abuse. Such reasoning also relieves any burden of guilt on their part by making it clear that they had nothing to do with causing it. This may be especially attractive to relatives if they are faced with a psychiatrist who implies that problems of child rearing or problems of family communication contributed to the genesis of the disease. In these cases relatives will often seize on drug-abuse-causes-schizophrenia as a defense against the psychiatrist.

> Ted was a promising college student who had his life well planned. Midway through his sophomore year he began having episodes of euphoria, strange bodily sensations, and ideas that he had been sent to save the world. His grades dropped sharply, he began going to church every day, and then began using LSD. Prior to that time he had only used marijuana occasionally at parties. His roommate, college authorities, and finally his parents became alarmed about his turn to drugs. Within one month he was admitted to the local hospital with overt schizophrenic symptomatology. His parents believe it was caused by his drug use and have never been persuaded otherwise.

In most such instances, a careful questioning of the patient will establish the existence of early symptoms of the disease prior to his or her turning to significant drug abuse.

Problems of drug abuse in persons who have schizophrenia will be discussed in Chapter 9.

PRESCRIPTION DRUG PSYCHOSIS

Our society is a drug-using society; young adults abuse street drugs, while older adults use extraordinary numbers of prescription drugs. One only has to randomly open a medicine cabinet in any American home to realize the number of prescription drugs available for ingestion.

Many of these drugs can cause psychiatric symptoms as side effects, ranging from confusion to depression to paranoid delusions or hallucinations. In the majority of cases the hallucinations will be visual, suggesting that the symptoms are due to drugs or other organic medical conditions. Occasionally the hallucinations may be auditory and the patient may appear to have a sudden onset of classical schizophrenia. For any first episode of psychosis, therefore, the physician should always ask the question: "What drugs are you taking?"

Prescription drugs that cause symptoms of psychosis as a side effect almost always do so when they are first started. The psychotic symptoms will go away, sometimes immediately and in other cases more slowly, as soon as the drug is stopped. The following is a list of prescription drugs which have been reported as causing symptoms that might be confused with schizophrenia. There are undoubtedly others, and just because a specific drug is not listed here does not mean that it cannot cause such symptoms. The interaction of two or more drugs can also produce such symptoms. This list is taken mostly from *The Medical Letter* (volume 35, July 23, 1993) and lists drugs generically with a common trade name in parenthesis. Many of these drugs have additional trade names.

acyclovir (Zovirax)
albuterol (Proventil)
amantadine (Symmetrel)
aminocaproic acid (Amicar)
amiodarone (Cordarone)
amphetamines and other drugs
   taken for weight reduction
anabolic steroids
anticonvulsants
antihistamines
asparaginase (Elspar)
atropine and anticholinergics
baclofen (Lioresal)
benzodiazepines
beta blockers
bromocriptine (Parlodel)
bupropion (Wellbutrin)
captopril (Capoten)
cephalosporins

chlorambucil (Leukeran)
chloroquine (Aralen)
cimetidine (Tagamet)
ciprofloxacin (Cipro)
clomiphene citrate (Clomid)
clonazepam (Klonopin)
clonidine (Catapres)
corticosteroids (prednisone, cor-
   tisone, ACTH, others)
cyclobenzaprine (Flexeril)
cycloserine (Seromycin)
cyclosporine (Sandimmune)
dapsone (Avlosulfon)
deet (Off)
diazepam (Valium)
diethylproprion (Tenuate)
digitalis glycosides
disopyramide (Norpace)
disulfiram (Antabuse)

dronabinol (Marinol)
enalapril (Vasotec)
ephedrine
ethchlorvynol (Placidyl)
ethionamide (Trecator-SC)
ethosuximide (Zarontin)
fenfluramine (Pondimin)
fluoxetine (Prozac)
ganciclovir (Cytovene)
gentamycin (Garamycin)
hydroxychloroquine
    (Plaquenil)
ibuprofen (Motrin)
indomethacin (Indocin)
isocarboxazid (Marplan)
isoniazid (INH)
ketamine (Ketalar)
levodopa (Dopar)
lidocaine (Xylocaine)
maprotiline (Ludiomil)
mefloquine (Lariam)
methyldopa (Aldomet)
methylphenidate (Ritalin)
methysergide (Sansert)
metrizamide (Amipaque)
metronidazole (Flagyl)
nalidixic acid (Neg Gram)
naproxen (Naprosyn)
narcotics
niridazole (Ambilhar)
nonsteroidal anti-inflammatory
    drugs
ofloxacin (Floxin)
oxymetazoline (Afrin)
pentazocine (Talwin)

pergolide (Permax)
phenelzine (Nardil)
phenmetrazine (Preludin)
phenteramine (Fastin)
phenylephrine (Neo-
    Synephrine)
phenylpropanolamine
    (Dexatrim)
phenytoin (Dilantin)
podophyllin (Podoben)
prazosin (Minipress)
primidone (Mysoline)
procainamide (Pronestyl)
promethazine (Phenergan)
propafenone (Rythmol)
propoxyphene (Darvon)
propranolol (Inderal)
pseudoephedrine (Actifed)
quinacrine (Atabrine)
quinidine
salicylates
selegiline (Eldepryl)
sulfonamides
sulindac (Clinoril)
tamoxifen (Nolvadex)
theophylline
thiabendazole (Mintezol)
thyroid hormones
tocainide (Tonocard)
trazodone (Desyrel)
triazolam (Halcion)
trimethoprim-sulfamethoxa-
    zole (Bactrim)
vincristine (Oncovin)
zidovudine (Retrovir)

The following is an example of such a case.

> Christopher, a 29-year-old lawyer with a severe alcohol problem, was
> noted to become increasingly paranoid over four days and to then begin

responding to auditory hallucinations. He was initially diagnosed as possible schizophrenia, but questioning by an emergency room doctor revealed that a psychiatrist had started Christopher on disulfiram (Antabuse) one week previously. The disulfiram was stopped and the symptoms went away within 48 hours. When disulfiram was again resumed the symptoms recurred. Subsequent withdrawal from alcohol without disulfiram produced no psychotic symptoms, suggesting that it had been the disulfiram and not alcohol withdrawal which had been the cause of the paranoia and hallucinations.

PSYCHOSIS DUE TO OTHER DISEASES

There are several diseases of the body that can produce symptoms similar to schizophrenia. In most cases there is no ambiguity because the disease is clearly diagnosable; in a few cases, however, there may be some confusion, especially in the early stages of the disease.

There is considerable dispute about how often other diseases mimic schizophrenia and go undetected. In a widely quoted study, Hall and his associates in Texas examined 38 hospitalized patients with schizophrenia and found 39 percent of them had a medical illness which "caused or exacerbated" the schizophrenia. On the other hand Koran and his colleagues in California thoroughly studied 269 patients with schizophrenia and found only one patient whose disease (temporal lobe epilepsy) had been missed and was apparently causing the schizophrenia-like symptoms. One English study of 318 hospital admissions with a diagnosis of schizophrenia found eight percent "with antecedent organic cerebral disorders." Another English study of 268 first admissions with schizophrenia found fewer than six percent with relevant organic disease findings. A postmortem study of 200 patients with schizophrenia "found organic cerebral disease thought to be causally related in 11 percent." What is clear is that there is a subgroup of patients with schizophrenia who have other medical diseases which are causing their schizophrenic symptoms, and that some of these other diseases are treatable.

The most important diseases that may produce symptoms of schizophrenia are:

Brain Tumors

Tumors of the pituitary gland are especially likely to cause symptoms of schizophrenia, but other tumors (e.g., a meningioma of the temporal lobe) may also do so. These are usually detectable on MRI scan and often curable by surgery in their early stages.

Viral Encephalitis

It has been known for many years that viral encephalitis can produce schizophrenialike symptoms following the encephalitis. What is becoming increasingly clear is that encephalitis occasionally mimics schizophrenia in the early stages of illness, before other signs and symptoms of encephalitis become apparent; how often this occurs is unknown. A recent review of twenty-two such cases identified a variety of viruses as capable of doing this, including herpes simplex, Epstein-Barr virus, cytomegalovirus, measles, coxsackie, and equine encephalitis. If suspected, most such cases can be diagnosed by lumbar puncture and EEG.

Temporal Lobe Epilepsy

The relationship between epilepsy and schizophrenia has been a controversial issue for many years. There is agreement, however, that one type of epilepsy—that of the temporal lobe—frequently produces symptoms like schizophrenia. One study found that 17 percent of patients with temporal lobe epilepsy had some symptoms of schizophrenia.

Cerebral Syphilis

Although not seen so much as in the past, syphilis should never be forgotten as a possible cause of schizophrenialike symptoms. A routine blood test will alert one to its possibility, and a lumbar puncture will confirm the diagnosis.

Multiple Sclerosis

Depression and intellectual deterioration are commonly found in the early stages of multiple sclerosis. Occasionally symptoms of schizophrenia may also occur, with one report of a woman with "paranoid schizophrenia" for ten years before her multiple sclerosis became fully manifest.

Huntington's Disease

Schizophrenia is said to be "a common initial diagnosis" and "the most frequent persisting mis-diagnosis" in Huntington's disease, a genetic disease beginning in midlife. Once choreiform movements begin in the patient, the correct diagnosis becomes clear.

AIDS

This is the newest addition to the list of diseases which may present with symptoms resembling schizophrenia. It has been clearly established that AIDS may occasionally manifest itself with symptoms of either schizophrenia or manic-depressive illness because of the effect of the human immunodeficiency virus (HIV) on the brain. With the incidence of AIDS increasing, a test for HIV should be included in all routine first admission diagnostic workups for serious mental illness.

Other Diseases

A large number of other diseases have been recorded as occasionally presenting with symptoms similar to schizophrenia. They include the following:

Wilson's disease
acute intermittent porphyria
metachromatic leukodystrophy
lupus erythematosus
congenital calcification of basal
  ganglia
progressive supranuclear palsy
aqueductal stenosis
normal pressure hydrocephalus
cerebral vascular accident (stroke)
narcolepsy
thyroid disease

adrenal disease
hepatic encephalopathy
pellagra
sarcoidosis
pernicious anemia
metal poisoning (e.g., lead, mercury)

insecticide poisoning (e.g., organophosphorus compounds)
leptospirosis
tropical infections (e.g., trypanosomiasis, cerebral malaria)

The best means of detecting these diseases are a competent physician and a complete diagnostic workup, as outlined in chapter 3.

PSYCHOSIS FOLLOWING CHILDBIRTH

Some degree of depression in mothers following childbirth is relatively common and on occasion may be severe. Much less common, occurring approximately once in every thousand births, are schizophrenia-like symptoms which develop in the mother. These usually begin between three and seven days postpartum and may include delusions (e.g., believing her baby is defective or has been kidnapped) or hallucinations (voices telling her to kill the baby). Depression may occur as well, and a schizoaffective diagnosis is frequent. Because of the unpredictability of such patients, the baby is usually separated from the mother until she improves. Treatment with medication usually produces rapid improvement, with resolution of the symptoms in most cases within two weeks. A small percentage of such cases persist and proceed to become a full-blown schizophrenic disorder or manic-depressive disorder.

The cause of this disorder is not known. Formerly it was believed that psychological factors, such as the mother's ambivalent feelings toward the baby, were primary. In recent years more attention has been focused on possible biochemical factors, especially the massive hormonal changes which take place following childbirth. Such theories receive added impetus from the observation that some female schizophrenic patients regularly become more symptomatic just prior to or at the time of their menstrual period. Those cases which go on to true schizophrenia may be women who would have done so even if they had not become pregnant. Since the onset of schizophrenia occurs most often during the same years in which most childbearing takes place, such a coincidence is occasionally inevitable.

Mary had just returned from the hospital after delivering her first child, a girl. Within the next three days her husband noted that she was talking strangely and appeared confused. She acknowledged that voices were telling her to kill the baby. Mary was hospitalized, treated with drugs, and completely returned to normal within ten days.

The use of the term "schizophrenia" is not appropriate for illnesses such as this.

PSYCHOSIS FOLLOWING TRAUMA

The fact that psychosis can occasionally follow severe head injuries has been well established since studies on soldiers during the Franco-Prussian War of 1870. Still very controversial, however, is how often this occurs and what kinds of head trauma can produce psychosis. Localized injury to the temporal or frontal lobe is seen more often in individuals who develop post-traumatic psychosis, as is a history of coma for more than 24 hours. It has also been claimed that thinking disorders are uncommon in these psychoses but that paranoid delusions are common.

The problem arises in trying to assess whether the head trauma is related to the onset of the psychosis. Head trauma and schizophrenia are both common in young adults and so will occur coincidentally from time to time. Most young adults can recall some instance of head trauma, and associating the trauma with the schizophrenia has an appeal to relatives who may be looking for an explanation for the sickness. Further complicating this assessment is the fact that individuals developing early symptoms of schizophrenia may do irrational things which produce head trauma; the family may not have been aware of the early symptoms, and so may associate the onset of the schizophrenia with the trauma. Finally there is the confounding issue of whether the trauma produces the psychosis by direct injury to the brain or by acting as a severe stressor, the straw that broke the camel's back.

John, a 22-year-old college student with no history of psychiatric symptoms, was struck by a car while riding his bicycle. He was semicomatose for 16 days, had signs of neurological damage, and seizures. Emerging from his semicomatose state, he told his mother that voices on the radio had accused him of being a homosexual. No further symptoms were noted over the following year except insomnia and headaches, until he became suicidal and was hospitalized. At that time paranoid delusions were noted and these became more severe. He had seven more admissions over the next five years. His delusions responded to antipsychotic medication, which he stopped taking each time he left the hospital.

INFANTILE AUTISM

Infantile autism, a brain disease of infancy, appears unrelated to schizophrenia. This syndrome, beginning within the child's first two-and-one-half years, is characterized by severe social withdrawal (e.g., child resists being held or touched), retarded language development, abnormal responses to sensory stimuli (e.g., sounds may overwhelm the child), and a fascination with inanimate objects (e.g., a faucet, the child's own shadow) or repititive routines (e.g., spinning). It occurs in approximately 4 children per 10,000 and thus is one twenty-fifth as common as schizophrenia. At one time it was said that autism was more common in higher socioeconomic groups but that has been disproven. It occurs four times more in males than in females.

Autism is almost certainly a collection of diseases rather than a single disease. Autisimlike behavior may also be observed in children with the fragile X syndrome, phenylketonuria, viral encephalitis, and other diseases. Epilepsy commonly accompanies autism; approximately one-half of autistic children may have some degree of mental retardation; and a higher than expected percentage of autistic children also have blindness or deafness.

Like schizophrenia, the evidence that autism has biological causes has become overwhelming in recent years; older psychogenic theories such as Kanner's "refrigerator mother" now are completely discredited. There definitely appears to be a genetic component to autism: neuropathological abnormalities occur in the brains of these children, especially in the cerebellum. MRI abnormalities have been found in some studies but not in others. Abnormalities in endocrine function and blood chemistry have also been found. One of the most interesting findings which may relate to the causes of autism is that mothers who give birth to autistic children report having had an unusually high frequency of bleeding during pregnancy, compared with controls. In addition to being found in retrospective studies, the increased bleeding has also been found in a prospective study in which information was collected on a large group of mothers, and only later was the data analyzed on those who gave birth to autistic children.

A variety of medications have been used to treat autism but so far with only modest success. As the autistic child gets older, a small percentage improve and function well. The majority, however, take on the characteristics of adult schizophrenia with an emphasis on "negative" symptoms (e.g., withdrawal, flattened emotions, poverty of thoughts), rather than "positive" symptoms (e.g., delusions, hallucinations).

Differentiation of infantile autism from childhood schizophrenia is in most cases not too difficult. Autism almost always begins before age two-and-one-half, while schizophrenia is rare before 5 and uncommon before age 10. The autistic child will have prominent withdrawal, language retardation, and repetitive routines, while the child with schizophrenia will have delusions, hallucinations, and thinking disorders. Half the autistic children will be retarded but far fewer of the children with schizophrenia will be. Finally, children with schizophrenia may have a family history of schizophrenia, but autistic children almost never have a family history of schizophrenia.

CULTURALLY INDUCED OR HYSTERICAL PSYCHOSIS

Occasionally confusion will arise between schizophrenia and culturally induced or hysterical psychosis. This is an altered state of consciousness usually entered into voluntarily by an individual; while in this altered state of consciousness the person may exhibit symptoms which look superficially like schizophrenia. For example, the person may complain of altered bodily sensations and hallucinations and may behave in an excited and irrational manner. In the United States these conditions are seen most commonly in connection with fundamentalistic religious services. In other cultural groups and in other countries these conditions are known by such names as moth craziness (Navajo Indians), windigo (Cree and Ojibwa Indians), zar (Middle East), koro (China), susto (Latin America), latah (Southeast Asia), and amok (worldwide).

Cecelia led a perfectly normal life except for the monthly all-night worship service at her fundamentalist church. During the service she claimed to hear voices talking to her, often spoke in tongues, and occasionally behaved in a wild and irrational way so that others had to restrain her.

Other members of the congregation regarded her with both fear and awe, suspecting that she was possessed by spirits.

People like Cecelia should not be labeled as having schizophrenia unless there are other symptoms of the disease. Occasionally persons who have schizophrenia will be attracted to fundamentalist religious groups or religious cults, however, since such groups often value hearing voices or "speaking in tongues."

CREATIVITY, SCHIZOPHRENIA, AND FAMOUS PEOPLE

An oft-debated question around firesides and pubs is whether there is a relationship between creativity and schizophrenia. John Dryden reflected the views of many people when he wrote three hundred years ago, "Great wits are sure to madmen near allied." Since then we have moved a little closer to a definitive answer to this question.

It is known that the creative person and the person with schizophrenia share many cognitive traits. Both use words and language in unusual ways (the hallmark of a great poet or novelist), both have unusual views of reality (as great artists do), both often utilize unusual thought processes in their deliberations, and both tend to prefer solitude to the company of others. When creative persons are given traditional psychological tests, they manifest more psychopathology than noncreative persons, and creative persons are often viewed as eccentric by their friends. Conversely, when people with nonparanoid schizophrenia are given traditional tests of creativity they score very high (people with paranoid schizophrenia do not).

Several surveys have shown that highly creative persons are not themselves more susceptible to schizophrenia. However, one study has suggested that the immediate relatives of creative persons may be more susceptible to schizophrenia. As a case in point one thinks of Robert Frost, whose aunt, son, and perhaps daughter all developed schizophrenia. Looking at the problem from the other side, the same study found that the immediate relatives of patients with schizophrenia scored higher on tests of creativity than would be expected by chance. Such studies need to be replicated before one can seriously suggest a link between schizophrenia and creativity. If such a link exists, it would most likely be a genetic predisposition to both conditions.

There is one fundamental difference between the creative person and the person with schizophrenia of course. The creative person has his/her unusual thought processes under control and can harness them in the creation of a product. The person with schizophrenia, on the other hand, is at the mercy of disconnected thinking and loose associations which tumble about in cacophonic disarray. The creative person has choices whereas the schizophrenia sufferer does not.

The list of creative individuals who have been suspected of having schizophrenia or schizoaffective disorder is remarkably short; this is not surprising when one considers how thinking disorders interfere with a person's ability to work. Artists and writers who almost certainly suffered from schizophrenia include Russian dancer Vaslav Nijinsky, French playwright Antonin Artaud, Swedish composer Jakob Adolf Hagg, German poet Johann Freidrich Holderlin, and English poet and composer Ivor Gurney. Schizophrenia or schizoaffective disorder has also been suggested as possible diagnoses for Swedish writer August Strindberg and French painter Vincent Van Gogh, and Irish writer James Joyce appears to have had some clearly schizotypal features in his thought processes. Finally, there is a group of painters who became well known for their art after they had been diagnosed with schizophrenia; Swiss Adolf Wolfli is probably the best known of these painters and is featured in John M. MacGregor's 1989 book, *The Discovery of the Art of the Insane*.

Nijinsky was the most famous dancer in the years immediately preceding World War I and, some have said, the greatest dancer who ever lived. At the age of 29 he developed schizophrenia and remained psychotic for the remainder of his life despite consultations from Drs. Adler, Bleuler, Freud, Jung, and Kraepelin. Portions of his diary, written while hospitalized, were edited and published by his wife:

> I love life and want to live, to cry but cannot—I feel such a pain in my soul—a pain which frightens me. My soul is ill. My soul, not my mind. The doctors do not understand my illness. I know what I need to get well. My illness is too great to be cured quickly. I am incurable. My soul is ill, I am poor, a pauper, miserable. Everyone who reads these lines will suffer—they will understand my feelings.

James Joyce is a particularly interesting study in psychopathology. A biography on him noted his "keen pleasure in sounds," his periods of depression, intermittent alcohol abuse, and at least one episode of mania during which "he could not sleep for six or seven nights . . . he felt as if he were wound up and then suddenly shooting out of water like a fish. During the day he was troubled by auditory hallucinations." A psychiatrist who studied Joyce's writings concluded that he was a schizoid personality with paranoid traits and claimed that *"Finnegans Wake* must ultimately be diagnosed as psychotic." Joyce's only daughter, Lucia, was diagnosed with classical schizophrenia at age 22, treated by Jung, and spent the rest of her life in mental hospitals. It was noted that "Joyce had a remarkable capacity to follow her swift jumps of thought, which baffled other people completely."

Vincent van Gogh was also troubled by episodes of depression, intermittent alcohol abuse, and periods of great energy. At Arles, while being "assailed by auditory hallucinations," he "suddenly cut off his left ear," then presented it to a prostitute as a gift. Hospitalized in Arles twice in the next two months, he displayed paranoid delusions, visual and auditory hallucinations, and mutism. He then was involuntarily committed to an asylum in St.-Rémy for a year, during which time he had to be periodically placed in isolation and complained of hearing "sounds and strange voices." Various diagnoses of van Gogh's illness have been offered, including schizophrenia, schizoaffective disorder, manic-depressive psychosis, temporal lobe epilepsy, porphyria, and cerebral syphilis. Although there is a tendency to romanticize his psychosis and view it as partially responsible for his great art, van Gogh's own letters make explicit how painful and unpleasant it was. He ultimately committed suicide after painting for just ten years. From St.-Rémy he wrote to his brother, Theo: "Oh, if I could have worked without this accursed disease—what things I might have done."

In contrast to schizophrenia, manic-depressive psychosis lends itself to creativity because of the high energy level and rapid thought processes experienced by many people with this disease. The list of people suspected of having manic-depressive psychosis among creative individuals includes Handel, Berlioz, Schumann, Beethoven, Donizetti, Gluck, Byron, Shelley, Coleridge, Poe, Balzac, Hemingway, Fitzgerald, Eugene O'Neill and Virginia Woolf. Alcoholism is also common among creative individuals; the first five Americans who won a Nobel Prize for literature were all alcoholics or nearly so (Sinclair Lewis, O'Neill, Faulkner, Hemingway, and Steinbeck).

RECOMMENDED FURTHER READING

Coleman, M., and C. Gillberg. *The Biology of the Autistic Syndromes.* New York: Praeger Publishers, 1985.

Davison, K. "Schizophrenia-like Psychoses Associated with Organic Cerebral Disorders: A Review." *Psychiatric Developments* 1 (1983): 1–34. This is an excellent review of psychosis due to medical conditions. An earlier version of the paper, widely referenced, was published by Davison and C. R. Bagley as "Schizophrenia-like Psychoses Associated with Organic Disorders of the Central Nervous System" in *Current Problems in Neuropsychiatry,* edited by R. N. Herrington, Ashford, England: Headley Brothers, 1969.

Fieve, R. *Moodswing: The Third Revolution in Psychiatry.* New York: Bantam Books, 1989.

Goodwin, F. K., and K. R. Jamison. *Manic-Depressive Illness.* New York: Oxford, 1990.

Lishman, W. A. *Organic Psychiatry: The Psychological Consequences of Cerebral Disorder.* Oxford: Blackwell Scientific Publications, 1987.

Papolos, D. F., and J. Papolos. *Overcoming Depression.* New York: Harper & Row, revised edition, 1992.

Torrey, E. F. "Functional Psychoses and Viral Encephalitis." *Integrative Psychiatry* 4 (1986): 224–36.

5

PROGNOSIS AND
POSSIBLE COURSES

Such a disease, which disorders the senses, perverts the reason and breaks up the passions in wild confusion—which assails man in his essential nature—brings down so much misery on the head of its victims, and is productive of so much social evil—deserves investigation on its own merits, by statistical as well as other methods. . . . We may discover the causes of insanity, the laws which regulate its course, the circumstances by which it is influenced, and either avert its visitations, or mitigate their severity; perhaps in a later age, save mankind from its inflictions, or if this cannot be, at any rate ensure the sufferers early treatment.

Dr. William Farr, 1841

When diagnosed with schizophrenia for the first time, the person and his/her family want to know what is likely to happen next. What are the chances for complete recovery? How independent is the person likely to be ten years later, or thirty years later? What are the chances for little recovery or for spending most of the person's life in a mental hospital? What is the risk of suicide? These are important questions, for the answers to them will determine how the family of a person with schizophrenia plans for the future.

PREDICTORS OF OUTCOME

Over the years it has been noted that some persons afflicted with schizophrenia recover completely, others recover partially, and some do not recover at all. This observation led many professionals to review the clinical data at the time of the original hospital admission to determine what factors might predict a good outcome and which might predict a poor outcome. The result of these efforts has been a series of predictive factors, each of which taken by itself has limited usefulness, but which taken together may be very useful. From this a subtyping of schizophrenia into good outcome (good prognosis) and poor outcome (poor prognosis) has emerged and is becoming widely used. It is probably the most valid way to classify the disease which has been found to date.

The factors which are included in determining whether the person fits the good outcome or the poor outcome group are:

History of Adjustment Prior to Onset of Illness

Patients who are more likely to have a good outcome are those who were considered to be relatively normal prior to getting sick. Thus, if as children they were able to make friends with others, did not have major problems with delinquency and achieved success levels in school reasonable for their intelligence level, their outcome is likely to be good. Conversely, if they are described by relatives as "always a strange child," had major problems in school or with their peers, were considered delinquent, or were very withdrawn, they are more likely to fall into the poor outcome group.

Gender

It has now been clearly established that women with schizophrenia have a much more favorable outcome than men (see chapter 3).

Family History

Patients with the best outcome are those with no history of relatives with schizophrenia. The more close relatives who have schizophrenia, the poorer the outcome becomes. If there is a history of depression or manic-depressive psychosis in the family, the person is likely to have a good outcome. Thus a good outcome is suggested by a family history with no mental disease or only depression and/or manic-depressive illness. A poor outcome is suggested by a family history of schizophrenia.

Age of Onset

In general, the younger the age at which schizophrenia develops, the poorer the outcome. A person who is first diagnosed with schizophrenia at age 15 is likely to have a poorer outcome than a person with the onset at age 25. Persons who are first diagnosed with schizophrenia in older age groups, especially over age 30, are likely to fall into the good outcome group.

Suddenness of Onset

This is an important predictor of recovery, with the best outcomes occurring in those patients whose onset is most sudden. A relative who describes the gradual onset of the person's symptoms over a period of many months is painting a bleak picture, for it is much more likely that the person will fall into the poor outcome group. Conversely, as a practicing psychiatrist I am very happy when a relative tells me that "John was completely normal up until about a month ago," for I know that such a history bodes well for the future.

Precipitating Events

These are very difficult to evaluate and therefore less reliable as predictors. The reason is that during the time of life when most persons become ill with schizophrenia for the first time (ages 15 to 25), there is a great deal—much of it stressful—happening in their lives. Changing girlfriends and boyfriends, separations and divorces, school failures and new jobs, vocational plans, the death of parents, and existential crises all flow naturally through these years. Ask anyone in the 15-to-25 age range on any given day what is going on in his/her life that is important and you will probably get a long list in answer. If, however, there have been major life events immediately preceding the breakdown, this points toward a good likelihood of a poor outcome.

Clinical Symptoms

The symptoms during the initial breakdown are often suggestive of the outcome of the disease and can be used as predictive factors. Some of the more important of these are:

A. Catatonic symptoms are a good sign.

B. Paranoid symptoms are a good sign.

C. The presence of depression or other emotions is a good sign. If the person is diagnosed as schizoaffective (see chapter 3), that is also a good sign.

D. The predominance of "negative" symptoms such as flattening of emotions, poverty of thoughts, apathy, and social withdrawal is a sign of a poor outcome.

E. Obsessive (compelled to think about a certain thing) and compulsive (repeated ritualistic behavior) symptoms are bad signs.

F. Symptoms which are atypical—which do not fit the established clinical patterns for schizophrenia—are a good sign.

G. The presence of confusion (e.g., "I don't understand what is happening to me") is a good sign.

CT or MRI Scan Findings

If a diagnostic CT or MRI scan is done and it is normal, that is a good sign. If it shows enlargement of the ventricles in the brain and/or atrophy of brain tissue, that is a bad sign.

Early Treatment with Medication

There is some evidence that suggests that long delays in treating early episodes of schizophrenia with medication may result in a poorer outcome. If this is substantiated, it would mean that psychoanalysts or other psychotherapists who treat schizophrenia with talk therapy

without using medications might be liable with legal action for malpractice.

Response to Medication

The initial response of the person to antipsychotic medication is a
strong indicator of prognosis: the better the response, the better the
outcome is likely to be.

It should be emphasized again that each of these factors *by itself*
has limited predictive value. It is only when they are all put together
that an overall prognosis can be assigned. Many patients will, of
course, have a mixture of good and poor outcome signs, whereas others will fall quite clearly into one category or the other.

It should also be remembered that all predictions are only statistical assertions of likelihood. There is nothing in the least binding about
them. All of us who regularly care for patients with schizophrenia have
seen enough exceptions to these guidelines to make us humble about
any predictions. Thus I have seen a patient with a normal childhood,
no family history of the disease, a rapid onset at age 22, clear precipitating events, and initial catatonic symptoms who never recovered
from even his initial illness and whose outcome is poor. More opti-
mistically, I have seen patients with virtually every poor prognostic
sign go on to almost complete recovery.

POSSIBLE COURSES: TEN YEARS LATER

For individuals hospitalized with schizophrenia for the first time, the
outlook at the end of one year is reasonably optimistic. Dr. Jeffrey
Lieberman and his colleagues in New York recently completed a study
of 70 such patients, and at the end of one year 74 percent of them
"were considered to be fully remitted" and 12 percent were "partially
remitted." For those who went into remission the mean time for those
with a diagnosis of schizophrenia was 42 weeks and for schizoaffective disorder 12 weeks.

The extended prognosis for schizophrenia is less optimistic than
this one-year outcome. From the early years of this century it has been
said that there is a rule of thirds determining the possible courses in

schizophrenia: a third recover, a third are improved, and a third are unimproved. Recent long-term follow-up studies of persons with schizophrenia both in Europe and in the United States suggest that this rule is simplistic and out-of-date. It is clear, for example, that the course of the disease over thirty years is better than it is over ten years. The use of medications has probably improved the long-term course for many patients, while the positive effect of deinstitutionalization has been to decrease dependency on the hospital and increase the number of patients able to live in the community. On the other hand, it is also clear that the mortality rate, especially by suicide, for persons with schizophrenia is very high and apparently increasing.

The best summary of possible courses of schizophrenia was done by J. H. Stephens, who analyzed twenty-five studies in which follow-up was for at least ten years. The percentage of patients "recovered," "improved," or "unimproved" varied widely from study to study depending on the initial selection of patients, e.g., inclusion of large numbers with acute reactive psychosis increased the percentage of fully recovered. Utilizing all studies done to date, the ten-year course of schizophrenia can be seen in the chart below and more nearly approximates a rule of "quarters," rather than a rule of "thirds".

THE COURSE OF SCHIZOPHRENIA

10 Years Later

25% Completely recovered	25% Much improved, relatively independent	25% Improved, but require extensive support network	15% Hospitalized, unimproved	10% Dead (mostly suicide)

30 Years Later

25% Completely recovered	35% Much improved, relatively independent	15% Improved, but require extensive support network	10% Hospital- ized, unim- proved	15% Dead

Twenty-five Percent Recover Completely

This assumes that all patients with symptoms of schizophrenia are part of the analysis, including those who have been sick for less than six months with schizophreniform disorders. If only patients with narrowly-defined schizophrenia are included (i.e., "continuous signs of the illness for at least six months"), then the percentage of completely recovered will be under 25 percent. Patients who recover completely do so whether they are treated with antipsychotic medication, wheat germ oil, Tibetan psychic healing, psychoanalysis, or yellow jelly-beans, and all treatments for schizophrenia must show results better than this spontaneous recovery rate if they are to be accepted as truly effective. Those who recover also do so within the first two years of illness and usually have had no more than two discrete episodes of illness.

> Andrea became acutely psychotic during her second year of college and was hospitalized for six weeks. She recovered slowly, with medication and supportive psychotherapy over the following six months while living at home, and was able to resume college the following year. She has never had a recurrence. She believes she got sick because of a failed romance and her family, when they refer to the illness at all, talk vaguely of a "nervous breakdown."

Such families often deny that their family member had schizo-phrenia and rarely join family support groups such as the National Alliance for the Mentally Ill (NAMI).

Twenty-five Percent Are Much Improved

These patients usually have a good response to antipsychotic medica-tion, and as long as they take it continue to do well. They can live rela-tively independently, have a social life, may marry, and often are capa-ble of working part- or full-time.

> Peter had a normal childhood and successful high school career. He then married and joined the army to get training and travel. There was no family history of mental illness. At age 21, while assigned to Germany, he began to have strange feelings in his body and later to hear voices. He started drink-ing heavily, which seemed to relieve the voices, then turned to the use of hashish and cocaine. His condition deteriorated rapidly, and he was arrested for hitting an officer who he believed was trying to poison him. He was hos-pitalized and eventually discharged from the army with a full service-con-nected disability. Over the next three years he was hospitalized three more

times.

Peter responded slowly to very high doses of medication and was released from the hospital almost completely well. He returned faithfully for an injection of medicine every week, lived in his own apartment, and visited his family (including his divorced wife and children) and friends during the day. He clearly was capable of holding a job, but declined to do so for fear that it would jeopardize his monthly army disability check. His only remaining symptoms were voices which he heard late in the day but which he was able to ignore.

Twenty-five Percent Are Modestly Improved

These patients respond less well to medication, often have "negative" symptoms, and have a history of poorer adjustment prior to the onset of their illness. They require an extensive support network; in communities where this is available they may lead satisfactory lives, but where it is not they may be victimized and end up living on the streets or in public shelters.

Frank was a loner as a child but had considerable musical ability and received a college scholarship. In his third year of college his grades slowly dropped as he complained of continuous auditory hallucinations. Hospitalization and medication produced a modest improvement so that he could eventually be placed in a halfway house in the community. He is supposed to attend a day program but usually walks the street talking to himself or composing music on scraps of paper. He stays completely to himself and needs to be reminded to change his clothes, brush his teeth, and take his medicine.

Fifteen Percent Are Unimproved

These are the treatment-resistant patients for whom until recently we had little to offer. Some have responded to new antipsychotic drugs such as clozapine (see chapter 6). Those who do not respond are candidates for long-term asylum care in a sheltered setting (see chapter 8). When released into the community, often against their will, the results are frequently disastrous.

Dorothy was known as a quiet child who attained straight A's in school. Her mother was hospitalized for schizophrenia for two years during Dorothy's childhood, and a brother was in an institution for the mentally retarded. She was first hospitalized at age 15 for one month; information on this hospitalization was not obtainable except for a diagnosis of "transient situational reaction of adolescence." Following this, Dorothy dropped out of school, went to work as a domestic, married, and had three children. She remained apparently well until age 22, at which time she believed people were trying to kill her, believed people were talking about her, and heard airplanes flying overhead all day. She neglected her children and housework and simply sat in a corner with a fearful expression on her face. On examination she had a marked thinking disorder and catatonic rigidity and was noted to be very shy and withdrawn.

Over the ensuing fifteen years Dorothy has been hospitalized most of the time and has responded minimally to medication. During the earlier years she was returned to her home for brief periods, with homemaker services; and in more recent years she lived for several months in a halfway house. There she was invariably victimized by men and was judged not to be capable of defending herself. She remains in the hospital, sitting quietly in a chair day after day. She answers politely but with absolutely no emotion and shows marked poverty of thought and of speech.

Ten Percent Are Dead

Almost all of these die by suicide or accident, and other factors will be discussed at greater length below.

POSSIBLE COURSES: THIRTY YEARS LATER

It has been clearly established in recent years that the thirty-year course of schizophrenia is more favorable for the average patient than is the ten-year course. This directly contradicts a widespread stereotype about the disease which dates to Kraepelin's pessimistic belief that most patients slowly deteriorate. A major reason for this better long-term prognosis is that aging ameliorates the symptoms of schizophrenia in most people. Symptoms of this disease tend to be most severe when the person is in his/her 20s and 30s, then become somewhat less severe in the 40s, and significantly less severe in the 50s and 60s. We do not understand why this is so and there are, of course, exceptions, but schizophrenia represents one of the few conditions in life for which aging is an advantage.

The definitive work on the long-term course of schizophrenia has come from studies carried out by Dr. Manfred Bleuler, Dr. Luc Ciompi and his colleagues, and Dr. Gerd Huber and his colleagues in Europe, and by Dr. Courtenay Harding and her colleagues on patients deinstitutionalized from the Vermont State Hospital. Some patients followed up by these groups were as much as forty years older than when they became ill, and the agreement between the results of the different studies is impressive. As summarized by Ciompi for patients followed for an average of thirty-six years: "About three-fifths of the schizophrenic probands have a favorable outcome; that is, they recover or show definite improvement." And for patients with chronic schizophrenia in Vermont, followed up by Harding, et al., twenty to twenty-five years after leaving the hospital, "the current picture of the functioning of these subjects is a startling contrast to their previous levels described during their index hospitalization." Approximately three-quarters of the Vermont patients required little or no help in meeting their basic daily needs.

In most patients with schizophrenia, the "positive" symptoms of hallucinations, delusions, and thinking disorders decrease over the years. A person who was severely incapacitated at age 25 by these symptoms may have only residual traces of them at age 50. It is almost as if the disease process has burned itself out over time and left behind only scars from its earlier activity. Patients also learn how to live with their symptoms, ignoring the voices and not responding to them in public.

The residual phases of schizophrenia are often referred to in psychiatric literature as a chronic defect state and are described as follows in a standard textbook:

The patient, living in an institution or outside, has come to an *arrangement with his illness.* He has adapted himself to the world of his morbid ideas with more or less success, from his own point of view and from that of his environment. Compared with the experiences during the acute psychosis, his positive symptoms, such as delusions or hallucinations, have become colorless, repetitive, and formalized. They still have power over him but nothing is added and nothing new or unexpected happens. Negative symptoms, thought disorder, passivity, catatonic mannerisms and flattening of affect rule the picture, but even they grow habitual with the patient and appear always in the same inveterate pattern in the individual case. There is a robotlike fixity and petrification of attitude and reactions which are not only due to poverty of ideas but also to a very small choice of modes of behavior.

As with all rules, there are exceptions, so this final course can vary. Occasional patients retain their more florid symptoms all their lives. For example, I had under my care a 75-year-old man who hallucinated all day every day and had been doing so for fifty years. His illness was virtually unaffected by medications. These kinds of patients are certainly exceptional, but they do exist.

It is currently popular to attribute many of the symptoms of schizophrenia to drug effects. The truth is that exactly the same picture was described for fifty years before the drugs were introduced. Drugs used in schizophrenia may certainly produce some sedation, especially in older patients, but such effects account for a minuscule portion of the total picture on a properly run hospital ward. Similarly these late symptoms are often blamed on the effects of chronic institutionalization; this also accounts for only a small portion of the picture. The late symptoms may be attributed to depression and hopelessness in a patient who is chronically ill and sees no possibility of leaving the hospital; this too may account for a small portion. The vast majority of the late clinical symptoms seen in patients with schizophrenia has been shown to be a direct consequence of the disease and its effects on the brain.

As seen in the chart on page 131, only 10 percent of patients with schizophrenia will require hospitalization (or a similar total-care facility) thirty years later. The vast majority are able to live in the community, with only about 15 percent requiring an extensive support network.

One of the mysteries which has perplexed mental health professionals in recent years is where all the persons with schizophrenia have gone. Comparisons of past hospitalization rates with the number of patients receiving care as outpatients invariably find that approximately half of the expected number of patients are missing. The answer is that the missing patients are living in the community, most taking no medication, with varying degrees of adjustment. A community survey in Baltimore, for example, found that half the persons with schizophrenia in the community were receiving no ongoing care or medication from any psychiatric clinic. An example of such a patient follows:

> A 72-year-old recluse was forcibly evicted from his rural decaying house by the police. He had been hospitalized for schizophrenia twice in his twenties, worked briefly as a clerk, then returned to live with his aging parents. After they died he had continued to live in the house for thirty years on Social Security disability checks. The house had no electricity or running water and the rooms were packed to the ceiling with piles of newspapers. He cooked over a sterno stove, did not bother anybody, and asked nothing except to be left alone.

The fierce independence and ability to live with his disease in such cases is commendable. The sad aspect, however, is how much better a life he might have led had well-organized rehabilitation services been available.

Many questions about the long-term course of schizophrenia are as yet unanswered. Do more episodes of schizophrenia cause progressively more damage to the brain? How much can the long-term course be affected by rehabilitation programs which provide jobs and social interaction? As basic as these questions are, there is remarkably little research in progress to find the answers.

WHY DO PEOPLE WITH SCHIZOPHRENIA
DIE AT A YOUNGER AGE?

It has been clearly established that individuals with schizophrenia die at a younger average age than do individuals who do not have schizophrenia. Between 1989 and 1991 three studies were published estimating the overall mortality in schizophrenia to be "about twice that of the general population," "nearly a threefold increase in overall mortality," and "5.05 times greater than expected" for males and "5.63 times greater" for females. The largest single contributor to this excess mortality is suicide, which is 10 to 13 times higher in schizophrenia than in the general population, as will be discussed in Chapter

9. In addition to suicide, however, there are other contributors to the excess mortality.

Accidents

Although individuals with schizophrenia do not drive as much as other people, studies have shown that they have double the rate of motor vehicle accidents per mile driven. A significant but unknown number of individuals with schizophrenia are also killed as pedestrians by motor vehicles; for example, one patient under my care accidentally stepped off a curb into the path of an oncoming bus. Confusion, delusions, and distraction by auditory hallucinations all contribute to such deaths.

Diseases

There is some evidence that individuals with schizophrenia have more infections, heart disease, type II (adult onset) diabetes, and female breast cancer, all of which might increase their mortality rate. Individuals with schizophrenia who become sick are less able to explain their symptoms to medical personnel, and medical personnel are more likely to disregard their complaints and assume that the complaints are simply part of the illness. There is also evidence that some persons with schizophrenia have an elevated pain threshold so that they may not complain of symptoms until the disease has progressed too far to be treatable.

Partially offsetting this increased mortality is the likelihood that individuals with schizophrenia have a lower than expected incidence of lung cancer (to be discussed in chapter 9), prostate cancer, type I (juvenile onset) diabetes, and rheumatoid arthritis (to be discussed in chapter 6). The prostatic cancer data are especially interesting because one recent study found a relationship between having been treated with higher doses of antipsychotic medication and having a lower rate of prostate cancer.

Homelessness

Although it has not been well studied to date, it appears that homelessness increases the mortality rate of individuals with schizophrenia by making them even more susceptible to accidents and diseases. A recent study in England followed 48 homeless seriously mentally ill individuals for 18 months; at the end of that time three had died of diseases (heart attack, suffocation during epileptic seizure, and ruptured aneurysm), one had been killed by a car, and three others had disappeared without taking their belongings with them. Scattered reports from around the United States suggest that homeless mentally ill individuals may have a very high mortality rate. For example, in Oklahoma a woman was released from a psychiatric hospital in January, sought shelter in an old chicken coop where she froze to death and was not found for two years. In Virginia, the skeleton of a seriously mentally ill woman was found a year after she had been apparently murdered. I predict that when we finally do a careful study of mortality rates among homeless individuals with schizophrenia in the United States, the results will be shocking.

RECOMMENDED FURTHER READING

Ciompi, L. "Aging and Schizophrenic Psychosis." *Acta Psychiatrica Scandinavica,* Supplementum no. 319, 71 (1985): 93–105.

Harris, A. E. "Physical Disease and Schizophrenia." *Schizophrenia Bulletin* 14 (1988): 85–96.

Harding, C. M., J. Zubin, and J. S. Strauss. "Chronicity in Schizophrenia: Revisited." *British Journal of Psychiatry* (suppl. 18), 161 (1992): 27–37.

6

WHAT CAUSES SCHIZOPHRENIA?

Something has happened to me—I do not know what. All that was my former self has crumbled and fallen together and a creature has emerged of whom I know nothing. She is a stranger to me—and has an egotism that makes the egotism that I had look like skimmed milk; and she thinks thoughts that are—heresies. Her name is insanity. She is the daughter of madness—and according to the doctor, they each had their genesis in my own brain.

Lara Jefferson, *These Are My Sisters*

The 1990s has been congressionally consecrated as the Decade of the Brain. The timing is appropriate, for we are in the midst of an explosion of knowledge in the neurosciences, and its effects are spilling over to schizophrenia. With each passing year we know more about how the brain functions, both normally and abnormally. The brains of individuals with schizophrenia are slowly beginning to yield their secrets to researchers. With luck, it is not unreasonable to hope for some major advances in knowledge about the causes and treatment of this disease by the end of the decade.

Before proceeding to a discussion of abnormalities in the brains of persons with schizophrenia, however, let us consider the normal brain—a mushroomlike organ with a stem narrowing into the spinal cord, which runs down the back. The bulk of the brain consists of four lobes (frontal, parietal, temporal, and occipital), which are divided in two by a deep vertical cleft. At the bottom of the cleft is the corpus callosum, a thick band carrying nerve fibers back and forth between the two halves of the brain. The four major lobes perform functions such as muscle coordination, thinking, memory, language, hearing, and vision. It is now established that the two halves of the brain are not

THE LOCATION OF THE LIMBIC SYSTEM
IN THE BRAIN

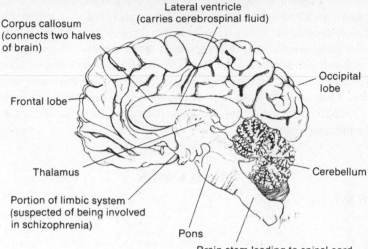

Lateral ventricle
(carries cerebrospinal fluid)

Corpus callosum
(connects two halves
of brain)

Occipital
lobe

Frontal lobe

Thalamus

Cerebellum

Portion of limbic system
(suspected of being involved
in schizophrenia)

Pons

Brain stem leading to spinal cord

identical; in most persons the left half controls language skills and conceptual thinking, whereas the right half is in charge of spatial skills and intuitive thinking.

The four lobes come together at the base of the brain beneath the corpus callosum. There lie the thalamus, hypothalamus, pituitary gland, limbic system, basal ganglia, midbrain, and brain stem tapering into the spinal cord. It is this area which controls all vital functions (e.g., heart, respiration, eating, and the body's endocrine [hormone] system), and which acts as a gatekeeper for all incoming and outgoing stimuli for the major lobes. Attached to the back of this area, as if by afterthought, is the cerebellum, which until recently was thought to function exclusively to coordinate muscle function; it is now thought to interact with the brain stem on other functions as well.

The entire brain is housed in the vaultlike bony skull and surrounded by a layer of cerebrospinal fluid for further protection. The fluid circulates around the brain and goes through the center of the major lobes by a series of canals which widen into ventricles. It is because the brain is so well protected that we understand comparatively little about it or its diseases. It has been facetiously suggested that if we could persuade the brain to change places with the liver we might then understand its functioning and what causes schizophrenia.

The actual work of the brain is performed by approximately fifty billion nerve cells. Each has branches with which it can transmit and receive messages from other cells; one cell can receive messages from as many as ten thousand other cells. The branches do not physically touch each other but rather release chemical messengers, called neurotransmitters, which carry the messages from the end of one nerve branch to the end of an adjacent branch. We already know of over sixty different kinds of neurotransmitters, and it is likely that there are many more. Some of these neurotransmitters, such as dopamine, norepinephrine, serotonin, GABA, and the endorphins, are of great interest to schizophrenia researchers.

WHAT IS KNOWN

It is a Brain Disease

The idea that schizophrenia is a brain disease is hardly new. Voltaire in 1764 wrote that "a lunatic is a sick man whose brain is in bad health, just as the man who has gout is a sick man who has pains in his feet and hands. . . . People have gout in the brain as in the feet." Throughout the nineteenth century insanity continued to be widely considered as a brain disease. For example, Wilhelm Griesinger, one of the most widely respected psychiatrists of the century, wrote in the 1860s that "psychiatry and neuropathology are not merely two closely related fields; they are but one field in which only one language is spoken and the same laws rule."

It was only in the twentieth century, when most psychiatrists drifted off into the land of Freudian fairy tales (see below), that the idea of schizophrenia being a brain disease was lost. It has now been rediscovered, and the evidence is so overwhelming that mental illness professionals who are unaware of it have either been on an extended trek in Nepal or have restricted their professional reading to the *National Geographic.* In fact, any mental illness professional who doubts that schizophrenia is a brain disease should be assumed to be incompetent until proven otherwise.

The evidence that schizophrenia is a brain disease is based on studies of brain structure and function. Such studies include the following:

Magnetic resonance imaging (MRI)

Magnetic resonance imaging (MRI), which utilizes magnetic fields and radio waves to produce pictures of the brain, was introduced in the 1980s and has proven to be a great boon for schizophrenia research. The pictures it produces are tenfold more detailed than the computerized axial tomography (CAT or CT) scans used in the 1970s and one hundredfold more detailed than pneumonencephalography used since the 1920s.

The most easily observed structural abnormality in schizophrenia is mild to moderate dilatation of the lateral and third ventricles, which carry cerebrospinal fluid through the brain. Such dilatation is found in many but not all individuals with this disease. It is not specific to schizophrenia and may also be found in manic-depressive psychosis as well as brain tumors, strokes, Alzheimer's disease, and other brain diseases, so it cannot be used as a diagnostic marker for schizophrenia. MRI studies of first-admission patients with schizophrenia, done before the patients have received any antipsychotic medication, show the same degree of dilatation as those done on patients who have received medication, so the dilatation also appears to be static and does not progress further with length of illness.

Other brain structural abnormalities in schizophrenia are not as easily observed as is ventricular dilatation, but they are probably more directly related to the disease process. There is a small but significant loss of brain tissue seen as generalized atrophy but especially in limbic system structures such as the hippocampus and amygdala. For example, in our study of 27 identical twin pairs in which one twin has schizophrenia and the other is well, the twin with schizophrenia was found to have a smaller hippocampus and amygdala 80 percent of the time. It should be emphasized that the loss of brain tissue in schizophrenia is not great, averaging 10 to 15 percent, but is probably part of the disease process.

Other brain structures are also under study in schizophrenia using MRIs. Loss of brain tissue has been reported in the left parahippocampal gyrus and left superior temporal gyrus, and other abnormalities found in the corpus callosum, cerebellum, basal ganglia, and planum temporale. Three-dimensional MRI reconstruction of brain structures using advanced computer technology is especially promising and we are likely to see a continuing flow of significant findings as the precise anatomical abnormalities in schizophrenia become clear.

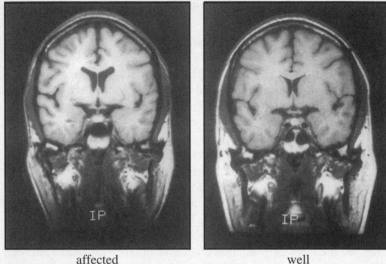

affected   well

34-year-old males

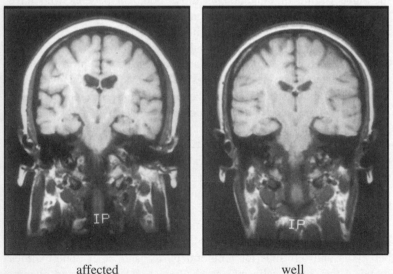

affected   well

35-year-old females

MRIs from two sets of identical twins in which one has schizophrenia and the other is well. The butterfly-shaped cerebral ventricles are enlarged in the affected twins due to the schizophrenia.

Microscopic abnormalities

At the same time as MRI studies have been elucidating macroscopic structural brain abnormalities in living individuals with schizophrenia, increasing numbers of microscopic studies, using postmortem brain tissue, have also reported abnormalities. The majority of these report a decreased number of neurons in specific brain areas or abnormalities in the arrangement of the cells. These abnormalities have been described in several brain areas, including the hippocampus, entorhinal cortex, cingulate cortex, prefrontal cortex, motor cortex, and thalamus.

An important question is whether these microscopic abnormalities are caused by the schizophrenia or by antipsychotic medications used to treat it. Several studies have now been completed using postmortem brain tissue that was collected prior to the 1950s when antipsychotic drugs first became available, and they show the same abnormalities as brain tissue collected after drugs were introduced. An example of such work is that being done by Dr. Bernhardt Bogerts and his colleagues in Germany. Utilizing brains collected from thirteen patients who died before the introduction of antipsychotic medication, Dr. Bogerts has shown "a considerable shrinkage of the limbic temporal structures (hippocampal formation, amygdala, and parahippocampal gyrus) and a moderate shrinkage of the inner pallidal segment in the schizophrenic group" compared with controls.

Another important question is whether those individuals with MRI or microscopic abnormalities of their neuroanatomy represent a specific clinical subgroup of patients or whether they are merely one end

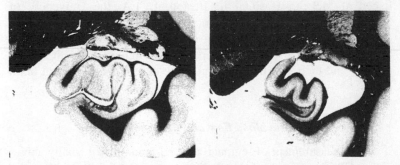

Identical microscopic sections from brains of normal control (left) and person with schizophrenia (right) showing impaired development of hippocampus. It is findings such as these that have convinced many researchers that some cases of schizophrenia are caused by brain changes that begin very early in life.

of a clinical continuum. For example, can specific structural defects be correlated with symptoms such as auditory hallucinations or negative symptoms, or are they found to some degree in most patients. The answer to this question is not yet clear. Some correlations have been reported, such as reduced temporal lobe volume on MRI and greater neuropsychological deficits, or reduced temporal gyral volume and severity of hallucinations. However, other studies have failed to find such correlations and so it is possible that these structural abnormalities represent merely one end of a spectrum.

Neurochemical abnormalities

In studies of postmortem brain tissue from individuals who had schizophrenia, a variety of neurochemical abnormalities have been reported. The most frequently found abnormality has been increased dopamine (especially D-2) receptors in the basal ganglia, nucleus accumbens, and other brain areas. Neurochemical abnormalities of serotonin, norepinephrine, cholecystokinin, and glutamate receptors have also been described but are not as clearly established. In contrast to the MRI and microscopic studies, it is not yet resolved whether the neurochemical findings are due to the schizophrenia or whether they are a consequence of the person having taken antipsychotic medication.

The neurochemical studies and the microscopic studies also illustrate the critical importance of the availability of postmortem brain tissue for researchers. Brain banks such as have been established at McLean Hospital in Boston, UCLA, the University of Miami, and the NIMH Neuroscience Center in Washington, D.C., are absolutely essential for furthering research on schizophrenia as well as on other brain disease. It is important for individuals with schizophrenia and their families to support the development of such brain banks.

Cerebral blood flow and PET scan studies

The measurement of regional cerebral blood flow (usually abbreviated CBF) and cerebral metabolism has received wide publicity in recent years, especially metabolic studies utilizing positron emission tomography (PET) scans. These studies utilize slightly radioactive isotopes that can be inhaled in a gas or injected intravenously; these then permit the measurement of glucose or oxygen metabolism in specific brain regions.

The most clearly established brain metabolic change in individuals with schizophrenia is decreased blood flow to the frontal lobe. This is often referred to as hypofrontality and is most clearly seen when the person is asked to do a task that uses frontal lobe function as the metabolism is being measured. Several studies utilizing individuals with schizophrenia who had never been treated with antipsychotic drugs also reported hypofrontality, so it does not appear to be a drug effect. In our study of identical twins in which one twin has schizophrenia and the other is well, the affected twin had more hypofrontality in every pair in which this was measured. Other parts of the brain may show metabolic abnormalities in schizophrenia; in 1992 metabolic abnormalities were also reported for the hippocampus and for the parahippocampal region. Additional technologies are being developed to combine the measurement of brain structures using MRI scans with measurements of cerebral metabolism using PET scans, and this methodology, called functional magnetic resonance imaging (FMR), is likely to yield valuable findings in the next few years.

Electrical abnormalities

One method the brain uses to send information from one area to another is by electrical impulses, and these have been shown to be abnormal in many patients with schizophrenia. This is true when the electrical impulses are measured as evoked potentials, a special electrical impulse elicited by auditory, visual, or sensory input, and abnormal evoked potentials (especially the P-300 component) have been reported in schizophrenia since the early 1970s. It is also true when electrical activity is recorded on electroencephalograms (EEGs); approximately one-third of persons with schizophrenia have abnormal EEGs. Abnormal EEGs in schizophrenia are twice as common as among persons with mania, and four times as common as among persons with depression. A review article summarizing electrical abnormalities in schizophrenia concluded that "a broad interpretation of the EEG and EP [evoked potential] findings supports the presence of brain disease in many patients with this disorder."

Neurological abnormalities

Neurological abnormalities in patients with schizophrenia are very common, were observed for many years prior to the introduction of antipsychotic medication, and strongly suggest abnormal brain function. The neurological abnormalities include some "hard" neurological signs such as a transient grasp reflex (a reflex found in infants who automatically close their hand around any object they feel, found in 6 percent of patients with schizophrenia) and an impaired gag reflex (in 26 percent of patients, not related to medication), but many more "soft" neurological signs—such as double simultaneous stimulation (being unable to feel two simultaneous touches), agraphesthesia (being unable to identify numbers traced on the palm of the hand), and confusion about the right and left sides of the body.

In a 1983 review of eight neurological studies of schizophrenic patients, Seidman concluded: "The frequency of abnormal neurological examinations using soft signs is consistently between 36 percent and 75 percent for those studies providing frequency data.... A second clearcut finding is that schizophrenics have more frequent neurologic abnormalities than other psychiatric patients (e.g., affective disorder) and normal controls.... The data are very consistent from study to study and consequently are rather convincing." Since 1983 at least 15 additional studies have been published showing that neurological soft signs occur more frequently in individuals than in normal controls, with most studies reporting abnormalities in between 50 and 60 percent of patients.

An important consideration in neurological studies of schizophrenia is the effects of antipsychotic medication. Since it is well known that these medications may cause tremors, movement disorders, and other neurological abnormalities in some patients, it is frequently assumed that all neurological abnormalities in individuals with schizophrenia are probably caused by medications. Counterbalancing this belief is the finding in several studies that individuals off medications had just as many neurological abnormalities as those on medications. Especially significant was the 1992 study by Schroder et al. that included 17 patients with schizophrenia who had never received antipsychotic medications and who had equally as many neurological abnormalities as those who had received medications. Thus it appears that many of the neurological abnormalities seen in individuals with schizophrenia are inherent in the disease process, with the remainder being probable side effects of the medications.

Eye abnormalities

Eye abnormalities can be considered as neurological signs, although they are usually considered separately. They were observed in individuals with schizophrenia in the early years of this century and include abnormal blink rates, abnormal eye reflexes, and abnormalities in eye movements. The abnormal eye movements, found in 50 to 85 percent of individuals with schizophrenia, have been extensively studied and are also said to occur in some relatives of the affected individuals. As such these abnormal eye movements have been suggested as being genetic markers for schizophrenia. Some of the data are supportive of this genetic interpretation but other data are not. At a minimum the eye abnormalities are further evidence of brain dysfunction in this disease.

Neuropsychological abnormalities

Neuropsychological abnormalities in schizophrenia can be regarded as yet another way to quantitatively document impaired functioning of the brain. Neuropsychological tests measure functions such as intelligence, visual-spatial ability, attention span, memory, problem-solving ability, and concept formation; the best-known such test is the Halstead-Reitan battery, which is especially sensitive to cerebral dysfunction. The literature is voluminous on these tests used on patients with schizophrenia and the results are remarkably consistent. As summarized by a review of over a hundred such studies: "Chronic or process schizophrenics may have a cerebral deficit because they performed much as did many of the diffusely brain-damaged patients and could not be statistically differentiated from them. . . . Neuropsychological impairment appears to be mild to moderate in severity and more likely to be diffuse or bilateral than focal."

It should be emphasized that schizophrenia affects only some cognitive processes and leaves others completely intact. The psychological functions that are most often impaired in schizophrenia are memory, attention, problem-solving, and the ability to abstract. It appears that approximately three-quarters of individuals with schizophrenia have some measurable impairment of cognitive function, although the degree of severity is in most cases only mild to moderate. The impairment of cognitive function in schizophrenia is not caused by antipsychotic medications, and in fact it is sometimes improved by the medications. However, even on medication most individuals with schizophrenia continue to have some cognitive deficits and these often make it difficult to engage in competitive employment or take academic courses. As summarized by the Goldberg et al. 1991 review of these studies: "It is possible at this point that cognitive and information-processing dysfunction becomes the crucial rate-limiting factor in treatment and rehabilitation."

In most individuals with schizophrenia the type of cognitive impairment that is easiest to detect is the person's ability to abstract. This can be tested by asking the person the meaning of various proverbs. In our study of identical twins in which one had schizophrenia and the other was well, we asked them to tell us the meaning of several proverbs. In response to "he who lives in a glass house shouldn't throw stones" we got answers such as the following:

Well twin	*Twin with schizophrenia*
"Don't do things that are against your principles."	"If you throw a stone it might break a glass house."
"Don't judge someone else when you don't know their situation."	"If you don't want your house to get ruined you shouldn't throw stones."

In summary, schizophrenia is now firmly established as a brain disease. MRI, microscopic, and neurochemical studies of brain structure and cerebral blood flow, electrical, neurological, eye movement, and neuropsychological studies of brain function are remarkably consistent in pointing in this direction. Many of these studies have been carried out on affected individuals who have never been treated with antipsychotic medication, proving that the abnormalities are caused by the disease process, not by the drugs. Schizophrenia is a brain disease just as surely as multiple sclerosis, Parkinson's disease, and Alzheimer's disease are established as brain diseases. The dichotomy used in the past, whereby schizophrenia was classified as a "functional" disorder as distinct from an "organic" disorder, is now known to be inaccurate; schizophrenia has impeccable credentials for admission to the organic category.

The Limbic System and
Its Connections Are Primarily Affected

In the early part of this century, when scientists began looking at autopsies for abnormalities in the brains of individuals with schizophrenia, they looked mostly in the outer layer of the brain. At that time it was believed that most of the important functions of the brain were closest to the surface. The limbic system, which lies deep below the surface in the center of the brain, was thought to be merely an ancestral remnant of the primitive system for smelling.

All this has changed radically. The limbic system is now known to be the gate through which most incoming stimuli must pass. It has "selective, integrative, and unifying functions by which raw experience is harmonized into reality and coherent activity is organized." According to Dr. Paul MacLean, the modern father of the limbic system, it is "able to correlate every form of internal and external perception."

All of this takes place in an area which is anatomically very small. It is composed of contiguous portions of the frontal and temporal lobes, and its main structures include the amygdala, hippocampus, hypothalamus, nucleus accumbens, ventral septum, mammillary bodies, stria terminalis, and olfactory area. However, its size is deceptive, for the limbic system has direct connections to all areas of the brain, including the upper brain stem and the cerebellum. Increasingly it has been realized that the brain works as a functionally interdependent and intricate system and an abnormality anywhere within it can throw the whole system off. It is analogous to an electrical system with a short circuit in it; the short circuit may occur at any one of several places, but the result will be the same.

Evidence that the limbic system is the site of pathology for some, if not most, cases of schizophrenia is strong. Abnormalities in this system in animals may produce profound changes in emotion, inappropriate behavior, and an impairment in the animal's ability to screen out multiple visual stimuli. Abnormalities in the limbic system in human beings may produce, in addition to the above effects, distortions of perception, illusions, hallucinations, feelings of depersonalization, paranoia, and catatoniclike behavior. In short, the symptoms of schizophrenia described in chapter 2 are a logical consequence of impaired limbic system dysfunction, given what we know about it.

Diseases of the brain which affect the limbic system are also more likely to produce schizophrenialike symptoms. This is seen, for example, with brain tumors located in the limbic system. Cases of encephalitis which produce schizophrenialike symptoms have been found in several studies to involve the limbic system, and epilepsy, when it originates in the limbic area, is more likely to be accompanied by schizophrenialike symptoms.

The strongest evidence linking the limbic system to schizophrenia has come from studies of electrical activity in this area. Robert Heath and his coworker in New Orleans found abnormal limbic electrical activity in patients with schizophrenia; these findings have been replicated by at least three other groups of researchers. One group found abnormal electrical impulses in the limbic area of sixty-one out of sixty-two patients tested, and as the electrodes were moved away from the limbic area, the abnormalities became less frequent. Another group was able to correlate the occurrence of abnormal electrical activity and bizarre behavior in a patient.

Also significant in this regard is the discovery that many of the structural changes described in the brains of persons with schizophrenia have been found in the limbic area, or in nearby areas with which it is closely connected. MRI abnormalities, microscopic abnormalities, and neurochemical abnormalities occur most frequently in the limbic system, both in the medial temporal lobe and in its immediate connections to the frontal lobe. One schizophrenia researcher, after reviewing these studies, recently concluded: "It is probable that all schizophrenics have abnormalities in the medial temporal lobe, which differ in degree but not in kind."

There is one other curious fact about the anatomical location of schizophrenia. In recent years there have been several studies suggesting that the left side of the brain is primarily affected in schizophrenia much more often than the right side of the brain. Patients with temporal lobe epilepsy, for example, will be more likely to have schizophrenialike symptoms if the epilepsy is in the left temporal lobe. Similarly, studies of visual evoked potentials, abnormal EEGs, lateral eye movements, auditory discrimination, galvanic skin response, information processing, and neurological signs, all suggest that the major problem may lie in the left hemisphere.

As both gross and microscopic pathlogical lesions have continued to be described in the brains of individuals with schizophrenia, a subject of great controversy has arisen among researchers in this field. Where precisely is the primary lesion (or lesions) which gives rise to schizophrenia? Each researcher has his or her favorite area to bet on and long hours are spent in debate on the merits of each choice. Most researchers believe that the limbic system is the site of the primary lesion(s), although a few are betting on a portion of the frontal lobe immediately adjacent to the limbic system (the dorsolateral prefrontal cortex). Scattered here and there can also be found proponents for other portions of the brain with intimate connections to the limbic system, such as the midbrain or the cerebellum.

To translate the research discussions into geographical terms, imagine that the brain is the equivalent of the United States. Most researchers are convinced that schizophrenia is caused by dysfunction in the greater New York area, although a few believe it is in Baltimore and occasional proponents can be found arguing for Cleveland or Detroit. Within the New York area many researchers have favorite sites which they are researching; these may be as large as Queens, Bergen, or Suffolk counties or the size of towns like Hicksville, New Rochelle, or Paterson. Although the area under investigation is still relatively large, many other areas of the country (e.g., the northwest and southwest) have been effectively eliminated from consideration. In schizophrenia research, as in geography, it is obvious that the more researchers you have looking, the greater the chances are of finding it.

The Brain Damage May Occur Very Early

Evidence has also accumulated that some cases of schizophrenia begin with damage to the brain in early childhood, perhaps even while the child is still growing in the uterus. This may be true even in persons who show no symptoms of schizophrenia until they are in their late teens or twenties.

Five different types of research studies point toward the importance of the *in utero* period and earliest months of life as being the time when the initial brain damage occurs in at least some cases of schizophrenia. These are:

A. *Minor physical anomalies.* Minor physical anomalies are nonobvious but measurable physical deviations of the head, hands, and feet that are caused by effects on the developing fetus. Examples of such anomalies include low-set ears, a high arched palate, a curved fifth finger, and a wide space between the first and second toes. Occasional anomalies are found in normal persons but they are found more frequently in people who have various kinds of brain dysfunctions. Since 1983 six separate studies have reported that individuals with adult onset schizophrenia have an excess number of minor physical anomalies compared to normal controls. Four additional studies have reported the same finding for childhood onset schizophrenia and autism.

B. *Fingerprint patterns.* The ridges on one's fingers, hands, toes, and feet are called dermatoglyphics and are formed by the fifth month of pregnancy. As a window onto the past, dermatoglyphics provide a useful measure of *in utero* events. Differences in fingerprint patterns have been observed in a variety of diseases, including schizophrenia. Since the 1930s more than 20 studies have shown that individuals with adult onset or childhood onset schizophrenia differ subtly in their dermatoglyphic pattern from normal controls.

C. *Pregnancy and birth complications.* Since 1966 there have been 11 controlled studies of pregnancy and birth complications in schizophrenia. Seven of the studies reported a statistically significant increase in such complications, two others found a trend in this direction, and two reported negative results. Despite these findings it should be noted that no single pregnancy or birth complication has been shown to be especially associated with schizophrenia. It should also be emphasized that the vast majority of women who have pregnancy and birth complications give birth to offspring who do not develop schizophrenia. It is also possible that the increased number of pregnancy and birth complications seen in schizophrenia do not *cause* the schizophrenia but rather that both the observable complications and the schizophrenia have been caused by other, nonobservable events, such as an *in utero* infection.

D. *Seasonality of births.* One of the most clearly documented facts about schizophrenia is that individuals who develop this disease had an excess number of births in the winter and early-spring months. It should be emphasized that this excess is a statistical association only and is not predictive for any given individual. The excess is in the range of 5 to 15 percent and has been shown to occur in over 50 studies from 18 countries. In southern hemisphere countries, the results are in the predicted direction of excess births in the winter and early spring in that hemisphere. Claims that the seasonal excess of births in schizophrenia is a statistical artifact have been conclusively put to rest. The excess is real and could theoretically be explained by infectious agents, nutritional factors, temperature, or other seasonal environmental variables.

A recent study has also shown that stillbirths, which also have a modest seasonal excess in the winter and spring months, have a pattern that is statistically linked to the schizophrenia birth pattern, suggesting that some stillbirths and some schizophrenia births may have a similar cause. This in turn may be linked to the pregnancy and birth complications discussed above.

E. *Microscopic studies of the brain.* Many of the microscopic studies that report abnormalities in brain structure show abnormalities in the number or arrangement of brain cells that could only have taken place during the period when the brain was developing. Thus there is neuropathological evidence to support the assertion that at least in some cases of schizophrenia the brain damage that causes the disease may occur very early in life.

MAJOR THEORIES

We now leave the world of facts (things known about schizophrenia) and enter the realm of theories, where researchers speculate about the ultimate causes of the disease. As knowledge accumulates, some theories lose favor and drop by the wayside, while others gain adherents.

We say that schizophrenia is a heterogeneous condition, which means that it has more than one subgroup and more than one cause. Virtually everything written about schizophrenia today includes that caveat, and it may well be true but it is not established as fact. A case can be made for the opposite approach—that schizophrenia may turn out to have a single major cause. Dr. Lewis Thomas has pointed out that syphilis, tuberculosis, and pernicious anemia were all conditions with a bewildering variety of manifestations that few scientists thought could constitute a single illness, yet in each case a single cause (spirochete, tubercle bacillus, and vitamin deficiency) was eventually found to be the primary cause. That this may be true for schizophrenia (and possibly for manic-depressive psychosis as well) is not beyond the realm of possibility.

Keep in mind that the theories of causation discussed below are not mutually exclusive. The cause or causes of schizophrenia may well turn out to be an amalgam of these components, such as a genetic predisposition to immunological and biochemical dysfunction, or a developmental anomaly triggered by a virus *in utero*.

The theories of causation of schizophrenia may be divided into major, minor, and obsolete theories.

Genes

Genetic theories of schizophrenia are among the oldest, most widely believed, and most extensively tested. These theories claim that schizophrenia is an inherited disorder, carried on one or more genes. The recent discoveries of genes that carry cystic fibrosis and Huntington's disease has stimulated genetic research on diseases in general, including research on schizophrenia. Studies are underway using families with several members affected, looking for the gene or genes that may be responsible for transmitting this disorder.

The strongest evidence for the genetic theory of schizophrenia is that the disease runs in some families. A brother, sister, or child or someone with schizophrenia is said to have approximately a ten percent chance of developing the disease, in contrast to a random person without such a family history, who has a 1.5 percent chance. Studies of identical twins show that when one twin develops schizophrenia, the second twin has approximately a 30 percent chance of also becoming affected. (Most books still cite a 50 percent chance in the second identical twin, but that figure is based on methodologically flawed studies.) Among fraternal twins the chance of the second twin becoming affected is approximately ten percent, the same as for brothers and sisters. Studies of children born to parents with schizophrenia who are then adopted by parents who do not have schizophrenia have shown that the children retain the risk acquired from their biological parents (i.e., about 10 percent) rather than assuming the risk of their adopted parents (i.e., about 1.5 percent).

Although virtually all schizophrenia researchers accept the fact that genes play *some* role in the development of schizophrenia, there continues to be much debate about what that role may be. If schizophrenia is truly a genetically transmitted disease, it does not fit existing dominant or recessive patterns. It is also difficult to understand why the disease has not died out since people with schizophrenia reproduce at an extremely low rate. Furthermore, first-cousin marriages or other inbreeding do not seem to affect the rate; the incidence of schizophenia is not higher in areas where such inbreeding is higher. Finally, it should be remembered that only approximately one-third of individuals with schizophrenia have a family history of this disease, which means that two-thirds do not.

An alternative explanation is that schizophrenia is not a genetic disease as such, but rather involves a genetic *predisposition* to the causative agent. This would put schizophrenia into the same category as rheumatoid arthritis, insulin-dependent diabetes, breast cancer, bowel cancer, and many other diseases. In each case the person is genetically predisposed to get the disease *if* they are exposed to the causative agent, but the diseases are not truly genetic diseases because the disease itself is not transmitted on genes.

Dopamine and other neurochemicals

Neurochemical theories of schizophrenia's causation date back to the early years of this century and have been widely tested. The center of attention for the past two decades has been the neurotransmitter dopamine, one of the brain chemicals in the class called catc-cholamines, which transmit information between nerve cells. Dopamine has come under suspicion because amphetamines, when given in high doses, cause a rise in the dopamine level at the same time that they produce symptoms which resemble schizophrenia. Similarly, when L-dopa, a drug which the body may turn into dopamine, is given to persons with schizophrenia, it often makes them worse. Finally, it is now known that drugs which are effective in schizophrenia block dopamine action. For all of these reasons many researchers suspect that an excess of dopamine is one of the causes of schizophrenia. Dopamine is broken down in the body to other compounds through the action of certain enzymes. One such enzyme is monoamine oxidase, known as MAO, and this enzyme has been the object of intensive research. Another metabolite of dopamine that has been widely studied is homovanillic acid (HVA). There are now known to be at least six different types of dopamine receptors in the brain.

Several other neurochemical transmitters have been studied in schizophrenia, including noradrenaline, serotonin, glutamic acid, gamma-aminobutyric acid (GABA), histamine, acetylcholine, and neuropeptides such as cholecystokinin, somatostatin, and neurotensin. Improving technology has made the measurement of these and other chemicals and their receptors more precise. Findings to date have not been consistent except for the findings of excess dopamine (D-2) receptors in some brain regions.

Despite the longevity and theoretical attractiveness of dopamine and other neurochemical theories, these theories also have several shortcomings. Most research is carried out on postmortem brain specimens, and it is often difficult to know how much the chemicals have changed after death. It is also known that antipsychotic medications may affect many of these chemicals, and many initially promising findings have been shown later to have been a drug effect. The most important criticism of dopamine and other neurochemical theories of schizophrenia, however, is that they are not really theories of causation but rather theories of the pathophysiology or process of the disease. If altered dopamine *is* the cause of schizophrenia, how did it become altered? Possible answers are a genetic defect, stress, a virus, etc., but some other theory must be invoked to explain the altered dopamine.

Viruses

During the early years of this century there was considerable interest in infectious agents as the possible cause of schizophrenia. This was stimulated initially by the finding of a bacteria (spirochete) that caused syphilis, a disease that also infects the brain and may mimic schizophrenia. Then during the 1918 influenza pandemic it was observed that some patients with influenza had psychiatric symptoms similar to schizophrenia or manic-depressive illness.

Current infectious disease theories of schizophrenia focus on viruses. Viruses are known to attack very specific areas of the brain while leaving other areas untouched; for example, the rabies virus and the herpes zoster virus will attack only one kind of cell in one part of the central nervous system. Viruses may also alter the function of brain cells without altering their structure; cell enzymes, for example, may be permanently disrupted by a viral infection yet the cell itself will continue to live and show no evident damage. This means that viruses could conceivably cause schizophrenia and leave no trace of their damage visible under a microscope.

Another intriguing fact about viruses as a possible cause of schizophrenia is that they may remain latent for many years at a time. This is true for some well-known viruses, such as those in the herpes family, but it is also true for a group of viruses called "slow" viruses, which may not cause disease for twenty years or more after they originally infect the person. Thus persons with schizophrenia could theoretically become infected while still in the uterus or shortly after birth and yet not show symptoms of the disease until their twenties or thirties.

If viruses are involved in the causation of schizophrenia, it may be that the timing of the original infection is critical. There are known viral diseases which cause brain damage if introduced at one stage of fetal brain development but not at another stage. German measles (rubella) is the best-known example of this, causing mental retardation and heart and other defects if it infects the baby in the first three months of pregnancy but often causing no damage if infection takes place a few months later.

The evidence supporting viruses as a cause of schizophrenia is mostly circumstantial. It has been clearly shown that several different viruses, in addition to influenza, can infect the brain and occasionally produce symptoms that mimic schizophrenia. Studies in Finland, Denmark, England, and Japan have also shown that women who were exposed to the influenza virus in the middle three months of pregnancy are more likely to give birth to children who later develop schizophrenia, although some other studies have not found this association.

Since many viruses are seasonal, they could account for the seasonality of births in schizophrenia. Viruses are also known that cause minor physical anomalies, alterations in fingerprint patterns, pregnancy and birth complications, and stillbirths, which might explain the increased occurrence of these phenomena in schizophrenia. Some viruses may also affect dopamine metabolism. Also, a genetic predisposition to viral infections is clearly established. For diabetes, for example, Abner Notkins and his colleagues at the National Institutes of Health have developed a strain of mice which, when injected with a particular virus, develop diabetes. Another strain of mice is completely resistant and never develop diabetes. It is clear that the first strain has a genetic predisposition toward reacting with the virus in such a way as to produce diabetes. The mice do not inherit the diabetes but rather the predisposition. Another possible virus-gene model for schizophrenia is the transmission of a virus on a gene, which is known to occur for retroviruses.

The shortcomings of a viral theory of schizophrenia include the fact that no specific virus has yet been identified. Studies of viral antibodies, antigens, genomes, cytopathic effect, and animal transmission experiments have yielded mixed and frequently contradictory results. The most promising work that has recently emerged is the finding of increased antibodies to pestiviruses in some individuals with schizophrenia and manic-depressive illness. This work, being carried out in the laboratory of Dr. Robert Yolken at Johns Hopkins University, is especially intriguing because pestiviruses have never previously been described in humans but cause a disease in cows that may produce microscopic brain lesions remarkably similar to those seen in human schizophrenia. One mode of transmission that is being explored for the pestiviruses is through housecats. Until pestiviruses or other viruses are firmly implicated as a cause of schizophrenia, however, the viral theory should continue to be regarded as simply one major theory of the disease.

Developmental defect

Regarding schizophrenia as a developmental defect is a comparatively new approach. It is a product of increasing findings from MRI, microscopic, neurochemical, minor physical anomaly, fingerprint, pregnancy and birth complications, and seasonality of births studies that have pointed toward the brain damage in schizophrenia as having occurred early in life. The developmental defect theory postulates that any one of a number of agents could cause the defect *if* that agent affected the brain at a crucial stage of development *in utero* or shortly after birth. The agents could include, in the words of Dr. Daniel R. Weinberger, one of its major proponents, "a hereditary encephalopathy or predilection to environmental injury, an infection or postinfectious state, damage from an immunologic disorder, perinatal trauma or encephalopathy, toxin exposure early in development, a primary metabolic disease, or other early developmental events."

Once the original insult has taken place at a critical stage of brain development, then the damage is done. In most cases, however, its effects would not be immediately noticeable, except perhaps for nonspecific signs such as lack of coordination or behavioral problems in childhood. Once the brain matured the signs and symptoms of schizophrenia would appear.

The strength of the developmental defect theory is that it accounts for many aspects of the disease, including genetic aspects because brain development is under genetic control. Its weakness is that only a minority of individuals with schizophrenia show any signs of brain dysfunction early in life, which would be surprising if brain damage did in fact occur in most of them at that time.

MINOR THEORIES

In addition to the major theories of causation outlined above, there are other theories that have received less attention.

Immune system dysfunction

There have been reports for the past 50 years of immune system dysfunction in individuals with schizophrenia. The majority of early reports focused on a hypoactive immune reaction in response to the injection of various substances beneath the skin. In recent years there have been reports of lymphocyte abnormalities, alterations in proteins in the cerebrospinal fluid, antibodies directed against the person's own body (called autoantibodies), and alterations in interferon and interleukin that help mediate the immune response. Some of the recent findings in this field look very interesting.

The major problems with immune system research in schizophrenia is telling the chicken from the egg: Are the immune system dysfunctions the *cause* of the schizophrenia or are they merely one of the *effects* of the disease? Another problem is that antipsychotic medications may also alter the immune system so that some of the changes that have been described in schizophrenia have been found to be drug effects. Nevertheless, immune system dysfunction remains as a potentially promising area of schizophrenia research.

Nutrition and food allergies

Nutritional theories of schizophrenia have had adherents since it was discovered that beriberi, pellagra, and pernicious anemia, all of which may have psychiatric symptoms, were vitamin deficiency diseases. Researchers have searched for a wide variety of nutritional deficiencies and food allergies with relatively little success, although it must be acknowledged that most of the studies were methodologically poor. In the 1950s, Drs. Humphrey Osmond and Abram Hoffer began treating patients with schizophrenia with high doses of niacin, other vitamins, and minerals and claimed remarkable success. Their claims have not been substantiated. Treating schizophrenia with vitamins and minerals became known as orthomolecular psychiatry and an organization of families, the American Schizophrenia Association, was formed.

At this time most schizophrenia researchers do not regard nutrition and food allergies as promising avenues for research. For many people, orthomolecular psychiatry has merged with food faddists and cultists, and is not considered scientifically respectable. This is unfortunate because there are occasional individual patients who appear to be helped by specific nutritional regimens and there may indeed be small subgroups of individuals with schizophrenia whose disease may have a nutritional basis.

Endocrine dysfunction

Interest in endocrine dysfunction as a possible cause of schizophrenia is linked to observations that severe hypothyroidism, hyperthyroidism, and hyperfunction of the adrenal gland (Cushing's syndrome) may all produce psychiatric symptoms that resemble schizophrenia. A related observation is that maternal psychosis following childbirth is thought to be triggered by massive hormonal changes that occur postpartum. Such observations have led some researchers to question whether more subtle endocrine dysfunction may contribute to the causation of schizophrenia.

One finding that points in this direction is the occurrence of compulsive water drinking (polydypsia) among some individuals with schizophrenia. Water intake is related to hormones in the posterior pituitary gland. The anterior pituitary has also been provisionally linked to schizophrenia in some patients who show altered response to growth hormone when given apomorphine, a dopamine-stimulating drug. There have also been claims that reproductive hormones (FSH and LH), which come from the anterior pituitary, are abnormal in individuals with schizophrenia. The interruption of menstrual periods in some female patients is well known. The fact that insulin coma produced brief remissions in some individuals with schizophrenia led to interest in insulin metabolism, and there have been claims that schizophrenia is less common than expected in type I (insulin-dependent) diabetics and more common than expected in type II (noninsulin-dependent) diabetics. There has also been extensive research in melatonin and the pineal gland in schizophrenia, although the current consensus is that these are not abnormal.

The precise meaning of endocrine dysfunction in schizophrenia is unclear. It could represent an endocrine response to the stress of the illness or an effect of antipsychotic drugs. The endocrine dysfunction may also be another aspect of the disease process; if so, it would not be surprising since the hypothalamus, which controls much endocrine function, is both proximate to and closely connected with the limbic system.

Inverse correlation with rheumatoid arthritis

One of the most curious yet most clearly established facts about schizophrenia is that it rarely occurs in a person who also has rheumatoid arthritis. Reports of this negative association date to 1936. Since that time 14 separate studies have been done, with 12 of them reporting a lower-than-expected incidence of rheumatoid arthritis in individuals with schizophrenia. Among the three studies that were methodologically the best, no individuals with rheumatoid arthritis were found among 111 and 301 inpatients with schizophrenia in two of the studies and a very low incidence was found in the third.

There are many similarities between schizophrenia and rheumatoid arthritis that make this inverse correlation even more interesting. Neither disease was clearly described until the beginning of the nineteenth century. Both diseases have a lifetime incidence of approximately one percent and a pairwise concordance rate in identical twins of approximately 30 percent (i.e., when one twin gets it, the second twin also gets it approximately 30 percent of the time). Both diseases are said to be more common in urban than in rural areas. A major difference between the diseases is that rheumatoid arthritis is more common in women than in men by a ratio of 3 to 1.

Several theories have been proposed to explain this inverse correlation but none has been proven. It is possible that there are genetic factors that render a person susceptible to schizophrenia and at the same time resistant to rheumatoid arthritis. Biochemical factors, including prostaglandins, essential fatty acids, beta-endorphins, and tryptophan, have all been hypothesized as playing a role by some researchers. Viruses could explain it if both diseases were caused by closely related types; becoming infected with one virus might confer immunity to the second virus. The most intriguing challenge is that if we are able to understand the causes of one of these diseases, then it may help to understand the other as well.

Stress

Stress is included as a minor theory of causation because it is invoked as a possible causative cofactor by some geneticists and developmental defect proponents and because it is prominently featured in many textbooks. It is discussed in this chapter as a cause of the initial onset of schizophrenia; in chapter 10 its role in relapses will be discussed. The belief that stress may cause schizophrenia has a long history and in fact "disappointment in a love affair" and similar stressors were regularly cited as causes of mental illness in the nineteenth century. The stress theory received an impetus during recent wars when it was noted that occasional soldiers, when under the extreme stress of battle, had the sudden onset of a brief psychotic disorder (see chapter 4) that transiently resembled schizophrenia.

Since Brown and Birley published their 1968 study claiming that life stresses were important causes of schizophrenia, at least 13 other studies have been carried out. Three of these studies provided some support for the Brown and Birley findings but the remainder did not. As early as 1980 Rabkin claimed that "no study found more events reported by schizophrenics than by other patient groups." In 1985 Tennant stated categorically that "there is no good evidence that life stress is causally related to episodes of schizophrenia." In 1993 Norman and Malla concurred: "There is no evidence for schizophrenia being related to higher levels of life event stressors than other psychiatric disorders."

The studies that reported an association between stressful events and schizophrenia have a major methodological flaw. In the early stages of schizophrenia, when the person is first becoming ill, the person often acts in unusual ways, thereby precipitating crises of one kind or another. The studies reporting a positive association view such crises as the cause of the schizophrenia rather than being one of its early effects. This distinction was perceptively noted by Dr. Eugene Bleuler in his classic 1911 book on *Dementia Praecox:*

> In cases in which we have excellent anamneses [histories], one regularly notes that signs of disease existed before the suspected psychic trauma so that it becomes difficult to impute to such trauma any causal significance. In the majority of cases, it is also quite evident without much searching that the unfortunate love affair, demotion from office, etc., were consequences and not causes of the disease if there was any connection between them at all.

Epidemiological observations also make it unlikely that stress is more than a very minor factor—perhaps the straw that broke the camel's back in causing schizophrenia. For example, if stress is important why do epidemics not occur in prisons or concentration camps? Why was the schizophrenia rate not high during the Inquisition or French Revolution? Why did the incidence of schizophrenia appear to go down, not up, during World War II? In summary, it appears very unlikely that stress is more than a very minor cause of schizophrenia, if indeed it plays any role at all.

OBSOLETE THEORIES

As knowledge evolves in every field of scientific enquiry, new theories arise to explain the observations. At the same time, older theories which no longer fit the facts are set aside and eventually discarded. All areas of science have dusty shelves full of discarded theories and schizophrenia research is no exception. Some of the more unusual discarded theories are as follows:

Masturbation

Masturbation was widely believed to be a cause of schizophrenia and other forms of insanity throughout the nineteenth century. Since many people were thought to masturbate and many people were afflicted with schizophrenia, it was theorized that the two were causally related. Only later was it realized that most people who masturbate do not get schizophrenia, and that some people who get schizophrenia do not masturbate. When it became clear that there was no scientific support for the masturbation theory, it simply died.

Bad mothering and Freudian theories

Bad mothering was widely believed to be a cause of schizophrenia for much of the twentieth century. Since many people were thought to have had bad mothers and many people were afflicted with schizophrenia, it was theorized that the two were causally related.

The strongest proponents of the bad mothering theory were psychoanalytic followers of Dr. Sigmund Freud. Freud himself knew virtually nothing about schizophrenia. In 1907 he acknowledged in a letter that "I seldom see dements [dementia praecox or schizophrenia] and hardly ever see other severe types of psychosis." In 1911 Freud published his analysis of a man, Daniel Schreber, who had paranoid schizophrenia. Freud concluded that Schreber had had a "conflict over unconscious homosexuality" that produced an inverted Oedipus complex. Incredibly, Freud never actually examined Schreber but merely read his memoirs. Freud later wrote to a friend that "I do not like these patients [with schizophrenia].... I feel them to be so far distant from me and from everything human. A curious sort of intolerance, which surely makes me unfit to be a psychiatrist."

Freud's lack of interest in schizophrenia did not dissuade his followers from applying his theories to this disease. By the 1940s and 1950s, Freudian theories of schizophrenia were widely believed in the United States. For example, in 1949, when Dr. Trude Tietze published her widely cited study of twenty-five mothers of individuals with schizophrenia, she concluded that "all mothers were overanxious and obsessive, all were domineering.... The mothers' own warped psychosexual development and their own distorted ideas about sex were reflected in their attitude toward their children's sexual development."

Like most studies of Freudian theory, Tietze used no controls in her study.

Several studies have now demonstrated that insight-oriented psychotherapy is of no value for schizophrenia. Probably the best-known of these studies was done by Philip R. A. May and his colleagues at Camarillo State Hospital, California. May randomly assigned 228 patients with schizophrenia to five separate wards where they were treated by (1) psychotherapy alone, (2) psychotherapy plus drugs, (3) drugs alone, (4) milieu alone, and (5) electroconvulsive therapy. The patients who did best were those treated by drugs alone or psychotherapy plus drugs, and there were virtually no differences between the two groups; the patients who did worst were those treated by psychotherapy alone or milieu alone. The inescapable conclusion is that psychotherapy added nothing to the treatment regimen in this study. These patients were followed up for from three to five years after the initial treatment and the results did not change: "Analysis of variance indicated an extremely significant effect from drug. . . , no significant effect from psychotherapy."

May's study was criticized by some for utilizing psychotherapy which was not "intensive" enough and for having it done by psychotherapists who were relatively inexperienced. Another study was therefore designed to treat patients with schizophrenia with explicitly psychoanalytically oriented psychotherapy (two hours a week for two years), using highly experienced psychotherapists. At the end of the study period the outcome was said to be that "psychotherapy alone (even with experienced psychotherapists) did little or nothing for chronic schizophrenic patients in two years." Such studies were summarized by Donald Klein, one of America's most respected psychiatrists: "There is no scientific basis for the affirmation of clinical benefit from the individual psychotherapy of schizophrenic patients."

There is some evidence that psychoanalysis and insight-oriented psychotherapy may not only be useless for treating schizophrenia, but may in fact be harmful. In the May study, for example, the "outcome for patients who received only psychotherapy was significantly worse than the outcome in the no-treatment control group." In other words, getting no treatment at all led to better outcomes than being treated with psychotherapy alone. This correlates with the individual experience of many psychotherapists who have given up treating such patients with insight-oriented psychotherapy, because many of their patients seemed to get worse. In following up Freud's original formula-

tion about unconscious homosexual impulses being the cause of paranoid schizophrenia, one psychiatrist "checked the therapeutic successes
of psychoanalysts and found to our surprise that it is common experience, frequently admitted and often implied, that not only are 'paranoid' patients not improved by homosexual interpretations, but even
made worse."

Given what we now know about the brains of persons with schizophrenia, it should not be surprising to find that insight-oriented psychotherapy makes them sicker. Such persons are being overwhelmed
by external and internal stimuli and are trying to impose some order on
the chaos. In the midst of this a psychotherapist asks them to probe
their unconscious motivations, a difficult enough task even when one's
brain is functioning perfectly. The inevitable consequence is to add
insult to injury, unleashing a cacophony of repressed thoughts and
wishes into the existing internal maelstrom. To do insight-oriented psychotherapy on persons with schizophrenia is analogous to directing a
flood into a town already ravaged by a tornado. Or, to use another
comparison from a recent review entitled "The Adverse Effects of
Intensive Treatment of Chronic Schizophrenia," insight-oriented psychotherapies are "analogous to pouring boiling oil into wounds
because they ignore the chronic schizophrenic's particular vulnerability
to over-stimulating relationships, intense negative affects, and pres-
sures for rapid change."

It is remarkable how many people (including even some mental
health professionals) still believe that insight-oriented psychotherapy is
effective for treating schizophrenia. I still regularly meet wealthy families who have paid exorbitant sums—$100,000 to $200,000 a year—to
have their son or daughter treated by psychoanalysis or insight-oriented psychotherapy in a private hospital. This is one of the last areas
of American medicine where a Laetrile-type treatment—not only useless but probably harmful—may be legally purchased.

Recognition of the harmful role played by insight-oriented psychotherapy in patients with schizophrenia is not new. In a 1976 study
of harmful effects of psychotherapy, Hadley and Strupp noted that
"psychotic breaks resulting from psychotherapy were also frequently
mentioned as a clear-cut negative effect . . . an occurrence would most
typically be due to ego disintegration brought on by therapy." In 1978
the President's Commission on Mental Health observed that "there is
some evidence that suggests that certain chronic schizophrenic patients
respond adversely to psychological treatments." Shortly thereafter Dr.

Gerald Klerman, at that time the highest-ranking government psychiatrist and a respected researcher, also acknowledged that "recent evidence suggests that high intensity psychotherapy may actually have negative effects in schizophrenia."

What, then, is the proper role for psychoanalysis and insight-oriented psychotherapy in the treatment of schizophrenia? It has none, and should be explicitly avoided. As summarized by Dr. T. C. Manschreck in a 1981 *New England Journal of Medicine:* "To offer traditional psychotherapy as the only treatment for schizophrenic disorder is generally regarded as inadequate and possibly negligent. Psychoanalysis and other insight-oriented psychotherapies have little demonstrated value in this illness." Given what is now known about schizophrenia, to treat it by utilizing these approaches is not only negligent, it is malpractice. Mental health professionals who advocate such treatment should be regarded as interesting relics of the past, much as we regard the last survivors of the Spanish-American War and other past eras.

Bad Families

Following World War II the bad mothering theory of schizophrenia was broadened to include the entire family constellation. The theorists who believed that family interaction caused schizophrenia were almost all psychoanalysts who had been trained in Freudian theory.

Foremost among them was Dr. Theodore Lidz at Yale University. In 1952 Lidz and his colleagues began a study of sixteen families of individuals with schizophrenia. No controls were used. Lidz et al. concluded that approximately half of the mothers were "strange, near-psychotic or overtly schizophrenic" but said that the fathers could also exert "an extremely noxious or pathogenic influence upon the family and the patient."

In 1956 the "double-bind" was born, destined to become the cornerstone of family interaction theorists. Basically it postulated that schizophrenia arises when parents give their children heads-I-win-tails-you-lose messages. The lead author of the original paper describing this theory was Gregory Bateson, an anthropologist who had undergone Jungian psychoanalysis; Don Jackson, Jay Haley, and John Weakland were also authors. According to a later essay by Bateson, the inspiration for the "double-bind" came from his studies of communications theory, cybernetics, rituals among natives in Papua New Guinea, the communications of dolphins, and Lewis Carroll's *Through the Looking Glass*. No control studies were done and Bateson freely acknowledged that "this hypothesis has not been statistically tested." In fact it never was, and in retrospect the single most important antecedent of the theory appears to have been the thinking of Lewis Carroll.

Family interaction theories of schizophrenia, like psychoanalytic theories, have by now been discarded and for many of the same reasons. Not only did they lack a scientific base, but when controlled studies were done on families of patients with schizophrenia by other researchers, the family interaction theories failed to hold up. As early as 1951, for example, Prout and White compared the mothers of twenty-five men with schizophrenia with the mothers of twenty-five normal men and reported no significant differences; several subsequent studies found the same results. The other major problem with family interaction theories is that they fail to distinguish family interactions which cause schizophrenia from those *caused by* schizophrenia. Clinicians experienced in dealing with schizophrenia are acutely aware of the disruptions to normal family life, including family communications, which can result from having a family member with this disease.

In addition to lacking any scientific basis, both the bad mothering and bad families theories of schizophrenia fell victim to common sense. Any parent who has raised a child knows that parents are not powerful enough to cause a disease like schizophrenia simply by favoring one child over another or giving the child inconsistent messages. Furthermore, families in which one child had developed schizophrenia usually contained one or more other children who were perfectly normal; they stood as the final refutation of these theories.

Bad Cultures

In addition to bad mothers and bad families, a few individuals have proposed that bad cultures may cause schizophrenia. This idea was first developed by anthropologists Margaret Mead and Ruth Benedict in the 1930s. In more recent years it has found expression among occasional intellectuals, most of whom have become enamored with sociology, socialism, or both.

One such writer is Christopher Lasch, who in his 1979 *The*

Culture of Narcissism, claimed that psychoses are "in some sense the characteristic expression of a given culture." He also quoted Jule Henry, who wrote that "psychosis is the final outcome of all that is wrong with a culture." Another example of this theory is included in the 1984 book *Not in Our Genes* by R.C. Lewontin, Steven Rose, and Leon Kamin who, in the Preface, claim that "we share a commitment to the prospect of the creation of a more socially just—a socialist—society." After disparaging biological research on schizophrenia, the authors write: "An adequate theory of schizophrenia must understand what it is about the social and cultural environment that pushes some categories of people toward manifesting schizophrenic symptoms." The social and cultural environment, they believe, produce biological changes in the brain that "might be the reflections or correspondents of that schizophrenia with the brain." Such theorizing, atavistic in view of contemporary knowledge, is now heard only rarely.

Thomas Szasz

Dr. Szasz, a psychoanalyst in Syracuse, New York, has become well known not for his theory of schizophrenia but rather for his theory of nonschizophrenia. According to Szasz, schizophrenia and other mental disorders are simply semantic artifacts and do not really exist. This will certainly be welcome news to the individuals afflicted with this disease and to their families. People with schizophrenia says Szasz, have a "fake disease," which is simply "the sacred symbol of psychiatry." To be a true disease, Szasz claims, "it must somehow be capable of being approached, measured, or tested in a scientific fashion."

Szasz' theories deserve refutation only because they have been so widely circulated. Szasz himself conducts a traditional psychoanalytic practice for individuals with problems of living; there is nothing in his writings to suggest that he has any experience with or ever treats patients with schizophrenia. Moreover, schizophrenia is now regularly "approached, measured, or tested in a scientific fashion" and the evidence that schizophrenia is a brain disease is overwhelming. The theories of Thomas Szasz about schizophrenia, therefore, have been relegated to the shelf of quirks of medical history.

R.D. Laing

Perhaps the most bizarre and puzzling of all obsolete theories of schizophrenia were those of British psychoanalyst R.D. Laing. He promoted the idea that schizophrenia was a sane response to an insane world and may even be a growth experience, a romantic if nonsensical idea that appealed to many 1960s radicals. Laing's ideas grew out of Freudian and family interaction theories. As expressed by Dr. Joseph Berke, one of his closest followers: "'Mental illness' reflects what is happening in a disturbed and disturbing group of people, especially when internalized in and by a single person. More often than not, a person diagnosed as 'mentally ill' is the emotional scapegoat for the turmoil in his or her family or associates, and may, in fact, be the 'sanest' member of this group." Laing's ideas about schizophrenia take on a poignant air when it is realized that his mother was seriously mentally ill and his eldest daughter was diagnosed with schizophrenia and hospitalized for many years.

Laing founded Kingsley Hall, a house in London in which people with schizophrenia were allowed to experience their psychosis amidst friends who were loving and understanding. He refused to treat patients with medication unless they requested it. Kingsley Hall failed and ultimately closed, and Laing became increasingly disillusioned and alcoholic as he grew older. In 1982 he commented to an interviewer: "I was looked to as one who had the answers but I never had them." He died in 1989.

FUNDING FOR SCHIZOPHRENIA RESEARCH

Funding for schizophrenia research is perhaps the single best news for sufferers and their families in the past decade. Research funding in the United States comes from one of three sources: the National Institute of Mental Health (NIMH) and other federal research agencies, the public via donations to public drives, and private foundations. All three of these sources have dramatically increased the funds available for schizophrenia research in the past decade.

Until the mid-1980s NIMH had badly neglected schizophrenia research. This was cruelly ironic since research on serious mental illnesses was the cornerstone on which NIMH had been founded in

1946. However, between 1980 and 1985 less than 10 percent of the NIMH research budget, or approximately $20 million per year, was spent on schizophrenia research. Then, through a combination of advocacy efforts by the National Alliance for the Mentally Ill and members of Congress, especially Senator Pete Domenici and his wife, Nancy, the federal funds were increased. In 1993 the NIMH research funds for schizophrenia research totaled $106 million, a fivefold increase in ten years.

It was during these same years that the National Alliance for Research on Schizophrenia and Depression (NARSAD) also was founded to solicit research funds from corporations and the public. This has become the major funder for young researchers on serious mental illnesses who are just embarking on their research careers. Although it has not yet achieved the visibility of public solicitations for diseases such as heart disease, cancer, or multiple sclerosis, NARSAD is making an important contribution both to research funding and to public education.

Until 1989 the only American foundation that had made any substantial contribution to schizophrenia research was the Scottish Rite of Freemasonry, headquartered in Boston. The Scottish Rite had done so in fact since 1934, funding many high-quality research projects during years when virtually no other research funds were available. It has continued to run this program, and to be an important source of funds for researchers on schizophrenia. In 1989 the Theodore and Vada Stanley Foundation began funding research on both schizophrenia and manic-depressive illness. Since that time it has become a major source of research funding for both diseases, including the support of the Stanley Foundation Neurovirology Laboratory on Schizophrenia and Manic-Depressive Disorder at Johns Hopkins University, six research centers in Europe, and a multisite Bipolar Disorder Treatment Outcome Network in the United States.

In summary, compared to where things were a decade ago, funding resources for schizophrenia research have dramatically improved. Funding still lags substantially behind other major diseases, such as cancer and heart disease, and no schizophrenia researchers to date have been heard to complain that they have too much money. However, there is no question that improved funding for schizophrenia research is part of the good news on this disease.

RECOMMENDED FURTHER READING

Andreasen, N. *The Broken Brain: The Biological Revolution in Psychiatry.* New York: Harper & Row, 1984.

Gottesman, I. I., and J. Shields. *Schizophrenia: The Epigenetic Puzzle.* New York: Cambridge University Press, 1982.

Gottesman, I. I. *Schizophrenia Genesis: The Origins of Madness.* New York: W. H. Freeman and Company, 1991.

Helmchen, H., and F. Henn, eds. *Biological Perspectives of Schizophrenia.* Chichester, England: John Wiley and Sons, 1987.

Nasrallah, H. A., and D. R. Weinberger, eds. *The Neurology of Schizophrenia.* Amsterdam: Elsevier, 1986.

Torrey, E. F., A. E. Bowler, E. H. Taylor, and I. I. Gottesman. *Schizophrenia and Manic-Depressive Disorder: The Biological Roots of Mental Illness as Revealed by the Landmark Study of Identical Twins.* New York: Basic Books, 1994.

7

THE TREATMENT OF SCHIZOPHRENIA

> To lighten the affliction of insanity by all human means is not to restore the greatest of the divine gifts; and those who devote themselves to the task do not pretend that it is. They find their sustainment and reward in the substitution of humanity for brutality, kindness for maltreatment, peace for raging fury; in the acquisition of love instead of hatred; and in the acknowledgment that, from such treatment improvement, and hope of final restoration, will come if hope be possible.
>
> Charles Dickens, *Household Words,* 1852

Contrary to the popular stereotype, schizophrenia is an eminently treatable disease. That is not to say it is a curable disease, and the two should not be confused. Successful treatment means the control of symptoms, whereas cure means the permanent removal of their causes. Curing schizophrenia will not become possible until we understand its causes; in the meantime we must continue improving its treatment.

The best disease model to explain schizophrenia is diabetes, a disease which has many similarities. Both schizophrenia and diabetes have childhood and adult forms, both almost certainly have more than one cause, both have relapses and remissions in a course which often lasts over many years, and both can usually be well controlled, but not cured, by drugs. Just as we don't talk of curing diabetes but rather of controlling its symptoms and allowing the diabetic to lead a comparatively normal life, so we should also do with schizophrenia.

HOW TO FIND A GOOD DOCTOR

There is no easy solution to this problem, one which is most frequently faced by friends and relatives of persons with schizophrenia. There are few doctors in the United States who either know anything about, or have any interest in, schizophrenia. This is both shocking and sad, since it is one of the most important chronic diseases in the world. In Europe, especially the British Isles and Scandinavia, it is somewhat easier to find a good doctor.

Since schizophrenia is a true biological disease, and since drugs are the mainstay of treatment, there is no avoiding the doctor-finding issue. If schizophrenia is to be properly treated, sooner or later a doctor will need to be involved. He or she will be needed not only to prescribe the proper drugs but also to do an initial diagnostic workup, including laboratory tests, in order to rule out other diseases which may be masquerading as schizophrenia. Before the schizophrenia is treated, one had better be certain that it is not really a brain tumor or herpes encephalitis in disguise. Only a doctor can do this.

The best way to find a good doctor for schizophrenia or any other disease is to ask others in the medical profession whom they would send their own family to if they had a similar problem. Doctors and nurses know who the good doctors are and pass the information freely among themselves; often they will tell you if you ask. If your brother-in-law has a sister who is a nurse, all the better. Use every contact and every relative you have, however distant, to locate and identify competent doctors who may know something about schizophrenia. It is an appropriate time to cash in all your IOUs, for the information is invaluable and may save you months of searching.

Another way to find a good doctor is through other families who have a family member with schizophrenia. They can often provide a quick rundown of the local resources and save weeks of hunting and false starts. Sharing this information is one of the most valuable assets of local chapters of the National Alliance for the Mentally Ill, and is an important reason to join. (Contacts for the state offices of the Alliance for the Mentally Ill are listed in Appendix D.)

Distinctly *un*helpful in searching for a good doctor are referral lists maintained by local medical societies or the local chapters of the American Psychiatric Association. Anyone can call these organizations and obtain three names. The names, however, are taken from a rotating list of those doctors who are looking for additional patients. Since any doctor who wishes to pay the annual dues can belong to these organizations, there is no screening or ascertainment of quality of any kind. Even those doctors who are under investigation for malpractice will continue to be listed by such organizations until they are specifically removed from membership, which is an all-too-rare occurrence. Thus referral lists from medical and psychiatric societies are really no better than picking a name at random from the physicians' list in the Yellow Pages.

What should one look for in a good doctor who can treat schizophrenia? Ideally he/she should combine technical competence with an interest in the disease and empathy with its sufferers. Training in psychiatry or neurology is helpful but not mandatory; there are some internists and family practitioners who have an interest in schizophrenia and can treat it very competently. As a general rule younger physicians who have been trained recently are more likely to view schizophrenia as a biological disease. However, there are major exceptions to this rule: some older practitioners who will tell you, "I've said all along it was a real disease" and some younger practitioners who still believe that what is needed is psychoanalysis of the mother-child relationship.

Another important quality possessed by doctors who are good in treating schizophrenia is an ability to work with other members of the treatment team. Psychologists, psychiatric nurses, social workers, case managers, rehabilitation specialists, and other members of the team are all part of the therapeutic process. Physicians who are reluctant to work as team members are not good doctors for treating schizophrenia no matter how skilled they may be in psychopharmacology.

In trying to find a good doctor it is perfectly legitimate to ask questions such as "What do you think causes schizophrenia?" "What has been your experience with clozapine?" "What do you think about risperidone (or any other new drug)?" "How important is psychotherapy in treating schizophrenia?" Such open-ended questions will quickly elicit the relative biological orientation of the doctor as well as some sense of how well the person is keeping up with new treatments. As families and consumers become increasingly knowledgeable and sophisticated about the treatment of schizophrenia, it is becoming increasingly common to find that they know as much (or more) than some of the treating doctors. The ultimate goal in looking for a good doctor, then, is to find one who is knowledgeable and who also views individuals with schizophrenia, in the words of one psychiatrist, "as a suffering patient, not a defective creation of abstruse, mystical, psychic body parts."

How important is it for the physician to be "board eligible" or "board certified" in his/her specialty? "Board eligible" means that the physician has completed an approved residency program in that specialty. "Board certified" means that the physician has taken and passed an examination in the specialty. Such board examinations are completely optional and are not required for licensure or for membership in any professional organization. They simply mean that the doctor had the theoretical knowledge required to be competent in that specialty at the time he/she took the examination. They do not indicate whether or not the doctor has kept up-to-date since the examination, and for that reason there is relatively little relationship between board certification and competency. All medical specialists should be required to become recertified by examination every five years. Until that time comes, families should give relatively little weight to selecting a "board certified" psychiatrist over a "board eligible" one unless all other things are equal.

What about foreign medical graduates? Psychiatry has attracted more foreign medical graduates than any other medical specialty in the United States. They comprise more than half of all psychiatrists in state mental hospitals and a substantial percentage in community mental health centers. On the plus side, some foreign medical graduates are highly competent and among the best psychiatrists I know for treating schizophrenia. They are the backbone of American public psychiatry and without them the disaster of deinstitutionalization would have been much worse than it has been.

On the minus side other foreign medical graduates range from being mediocre to incompetent. The two foreign medical schools which contributed the greatest number of psychiatrists to American state hospitals both had very low pass rates on the Education Council for Foreign Medical Graduates (ECFMG) examination. Some of the foreign graduates who cannot pass basic licensing exams are given special exemptions by the state to practice only in the state institutions. In essence the state is saying that it does not consider them competent to treat the "worried well" in private practice but will accept them if they treat the truly sick in the state hospitals.

The most disturbing aspect of utilizing large numbers of foreign medical graduates to treat patients with schizophrenia is the inevitable difficulties in communication. Verbal language skill is only one part of this; beyond it are many other levels of communication which involve nonverbal language, shared ideals and values, and other components of what is called culture. Communication between a psychiatrist and a person with schizophrenia is difficult enough even when they share a common language and culture; when they do not share these things, communication becomes virtually impossible. Delusions must be assessed in the context of the patient's culture. Affect which may appear appropriate within one culture context may be inappropriate within another. The evaluation of subtle disorders of thinking assumes a complete command of the idioms and metaphors of a language. One psychiatrist, for example, argued for an increase in medication for a patient who complained about "butterflies in her stomach." Another used as evidence of a patient's delusions the fact that she had talked of "babies coming from birds." "Do you mean storks?" asked the psychologist present. "Yes, that's the one," exclaimed the psychiatrist. "Isn't that crazy!" Still another foreign-trained psychiatrist was observed asking a patient the following proverb during a diagnostic interview: "What does mean, a stitch in time gathers no moss?" That kind of question inspires neither confidence nor clarity of thought in a person with schizophrenia.

What about nonphysicians for treating schizophrenia? In fact psychologists, nurses, social workers, case managers, rehabilitation specialists, and other nonphysicians treat people with schizophrenia regularly and are often the primary contact on the treatment team. It is not uncommon to have the physician on the team merely be the manager of medication and to play a relatively small role in the overall treatment plan.

The other aspect of using nonphysicians to treat schizophrenia is using them to prescribe medication. In many states physician assistants and nurse practitioners are already licensed to prescribe medications. Psychologists are currently lobbying for similar privileges that, not surprisingly, are being vigorously opposed by psychiatrists. With proper training in the use of medications and appropriate supervision, any one of these nonphysician groups can competently treat routine cases of schizophrenia while referring difficult diagnostic or therapeutic problems on to a supervising psychiatrist. It is extremely difficult to attract psychiatrists to work in state mental hospitals or public clinics, or in rural areas. Utilizing these nonphysician groups is one reasonable solution to the chronic shortage of psychiatrists in these settings.

To those looking for a good doctor to treat schizophrenia, one final word of caution. Doctors are human beings and, as such, run a wide range of personality types. Throughout the medical profession can be found occasional physicians who are dishonest, mentally ill, addicted to alcohol or drugs, sociopathic, or who have some combination of the above. I have a sense that psychiatry attracts more than its share of such physicians, often because the physician has become interested in his/her own mental aberrations. Thus one should not make an absolute assumption that physicians who treat persons with schizophrenia are themselves beyond question. If the physician seems strange to you, move on quickly to another. There *are* occasional strange birds in the psychiatric aviary.

HOSPITALIZATION: VOLUNTARY AND INVOLUNTARY

In most cases persons *acutely* ill with schizophrenia need to be hospitalized. Such hospitalization accomplishes several things. Most important, it enables mental health professionals to observe the person in a controlled setting. Laboratory tests can be undergone to rule out other medical illnesses which may be causing the symptoms, psychological testing can be done, and medication can be started in an environment in which trained staff can watch for side effects. In addition, the hospitalization often provides the family with a respite from what have often been harrowing days and nights leading up to the acute illness.

Hospitalization is frequently necessary to protect such patients. Some will try to injure themselves or others because of their illness (e.g., their voices tell them to do so). For this reason most hospitals utilize a locked ward for acutely agitated patients, and its use is often needed. Even in a locked setting the person occasionally may be dangerous and require additional restraints. These may include wrist or ankle restraints (usually made of leather), a special jacket which keeps the arms next to the body (the famous straitjacket of popular lore), or a seclusion room. None of these measures should be necessary for more than a few hours if the person is being properly medicated. It is currently chic in some circles to condemn locked wards and all use of restraints as "barbaric" and antiquated; the people who make such statements have usually never been faced with the task of providing care for persons with acute schizophrenia. It certainly will be nice when we arrive at the point where medications are instantly effective in acutely disturbed patients and restraint is not necessary, but we have not reached that nirvana yet.

There are ancillary benefits of hospitalization for persons with schizophrenia. Well-functioning psychiatric units have group meetings for the patients; this often allows each of them to see that his or her experience is not unique. Occupational therapy, recreational activities, psychodrama, and other forms of group interaction often accomplish the same thing. For someone who has been acutely schizophrenic and who has experienced many of the disturbances described in chapter 2, it is usually a relief to learn that other people have experienced them too. None of the above activities are likely to be of much benefit, however, unless the person is also being properly medicated to relieve the acute symptoms.

There are several different types of hospitals available in which people can be treated for schizophrenia. Psychiatric wards in community hospitals have become increasingly common in recent years and are often satisfactory. Psychiatric wards in university (teaching) hospitals generally have good reputations. Private psychiatric hospitals run a wide gamut from those of excellent reputation to fly-by-night operations in which making a profit is the main incentive and quality of care is often sacrificed. Of special concern are private hospitals which are owned by the psychiatrists themselves; in these instances there is an inherent conflict of interest between the needs of the patient and the need of the psychiatrist to make money. This may be seen vividly, in the frequent instances in which the length of hospitalization in such hospitals coincides with suspicious closeness with the maximum period covered by the patient's hospitalization insurance. When the insurance runs out, the patient is declared well and discharged.

In addition to community, university, and private hospitals, there are also state and Veterans Administration (VA) hospitals. The VA hospitals are very similar to state hospitals except that only those who have served in the armed forces are eligible for admission to them. State hospitals, by contrast, are open to everyone and run as wide a range in quality as do the private psychiatric hospitals.

In selecting a hospital for treatment, the most important factor by far is the competence of the treating psychiatrist. The type of hospital is relatively insignificant compared with this factor. Thus, in some state hospitals there are well-run wards with a competent psychiatrist offering excellent treatment for schizophrenia; and there are other wards in state hospitals which are still proverbial snake pits. The same can be said for private psychiatric hospitals and VA hospitals. As a general rule, community hospitals and university hospitals offer a more predictably high level of care than state, VA, or private hospitals, but this is not always so. I have treated patients who have received abysmal care in both community and university hospitals.

A measure of hospital quality which has become increasingly useful in recent years is accreditation by the Joint Commission on Accreditation of Health Care Organizations (JCAHO). At the invitation of a hospital, JCAHO sends a survey team to evaluate it, as well as provide consultation and education. The survey is very thorough, focusing especially on patient care and services but also including such related issues as the therapeutic environment, safety of the patient, quality of staffing, and administration of the hospital. The survey team then recommends that the hospital receive full three-year accreditation, full accreditation with a contingency (which may necessitate a followup inspection to ensure that the contingency has been corrected), or no accreditation. Full accreditation by JCAHO probably means that the hospital is a good one although, since the accreditation is for the hospital as a whole, there may be individual wards in an accredited hospital which are below standard. The JCAHO certification of accreditation is usually displayed by hospitals in the entryway or lobby; alternatively, anyone in the hospital administrator's office can tell you, or you can find out by writing to JCAHO, 1 Renaissance Boulevard, Oak Brook Terrace, IL 60181. Currently, approximately one-half of the state psychiatric hospitals and three-quarters of the private psychiatric hospitals and general hospitals are accredited.

A yardstick for measuring hospital quality which is *not* very useful is the fees charged. People throughout the world have a strong inclination to equate higher cost with higher quality of medical care, but this is erroneous; in psychiatry, as in the rest of medicine, that which costs more is not necessarily better.

How, then, should a hospital be chosen? The answer is, again, first to identify a good doctor. Since doctors have admitting privileges in a limited number of hospitals, you will probably have to hospitalize the person where the doctor you choose has access. If you have a choice, because the doctor has more than one hospital affiliation, always opt for a JCAHO-accredited facility.

One aspect of hospitalization that has changed markedly in recent years is the length of hospitalizations. In the recent past hospitalizations for schizophrenia were usually measured in weeks or even months. However, with the pressure of managed care and insurance companies, the average length of stay has decreased dramatically and is now often measured in days. This is sometimes adequate, especially if skilled follow-up is available, but at other times is not adequate and results in the premature discharge of the individual.

It is ideal when people with schizophrenia recognize that they are becoming sick and voluntarily seek treatment for their sickness. Unfortunately, however, this is often not the case. Schizophrenia is a disease of the brain, the body organ charged with the responsibility of recognizing sickness and the need for treatment—the same organ which is sick. Out of this unfortunate coincidence arises the frequent need for persons to be committed to psychiatric treatment settings against their will.

How does the commitment process work? All laws governing commitment of psychiatric patients are state laws, not federal laws. Therefore commitment laws vary from state to state, especially those governing long-term commitment. Between 1970 and 1980 there was a broad shift in the United States to change state laws to make it more difficult to involuntarily hospitalize individuals with psychiatric illnesses. The effect of this shift has been to make it virtually impossible in some states to hospitalize an individual with schizophrenia until that person has demonstrated overt danger to self or others. Because of the problems produced by these stringent laws, there is growing sentiment to modify the laws so that such persons can be involuntarily hospitalized and treated.

Legally there are two rationales for the commitment of mental patients. The first is referred to as *parens patriae* and is the right of the state to act as parent and protect a disable person; it arose in early English law from the belief that the king was the father of all his subjects. The second is the right of the state to protect other people from a person who is dangerous. The first right may be invoked when persons are so disabled that they do not recognize their own need for treatment or cannot provide for their own basic needs and therefore may be dangerous to themselves. The second may be invoked when persons, because of their mental illness, are dangerous to other people.

There are also two kinds of commitment—emergency and long-term. The basic purpose of commitment laws is to enable persons who are psychiatrically ill to be put forcibly into hospitals so that they will not harm themselves or others and can be treated. This can be done as follows:

1. A petition for commitment of the person thought to be psychiatrically ill must be initiated. In most states this can be done by one of several persons; for example, Tennessee allows petitions to be filed by "the parent, guardian, spouse, or a responsible adult relative of the individual or by any licensed physician or licensed psychologist or by any health or public welfare officer, or by the head of any institution in which the individual may be, or by any officer authorized to make arrests in Tennessee."

2. The person initiating the petition asks a physician (not necessarily a psychiatrist) to examine the person for whom commitment is sought. Some states require two physicians to be examiners while others allow psychologists. If the examiner(s) conclude that the person is mentally ill and meets the grounds for commitment in that state, then the examiners' report is attached to the petition and it is filed.

3. The examination may take place anywhere, including in the person's home.

4. If the person for whom commitment is sought refuses to be examined, many states have a provision for the petitioner to file a sworn written statement. In, for example, Nevada, this says, "such person is mentally ill and, because of such illness, is likely to harm himself or others, or is gravely disabled."

5. Once the petition has been filed, a police officer can bring the person to the hospital for examination by a psychiatrist.

6. Alternatively, if any person is acting strangely in public, a police officer can bring the person to the hospital for examination by a psychiatrist.

7. The examining psychiatrist at the hospital decides on the basis of his/her examination whether the person meets the criteria for commitment in that state. If the person does, emergency commitment is effected and the person is kept at the hospital. If not, the person is released.

8. An emergency commitment lasts for seventy-two hours in most states, not including weekends and holidays. At the end of that period the person must be released unless either the director of the hospital or the family has filed a petition with the court ask-

ing for long-term commitment. If this has been filed, then the
person can be held until the hearing.

9. The hearing for long-term commitment may be held in a room
in the hospital or in a courtroom. The person alleged to be mentally ill is expected to be present unless a psychiatrist testifies
that the person's presence would be detrimental to his/her mental state. The person is represented by a lawyer appointed by the
state if necessary, and normal judicial rules of evidence and due
process apply. Testimony may be taken from the examining psychiatrist, from family members, and from the person alleged to
be mentally ill.

10. The hearing is held before a mental health commission, judge,
or similar judicial authority depending on the state. In many
states the person has the right to a jury trail if he/she so wishes.

The major differences in commitment procedures among states are
the grounds which are used for commitment and the standard of proof.
In states that utilize only dangerousness to self or others and define dangerousness stringently, it is generally more difficult to get a commitment than in states which define dangerousness vaguely (for example,
Texas laws say a mentally ill person can be committed "for his own
welfare and protection or the protection of others"). Similarly, in states
in which "gravely disabled" or "in need of treatment" are grounds for
commitment by themselves, it may be easier to get a commitment.

The standard of proof utilized by states is also a major source of
variation. The most stringent level of proof is "beyond a reasonable
doubt," the same standard used to judge persons charged with crimes.
Currently eight states utilize this (California, Hawaii, Kansas,
Kentucky, Massachusetts, New Hampshire, Oklahoma, and Oregon). If
all other things are equal (see below), then it should be theoretically
more difficult to commit a mentally ill person in these states. A lesser
level of proof is "clear and convincing evidence," which is utilized in
the rest of the states. In 1979 the United States Supreme Court ruled
that the use of "clear and convincing evidence" was an acceptable level
of proof under the Constitution and that "beyond a reasonable doubt"
could be utilized by individual states if desired but was not required.
The ruling in effect says that the same level of proof is not required to
commit a person to a mental hospital as is required to convict a person
of a crime and commit him/her to jail. Civil rights lawyers interested in

the mentally ill continue to fight for more stringent standards of proof, whereas many psychiatrists and families of persons with schizophrenia would prefer to see the standard of proof remain more flexible.

In the past some states utilized standards of proof more lenient than "clear and convincing evidence." Texas, New Jersey, and Mississippi, for example, required only "a mere preponderance of the evidence" for a person to be involuntarily committed; this was generally interpreted to mean that the evidence on each side was added up and the side with the "preponderance of the evidence" won. Since the 1979 Supreme Court ruling, however, these states have had to adopt stricter criteria.

Probably the most important variables in determining how easy or difficult it is to commit psychiatric patients to hospitals are the specific judge involved and the local community standards. As lawyers well know, laws are written one way but can be interpreted in many ways, and this is certainly true for those concerned with psychiatric commitment. Thus in the same state one judge may interpret dangerousness much more stringently than another, and what for one judge is "clear and convincing evidence" is for another judge not at all persuasive. The standards of the community vary as well, with some localities more inclined to "lock up all those crazies" whereas another part of the same state may be reluctant to commit people unless absolutely necessary. Also important is the current local milieu. For example, if a former psychiatric patient has recently been accused of murder in the local newspaper, the tendency may be to commit everyone with acute symptoms. If, on the other hand, the local newspaper is doing an exposé on the poor conditions in the state hospital, the tendency may be to commit nobody unless absolutely necessary.

Individual horror stories abound of clearly psychotic persons who could not be involuntarily hospitalized because of the stringent interpretation of "dangerousness to self or others" by law enforcement and judicial officials. In 1984 in the District of Columbia, I personally examined a homeless woman who was blatantly hallucinating and carrying an axe around town; the police refused to take her to a hospital for possible commitment because they said she had not yet *done* anything to demonstrate dangerousness. In Wisconsin "a man barricaded himself in his house and sat with a rifle in his lap muttering 'Kill, kill, kill.' A judge ruled that the man was not demonstrably violent enough to qualify for involuntary commitment." At another commitment hearing in Wisconsin, a man with schizophrenia, mute and refusing to eat food or bathe, was noted to be eating feces while being held in jail. He was released because such behavior did not qualify as dangerous. The dialogue at the commitment hearing included the following:

Public defender: "Doctor, would the eating of fecal material on one occasion by an individual pose a serious risk of harm to that person?"

Doctor: "It is certainly not edible material. . . . It contains elements that are considered harmful or unnecessary."

Public defender: "But, Doctor, you cannot state whether the consumption of such material on one occasion would invariably harm a person?"

Doctor: "Certainly not on one occasion."

The public defender then moved to dismiss the action on the grounds that the patient was in no imminent danger of physical injury or dying.

The case was dismissed.

It is such absurd and inhumane legal decisions as these that have spurred a growing movement toward broadening grounds for commitment. The State of Washington was one of the first to move in this direction in 1979, and since then several others have begun to follow. In North Carolina, for example, "impairments to judgment" was added as a legal ground for commitment. In 1983 the American Psychiatric Association proposed a model commitment statute which would allow commitment of psychiatrically ill persons whose behavior indicates "significant deterioration" of their psychiatric state and who clearly are in need of treatment. I believe it is a good model for state laws because it permits the treatment of a relapsing schizophrenic patient *before* the person has had to demonstrate dangerousness, with its frequent tragic consequences.

What does all this mean for a family with a member who is in need of treatment and who refuses to go to the hospital? It means that the family must first learn the commitment procedures and criteria which apply in that state. The quickest way to do this is to telephone or visit the admission unit of the nearest psychiatric hospital, whose personnel are usually experts in this area. Other potential resources for this information are the local or state Department of Mental Health, public defenders, psychiatrists, or policemen. The family must also know what kinds of evidence are necessary and admissible to prove dangerousness. Are threats to other people sufficient, or does the person actually have to have injured someone? Families who wish to can usually testify at the commitment hearing, and their knowledge of what proof is necessary will often determine whether the person with schizophrenia is or is not committed. Indeed, many persons with family members with schizophrenia have become amateur lawyers in order to survive!

The long-term consequences of involuntarily hospitalizing a person with schizophrenia are quite variable. On one end of the spectrum are individuals who, following an involuntary hospitalization, refuse to have anything to do with their families or may even run away from home. The more radical consumer groups of so-called "psychiatric survivors" (see chapter 10) appear to be primarily made up of individuals who were once involuntarily hospitalized and who then decided to turn their resentment into a career.

On the other end of the spectrum are individuals who retrospectively regard their involuntary hospitalization very positively because it got them into treatment. In one of the few studies done on this question, Dr. John Kane and his colleagues in New York interviewed 35 involuntarily admitted patients shortly after their admission and again just prior to discharge approximately two months later. They found that most patients had "significant changes toward recognition of the original need for involuntary treatment." I have personally participated in an involuntary commitment hearing in which a woman with schizophrenia told her daughter, who was testifying for the commitment, that she would never speak to her again; a year later the woman, on medication and in complete remission, expressed profound thanks to the daughter for being the only family member who had the courage to put her into the hospital.

ALTERNATIVES TO HOSPITALIZATION

Hospitalization is usually necessary for patients with schizophrenia who are sick for the first time, for the reasons described above. For those who have already been clearly diagnosed and who have relapsed (often because they have stopped taking their medicine), hospitalization can sometimes be avoided. There are several possible alternatives.

One such alternative is the use of drugs given by injection in an emergency room or clinic. A skilled physician can dramatically reduce the psychotic symptoms in approximately half of patients with schizophrenia within six to eight hours, thereby allowing the person to return home. One problem with this technique, however, is that frequently the family members are so worn out by the person's recent behavior that *they* need the rest and understandably are not prepared to accept the person home again immediately.

Another increasingly popular alternative to hospitalization is the use of mobile treatment teams that go to the individual's home, assess the situation, and frequently begin treatment on the spot. This can effectively decrease the use of hospitalization but only works where there is skilled and coordinated follow-up.

Another recent development is the increasing use by states and counties of psychiatric beds for short-term hospitalization in institutions other than hospitals, primarily because such beds are less expensive. These institutions have different names in different places, such as IMDs (Institutes for Mental Diseases) or crisis homes. Some IMDs in California have over 200 beds and are similar to state mental hospitals in everything except name.

Another alternative is the treatment of the patient at home, using public health nurses or, rarely, physicians to make home visits. This technique is used much more often in England, with apparent success. It was also demonstrated to be feasible in a study done in Louisville by Benjamin Pasamanick and his colleagues, who concluded that "the combination of drug therapy and public health nurses' home visitation is *effective* in preventing hospitalization, and that home care is at least as good a method of treatment as hospitalization by any or all criteria, and probably superior by most." It has also been used successfully in the model treatment program in Dane County, Wisconsin, described in chapter 8.

I utilized it once when practicing in a rural village, when the family expressed a wish to keep the person at home if possible; it required home visits for injections twice a day for a week, but it was successful.

The use of partial hospitalization is another good alternative. Day hospitals, in which the patient goes to the hospital for the day and returns home at night, and night hospitals, in which the patient goes to the hospital only to sleep, can both be effective in selected cases. Since both cost less than full hospitalization they may be useful in communities in which they are available. They are usually affiliated with a full-time institution. Unfortunately both are much less available than they should be in the United States. When present, they are inspected by the JCAHO accreditation team at the same time as the parent institution is surveyed.

ANTIPSYCHOTIC DRUG TREATMENT

Once a competent doctor has been located and the intricacies of hospitalization have been mastered, then the treatment of schizophrenia becomes comparatively simple. Drugs are the most important treatment for schizophrenia, just as they are the most important treatment for many physical diseases of the human body. Drugs do not *cure,* but rather *control,* the symptoms of schizophrenia—as they do those of diabetes. The drugs we now have to treat schizophrenia are far from perfect, but they work most of the time for most of the people with the disease if they are used correctly.

The main drugs used to treat schizophrenia are usually called antipsychotics. They have also been called neuroleptics and major tranquilizers, but the best term is "antipsychotic" because that is what they are. They frequently do not produce tranquilization, so that term is a misnomer. The antipsychotic drugs were discovered in 1952 in France; chlorpromazine (Thorazine) was the first such drug discovered.

Six different chemical families of antipsychotic drugs are used in the United States—phenothiazines, thioxanthines, butyrophenones, dibenzoxazepines, dihydroindolones and benzodiazepines (table 1). The drugs in each family are listed by their generic name (the official name for that chemical compound), and their trade names (the brand names used by drug companies for that product; e.g., Thorazine and Largactil are both chlorpromazine, exactly the same drug chemically, though marketed by two different drug companies under their own registered trade names).

Antipsychotic drugs are usually given as tablets or liquid. Tablets can be taken once a day and are more effective if taken on an empty stomach. If ingested at the same time as antacids containing aluminum or magnesium (information that appears on the lists of ingredients on their labels), their effectiveness is reduced. Some people believe that antipsychotic medications should not be taken with coffee, tea, or cola drinks because it will reduce their effectiveness. This is probably true for the liquid form of these medications but not for the tablet form. The tablets may also be crushed for ease of administration. The liquid form may be mixed with juices (other than apple juice) and used in individuals in which there is doubt whether the person is swallowing their tablets; however, the liquid form is more expensive than the tablet form. Many of these drugs can also be given as a short-acting intramuscular injection, and two (fluphenazine and haloperidol) can be given as long-acting injections which need be given only every one to four weeks. Such long-acting injections are extremely useful for individuals who find it difficult (or refuse) to take pills; they have to return to the clinic for another injection only once every few weeks in order to stay well. Injections are usually given in the buttocks, although they may be given in the arm if preferred.

Types of Antipsychotic Drugs

Type	Generic Name	Trade (Brand) Names
Aliphatic phenothiazines	chlorpromazine	Thorazine, Largactil, and others
Piperidine phenothiazines	thioridazine	Mellaril
	mesoridazine	Serentil
Piperazine phenothiazines	fluphenazine	Prolixin, Permitil
	trifluoperazine	Stelazine and others
	perphenazine	Trilafon
	prochlorperazine	Compazine
Thioxanthines	thiothixene	Navane
	chlorprothixene	Taractan
Butyrophenones	haloperidol	Haldol
	pimozide	Orap
Dibenzoxazepines	loxapine	Loxitane
Dihydroindolones	molindone	Moban
Benzodiazepines	clozapine	Clozaril

The antipsychotic drugs are roughly divided into high, intermediate, and low potency depending on how high a dose is required to produce an equivalent effect. Thus chlorpromazine (Thorazine) and thioridazine (Mellaril) are categorized as low potency because it takes 20 milligrams to produce the same effect as 1 milligram of fluphenazine (Prolixin) or haloperidol (Haldol), which are categorized as high potency. In other words, milligram for milligram fluphenazine and haloperidol are 20 times as strong as chlorpromazine and thioridazine. Molidone (Moban) and loxapine (Loxitane) are examples of antipsychotic drugs that are intermediate in potency.

General Principles

Do they work?

The efficacy of antipsychotic drugs is well-established. Studies show that approximately 70 percent of patients with schizophrenia clearly improve on these drugs, 25 percent improve minimally or not at all, and 5 percent get worse. This is approximately the same level of effectiveness that penicillin exerts in pneumonia or streptomycin in tuberculosis. Antipsychotic drugs reduce symptoms of the disease, shorten the stay in the hospital, and reduce the chances of rehospitalization dramatically. Whereas persons with schizophrenia entering a psychiatric hospital used to stay for several weeks or months, the average stay with these drugs is now reduced to days. And the data on their preventing rehospitalization are even more impressive. John Davis, for example, reviewed twenty-four scientifically controlled studies testing whether antipsychotic drugs were effective. All twenty-four studies found that persons with schizophrenia who took antipsychotic drugs were less likely to have to return to the hospital than those who did not take these drugs. The differences between the two groups were highly significant, especially for persons with chronic schizophrenia. On the average, a person who takes the drugs has a 3-out-of-5 chance (60 percent) of not being rehospitalized, whereas the person who does not take the drugs has only a 1-out-of-5 chance (20 percent) of not being rehospitalized.

When studies have been done on the long-acting, injectable form of antipsychotics (where compliance in taking the drug is assured), the results are even more impressive. In one study of chronic patients, only 8 percent of the patients who were taking the drug relapsed within one year, but 68 percent of those not taking the drug relapsed. In another study of patients taking injectable antipsychotics, 80 percent relapsed within two years when the drug was stopped. What all this means is that though taking the drugs does not guarantee you will *not* get sick again, and not taking the drugs does not guarantee you *will* get sick again, their use improves the odds toward staying out of the hospital tremendously. The data on the effectiveness of drugs are so clear that any physician or psychiatrist who fails to try them on a person with schizophrenia is probably incompetent. It is not that drugs are the *only* ingredient necessary to treat schizophrenia successfully; they are just the most essential ingredient.

Antipsychotic drugs are not equally effective for all the symptoms of schizophrenia. They are most effective at reducing delusions, hallucinations, aggressive or bizarre behavior, thinking disorders, and the symptoms having to do with the overacuteness of the senses—the so-called "positive" symptoms. For example, against auditory hallucinations, one of the most common and disabling symptoms of schizophrenia, antipsychotic drugs are 80 to 90 percent effective in being able to relieve the hallucinations, usually making them disappear altogether. The drugs have less efficacy (sometimes none) against symptoms such as apathy, ambivalence, poverty of thought, and flattening of the emotions—the "negative" symptoms.

How do they work?

It has been widely assumed that antipsychotic drugs work by blocking dopamine receptors on brain cells that use dopamine as a neurotransmitter. Recently, data have become available that throw some doubt on this assumption. It is known, for example, that the dopamine blockade is complete within 24 hours of starting the drug, yet the therapeutic effectiveness may be delayed for days or even weeks. It is also known that the cells that use dopamine as a neurotransmitter are not most numerous in the hippocampus and some other parts of the limbic system that are thought to be involved in schizophrenia. Finally, clozapine is a relatively weak blocker of dopamine receptors and yet it is a very effective antipsychotic.

The fact is that we do not know precisely how antipsychotic drugs work. Perhaps their major therapeutic effect is on another neurotransmitter system such as the sigma receptors or those utilizing serotonin, histamine, glutamic acid, acetylcholine, or noradrenalin. Perhaps their therapeutic effect has little to do with neurotransmitters but instead is dependent on another property such as their known antiviral effects. Since we do not understand yet precisely how aspirin works, it should not surprise us that we do not understand how antipsychotics work either.

Can we predict who will respond
and which drug they will respond to?

The current answer to both questions is no. People who do not respond to medications are more likely to have been sick longer, to have more neurological abnormalities, and to have more evidence of organic brain damage on neuropsychological testing but such predictors are relatively weak. And there is currently no way to predict which drug is best for which person with schizophrenia, and the only way to find out is by trial and error. Three clues to predicting response should be noted, however. First, if a person responds well to a certain drug one time, then he/she is likely always to respond well to that drug. Second, if another person in the same family has been psychiatrically ill and responded well to a certain drug, then other members of the same family who become ill will probably respond well to that drug. This suggests that there is a genetic predisposition to how well one responds to these drugs. Third, at least two groups of investigators have shown that if the person with schizophrenia has a very unpleasant subjective reaction (called a dysphoric effect) to the first dose of the medication, then the chances of the person's ultimately responding favorably to this medication are low.

It is likely that in the future we will be able to predict who will respond and which drug they will respond to. One example of research on this problem is the use of electroencephalographic (EEG) patterns of brain waves. In one such study reported in 1994, EEG patterns recorded six hours following the initial dose of haloperidol, correctly predicted which patients would respond to the drug at a high level of certainty.

At a practical level, every person with schizophrenia or the family members should keep a list of which drugs they have been tried on, what dosage level (i.e., how many milligrams), and what the response was. This can be extremely helpful and save weeks of trial-and-error medications in future treatment.

High dose, low dose, no dose

It has become clear in recent years that people require widely varying doses for these drugs to be effective. This is probably a genetic trait and is not surprising in view of how differently our bodies handle other chemical compounds. One ounce of alcohol will make one person intoxicated and will not even be felt by another. Similarly, when 20 milligrams a day of fluphenazine was given to a group of patients with schizophrenia and then the blood level of the drug was measured, the difference between the lowest and highest blood level was *fortyfold*. The absorption and excretion of antipsychotic drugs varies widely from person to person, so that one patient requires 10 milligrams and another patient 400 milligrams to achieve identical blood levels. In another experiment into the same phenomenon, some patients with schizophrenia proved to need *thirty-two times* more fluphenazine than other patients to produce a similar blood level of the drug.

The practical implications of this dose variability is that both physicians and patients must be flexible in thinking about dosage. Minidoses may suffice for some patients, with as little as 1 mg. a day of fluphenazine, haloperidol, or thiothixene keeping them well. And long-acting injectable fluphenazine doses as low as 1.25 mg. every two weeks have proved effective in some patients. On the other end of the spectrum, some patients with schizophrenia require megadoses of antipsychotic drugs in order to achieve a blood level which will be effective. Daily megadoses of haloperidol 270 mg., thiothixene 480 mg., and loxapine 500 mg. are described in the psychiatric literature, and I personally have had patients who failed to respond at daily doses of less than fluphenazine 150 mg. or chlorpromazine 3,000 mg. One well-known psychiatric researcher in New York claims to have had a patient take as much as 1,200 mg. a day of fluphenazine by mouth—and the patient continued working as a taxi driver! For long-acting injectable fluphenazine, Dr. Sven Dencker in Sweden has used weekly injectable doses of 900 mg. on rare treatment-resistant patients with good results; he has followed such patients for over ten years and reports no more side effects from the megadoses than from standard doses. Dr. Dencker's top dose is *over 1,400 times* the minidoses found to be effective in other patients. The findings on dose variability also suggest that many patients who received drugs failed to respond because the drug was administered in too low a dosage. This information conflicts with a presently popular stereotype of mental hospitals which portrays all the patients as being overmedicated. The truth is quite the opposite, and in every state hospital I have been in I find at least two *undermedicated* patients with schizophrenia for every one who is over-medicated.

But stereotypes die slow deaths, and the image of the over-medicated, "zonked-out," "zombied" patient is a very strong one. It has its principal origin in the fact that the *symptoms* of schizophrenia are often confused with the *effects* of the drugs used in its treatment. Thus when families see their relatives with schizophrenia sitting lethargically, apathetic, ambivalent, and suffering poverty of thought, they assume that the drugs made them that way. All one has to do to prove this is not so is to talk with anyone who had to care for patients *before* antipsychotic drugs were introduced in the 1950s; you will invariably be told that *more* patients were "zonked-out" in the old days.

This is not to say that antipsychotic drugs are never abused or that patients are not sometimes overmedicated for the convenience of the hospital staff who want to calm them down. These things certainly do happen. But stereotypes to the contrary, this problem is relatively minor in the treatment of schizophrenia, compared with the number of patients who have never been given an adequate trial of available medications.

In recent years there has also been considerable interest in an intermittent "no dose" strategy, in which medication is stopped until the person begins to relapse, at which time it is restarted. Two American and two European research groups have now completed controlled trials using intermittent medication. It seems clear that for most individuals with schizophrenia the intermittent strategy is not effective and results in a much higher rehospitalization rate than does continuous medication.

How long should antipsychotic drugs be continued?

Given the wide variation in blood levels in different individuals who take the same dose of medication, it is not surprising to find that their rate of response also varies widely. On one end of the clinical spectrum are individuals who respond dramatically within 48 hours of being started on medication, whereas on the other end are individuals who respond very slowly over several months. Dr. Jeffrey Lieberman and his colleagues in New York recently studied the treatment response in newly admitted, first-episode patients with schizophrenia and reported that the mean interval between beginning medication and achieving the maximum clinical improvement was 35 weeks, although half the patients had achieved it by 11 weeks. This means that a few patients respond rapidly but the remainder may take much longer. Patience is indeed a virtue when treating schizophrenia.

Once started, how long should the medications be continued? If a person has had an initial episode of schizophrenia and recovered, it is known that one-quarter of such individuals will not get sick again and will not need medication. There is currently no way to identify for certain which patients fall into that group. Within a few weeks following recovery, therefore, medication should be slowly decreased and then discontinued.

The three-quarters who eventually relapse will again be treated with medication. For this group, medication should probably be continued for several months after recovery. If patients relapse a third time, then it is known that they will need the medication continuously for several years, and I encourage them to think of themselves as similar to a diabetic who needs insulin. In summary, then: first episode, continue medications for several weeks; second episode, for several months; and third episode, for several years.

As persons with schizophrenia age, can they reduce and eventually discontinue their medication? Many can do so in their forties or fifties, and most can do so by their sixties. Usually the older a person gets, the lower the required dose of antipsychotic medication.

Are antipsychotic drugs addicting?

The abuse of antipsychotic drugs to achieve a "high" is extremely rare and has been reported only for loxapine. Antipsychotic drugs do not produce a pleasant or euphoric effect on normal people. I have had street-wise patients try to sell them and I always tell them: "If you can find somebody who will buy these from you, tell them I'll gladly give them an additional supply free because they undoubtedly need them."

In terms of addiction to antipsychotic drugs, this is unknown. The person's body does not slowly get used to them and therefore require higher and higher doses, and the stopping of these drugs does not usually cause withdrawal symptoms. The one possible exception to this is clozapine, which is discussed on page 204. Antipsychotic drugs for schizophrenia are exactly the same as insulin for diabetes or digitalis for heart failure—they are drugs needed by the body to restore the functioning of the respective organs (brain, pancreas, and heart) to more normal levels.

Does early treatment help?

Recent studies have suggested that early treatment may lead to a better clinical outcome in schizophrenia and, conversely, that delayed treatment may lead to a worse outcome. Dr. Richard Wyatt of the National Institute of Mental Health reanalyzed 22 studies on the course of schizophrenia and concluded that "early intervention with neuroleptics in first-break schizophrenic patients increases the likelihood of an improved long-term course." An analysis of the Lieberman et al. recent study of individuals undergoing their first episode of schizophrenia similarly concluded that "greater duration of illness [prior to beginning treatment] was found to predict increased time to remission" in younger but not in older patients. An Irish study of untreated patients with schizophrenia also found that "untreated psychosis in schizophrenia appears to have a progressive and, ultimately, a profoundly debilitating effect on long-term outcome." The implication of these studies is that the failure by mental illness professionals to treat individuals with schizophrenia with antipsychotic medications as early in the course of their illness as possible, probably constitutes malpractice.

Side effects

"The antipsychotic agents," says Dr. Ross J. Baldessarini, "are among the safest drugs available in medicine." As one of the foremost experts on these drugs, Dr. Baldessarini should know, yet his claim is at variance with popular stereotypes of the drugs. It is widely believed that antipsychotic drugs have terrible side effects, are dangerous, and almost invariably produce tardive dyskinesia (involuntary muscle movements) and other irreversible conditions which may be worse than the original schizophrenia.

Dr. Baldessarini is in fact correct, and the popular stereotype is wrong. Antipsychotic drugs are among the safest group of drugs known. It is almost impossible to commit suicide with them by overdosing, and their serious side effects are comparatively rare.

Then why is there such a strong misperception and fear of these drugs? Much of the reason can be traced to theories of causation of the disease. As we have noted, it is only in the past few years that the evidence for schizophrenia's being a real biological disease has become clear. The resistance to this idea among mental health professionals trained in the psychogenic belief systems has been impressive. And one of the ways this resistance is shown is by strongly opposing the use of drugs; implicitly, if the drugs are too dangerous to be used, then patients will again have to rely on psychotherapy and other nondrug modes of treatment. For this reason it is not uncommon to find psychiatrists—who should be better informed—warning patients with schizophrenia about all kinds of terrible calamities which will befall them if they take antipsychotic drugs. Additional opposition to antipsychotic drug use comes from the Church of Scientology whose founder, L. Ron Hubbard, was virulently antipsychiatry.

This is *not* to say that antipsychotic drugs are perfectly safe and have no side effects whatsoever. They do have side effects, sometimes so severe that the drug must be stopped. The side effects have on occasion even been fatal, but this is very rare. One of the main goals of the current search for newer antipsychotic drugs is to find effective compounds which will continue to suppress psychotic symptoms while producing minimal undesirable side effects. But it is important to repeat that the point to be remembered is that antipsychotic drugs, as a group, are one of the safest groups of drugs in common use and are the greatest advance in the treatment of schizophrenia which has occurred to date.

The side effects of antipsychotic drugs can be discussed as a group. Some side effects are more common with particular drugs, but the differences are not great. And, like side effects to all drugs used in medicine, it is not possible to predict with any accuracy which person is likely to get which side effect.

Common

Among the most common side effects of antipsychotic medications are the following:

Sedation: This occurs most commonly with chlorpromazine, thioridazine, mesoridazine, and clozapine. It usually decreases as the person takes the drug for a longer period of time. Taking the drug at bedtime will minimize this side effect.

Dry mouth, blurred vision, and constipation: This occurs most commonly with high potency drugs such as haloperidol and fluphenazine. It usually decreases as the person takes the drug over a longer period of time.

Acute dystonic reaction: This side effect is frightening for patients and their families. It usually occurs within the first few days after beginning antipsychotic drug therapy, is more common in younger people and in men, and consists of the stiffening of muscles on one side of the neck and jaw. Usually the neck becomes rigid so it cannot turn, talking becomes difficult because of stiffening of the tongue, and occasionally it also affects the eye muscles, causing the eyes to look upward. This side effect can be reversed within minutes by giving the patient an anticholinergic drug such as benztropine (Cogentin), biperiden (Akineton), procyclidine (Kemadrin), or trihexyphenidyl (Artane), or by giving diphenhydramine (Benadryl) or diazepam (Valium). Dystonic reactions can also be prevented by giving anticholinergic drugs prophylactically. Although frightening, acute dystonic reactions cause no permanent damage.

Stiffness and tremor: These side effects are grouped together because they usually occur together and are similar to the symptoms of Parkinson's disease. They may be accompanied by slowed body movements, loss of facial expression owing to stiffness of the facial muscles, and drooling. A tremor can be very annoying, especially if the person has a job that requires writing or other fine hand movements. These side effects can often be improved using the anticholinergic drugs mentioned above or bromocriptine (Parlodel). It should also be emphasized that stiffness and tremor may occur as part of the schizophrenic disease process in addition to being side effects of the medication. One recent study of individuals with schizophrenia who had never been treated with antipsychotic drugs reported that 29 percent of them had some stiffness and 37 percent had a tremor.

Akinesia or decreased spontaneity: This side effect is not usually noticed until several weeks after beginning antipsychotic drugs. It often occurs in the same persons who have stiffness and tremors. It is an especially difficult side effect to evaluate because decreased spontaneity may also be a symptom of the person's schizophrenia or a symptom of the depression that often accompanies schizophrenia. Decreased spontaneity that is caused by the medication can often be successfully reversed with the anticholinergic drugs mentioned above.

Akathisia or restlessness: This is one of the most uncomfortable side effects of antipsychotic drugs and occurs in approximately 25 percent of all patients. It consists of feelings of restlessness, jumpiness, and a need to keep moving. Individuals experiencing it will sometimes shift from one foot to the other or pace back and forth. It may begin within three days of starting the antipsychotic drug and is a major reason why some individuals refuse to continue taking their drugs. It can be successfully treated in many individuals with propranolol or other beta blockers, clonidine, or diazepam. In other individuals it may be necessary to change to another antipsychotic.

Weight gain: This is also a serious and moderately common side effect of antipsychotic medication. The precise mechanism is not well understood but in some individuals involves increased appetite. The weight gain caused by the medication is also exacerbated by weight gain caused by the decreased activity and depression that are often part of the schizophrenic disease process. As the person gains weight he/she may exercise less, producing still further weight gain. The best ways to combat weight gain in individuals with schizophrenia are the same as in individuals who do not have schizophrenia—control of diet and exercise. There is also some evidence that molindone is less likely to cause weight gain and individuals for whom this is a problem should probably be given a trial on this antipsychotic.

Uncommon

Among the less common side effects of antipsychotic drugs are the following:

Impaired sexual function: Impairments in sexual functioning definitely occur as a side effect of antipsychotic drugs, but both their frequency and their seriousness are matters of dispute. Decreased sexual desire may be found in both sexes and impotence or retrograde ejaculation may occur in men; the latter occurs especially with thioridazine (Mellaril). It is difficult to evaluate how many of these effects are due to the drugs, how many are due to the schizophrenia, and how many antedated the disease altogether. For example, impotence is a common condition among men, and it is obviously inaccurate to blame all impotence in men who take antipsychotic drugs on these medications. There is a general consensus among clinicians that thioridazine (Mellaril) is most likely to cause sexual problems as a side effect, and some belief (although unproven) that molindone (Moban) and loxapine (Loxitane) are least likely to do so.

It is similarly difficult to evaluate the seriousness of these symptoms since sexual functioning varies so widely in people who do not have schizophrenia. For some people with comparatively little interest in sex, the decreased libido from antipsychotic drugs may not even be noticed. For others it may be a disaster of monumental proportions and they may insist on stopping the drugs for that reason. I had one patient, for example, who definitely was impotent when he took antipsychotic drugs and who became acutely psychotic whenever he did not. He was faced with a painful dilemma; the role of the physician in such cases should be to outline the choices and consequences as clearly as possible and then support the person's choice. This kind of dilemma is fortunately not common.

Menstrual changes: Missed menstrual periods sometimes occur in women taking antipsychotic drugs. They may also occur because of the schizophrenia disease process and this phenomenon was well described prior to the introduction of antipsychotic drugs.

Breast discharge: This may occur in either women or men and is a result of the effect of the medication on the pituitary gland.

Urinary retention: This may occur in older patients, especially in men who have enlarged prostate glands.

Fast heart beat or fainting: These occur more commonly in people with heart disease or problems with blood pressure.

Seizures: These are rare except for individuals taking clozapine, which has a seizure incidence of 3 to 5 percent.

Photosensitivity: Photosensitivity is an increased susceptibility to sunburn. It can be prevented by the liberal use of sunscreens and wide-brimmed hats.

Damage to white blood cells: This occurs very rarely except with clozapine, discussed below.

Liver damage: This was seen more commonly when chlorpromazine was first introduced in the 1960s but now is rarely seen.

Eye damage: Damage to the retina may occur with thioridazine (Mellaril) when high doses are used. For this reason thioridazine should never be given in doses of more than 800 mg per day.

Tardive dyskinesia

Tardive dyskinesia is an important side effect of antipsychotic drugs. Much of the fear of using these drugs is in fact linked to this side effect and it has become a banner regularly waved by the Church of Scientology and other antipsychiatry zealots. Tardive dyskinesia is certainly a serious problem but it is not nearly as serious as those apostles of hysteria have claimed.

Tardive dyskinesia consists of involuntary movements of the tongue and mouth, such as chewing movements, sucking movements, pushing the cheek out with the tongue, and smacking of the lips. Occasionally these are accompanied by jerky, purposeless movements of the arms or legs or, rarely, even the whole body. It usually begins while the patient is taking the drug, but rarely may begin shortly after the drug has been stopped. Occasionally it persists indefinitely, and no effective treatment has been found to date.

The incidence of tardive dyskinesia is difficult to ascertain because it may occur as part of the schizophrenic disease process as well as being a side effect of medication. A study of the records of over 600 patients admitted to an asylum in England between 1845 and 1890 found an "extraordinary prevalence of abnormal movements and postures.... Movement disorder, often equivalent to tardive dyskinesia, was noted in nearly one-third of schizophrenics." Most estimates of the incidence of tardive dyskinesia have assumed that all such cases are drug-related when in fact a substantial percentage are not. In a study of this problem aptly titled "Not All That Moves Is Tardive Dyskinesia," Khot and Wyatt concluded that the true incidence of drug-related tardive dyskinesia was under 20 percent. This also falls within the 10 to 20 percent range estimated by the American Psychiatric Association's 1980 task force on the subject.

Much current research is taking place in an attempt to identify which persons with schizophrenia are most likely to get tardive dyskinesia. It is clear that the older the person, the more susceptible he or she is. It is also clearly established that women are more susceptible than men and that patients with more affective symptoms (for example, depression or mania) are more susceptible. Many other risk factors are being investigated including ethnicity (higher in Jews, lower in Chinese), dose of medication, duration of medication, use of depot injectable medication, use of anticholinergic drugs, concurrent diabetes, concurrent alcohol or drug abuse, concurrent evidence of organic brain disease, and concurrent Parkinson-like symptoms, but none of them has yet been clearly established. There is also no firm evidence that any particular antipsychotic is more or less likely to cause tardive dyskinesia, with the exception of clozapine, which causes it rarely, if at all.

New information has become available on the course of tardive dyskinesia. Previously, most people believed that once the symptoms began they would almost always get worse if the person continued taking the antipsychotic medication. This put many individuals with schizophrenia into a cruel bind, needing the medication to remain well but not wishing to worsen the early symptoms of tardive dyskinesia. A recent ten year follow-up of 44 patients with tardive dyskinesia who remained on the same antipsychotic medication found that in 30 percent the tardive dyskinesia got worse, in 50 percent it remained the same, and in 20 percent the tardive dyskinesia actually improved. In another 10-year follow-up study it was reported that approximately five percent of existing cases of tardive dyskinesia disappeared each year *even while continuing to take the antipsychotic medications.*

According to Dr. Daniel Casey, a leading researcher on tardive dyskinesia, 20 patients out of every 100 with schizophrenia will get tardive dyskinesia; among these five patients will have their tardive dyskinesia completely disappear and five others will have at least a 50 percent improvement. Casey then added: "Of the 10 remaining TD [tardive dyskinesia] patients, almost all of them will have mild to moderate symptoms. Severe TD is a very uncommon syndrome which probably occurs in approximately 1 in 100 to 1 in 1,000 TD patients."

The best treatment for tardive dyskinesia is prevention by using antipsychotic drugs only when necessary. All patients taking these drugs should be watched for early signs such as tongue movements. The use of the Abnormal Involuntary Movement Scale (AIMS) is useful for measuring the progression of tardive dyskinesia. If a person appears to be developing tardive dyskinesia, serious consideration should be given to switching the person to clozapine. For fully developed cases of tardive dyskinesia there is no known effective treatment despite trials of levodopa, vitamin E, tetrabenazine, and many other drugs.

Neuroleptic Malignant Syndrome

While rare, this side effect of antipsychotic medication merits serious study. Its prevalence appears to be less than 1 in 500 patients; men are affected twice as often as women. It may occur at any time while taking antipsychotic drugs, even in a person who has been taking them for several years, but in most cases it begins within ten days of starting medication. The symptoms come on slowly over a period of one to three days and consist of rigidity of the muscles, fever, confusion or coma, pallor, sweating, and rapid heart rate. Laboratory tests show elevations of the white blood cell count and of the blood creatine phosphokinase level.

The precise mechanism causing the neuroleptic malignant syndrome is unknown, other than being a kind of toxic reaction to the drug. There is no evidence that one type of antipsychotic drug causes it more than another, and it has been documented as occurring with clozapine. Between 15 and 20 percent of its victims die of it, although this may now be reduced because there are specific drugs for treating it (dantrolene, bromocriptine), which appear to be effective. It is not yet clear what relationship the neuroleptic malignant syndrome has to malignant hyperthermia, a rare but potentially fatal allergic reaction to anesthetic agents used in medicine. The neuroleptic malignant syndrome may also appear similar to lethal catatonia, a very rare but often fatal development in some patients with schizophrenia, in which the person's temperature becomes extremely high. Lethal catatonia was clearly described before antipsychotic medications began to be used and is presumably a complication of the schizophrenia itself on the brain center controlling temperature regulation.

Clozapine

Clozapine, marketed as Clozaril, is a benzodiazepine and thus a member of the same chemical family as Valium, Halcion, Dalmane, Ativan, and Xanax. It is an important new antipsychotic but its introduction has been mired by the exorbitantly high price set by its manufacturer, the Sandoz Pharmaceutical Corporation. The high price and linkage of clozapine to a mandatory blood-monitoring system led 23 states to file suit against Sandoz in 1990; the suit was settled in 1992 when Sandoz agreed to a $20 million settlement to rectify the overcharges.

Clozapine has been acclaimed because at least one-third of individuals with schizophrenia who are treatment-resistant and who have not responded to other antipsychotics will show at least some improvement. In a few cases the improvement has been so dramatic that clozapine was featured in a *Time* magazine cover story in July 1992. The majority of patients who improve do so less dramatically and a substantial percentage show no improvement at all. The other major advantage of clozapine is that it rarely, if ever, causes tardive dyskinesia and so has become a first-choice drug for any individual who is showing signs of the condition.

Clozapine has been called an "atypical" antipsychotic because it is not thought to work primarily on the dopamine receptors in the brain. It is in fact a weak D2 blocker but a reasonably good D4 blocker. It is a good serotonin (5-HT2) blocker and also blocks norepinephrine, acetylcholine, and histamine receptors. It is, however, premature to label clozapine as "atypical" because we do not really know how it works or, for that matter, how the so-called "typical" antipsychotics work.

The most important side effect of clozapine is agranulocytosis, a decreased number of white blood cells. Since these cells are used by the body to fight infections, if their number drops too low the body can be overwhelmed quickly by an infection. Approximately one percent of persons will develop agranulocytosis while taking clozapine, and for that reason blood counts must be monitored. Women and older persons have a higher risk. Of all the people who will develop agranulocytosis on clozapine, it is known that 23 percent will do so by the end of the first month, 61 percent by the end of three months, and 70 percent by the end of six months. Blood counts must therefore be done every week initially to detect those individuals whose white blood cell count is falling; if a significant fall is noted then clozapine is stopped. In the United States blood counts continue to be done weekly indefinitely, although this policy was under review in 1994 and was expected to be changed. After the first six months counts are reduced to every two weeks in England and to monthly in Germany and Finland. A blood count home testing kit is under development in Canada that would simplify this weekly ritual for individuals taking the drug.

Despite blood monitoring, there were still eleven deaths in the United States from agranulocytosis from 1990 to 1993. Since approximately 60,000 individuals took clozapine during that period, the mortality rate was 1 in 5,500. Because of this risk, clozapine should not be considered to be a first-choice antipsychotic for individuals with schizophrenia but rather a second-choice antipsychotic for those who are treatment resistant and for those who are developing tardive dyskinesia.

In addition to agranulocytosis, clozapine has several other important side effects. Sedation (39 percent) and excess salivation (31 percent) are both common and can be quite troublesome. The sedation caused by clozapine can be minimized in some patients by adding methylphenidate. Weight gain appears to be at least as common as for other antipsychotics. In one study patients started on clozapine gained an average of 14 pounds in the first four months and in another study they gained an average of 17 pounds in the first six months; in the latter study three-quarters of the patients gained at least 10 pounds. Seizures are another side effect, occurring in three to five percent of all individuals taking clozapine and occurring more commonly with higher doses. Fast heart rate, dizziness, low blood pressure, constipation, and nausea and vomiting also may occur.

There is one other aspect of clozapine that is important but not yet well studied. Since clozapine is a benzodiazepine, it may produce an additive effect when given to individuals who are also taking other benzodiazepines such as Valium, Halcion, Dalmane, Ativan, and Xanax. Respiratory depression is one side effect of benzodiazepines, and a few cases of respiratory arrest and death have been described in individuals given clozapine who were also taking these other drugs. Therefore, starting a patient who is on other benzodiazepines on clozapine should only be done in an inpatient setting with careful monitoring of their blood pressure.

The fact that clozapine is a benzodiazepine also raises the question of whether withdrawal symptoms may occur if the drug is stopped suddenly after the person has taken it for several months. Most benzodiazepines do produce withdrawal symptoms if stopped quickly. As early as 1984 it was reported in Europe that clozapine could produce a marked increase in psychotic symptoms and suicidal ideation if it was suddenly stopped after several months. For this reason individuals being taken off clozapine should be tapered slowly, except in cases where agranulocytosis necessitates immediate cessation.

Risperidone

Risperidone, marketed as Risperadal, became available as a new antipsychotic in the United States early in 1994. It costs approximately $2,000 per patient per year and is thus much less expensive than clozapine. It is a strong blocker of serotonin (5-HT2) receptors and also D2 receptors and so, like clozapine, has been labeled as "atypical."

It is too early to assess the place of risperidone in the antipsychotic drug treatment of schizophrenia. Early use has been encouraging and has suggested that it is probably more effective than haloperidol against symptoms such as delusions and hallucinations and perhaps more effective against "negative" symptoms such as withdrawal, apathy, and blunted affect. Its relative effectiveness compared with clozapine is not yet known; in a preliminary trial reported in 1994 only one of ten patients who were tried on both drugs responded better on risperidone than on clozapine. It does not appear to cause agranulocytosis so blood monitoring is not necessary. It also causes less stiffness and tremor than haloperidol, but it is not yet known whether it can cause tardive dyskinesia. Side effects of risperidone include sedation, dry mouth, blurred vision, dizziness, and weight gain.

New and Experimental Antipsychotics

Between 1975 and 1990 there were virtually no new antipsychotic drugs introduced for the treatment of schizophrenia in the United States. The remarkable success of clozapine since 1990 has changed that picture dramatically and there are now many new antipsychotic drugs in various stages of development. Pharmaceutical companies increasingly realize the market potential for better drugs to treat this disease, and increased research funds from the National Institute of Mental Health, the National Alliance for Research on Schizophrenia and Depression, and foundations such as the Theodore and Vada Stanley Foundation and the Scottish Rite have opened up new neurochemical avenues for drug development. The newer drugs work on a variety of receptors, including D2 (e.g., raclopiride, amisulpiride), serotonin (5-HT2) (e.g., ritanserin), D2 plus 5-HT2 (e.g., olanzapine), D2 plus 5-HT2 plus alpha adrenergic (e.g., amperozide), and 5-HT (e.g., ondansetron), but in fact the relationship between such receptor blockade and the clinical efficacy of the drugs is not well understood.

Among these newer drugs are the following:

remoxipride: Closely related to sulpiride, which has been available in Europe for many years. Said to be more effective against "negative" symptoms and to cause less stiffness, tremor, and akathisia. Must be taken more than once a day. However, in late 1993 cases of fatal aplastic anemia were reported in some patients so clinical testing was stopped; if and when testing will be resumed was uncertain.

amisulpiride: Also related to sulpiride. Said to not cause much sedation.

raclopride: Also related to sulpiride. Said to cause less stiffness, tremor, and akathisia but must be taken more than once a day.

ritanserin: A potent serotonin receptor blocker but questionable potency as antipsychotic.

ondansetron: Blocks serotonin (5-HT3) receptors and appears to have relatively few side effects.

amperozide: Like clozapine it blocks both dopamine and serotonin receptors. Appears to cause less sedation.

clocapramine: Available in Europe and appears to not cause sedation. Side effects include stiffness, tremors, and probably tardive dyskinesia.

melperone: Also available in Europe and is related to haloperidol but also blocks serotonin receptors.

olanzapine: Blocks serotonin (5-HT2 and 5-HT1C), dopamine (D2, D4, D1), and muscarinic receptors. Currently undergoing clinical trials and as of early 1994 was considered by many researchers to be one of the most promising new drugs.

savoxepine: Receptor blockade similar to clozapine.

In addition to the above 10 new and experimental drugs there is a long list of others in various stages of development. Some are listed by name and other identification number. Any one of these could emerge as a major treatment advance for schizophrenia. These include:

- B-HT 920
- BMY 14802
- BROFARAMINE
- CLEBOPRIDE
- CP 88059
- ELTOPRAZINE
- EMONAPRIDE
- GEVOTROLINE
- ICI-204,636
- IDAZOXAN
- ISOFLOXYTHEPIN
- MANZIDOL
- MDL 100,907
- ORG 5222

- OXYPROTHEPINE
- PRAMIPEXOLE
- ROXINDOLE
- RWJ37796
- SDZDOD-647
- SEROQUEL
- SERTINDOLE
- SETOPERONE
- TERGURIDE
- TIOSPRIONE
- ZACOPRIDE
- ZATOSETRON
- ZETEPHINE
- ZOTEPINE

In evaluating claims of efficacy for these new drugs, it is important to keep in mind that some of the scientists making the claims have received substantial support and/or travel expenses from the pharmaceutical companies that make the drugs. Families, consumers, and mental illness professionals should therefore be skeptical of initial claims for new drugs until these claims have been substantiated by independent clinicians who do not have a vested interest in the drugs' success.

Interactions of antipsychotics with other drugs

Antipsychotic medications not only may cause side effects by themselves but may interact with other drugs in the body as well. Physicians prescribing antipsychotic medications and individuals taking them should be aware of interactions which have been reported to occur between antipsychotics and other drugs. Many of these are rare. They do not necessarily mean that the two drugs should not be given at the same time, but only that caution should be used. The majority of interactions reported to date are for the phenothiazines, which have been in use the longest; it should be assumed that any antipsychotic drug may cause such reactions until proven otherwise.

Antipsychotic drug may interact with	Causing
alcohol	impaired motor coordination
ammonium chloride	antipsychotic to be less effective
amphetamines	increased psychotic symptoms
anesthetics	severe hypotension
antacids	antipsychotic to be less effective
antidepressants	severe drowsiness
antihistamines	severe drowsiness
barbiturates	severe drowsiness
benzodiazepines	severe drowsiness
beta blockers	increased antipsychotic blood level
bethanidine	bethanidine to be less effective
clonidine	clonidine to be less effective
coumarin	increased clotting time
debrisoquine	debrisoquine to be less effective

Antipsychotic drug may interact with	Causing
epinephrine	hypotension
fluoxetine (Prozac)	increased tremors and stiffness
griseofulvin	antipsychotic to be less effective
guanadrel	guanadrel to be ineffective
guanethidine	guanethidine to be ineffective
insulin	increased need for insulin
isoniazid	liver problems, mental changes
levodopa	levodopa to be less effective
MAO inhibitors	hypotension
narcotics (e.g., codeine)	severe drowsiness

There are also a few reactions that appear to be specific to certain antipsychotics:

Antipsychotic	May interact with	Causing
clozapine	benzodiazopines	respiratory arrest
fluphenazine	vitamin C	fluphenazine to be less effective
haloperidol	indomethacin (Indocin)	severe drowsiness
haloperidol	methyldopa (Aldomet)	mental changes
perphenazine (Trilafon)	disulfiram (Antabuse)	perphenazine to be less effective
thioridazine	quinidine	heart problems
thioridazine	phenylpropanolamine	heart problems

OTHER DRUGS USED TO TREAT SCHIZOPHRENIA

In addition to the antipsychotic drugs, a variety of other drugs have been used to treat schizophrenia. Some of these, such as the anticholinergics and lithium, are used frequently, whereas others, such as valproic acid or verapamil, are used only in unusual cases or in patients who do not respond to the antipsychotics. Research studies on these drugs are surprisingly few in number, as was noted in a recent review: "One cannot help being struck by how relatively small the literature is on adjunctive and alternative somatic treatments in neuroleptic-resistant patients with schizophrenia, given the magnitude of the problem."

Anticholinergics

The anticholinergics are a class of drugs which include benztropine (Cogentin), biperiden (Akineton), procyclidine (Kemadrin), and tri-hexyphenidyl (Artane) among others. They have been used in schizo-phrenia since shortly after the antipsychotic drugs were introduced, because of the known ability of anticholinergics to block dystonic reac- tions. They are also used to treat tremors and akathisia caused by antipsychotic drugs.

For many years it was considered good practice to withhold anti-cholinergic drugs until side effects actually appeared. More recently it has become accepted practice to use them prophylactically, especially in patients who are younger and/or male (in whom dystonic reactions are more common) or who are paranoid (and in whom a dystonic reac-tion would be construed as "proof" that the doctor was trying to poison him or her). One study suggests that giving anticholinergics for seven days to all patients being started on antipsychotic drugs has many more benefits than risks.

The use of long-term anticholinergics in schizophrenia, concurrent with antipsychotics, continues to be controversial. On the one hand, certain psychiatrists claim that anticholinergics do more than simply block side effects and may *enhance* the effect of antipsychotic medica-tion in many patients. On the other hand, some psychiatrists are con-vinced that the anticholinergics *decrease* the effect of antipsychotic medication but may increase the chances of getting tardive dyskinesia.

Anticholinergic drugs may interact with amantadine (Symmetrel) to cause confusion and hallucination, so the two should be used cau-tiously together. They may also decrease the effectiveness of cimeti-dine (Tagamet) used to heal ulcers. There have been reported instances of occasional patients with schizophrenia getting a mild "high" from anticholinergics; I had one patient who was known in every emergency room in the city of Washington for his ability to mimic the symptoms of an acute dystonic reaction in his nightly quests for an injection of benztropine (Cogentin).

Lithium

Lithium is the most useful drug to be introduced to psychiatry since the antipsychotics were discovered in the early 1950s. In fact, lithium was originally discovered even earlier—by Dr. John Cade in Australia in 1948—but for a variety of reasons it was not introduced to the United States until the 1970s. It rapidly became a mainstay of treatment and prevention for manic-depressive psychosis, and in recent years has been found effective in many patients with schizophrenia as well.

Like the antipsychotics, precisely how lithium works is as yet unknown; its effectiveness may be related to its ability to control the transport of substances across the cell membrane. What is clear is that, when used in conjunction with an antipsychotic, lithium is effective in decreasing symptoms such as hallucinations, delusional thinking, and thought disorders in perhaps one-third of patients with schizophrenia and that it often works when antipsychotics by themselves have failed. Patients with schizophrenia should not be categorized as "treatment unresponsive" until they have been given a trial on lithium with an antipsychotic.

Lithium is available as tablets or liquid. Previously it was thought that lithium must be given in divided doses two or three times a day, but recent studies have suggested that it can be given once daily or even every other day. Before starting lithium, the patient should have a blood test for kidney and thyroid function (usually a TSH and creatinine), and women should certainly have a pregnancy test; lithium may harm the fetus and should not be given in the first 3 months of pregnancy except in very unusual circumstances. Women on lithium should also bottle-feed rather than breast-feed their babies.

Lithium differs from the antipsychotic drugs in being potentially much more dangerous if taken in overdose. For this reason blood must be drawn for lithium level testing initially every few days, then in decreasing frequency as the person becomes stabilized on the drug. Blood tests should also be done approximately every six to twelve months to check thyroid and kidney function. The therapeutic blood level of lithium is 0.6–1.2 meq (milliequivalents) per liter, although a few patients can be maintained successfully in the 0.4–0.6 meq range and a few require a 1.2–1.6 meq range to be effective. To get a therapeutic blood level may require 2 or 3 tablets a day in one patient, 6 or 8 tablets in another. Older patients need lower doses.

Side effects of lithium in a normal dose range may include thirst, frequent urination, a tremor of the fingers or hands, diarrhea, fluid retention (edema) of the hands or lower legs, weight gain, altered hair texture, acne, or the worsening of psoriasis if the person has it. In my experience the two most troublesome side effects are tremor and frequent urination, especially at night. If the person is clearly responding to the lithium, then the tremor can often be treated using beta blocker drugs (e.g., propranolol) and the frequent urination with amiloride or other diuretics; the use of diuretics with lithium, however, may be risky in some cases and should be done only by physicians who are very familiar with these drugs.

If the lithium level goes too high, it can be a serious, even life-threatening, situation. Symptoms of toxicity include vomiting, diarrhea, weakness, confusion, stupor, staggering, incoordination, slurred speech, dizziness, blurred vision, convulsions, and coma. Lithium should *never* be given to a patient with any of these symptoms without first checking with a doctor. Even if the person has only vomiting or diarrhea from a suspected gastrointestinal upset, stop the lithium until the person is better. Lithium levels also tend to rise in very hot weather when the person is sweating heavily, and fluid intake should be increased.

Lithium interacts unfavorably with many other drugs. There has even been controversy regarding the advisability of using lithium with antipsychotic drugs, such as is useful in schizophrenia, because of rare reports of serious toxicity between lithium and haloperidol. The general consensus is that using lithium in combination with antipsychotic drugs is safe as long as a physician is involved in following the patient. Many other drugs interact with lithium by increasing the lithium blood level and thus increasing the chances of lithium toxicity. These drugs include amiloride, aspirin, captopril, clonazepam, diclofenac, diltiazem, enalapril, fluoxetine (Prozac), furosemide, ibuprofen, indomethacin, ketamine, lisinopril, mazindol, methyldopa, metronidazole, naproxen, phenylbutazone, piroxicam, spectinomycin, sulindac, thiazide diuretics (e.g., hydrochlorthiazide and others), tetracycline, and zomepirac.

Benzodiazepines

With the recent success of clozapine, a member of the benzodiazepine family, there has been renewed interest in the possible use of these drugs to treat schizophrenia. Diazepam (Valium), lorazepam (Ativan), alprazolam, estazolam, and clonazepam (Klonopin) have all been studied. Overall the studies suggest that a small number of patients with schizophrenia get some symptom improvement from benzodiazepine treatment but the number of such patients is not large. In addition, the benzodiazepines have the disadvantage of being addicting if taken for several months and of causing withdrawal symptoms such as seizures if stopped abruptly.

Antidepressants

Individuals with schizophrenia often have depression that may be part of their illness or a reaction to their illness. It is seen especially frequently in those cases that fall within the schizoaffective clinical spectrum. The symptoms of depression may be confused with other symptoms of schizophrenia, such as withdrawal and anergia, and the depression may make all the symptoms of schizophrenia seem more severe. The relatively high incidence of depression in schizophrenia is attested to by the fact that at least 10 percent of individuals with schizophrenia commit suicide.

When depression occurs in schizophrenia it should be treated with antidepressant drugs. The major types of antidepressants are the tricyclics, the MAO inhibitors, and the newer serotonin reuptake inhibitors such as fluoxetine (Prozac), sertraline (Zoloft), and paroxetine (Paxil). All of these have been used to successfully treat depression in schizophrenia. However, each type of antidepressant has side effects and each may interact with antipsychotic medications so they should be prescribed under the supervision of physicians who are knowledgeable in their use.

Carbamazepine

Carbamazepine (Tegretol) is widely used to treat some forms of epilepsy. In recent years it has also been found to be effective in treating manic-depressive illness (bipolar disorder), either in place of, or in conjunction with, lithium. It has been used as an ancillary drug to treat schizophrenia with modest results reported, especially for reducing aggression, violence, and paranoia. It should be considered as an ancillary drug for any patient with schizophrenia who has an abnormal electroencephalograph (EEG). There is some evidence that it may decrease the effectiveness of haloperidol when both drugs are taken simultaneously. One of carbamazepine's most serious side effects is to cause agranulocytosis, and for this reason it should not be given with clozapine which also may cause agranulocytosis.

Others

A variety of other drugs have been tried for treating schizophrenia, including apomorphine, baclofen, beta blockers such as propranolol and nadolol, bromocriptine, calcium channel blockers such as verapamil, cholecystokinin, clonidine, methadone, naloxone, naltrexone, reserpine, thyroid-releasing hormone, and valproic acid. Of these, clonidine, propranolol, and reserpine have shown some promise and may be worthwhile trying on patients who are truly treatment-resistant and on whom all else has failed.

COST OF MEDICATIONS AND USE OF GENERICS

Medications used to treat schizophrenia run a wide range in cost, from inexpensive drugs like lithium to very expensive drugs like clozapine. A 1985 study of the cost of antipsychotic drugs prescribed for outpatients (*not* including those in hospitals) calculated the total annual cost at $263 million. The breakdown by type of drug was phenothiazines $147 million, haloperidol $65 million, thiothixene $26 million, loxapine $10 million, molindone $1 million, and lithium $14 million. Since that time the increase in drug prices and additional costs of clozapine have increased that total cost substantially.

Many of us have been very critical of pharmaceutical companies for the high costs of drugs and the excess profits of the industry. For example, during 1991, when Eli Lilly was charging approximately $40 per month for fluoxetine (Prozac), its Chief Executive Officer was paid $2.8 million. During the same year Squibb Bristol-Myers was increasing the costs of fluphenazine (Prolixin) while its Chief Executive Officer was receiving $12.7 million in compensation. The most egregious example of overpricing of an antipsychotic drug has been the Sandoz Corporation's pricing of clozapine (Clozaril) at $6,000 per patient per year, not including blood tests, at the same time as they were selling Clozaril in European countries for less than $2,000 per patient per year. This unnecessarily high cost has made the drug unavailable to many severely ill individuals who need it.

There are some things that families and consumers can do to reduce the cost of medications. They include:

A. Use generic drugs when available. Despite recent scandals involving a few generic drug companies, most generic drugs are equivalent to their brandname counterparts and are usually much less expensive. In 1989 the U.S. Food and Drug Administration tested 2,500 samples of various generic drugs and found that only 1.1 percent of them did not conform to production quality specifications. One should, however, always be alert for clinical changes in a person whenever the person is switching from a brandname to a generic or from one generic to another because the clinical change may indicate that the new drug is not as effective. The majority of antipsychotic drugs are available as generics, including chlorpromazine, thioridazine, fluphenazine, and haloperidol. The Food and Drug Administration publishes a listing of approved generic drugs called *Approved Drug Products With Therapeutic Equivalence Evaluations.*

B. Use the largest-size tablet available, consistent with the dose needed. For example, a 20 mg. tablet of Haldol costs only slightly more than a 10 mg. tablet. A patient on Haldol 20 mg. per day who takes the daily dosage as two 10 mg. tablets will be paying almost twice as much as the patient taking a single 20 mg. tablet.

C. Consistent with the above, give all antipsychotic medication at a single dose at bedtime. Except in unusual instances, it is not necessary to take antipsychotic medication more than once a day; for example, it is just as effective to take fluphenazine 30 mg. at bedtime, as it is to take 10 mg. three times a day. It used to be thought that lithium had to be given in divided doses two or three times a day, but recent research suggests that lithium, like the antipsychotics, can be given once a day. Once-a-day dosing makes it easier for the patient and family and so improves compliance.

D. Shop around for the best price, since pharmacies vary so widely. Buy the largest quantity of drugs possible at one time since they are less expensive in larger numbers. Families using the same medication may even want to band together and negotiate a joint price with one pharmacy such as is done by food-buying cooperatives.

NONDRUG TREATMENTS OF SCHIZOPHRENIA

Medications are not only the treatment of choice for schizophrenia, they are virtually the only effective treatment. Of nondrug treatments that have been tried, only electroconvulsive therapy (ECT) has proven to be effective. Older nondrug treatments such as psychosurgery and hemodialysis are no longer used.

Electroconvulsive Therapy (ECT)

Electroconvulsive therapy (ECT) has a modest but definite role to play in the treatment of schizophrenia despite the adverse publicity it has received. It is a favorite whipping boy for Scientologists and antipsychiatry advocates and was even banned from use in Berkeley, California, in 1982 by a local referendum. In European countries it has been used more widely for the treatment of schizophrenia than in the United States.

Indications for use of ECT in schizophrenia were recently summarized in the *New England Journal of Medicine* as being "when the onset is acute and confusion and mood disturbance are present; and catatonia from almost any underlying cause." It may also be useful in some treatment-resistant cases, although it should be used in conjunction with an antipsychotic in such cases. Modern ECT is done using unilateral electrodes over the nondominant lobe to minimize memory loss. Some memory loss may nevertheless occur and is the major side effect of the procedure. Despite Scientologist claims to the contrary, there is no evidence that ECT causes any damage to the brain. Some patients respond to as few as 12 ECT treatments, whereas others need 20 or more. For individuals who respond well to ECT but rapidly relapse, it is possible to use monthly maintenance treatments.

Diet

Throughout this century various kinds of diets have been proposed as being helpful in the treatment of schizophrenia. The diet that has been researched most extensively is a gluten-free diet that contains no milk or meat. Unfortunately, most of the studies were done with small samples and so the results have been statistically inconclusive. The fact that only a small percentage of patients with schizophrenia may theoretically be improved by such dicts makes research very difficult because very large numbers of patients would have to be used in order to demonstrate a statistical difference. Diets emphasizing various vitamins have also been advocated. In 1990 a study was published showing significant clinical improvement in 17 individuals with schizophrenia who were given folic acid (vitamin B12) supplements for six months. To date this study has not been replicated.

At this time there is no solid data supporting the use of any particular diet to treat schizophrenia. Good eating habits and a healthy diet will help people with schizophrenia to feel better just as they will help anybody to feel better.

RECOMMENDED FURTHER READING

Baldessarini, R. J. *Chemotherapy in Psychiatry: Principles and Practice.* Cambridge, MA: Harvard University Press, 1985.

Biological Therapies in Psychiatry. Subscriptions from PSG, Inc., 545 Great Rd., Littleton, MA 01460. A monthly newsletter which provides accurate and current assessments of medications for schizophrenic patients and is the easiest way to stay up-to-date in this rapidly changing area.

Bouricius, J. K. *Psychoactive Drugs and Their Effects on Mentally Ill Persons.* Arlington, VA: National Alliance for the Mentally Ill, 1989.

Gorman, J. M. *The Essential Guide to Psychiatric Drugs.* New York: St. Martin's Press, 1990.

Lickey, M. E., and B. Gordon. *Medicine and Mental Illness.* New York: W. H. Freeman, 1991.

Yudofsky, S. C., R. E. Hales, and T. Ferguson. *What You Need to Know about Psychiatric Drugs.* New York: Ballantine Books, 1991.

8

THE REHABILITATION OF SCHIZOPHRENIA

Expecting the chronically ill patient to use the current mental health system is like expecting a paraplegic to use stairs.

J. Halpern et al.,
The Illness of Deinstitutionalization, 1978

The basic concept that underlies the rehabilitation of schizophrenia was clearly articulated by Dr. Werner M. Mendel, a psychiatrist who spent over 40 years treating patients with this disease in both the private and the public sector. In his book, *Treating Schizophrenia,* Mendel likens an individual with schizophrenia to an individual with a physical disability:

> If, for example, someone has a paralyzed right arm that cannot be fixed, we then provide her with a brace to help with function. We may modify her car so that she can drive and work the controls with only one hand. We may retrain her to use her left hand for all the things she used to do with her paralyzed right hand. We may also give her psychological support for accepting herself with the defect and help her focus on what she can do rather than what she cannot do.

Some individuals, of course, have more severe disabilities than others and a well-planned rehabilitation system must make provisions for those at all levels.

MEDICATION AND COUNSELING

Almost all individuals with schizophrenia need to continue taking antipsychotic medication for many years. These medications may be obtained through outpatient psychiatric services that include private psychiatrists, community mental health centers (CMHCs), or outpatient clinics attached to public, community, or Veterans Administration hospitals. Many individuals with schizophrenia have insight into their illness and recognize their need to take medication to control their symptoms. Others, however, have impaired insight and will only take medications if bribed or coerced to do so (see chapter 9, Medication Noncompliance).

There are three important principles that determine the quality of outpatient psychiatric services:

Competency of the Professionals

Psychiatrists, psychologists, social workers, and psychiatric nurses run a very broad spectrum of competency. Most training programs, unfortunately, continue to train these professionals to be mental *health* professionals rather than mental *illness* professionals. There are a handful of good programs in which the professionals are being well-trained to treat mental illness, but such programs stand out as exceptions rather than the rule.

Targeting the Seriously Mentally Ill as First Priority

Psychiatric outpatient services are obviously a finite resource for an almost infinite series of demands which may be placed upon such services. Married couples having problems, poor or minority groups with no jobs and low self-esteem, elderly persons who are lonely, and children underachieving in school because of emotional problems are only a few of the groups which may view local psychiatric outpatient services as a primary solution to their problems. The needs of these groups are both worthy and compelling, yet if psychiatric resources are utilized for them in large numbers, soon no resources are left for the seriously mentally ill. This is precisely what has happened in many CMHCs in the United States. It is, in short, a choice between promoting "mental health" or treating mental illness.

The allocation of public psychiatric resources is ultimately an ethical question. Which group is most worthy? Which group needs the services more? Which group can utilize the services best? What is the benefit to society of providing psychiatric services to each group? Dr. J. R. Elpers, in a discussion of this question, argued that the seriously mentally ill have fewer alternative resources and are also sicker, and on these grounds require first priority. What has become abundantly clear in recent years is that state programs which have targeted the seriously mentally ill as having priority for psychiatric services have much better programs than states which have not done so.

Continuity of Care

Although frequently given lip service, continuity of care for individuals with schizophrenia is rarely achieved in the United States. Sadly typical is an appalling lack of continuity such as was offered to Sylvia Frumkin, the focus of Susan Sheehan's *Is There No Place on Earth for Me?*, who over an 18-year period had 27 separate admissions to 8 different hospitals with a total of 45 changes in treatment settings.

It may well be that the key element in continuity of care is continuity of the caregiver. In other words, a single individual or team should be responsible for the psychiatric care of a person with serious mental illness, no matter where that person goes within a defined geographic area. A description of such an arrangement was provided by Dr. Mary Ann Test, one of the nation's acknowledged leaders on the organization of psychiatric services, who defined continuity of caregiver as taking "responsibility for seeing to it that a chronically mentally ill person's needs are met. . . . The team members do not necessarily meet all the client's needs themselves (they may involve other persons or agencies). However they never transfer this obligation to someone else. The buck stops with the team . . . the team remains responsible for the client no matter what his or her behavior is. This fixed point of responsibility means that the client always has a consistent resource." Elsewhere I have called such an arrangement "continuous treatment teams."

Continuity of caregivers is logical in theory, considering the needs of patients. People with serious mental illness, especially schizophrenia, often have great difficulties in establishing human relationships and to expect them to transfer their trust from one treatment team to another is exceedingly unrealistic. Continuity of caregivers also has many advantages from the point of view of mental health professionals, allowing them to get to know patients in depth, assessing their medication history and potentials for rehabilitation, and working with their family. Continuity of caregivers is nicely exemplified by continuous treatment teams that are patterned after the widely praised PACT (Program of Assertive Community Treatment) in Madison, WI. Continuous treatment teams have been widely used in Wisconsin, Michigan, Rhode Island, New Hampshire, and Delaware and are being implemented in Tennessee and Idaho. Exemplary programs following the PACT model are shown on the map under "Examples of Good Services" and listed in Appendix C.

Another part of outpatient psychiatric services is counseling and supportive "psychotherapy," which can be helpful for individuals with schizophrenia, especially if the person providing these services remains constant for long periods of time. I put the term "psychotherapy" in quotations to differentiate it clearly from insight-oriented psychotherapy, discussed in chapter 6, which for schizophrenia sufferers is a discredited and even harmful mode of treatment.

Supportive "psychotherapy," on the other hand, may provide a patient with friendship, encouragement, practical advice such as access to community resources or how to develop a more active social life, vocational counseling, suggestions for minimizing friction with family members, and, above all, hope that the person's life may be improved. Discussions focus on the here-and-now, not the past, and on problems of living encountered by the patient as he or she tries to meet the exigencies of life, despite a handicapping brain disease. The opening approach I take with my own patients is something like the following: "Look, I'm sorry you have this lousy brain disease, which is not your fault, but let's see what you can do to live better with it." It is exactly the same approach which one might take for a patient with multiple sclerosis, polio, chronic kidney disease, severe diabetes, or any other long-term disease.

The person who provides counseling or supportive "psychotherapy" can be the physician who is overseeing the medication or it can be any other mental illness professional or paraprofessional, such as consumers, who are on the care team. "Case manager" has become a popular term in recent years, although it is not clear to me how a case manager's job differs from what psychiatrists, psychologists, social workers, and psychiatric nurses are supposed to have been doing all along. The term "case manager" has the added disadvantage of implying that individuals with schizophrenia are "cases" who need to be "managed," when in fact a collaborative relationship between patient and mental illness professional is the ideal. An additional disadvantage of the term is that "case manager" is a term also used by insurance companies to manage insurance benefits. Thus it is not uncommon to have an insurance company's case manager telling the mental health center's case manager what reimbursements will be allowed. Not surprisingly this is frequently confusing to patients and their families.

Case managers on mental health teams may play a variety of roles. They may be the person's primary counselor, provide education about the illness, assist with applying for benefits and housing, provide transportation for clinic appointments, and make arrangements for rehabilitation programs. The effectiveness of a case manager depends in part on the case manager's personality characteristics but also on the availability of the benefits and programs that are available. All too often in the United States case managers are employed by mental health programs that offer meager housing, rehabilitation programs, or other benefits, and they are "managers" in name only.

The frequency of meetings between the person with schizophrenia and the counselor may vary from once a week or more often to once a year. Regarding the last, Dr. Werner M. Mendel once related the story of a man whose schizophrenia was in good remission but who always carried a small vial of antipsychotic medication because the rattling of the pills was reassuring to him. After about a year the pills became powder and rattling stopped and the man would return to Dr. Mendel for a refill.

There is scientific evidence that such a supportive relationship, when it is used *in addition to drug therapy,* is helpful in reducing the rehospitalization rate for schizophrenia. In one study patients were followed for one year after release from the hospital and offered one of four modes of follow-up: (1) placebo alone (a placebo is an inert or dummy medication with no physiological action), (2) placebo plus supportive "psychotherapy," (3) drugs alone, and (4) drugs plus supportive "psychotherapy." At the end of the year the rehospitalization rates were:

Treatment	Percentage of Patients Hospitalized
Placebo alone	72
Placebo plus "psychotherapy"	63
Drugs alone	33
Drugs plus "psychotherapy"	26

The "psychotherapy" used in this study included social services and vocational counseling provided by someone who was predictably available to the patients. The results suggest again that drugs are the single most important element in preventing rehospitalization but that a supportive relationship provides a measure of additional improvement.

In recent years much more emphasis has been placed on educating patients about their illness. This can be done in a variety of formats, such as the Skills Training Modules developed by Dr. Robert P. Liberman and his colleagues at UCLA and Camarillo State Hospital in California. Other similar programs are listed in Appendix C.

MONEY, FOOD, AND HOUSING

For almost two centuries, most individuals with schizophrenia were locked away in state psychiatric hospitals, usually for many years at a time. If they got out at all it was usually to live with their families. It was not until the advent of deinstitutionalization that money, food, and housing became major problems for the hundreds of thousands of individuals who were released from the hospitals.

Some persons with schizophrenia can work part-time or full-time and are self-supporting. The majority, however, must rely on their families or two government programs, Supplemental Security Income (SSI), and Social Security Disability Insurance (SSDI), for the money to pay for their food and housing.

SSI, a program to provide income for needy aged, blind, and disabled persons, is administered by the Social Security Administration. It defines disability as "an inability to engage in any substantial gainful activity by reason of any medically determined physical or mental impairment which . . . has lasted, or can be expected to last, for a continuous period of not less than twelve months." SSDI is a similar operation, except that to be eligible the person must have worked prior to becoming ill and accumulated sufficient credit under Social Security.

Benefits from both programs vary; SSDI functions according to how long the person had worked before becoming ill, while SSI varies from state to state depending upon how much that state supplements the federal SSI payment. Alaska, California, Connecticut, Massachusetts, and Wisconsin have been the most generous states in supplementing federal SSI benefits, whereas approximately half of all states do not supplement it at all. SSDI and SSI are the most important sources of financial support for individuals with schizophrenia in the United States. In 1991 a total of 731,500 people were receiving SSDI because of mental impairment and 596,800 more were receiving SSI for the same reason. These 1,328,300 people were 22 percent of all recipients of SSDI and SSI. It is not known what percentage of the 1,328,300 had a diagnosis of schizophrenia but it is almost certainly more than half.

During the early 1980s considerable public attention focused on the SSI and SSDI programs when officials in the Reagan administration decided to tighten the criteria for eligibility for such payments. In 1981 and 1982 it was estimated that almost one-half million disabled persons were dropped from the program, including many persons with schizophrenia. Court challenges to these changes followed, and in 1986 the U.S. Supreme Court ruled in favor of the disabled, and the majority of those who had been cut off the SSI and SSDI programs were reinstated.

Applications to establish disability and receive SSI funds should be made at the local Social Security office. The person's assets and other income are taken into consideration in computing eligibility. If he or she has savings worth more than $2,000 he may not be eligible; in computing assets, a home and basic household goods do not count toward the $2,000. Income from a job may also reduce the amount of the SSI payment. Thus a person with schizophrenia who is trying to go back to work must compute work income carefully to be certain that this income offsets the loss of SSI benefits. SSDI is more liberal in allowing individuals to work part-time before benefits are reduced.

The application for SSI is evaluated by a team consisting of a disability examiner and a physician; they may request additional medical information or even request an examination of the applicant in selected cases. In evaluating the application they pay special attention to evidence of a restriction of daily activities and interests, deterioration in personal habits, marked impairment in relating to other people, and the inability to concentrate and carry out instructions necessary to hold a job. Assessing eligibility for SSI is necessarily a subjective task, and studies have reported disagreement among SSI reviewers as much as 50 percent of the time.

If the applicant is denied SSI, he/she has the right to appeal. This must be done within sixty days of the denial, and additional evidence of disability can be included at that time. The initial reconsideration of the appeal occurs in the local Social Security office and results in approval only 15 percent of the time. However, the applicant may appeal again, and this time the hearing is before an administrative law judge of the Bureau of Hearings and Appeals of the U.S. Department of Health and Human Services. At this level 58 percent of appeals were approved in 1980. Further appeals are possible to a Department of Health and Human Services appeals council and then to a U.S. district court. It is clear that persistence in pressing a legitimate claim for SSI benefits will result in success most of the time.

People with schizophrenia usually require assistance with SSI applications and, when necessary, with the appeals processes. Social workers who are doing these on a regular basis are often very helpful, especially in ensuring that the correct clinical information is included so that the person's degree of disability can be assessed fairly. Persons applying for SSI for psychiatric disability for the first time would be wise to utilize the services of a knowledgeable social worker. Application forms and appeals processes are confusing even for persons whose brains are working perfectly; to a person with schizophrenia they must appear completely Kafkaesque.

SSI payments, but not SSDI payments, are reduced when the disabled recipient lives with his/her family. In theory this takes account of the room and board the person receives, but in fact it penalizes people with schizophrenia for living at home. Many families resent this discriminatory living aspect of the SSI program and claim that they have expenses for the person just as surely as a boarding house operator does. SSI payments are also stopped if a person is hospitalized for more than ninety days. A portion of the SSI monthly payment is intended for the disabled person to use as spending money for clothes, transportation, laundry, and entertainment. The amount of spending money varies by state.

It is important for persons with schizophrenia to establish eligibility for SSI benefits if they can. Even if they have other income, thereby reducing the monthly SSI check to a very small amount, it is still worthwhile. The reason is that eligibility for SSI may also establish eligibility for several other assistance programs which can be worth much more than the SSI benefits by themselves. Such programs include Medicaid, vocational rehabilitation services, food stamps, and some housing and rental assistance programs of the Department of Housing and Urban Development. In some states, eligibility for SSI automatically confers eligibility for the other programs, while in other states a separate application must be submitted.

Individuals with schizophrenia who do not receive support from their families or from the SSI and SSDI programs must rely on other income. Many of them, especially those living in public shelters, utilize public assistance or welfare checks. Individuals who were in the military at the time they first became ill often qualify for disability payments from the Veterans Administration; these are often very generous and may total over $2,000 a month when all benefits are included.

Food stamps are another supplementary source of support for persons with schizophrenia and are underutilized. To be eligible a person must have an income below the poverty level; this level includes many or most persons with schizophrenia. The amount of food stamps a person can receive varies by state and with income. It also varies with the cost of food and so has been rising as food prices have been rising. Food stamps can be obtained through local welfare or social services offices.

Housing for individuals with schizophrenia includes facilities with varying degrees of supervision, independent living, and living at home.

Professional Supervision

This type of housing has professionally trained persons who provide supervision for most or all of the 24-hour day. It includes crisis houses, halfway houses, quarter-way houses, and similar facilities. An excellent description of one such home can be found in Michael Winerip's 1994 book, *9 Highland Road*.

Nonprofessional Supervision

These facilities have a supervisor in residence, part or all of the time, but the supervisor has no training. These include foster homes, board-and-care homes, boarding houses, group homes, congregate care homes, and similar facilities which go by different names in different locales.

Intermittent Supervision

These residences include apartments and group homes set up for persons with schizophrenia to live basically on their own. Usually a case manager or other mental health professional stops by periodically (e.g., once a week) to make certain that there are no major problems.

The quality of supervised housing for persons with schizophrenia varies widely. On one end of the spectrum are small foster homes where each patient has a room, the food is adequate, and the foster home sponsors watch over and worry about their charges as if they were their own children. A larger version of this may be a renovated hotel where the manager hires staff which organizes social activities for the residents, checks to be sure they are taking their medicine, reminds them of dentist appointments, and helps them fill out applications for food stamps.

But at the other extreme are foster homes with sponsors who provide insufficient heat, blankets, and food, steal the patients' meager funds, use them as cheap labor, and sometimes even rape them or pimp for them. The larger versions of these homes are old hotels that provide no services other than a rundown room and perform similar kinds of exploitation.

Supervision in many homes for released psychiatric patients often exists on paper only. In a group home in Baltimore, which was licensed as a "graduated independent living program" with 24-hour supervision, the staff failed to discover a young diabetic until three days after he had died in his room. And in New York City "the police found the decaying corpse of a former patient lying undisturbed in one home inhabited by six other residents."

Because the living facilities are so poor in many places, the professionals in charge of discharging patients from state hospitals are frequently caught in an ethical dilemma. Is the patient really better off in the community than in the hospital? Are the living conditions and exposure to potential victimization really an improvement? I am always surprised to find how many released patients with schizophrenia express satisfaction with their living conditions in the community when I know how shoddy the living conditions are. In one study of patients living in board-and-care homes in Los Angeles, 40 percent claimed to be content or reasonably content. I suspect the contentment is in comparison to being back in the hospital or having to live in public shelters or on the streets.

What are the common denominators of good supervised housing for patients living in the community? There are four characteristics which can be identified. First, the people living there are treated with dignity and warmth, not simply as sources of income. Second, the best housing appears to set a maximum of ten to twelve persons living in a single facility. Boarding homes or congregate care homes for 50, 100, or even more released patients almost invariably become mental hospital wards called by another name; this is transinstitutionalization rather than deinstitutionalization.

Third, good community housing for psychiatric patients exists in a coordinated continuum whereby a person can be moved to a residence with more or less supervision depending on the needs of the person. Because schizophrenia is a disease of remissions and relapses, it is unrealistic to expect a patient to remain in the same kind of facility indefinitely.

Finally, community housing for patients with schizophrenia is most useful where it is integrated with other activities of the patients. An excellent example of this principle is the Fairweather Lodges, in which patients live together and contract for jobs as a group. Such facilities have been deemed to be very successful where they have been tried.

A practical problem that frequently arises with community housing for psychiatric patients is the issue of zoning and community resistance to such housing. Everybody applauds the placement of patients in the community, it is said, as long as the placement is not in their neighborhood. In some towns and cities in the United States, local fights over this issue have been very bitter. There have now been forty studies done on the effect of residential group homes for the mentally ill and mentally retarded on the surrounding neighborhood. A review of these studies found that "the presence of group homes in all the areas studied has *not* lowered property values or increased turnover, *not* increased crime, *not* changed the character of the neighborhood." Persons with schizophrenia in fact make very good neighbors. This assumes, of course, that they are being followed for their illness and supervised for medication by responsible mental illness professionals.

Independent Living

A large and growing number of individuals with schizophrenia live independently, either by themselves or with other people. In recent years this has been referred to as supported housing, implying that the mental illness professionals will support the choice of housing made by the consumers. Independent living may run a wide range in quality from rundown SROs (single-room-occupancy hotels) to nicely furnished apartments or homes. Some individuals with schizophrenia, especially those with limited insight into their illness, cannot live independently.

Living at Home

A large number of individuals with schizophrenia live at home or with relatives. For some patients and their families this may be a perfectly satisfactory arrangement and cause minimal problems. For many others, however, living at home is quite unsatisfactory and this is especially true for men. This is not surprising since most grown individuals who do not have schizophrenia also encounter problems living at home. For those who do live at home, some suggested rules are discussed in chapter 10.

EMPLOYMENT

In their interest in working, people with schizophrenia extend over the same broad range as persons without schizophrenia. At one end of the spectrum are individuals who will do anything to work and will often continue working even when not being paid; individuals at the other end will do anything to avoid work. The only difference in work attitudes between persons with and without schizophrenia is that those with the disorder often have problems working closely with other people, thereby making work more difficult for them.

A large number of persons with schizophrenia have residual disabilities, such as thinking disorders and auditory hallucinations, which are sufficiently severe that full-time employment is impossible. Some of these people can do part-time jobs, however. Estimates of the number of persons with schizophrenia capable of full-time work range as low as 6 percent; from my own experience I would estimate that approximately 20 percent of people with schizophrenia can work full-time and probably another 20 percent can work part-time *if* proper medication maintenance and rehabilitation programs are available. Past employment is the best single predictor of future employment for a person with schizophrenia; a person who becomes sick after having a job is more likely to find work than a person who becomes sick without ever having worked.

Work provides several potential benefits for people, not the least of which is additional income. Improved self-esteem is equally important, for to hold a job is evidence that one is like other people. England's Douglas Bennett, one of the few mental illness professionals who has fought for vocational opportunities for persons with schizophrenia, says that a job magically transforms a patient into a person. Patients will often work very hard to control their psychiatric symptoms in work situations because work is so important to them. It has been observed, for example, that "in the morning at the day center, the same person is fulfilling the role of patient and acts like a patient, exhibiting symptoms and bizarre behavior never seen in the workshop the same afternoon." Work also provides people with a daily structure, a reason to get out of bed in the morning, an identity, and an extended social network.

It is ironic that the civil rights efforts which led to the release of so many patients from psychiatric hospitals also led to sharply decreased availability of jobs for them. In the past, many of these patients had worked on the hospital farms, on the grounds, and on housekeeping and kitchen details. Undoubtedly there was some abuse of this captive work force, and civil rights lawyers went to court with cases of "peonage." The result was a pendulum which swung too far in efforts to correct the situation; hospitals became reluctant to employ patients at all because they could not afford to pay them the minimum wage and other employee benefits. The consequence is thousands of patients in hospitals and in the community who are capable of, and enjoy, working for brief periods but who are not capable of full-time employment. The jobs of the past which were often tailored to their needs are gone.

The largest impediment to vocational opportunities for persons with schizophrenia is stigma. Employers, like most people in our society, do not understand what schizophrenia is and so react negatively when asked if they would consider employing persons with this disease. "I can't have any psychos working in my place" is a common visceral reaction. Another major impediment is that government rehabilitation programs and sheltered workshops have traditionally shunned the mentally handicapped in favor of the physically handicapped. Vocational rehabilitation in the United States is still stuck in the polio era, and if you don't have a visible physical disability you need not apply. Some other countries do a much better job of providing job opportunities for patients. Sweden, England, and the Netherlands all have a greater availability of sheltered workshops for long-term partial employment of psychiatric patients.

There are several kinds of vocational rehabilitation programs for individuals with serious mental illnesses.

Sheltered Employment

These are sheltered workshops in which the person is not necessarily expected to graduate to competitive employment. In the United States, Goodwill Industries operates many of them. The most impressive example of a sheltered workshop that I have seen is the Broadway Industries, part of the Greater Vancouver Mental Health Services in Vancouver, British Columbia. It accommodates about 70 individuals per month and has developed more than 600 product design lines to allow one or more severely disabled individuals to be involved in production. Its high-quality crafts are sold at several locations in the city.

Transitional Employment

This model of vocational rehabilitation was developed by Fountain House, a clubhouse in New York City, and is used in many other club-

houses. Consumers are assigned to real jobs in commercial establishments and accompanied by a rehabilitation specialist. Two consumers
will often divide a single job (e.g., each working half-time) as they
learn the job. The graduation rate from transitional employment to
competitive employment is impressive and a 1991 study of transitional
employment showed it to be highly cost-effective.

Supported Employment

In this model the individual is encouraged to select the employment of
his/her choice, then is trained intensively in job and related social skills
before starting the job. An example of supported employment is the
Access program affiliated with the Boston University Center for
Psychiatric Rehabilitation. The person attends pre-employment classes
for 15 hours a week for seven weeks, then is given a job coach and
extensive support in the initial months on the job.

Job Skills Training

This model utilizes commercial establishments that are specifically
set up to train individuals with serious mental illnesses in job skills.
An impressive example is a restaurant in Hayward, California,
called the "Eden Express," in which consumers do all jobs including
food preparation, catering, aide to cook, busing, waiting on tables,
hostessing, cashiering, dishwashing, and janitorial. Between 1980
and 1985 a total of 315 persons completed the 15-week training program, which was 80 percent of those who enrolled. Approximately
25 trainees are enrolled at any given time, and several job counselors make up the training staff. The staff also teaches trainees how
to interview for jobs at the completion of their training, and 94 percent of the graduates have obtained jobs. The "Eden Express" is
largely self-supporting, serving over 4,000 customers each month.
Salaries for the job counselors are derived primarily from training
funds from the California State Departments of Rehabilitation and
Education.

Competitive Employment

Many people with schizophrenia can return to competitive employment but not necessarily at the level they would have achieved if they had not become ill. An especially interesting example of competitive employment is the use of people with schizophrenia to be consumer case managers for others with this illness. It is described in chapter 10.

FRIENDSHIP

Friendship is needed by persons with schizophrenia, just as it is by everyone. For the person with schizophrenia, however, there are often barriers to friendship. One such barrier encompasses the symptoms and brain dysfunction from the disorder.

One young man I provided care for recovered from most of his symptoms and was living at home. He attempted to return to his social group of peers, going to taverns and drinking with them as he had done prior to his illness. He found this very difficult, however, complaining that "I can't make out their words, I don't know what to say. It's just not like it used to be." Another patient complained that in social situations "I get lost in the spaces between words in sentences. I can't concentrate, or I get off into thinking about something else." In view of such difficulties it is not surprising that many people with schizophrenia often respond inappropriately in social situations and eventually withdraw. Studies of patients living in the community report that 25 percent are described as very isolated, 50 percent as moderately isolated, and only 25 percent as leading active social lives. Almost half have no recreational activity whatsoever, other than watching television.

In addition to their brain dysfunction that may interfere with social relationships, individuals with schizophrenia must also contend with the stigma that accrues to their illness. One older man, who returned to the hospital because the stigma encountered was so pervasive, expressed it well:

> I just can't make it out there. I know who I am and they know who I am—most of the people out there won't come near me or they spit me in the eye. I'm just like a leper in their eyes. They treat most of us like that.

They're prejudiced, you know. They are either afraid or hate us. I've seen
it a thousand times. I don't feel good on the outside. I don't belong. They
know it and I know it.

There are possible several solutions to the need for friendship
among individuals with schizophrenia. One is consumer self-help
groups, which are discussed in chapter 10. Another is the Compeer
Program that was begun in Rochester, New York, in 1981 and that has
spread to more than 300 cities. Compeer volunteers who are not mentally ill are matched with individuals who have schizophrenia and
other serious mental illnesses on a one-to-one basis. The two people
then get together once a week to shop, go to a movie, go to dinner, play
checkers, or share some common interest.

A direct solution to the friendship problem is offered by the
Friendship Exchange in New York, which is a dating service set up
specifically for persons who have schizophrenia or bipolar disorder. I
have personally been impressed by how much support two individuals
with schizophrenia can give each other and the strength of the bond
that comes from sharing the disorder. Some of the relationships are, of
course, disasters, but others are the most important thing that has happened to the people; as such, they essentially mirror the range of relationships found among people who do not have schizophrenia.

Another approach to friendship is by improving the person's social
skills through didactic instruction and supervised group interaction.
Social skills training is built into many of the vocational rehabilitation
programs mentioned in the previous section but may also be done on
its own. Some social skills training programs for individuals with
schizophrenia are highly structured programs to make the person more
aware of social cues, facial expressions, and the subtleties of normal
social interactions. One of the most widely used such programs is the
UCLA Skills Training Modules, listed in Appendix C, which since
1981 has provided skills training for over 3,000 mentally ill individuals
at the West Los Angeles Veterans Administration Medical Center as
well as at many other facilities. It consists of ten training modules,
each of which has a trainer's manual, patient's workbook, user's guide,
and video cassette. Such educational methods can be extremely useful
in helping consumers function better and thereby better survive schizophrenia.

One of the best solutions to the friendship problem are clubhouses.
Modeled after Fountain House, which began in New York City in

1948, there are now over 200 clubhouses in the United States. Some of them are excellent and are listed under "Examples of Good Services" (see p. 241). Clubhouses are especially numerous in Virginia and Massachusetts because these states have made their development an official policy of the state department of mental health. Clubhouses provide their "members," as the consumers are called, not only with a location for friendship and social activities but with vocational, educational, and housing programs as well.

Clubhouses have also been shown to be cost-effective, because they decrease the rehospitalization rate of members. In studies done at Thresholds in Chicago and its allied program, The Bridge, the rehospitalization rate after nine months among members was 14 percent, compared with a rate of 44 percent for a control group that utilized existing community resources. For people with schizophrenia, who regularly go through the revolving door of community-hospital-community-hospital, it was found that the savings in treatment costs averaged $5,700 per member per year: "These findings imply that an outreach program like The Bridge can literally pay for itself while producing tangible benefits for the members it serves." One wonders how much better off persons with schizophrenia would be in the United States if the $3 billion in federal funds that were used to set up Community Mental Health Centers had been used instead to set up clubhouses.

Another aspect of friendship for a person with schizophrenia is the nonhuman variety. Pets often make excellent companions, just as they do for some persons without schizophrenia. Dogs are especially good, for they love indiscriminately, are not at all bothered by a person's thought disorders or auditory hallucinations, and are usually understanding when things are not going well. Providing pets for persons with schizophrenia can often bring them much pleasure; this has been discovered by families as well as by some mental hospitals that have allowed the patients to keep pets or to utilize visiting "pets on wheels" programs.

MEDICAL CARE

Like everyone else, individuals with schizophrenia get sick with other illnesses and require medical care. Obtaining medical care may be difficult, however, for a variety of reasons. Perhaps the most important one is that most people with schizophrenia do not have medical insurance and so must utilize Medicaid and Medicare. Medicaid benefits vary widely from state to state, and many physicians will not accept Medicaid patients.

Other impediments to obtaining medical care include the inability of some people with schizophrenia to give a coherent account of their symptoms to a physician or other health care practitioner, the higher pain threshold found in some individuals with schizophrenia leading to a delay in diagnosis, and the difficulty that some people with schizophrenia have in understanding or following instructions for treatment. In addition, side effects of the person's antipsychotic medications may confuse the clinical picture, and the antipsychotic medication may interact with medication prescribed for the medical problems.

For all these reasons there is known to be a comparatively high incidence of untreated medical problems among persons with schizophrenia, with studies reporting such problems in 26 to 53 percent of patients. A 1991 study by Adler and Griffith concluded that "the treatment of the medically ill schizophrenic patient can be one of the most challenging tasks a physician will face." The failure to provide such treatment, however, is one reason why individuals with schizophrenia have a higher mortality rate, as discussed in chapter 5.

SERVICES FOR CHILDREN

Children with schizophrenia require the same services as adults with this disorder but, in addition, have special needs as well. Schizophrenia almost never begins before age five and increases slowly in incidence between five and 16, at which time its incidence rises sharply.

One special problem with schizophrenia in childhood is clarifying the diagnosis. Children with schizophrenia may also have behavioral problems, drug or alcohol abuse, severe depression, or neurological problems such as seizures and are sometimes mislabeled with these other conditions. For this reason it has become common in the United States to label children as "seriously emotionally disturbed," or SED, children rather than specifying a specific condition. In recent years Dr. Enid Peschel and others have promoted the term "neurobiological disorders," or NBD, to encompass schizophrenia, autism, severe depression, bipolar disorder, obsessive-compulsive disorder, Tourette's syndrome, and other known brain diseases of childhood.

Another problem peculiar to childhood schizophrenia is that over half of the states encourage or require parents to give up custody of their child in order to be eligible for state residential services. The reason for this Draconian practice is purely fiscal: Federal Medicaid under Title IV-E (Adoption Assistance and Foster Care Act) will pay much of the cost for residential services for children who are under state custody but not for those who are not under state custody. Therefore, to save state funds and shift the cost to the federal government, states encourage, and sometimes require, parents to give up custody of their child with schizophrenia as a condition for receiving residential services.

A third aspect of childhood schizophrenia that is not found in the adult variety is that, until recently, the majority of states sent large numbers of these children to other states to be treated in private facilities rather than provide the treatment themselves. For example, in 1990 Maryland sent 680 seriously emotionally disturbed children out of state for treatment, some as far as Vermont and Florida, at a cost to the state of $31.5 million. This practice is slowly becoming less common in most states.

There are three important principles that should be incorporated into services for children with schizophrenia or other neurobiological disorders.

1. Treatment must be integrated with education and job skills training. Children with schizophrenia, in contrast to adults with the disorder, have not completed their education. Model programs such as Kaleidoscope and Thresholds in Chicago have demonstrated how this can be done.
2. The child should continue to live home whenever possible unless there is some contraindication. The Homebuilders program in Tacoma, Washington, is considered to be a model for such services.
3. Services must be flexible and well coordinated. A variety of services may be required, including residential group homes, foster care, day programs, wilderness camps, and transition services when the person graduates to adult services. Services for children with schizophrenia often involve a variety of local, county, and state agencies, including education, juvenile justice, social services, and child welfare as well as mental health; the coordi-

nation of these services can be a bureaucratic nightmare. The Alaska Youth Initiative and Ventura County, California, have been widely praised as ambitious attempts to coordinate such services.

SERVICES IN RURAL AREAS

Rehabilitation services for individuals with schizophrenia who live in rural areas are very deficient in most states. Long distances, bad roads, and few mental illness professionals or facilities make the provision of good services an ongoing challenge. It *is* possible to provide quality services, however, utilizing some of the following principles.

1. Family physicians, internists, physician assistants, nurse practitioners, and public health nurses must be utilized as the primary person to prescribe and monitor medication. In order to do so they must be given some training, periodic continuing education, and consultation back-up by a psychiatrist who is available by telephone 24 hours a day. In Canada, the province of Saskatchewan has utilized family physicians and public health nurses very successfully to provide ongoing care for individuals deinstitutionalized from the provincial hospital. Similarly, in British Columbia family physicians provide extensive psychiatric services in rural hospitals and are visited on a monthly basis by psychiatrists from Vancouver. The feasibility of using public health nurses to provide primary care for individuals with schizophrenia living in the community was demonstrated more than 30 years ago by Dr. Benjamin Pasamanick and his colleagues in Louisville. More recently they have been successfully used to follow elderly mentally ill persons in rural Iowa.
2. Brief psychiatric hospitalizations can be done utilizing the medical wards of general hospitals as well as crisis beds in nursing homes or other medical or social service facilities. Over 20 years ago Reading and Maguire demonstrated the effective use of general hospital beds for acute psychiatric admissions in upstate New York.
3. Continuity of care is equally as important in rural areas as it is in urban areas. Recently, in South Carolina it was shown that

continuity of care could be achieved in a rural area using the PACT model, as described above.

4. Mobile clinics, which go to a different town each day, are very useful in rural areas. Mobile day programs, which cover five areas each for one day a week, have also been successfully utilized.

5. Given the paucity of mental illness professionals in most rural areas, it is even more important to train local and state police, emergency medical technicians, and ambulance personnel on the proper management of individuals with acute psychosis. A good model for this is the training courses run by Dartmouth Medical School for rural areas in New Hampshire and Vermont.

EXAMPLES OF GOOD SERVICES

The following are some examples of good outpatient, housing, vocational, social, and children's services for individuals with serious mental illnesses that were reported as being especially noteworthy as of early 1994. The fact that such services exist at all proves that it is possible to deliver quality services. The list is useful for identifying programs that mental illness service providers, families, and consumers may wish to visit. Be aware, however, that many service programs are in flux; a program that was good in early 1994 may not necessarily be so by 1995 because of loss of funding, loss of key staff, or other reasons. None of these programs is perfect nor is the list all inclusive; many other good programs exist.

The best overall program for mental illness services in North America is not in the United States but in Vancouver, British Columbia. The Greater Vancouver Mental Health Services covers a population of approximately 600,000 ethnically diverse individuals with an acute-care inpatient facility; some exemplary outpatient services; mobile emergency evening services, which are coordinated with the local police; extensive outreach to seriously mentally ill individuals in shelters, on the streets, and in jail; some model vocational services, such as Broadway Industries; and extensive housing for over 1,100 individuals. A 1993 study found that the relatively high quality mental illness services in British Columbia were less expensive per capita than in eight states in the United States. Several other Canadian provinces, especially those in Western Canada, provide an impressive array of high quality services.

Among the states, the best overall programs are in New Hampshire. The collaboration between Dartmouth Medical School's Department of Psychiatry and the New Hampshire State Hospital has made that hospital one of the best state hospitals in the United States. The Mental Health Center of Greater Manchester is among the strongest in the country. Continuous treatment teams are used to promote continuity of outpatient care in all 10 CMHCs in the state, with one team being used to focus exclusively on individuals with severe mental illness and substance abuse. There are some excellent housing programs (e.g., Harbor Homes in Nashua, Independent Living Program in Concord) and rehabilitation programs (e.g., The Job Store in Portsmouth, Wyman Way Co-op in Keene, Cornerstone House in Laconia, Wyndham Inn in Wyndham). One reason for New Hampshire's fine services compared to other states is effective and stable leadership in the State Division of Mental Health and Developmental Services as well as a strong state AMI group.

Other states that also provide comparatively good services for individuals with serious mental illnesses are Vermont (e.g., Washington County Mental Health Services), Rhode Island (e.g., Northern Rhode Island Mental Health Center), and Connecticut (e.g., Genesis Center in Manchester). Ohio is another state that has improved markedly in recent years, and services in Akron (e.g., Community Support Services), Columbus (e.g., Center on Vocational Alternatives and Community Housing Network), Toledo (e.g., MERIT rehabilitation program), and Cincinnati (e.g., Excel Development Corporation for housing) are among the best urban services in the nation; the last three received assistance in developing services from the Robert Wood Johnson Foundation.

Many states have one or two areas with impressive services, usually because of a single good mental health center. Salt Lake County (UT) does as well as anywhere in the country with an excellent mental health center, a good clubhouse (Alliance House), crisis housing, and impressive services for the mentally ill in jail and on the streets. Other places that also are noteworthy for their comprehensive mental illness services are northern Maine (Aroostock MHC), Lowell, MA (Solomon MHC), Fall River, MA (Corrigan MHC), Pomona, NY (Rockland MHC), Rochester, NY (Rochester MHC), Frederick, MD (Way Station), Huntington, WV (Shawnee Hills MHC), Louisville, KY (Seven Counties MHC), St. Petersburg, FL (Boley Foundation programs), Virginia, MN (Range MHC), Mission, KS (Johnson County

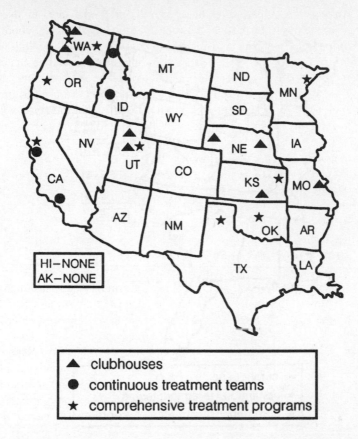

- ▲ clubhouses
- ● continuous treatment teams
- ★ comprehensive treatment programs

Map Showing Location of Some Exemplary Clubhouses, Continuous Treatment Teams, and Comprehensive Treatment Programs. (See Chapter 8 and Appendix C.)

MHC), Amarillo, TX (Texas Panhandle MH Authority), Oklahoma City, OK (Red Rock MHC), San Mateo, CA (San Mateo County MHC), Eugene, OR (Laurel Hill Center), Spokane, WA (Spokane MHC), and Tacoma, WA (Comprehensive MHC). The locations of these especially noteworthy comprehensive programs are indicated on the maps (see pp. 243–244).

Good examples of programs designed specifically for individuals dually diagnosed with serious mental illnesses and substance abuse, in addition to the New Hampshire program cited above, are Caulfield

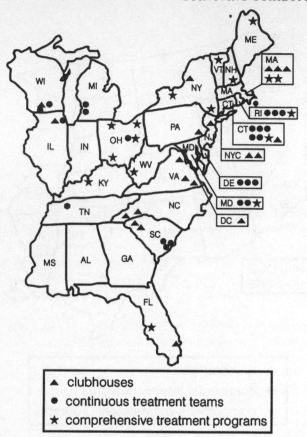

- ▲ clubhouses
- ● continuous treatment teams
- ★ comprehensive treatment programs

Map Showing Location of Some Exemplary Clubhouses, Continuous Treatment Teams, and Comprehensive Treatment Programs. (See Chapter 8 and Appendix C.)

Center in Woburn, MA, and Harbor House in Bronx, NY. Exemplary programs for diverting seriously mentally ill individuals from jails include those in Montgomery County (Norristown), PA, Shelby County (Memphis), TN, and King County (Seattle), WA. Noteworthy programs that target seriously mentally ill individuals who are also homeless are Step Up On Second in Santa Monica, CA, Weingart Center in Los Angeles, and programs at Bellevue Hospital in New York City.

Continuity of care is one of the essential ingredients in good mental illness services and, as noted above, nobody has devised a better way to do this than PACT-type continuous treatment team programs. There are now many exemplary continuous treatment teams based on the PACT model, including those in Connecticut (Bridgeport, Middletown, Danbury, Norwich, and West Haven), Rhode Island (Pawtucket, Wakefield, and Warren), Delaware (Wilmington and New Castle), Maryland (Baltimore), South Carolina (Charleston and Summerville), Tennessee (Nashville), Ohio (Columbus), Illinois (Chicago), Michigan (Grand Rapids and Kalamazoo), Wisconsin (Madison and Monroe), Idaho (Boise and Coeur d'Alene), and California (San Jose and Long Beach). The locations of these programs are indicated on the accompanying map and their addresses are listed in Appendix C.

Clubhouses are also an extremely effective way to blend together social, vocational, and housing programs for seriously mentally ill individuals. Examples of well-functioning clubhouses in large urban areas can be found in New York (Fountain House and Venture House); Chicago (Thresholds and its associated Bridge programs); Miami (Fellowship House); Washington (Green Door and Clarendon House in suburban Arlington, VA); Philadelphia (Chestnut Place); St. Louis (Independence Center); and Salt Lake City (Alliance House). Outstanding clubhouses in smaller cities include Worcester, MA (Genesis Club); Paterson, NJ (Harbor House); Richmond (Lakeside House) and Virginia Beach (Beach House), VA; Madison, WI (Yahara House); and Wichita, KS (Breakthrough Club). Excellent clubhouses can also be found in some smaller cities and towns such as Salem (Pioneer House) and Hopedale (Crossroads), MA; Torrington, CT (Prime Time); Watertown, NY (Bridges); Hendersonville (Sixth Avenue West) and Shelby (Adventure House), NC; Spartanburg (New Day Clubhouse) and Greenville (Gateway House), SC; Scottsbluff (Cirrus House) and Norfolk (Liberty Center), NV; Brigham City, UT (Rainbow Club); and Everett (New Frontier Club), Longview (Cowlitz River Club), and Pasco (Wilson House), WA. The locations of these clubhouses are indicated on the accompanying map and their addresses are listed in Appendix C.

Turning to vocational rehabilitation programs for seriously mentally ill individuals, some of the best transitional employment programs are found in the clubhouses. Fairweather Lodges also combine residential and vocational programs; good examples of these can be found in Detroit (Rademacher Lodge) and Mount Clemons (North Avenue Lodge) MI; Minneapolis, MN (Tasks Unlimited); Hartford, CT (Sunshine Projects); and Austin, TX (Harbor House).

Many examples of good supported employment programs can be found in Massachusetts, such as Incentive Community Enterprises and Career Development Services in Northampton; Greater Boston Rehabilitation Services in Cambridge; Eastern Middlesex MHC in Wakefield; and Center for Psychiatric Rehabilitation in Boston. New York State has Buy OMH, an exemplary vocational program run by the Office of Mental Health, as well as a variety of other programs in New York City (Choices); West Brentwood (Long Island Industries); Hicksville (Nassau Day Training); Ronkonkoma (Club House of Suffolk County); New Rochelle (Guidance Center); Syracuse (Provisions); Niagara Falls (Community Missions); Orchard Park (Spectrum Human Services); and Buffalo (STEPS, Center for Choice and Achievement, Residential Care Center for Adults). Other examples of good vocational programs are scattered across the country in Fairfax, VA (Social Center for Psychiatric Rehabilitation); Atlanta, GA (Community Friendship); Ft. Lauderdale (Path Project), Hypoluxo (Jeff Industries), and Clearwater (Boley Foundation), FL; Denver CO (Bayaud Industries); and San Diego (Employment Services) and Hayward (Eden Express Restaurant), CA.

Despite the generally poor quality of housing for seriously mentally ill individuals in the United States, there are a few very good programs. Vermont, Ohio, Minnesota, Wisconsin, and Tennessee are examples of states with good rent subsidy programs, whereas Baltimore (Community Housing Associates), MD, Providence, RI (Thresholds), and Raleigh, NC (Community Alternatives for Supportive Abodes) are cities with good housing finance and development agencies. Many of the comprehensive programs and clubhouses mentioned also have good housing programs.

Other noteworthy housing programs can be found in Rutland, VT (Rutland Mental Health Services); Whitinsville, MA (Alternatives); Pawtucket, RI (Community Counseling Center); Albany, NY (Housing Opportunities Made Easier); Bronx, NY (Pibly Residential Services); Prince Frederick, MD (Southern Maryland Community Network); Little Rock, AR (Greater Assistance for Those in Need); Forth Worth, TX (Tarrant County MH Services); Lubbock, TX (Lubbock Regional MHC); Oakland, CA (Oakland Independence Support Center); Everett,

WA (Olympic MH Services); and Kenai, AK (Central Peninsula Counseling Services). A model halfway house can be seen in Haverford, PA (Torrey House—I will admit to some partiality). The nicest group homes I have seen anywhere are on the bucolic grounds of the Chilton-Shelby Mental Health Center in Calera, AL.

Compeer programs, in which seriously mentally ill individuals are paired with volunteers for regular social activities, are an effective way to promote socialization. Among the best Compeer programs are those in Rochester and Buffalo, NY; Manchester, NH; Norristown, PA; Tiffin, OH; Harrisonburg, VA; Charlotte, NC; Decatur, GA; Wichita, KS; Hampton, IA; Phoenix, AZ; and Anchorage, AK.

Finally, there are a few programs for children with serious mental illnesses that are highly regarded. These include the Homebuilders program in Tacoma, WA; Kaleidoscope and Thresholds in Chicago; the Alaska Youth Initiative; and the coordinated services offered by Ventura County and Riverside County, CA.

QUALITY OF LIFE MEASURES

The outcome of the rehabilitation of schizophrenia is usually conceptualized using objective outcome measures that are either positive, such as the number of persons employed or living on their own, or negative, such as severity of symptoms, rehospitalization rates, or arrest rates. Occasional attempts have been made to also include objective measures of the person's standard of living, such as the quality of their housing or amount of disposable income.

By contrast, very little effort has been made to assess the rehabilitation of schizophrenia using subjective measures such as consumers' opinions as the outcome measure. Two American research groups which have attempted to do so by developing quality of life rating scales are Dr. Douglas A. Bigelow and colleagues at the University of Oregon Health Sciences Center and Dr. Anthony F. Lehman and colleagues at the University of Maryland Center for Mental Health Services Research. Bigelow et al. defined quality of life as "an abstraction which integrates and summarizes all those features of our lives that we find more or less desirable and satisfying" and developed a 263-item questionnaire. Lehman defined quality of life as "measures covering patients' perspectives on what they have, how they are doing, and how they feel about their life circumstances" and developed a 143-

item questionnaire. Both questionnaires take less than an hour to administer and have been extensively tested and validated. They include such issues as the person's living situation, family relations, social relations, employment, health, finances, safety, and legal problems. Some quality of life surveys also include questions regarding the person's inner experiences, such as pleasure, self-reliance, and self-fulfillment.

To date these quality of life measures are little known and even less used by mental illness professionals. However, they may well be the wave of the future. Imagine how different services for mentally ill individuals would be if measures of the quality of their lives were included as a routine part of rehabilitation. Imagine, moreover, how different the service system would be if rehabilitation outcome measures, both objective (e.g., rehospitalization rates) and subjective (quality of life), were used to determine the promotion and compensation of the mental illness professionals.

Such changes will not come easily. The traditional mental illness service system is strongly embedded and will resist change. I personally found this out when I was administering ten wards at St. Elizabeths Hospital in Washington, D.C., in 1980. I suggested that we set aside some money each year and at the end of the year have the patients on each ward vote by closed ballot on which mental illness professionals should receive bonuses. The cries of protest from some mental illness professionals and the union were deafening and the plan had to be abandoned.

THE NEED FOR ASYLUM

When the deinstitutionalization of seriously ill psychiatric patients began in the early 1960s, most people assumed that some patients could be placed in the community but that many others would continue to need long-term hospitalization. By the early 1970s that assumption had been steadily eroded, and in some states (e.g., California, Massachusetts) there was serious talk of closing state hospitals altogether. Two decades later we have come back, full circle, to where we began, and most mental illness professionals who work with seriously ill patients believe that there is, and will continue to be, a need for state hospitals for some patients.

The kinds of patients who will continue to need state hospitals are those whose symptoms are the most severe and/or whose behavior makes placement in the community very difficult. They include the 10 to 20 percent of seriously mentally ill who respond minimally or not at all to antipsychotic drugs, those with a propensity toward aggression or violence, those with inappropriate behaviors such as setting fires or disrobing in public, and those who are so helpless and/or dependent that they need the protection of the institution. It would be nice if there were no such patients, but there are and—until we learn the causes of brain disease like schizophrenia—there will continue to be. Because of the push to close down hospitals and because of legal decisions mandating the placement of patients in the community as "the least restrictive setting," many patients are currently being returned to the community who should not be.

How big a group of patients is this? The answer will depend in large measure on the quality of outpatient psychiatric and rehabilitation services available. A county with good programs, such as Dane County, Wisconsin, may be able to successfully maintain in the community all except 10 percent of the seriously mentally ill, whereas in an area with few services less than half of all seriously ill patients may be better off in the community. The point is that in every system there comes a point where you have to ask hard questions. Is this patient really better off living in the community than remaining in the hospital? Is the quality of his/her life really going to be better? Is the community truly the "least restrictive setting" for this person? In our rush to return everybody to the community, we have avoided asking such questions in recent years, and yet many of them have ended up in nursing homes, boarding homes, and public shelters much worse than the hospital ward they left. In my eight years of placing patients in the Washington, D.C., community from St. Elizabeths Hospital, I would estimate that at least one-quarter of them were *worse* off, in terms of quality of life, than they had been in the hospital. And such patients often told me that they would gladly return to the hospital if they had the opportunity.

We need to acknowledge, then, the need for some long-term psychiatric beds for the severely disabled. It is reviving the concept of asylum in the benevolent sense that the term was originally used—as protection for those who cannot protect themselves. We do not expect everyone who gets paralytic polio to necessarily be able to walk again, and we do not place them in boarding homes in the community if they are clearly unable to look after themselves. We maintain long-term hospital beds for patients with other severe brain diseases, such as multiple sclerosis and Alzheimer's disease, who are unable to care for themselves. Why shouldn't we do the same for schizophrenia?

RECOMMENDED FURTHER READING

Anthony, W., M. Cohen, and M. Farkas. *Psychiatric Rehabilitation.* Boston: Center for Psychiatric Rehabilitation, 1990.

Bond, G. R. "An Economic Analysis of Psychosocial Rehabilitation." *Hospital and Community Psychiatry* 35 (1984): 356–62.

Carling, P. J., F. L. Randolph, and P. Ridgway. *Providing Housing and Supports for People with Psychiatric Disabilities.* Boston: Center for Psychiatric Rehabilitation, 1986.

Lehman, A. F. "Measures of Humanistic Outcomes (Quality of Life) Among Persons with Severe and Persistent Mental Disorders." *Social Psychiatry and Psychiatric Epidemiology,* in press.

Peschel, E., R. Peschel, C. W. Howe, et al. *Neurobiological Disorders in Children and Adolescents.* San Francisco: Jossey-Bass, 1992.

There Goes the Neighborhood. White Plains, NY: Community Residences Information Services Program (CRISP), 1986. This summarizes studies showing that community residences for the mentally disabled do not depreciate property values or the neighborhood.

Torrey, E. F., D. A. Bigelow, and N. Sladen-Dew. "Quality and Cost of Services for Seriously Mentally Ill Individuals in British Columbia and the United States." *Hospital and Community Psychiatry* 44 (1993): 943–50.

Torrey, E. F., K. Erdman, S. M. Wolfe, et al. *Care of the Seriously Mentally Ill: A Rating of State Programs.* Washington, D.C.: NAMI and Public Citizen Health Research Group, 1990.

Uhlhorn, B. *Creating a Caring Community: Developing Housing for Persons with Mental Illness.* Arlington, VA: National Alliance for the Mentally Ill, 1987.

Winerip, M. *9 Highland Road.* New York: Pantheon, 1994.

Wing, J. K. "The Functions of Asylum." *British Journal of Psychiatry* 157 (1990): 822–27.

9

SIX MAJOR PROBLEMS

Although insanity is a disease to which every man is liable, a feeling prevails regarding it obviously different from any that prevails regarding most diseases. It is so incapacitating, and involves such complete dependence; its effects upon the civil and social condition of a man are so distinctive; and it is the subject of so much popular apprehension and horror, that it demands a consideration, especially if a cure is expected, that is peculiar to itself.

American Journal of Insanity, 1868

Having the misfortune to be afflicted with schizophrenia brings with it many problems, both for those affected and for their families. Of all those problems, six stand out as among the most common, the most persistent and the most perplexing. These problems are cigarettes and coffee; alcohol and street drugs; sex, pregnancy, and AIDS; medication noncompliance; assaultive and violent behavior; and suicide.

CIGARETTES AND COFFEE

One cannot overstate the importance of cigarettes and coffee in the daily lives of many people with schizophrenia. They are a major focus of social interaction, expenditure of funds, accumulation of debt, and trading of favors. Some individuals with schizophrenia are so obsessed with obtaining cigarettes and coffee that it appears to dominate their daily activities.

Several studies have shown that between 80 and 90 percent of individuals with schizophrenia smoke cigarettes. This is significantly higher than the approximately 50 percent smoker rate among psychiatric patients with other diagnoses or the 30 percent rate in the general population. Studies have also shown that individuals with schizophrenia are more likely to be heavy smokers and to smoke high-tar cigarettes. One study conservatively estimated that individuals with schizophrenia in the United States smoke over 10 billion packs of cigarettes each year, costing a total of over $20 billion.

Many explanations have been proposed to account for heavy smoking among individuals with schizophrenia. Boredom from sitting on inpatient wards may account for some of it, but the incidence of heavy smoking among outpatients is almost as high as it is among inpatients. Nicotine reduces anxiety, reduces sedation, and improves concentration in some people, which might be a form of self-medication for the person with schizophrenia. The self-medication theory received support when a study of people with schizophrenia reported that smoking transiently improved specific brain functions (auditory sensory gating) that are known to be impaired in this disease. There are also two studies showing that smoking decreases the Parkinson-like stiffness and tremor that often occur as side effects of antipsychotic medication.

Nicotine is known to affect the receptors for many brain neurotransmitters and to promote the release of dopamine, serotonin, acetylcholine, and norepinephrine. There are also nicotine receptors in the brain and it is possible that these might be related to schizophrenia. Nicotine has been shown in some studies to decrease the blood level of antipsychotics by increasing excretion by the kidneys. Smokers with schizophrenia are known to require higher doses of antipsychotic medication than nonsmokers, but whether this is a result of the increased excretion is less certain. On the other hand, a study of Tourette's disease reported that nicotine potentiated the effects of haloperidol in decreasing tics. In summary, we really do not know why individuals with schizophrenia are such heavy smokers.

The consequences of smoking are well known. Individuals with schizophrenia have elevated death rates from pneumonia and heart disease but it is not known how much of this is because of smoking and how much is because of the relatively poor medical care most of them receive. Smoking, especially in individuals who are mentally confused, can be dangerous, and serious fires in group homes caused by careless smoking are not uncommon. One study found an increased incidence of akathisia among individuals with schizophrenia who were smokers.

Two studies reported that smoking also increased the risk for developing tardive dyskinesia but a third study did not find this association.

One would also predict that individuals with schizophrenia should have a very high incidence of lung cancer. One of the intriguing mysteries about this disease, however, is that the lung cancer rate in schizophrenia appears to be *lower* than the general population, not higher. There has been speculation whether antipsychotic medication might in some way be protective and account for this, but this explanation seems unlikely since at least two studies reported a lower lung cancer rate in schizophrenia before antipsychotic drugs were introduced.

Caffeine intake among individuals with schizophrenia is also very heavy but has not been quantified as precisely as has smoking. Patients have been documented drinking 30 or more cups of coffee each day as well as drinking many colas, which also contain caffeine. There are also occasional individuals with schizophrenia who buy instant coffee and eat it directly from the jar with a spoon. Like nicotine, it is not understood why individuals with schizophrenia are so strongly addicted to caffeine, although caffeine is known to affect adenosine receptors in the brain and, through them, the metabolism of dopamine, serotonin, GABA, glutamate, and norepinephrine. One study also suggests that caffeine may decrease Parkinsonian symptoms such as rigidity and tremor.

It is known that high caffeine intake in anyone can produce the symptoms of caffeine intoxication, including nervousness, restlessness, insomnia, excitement, flushing of the face, rapid heart beat, and muscle twitching. Studies of individuals with schizophrenia who ingest large amounts of caffeine have demonstrated that some patients have a worsening of their symptoms. Some of this effect may be brought about by the fact that coffee, and especially tea, are known to interfere with the absorption of antipsychotic drugs. Three controlled studies have been done in which psychiatric inpatient units were switched from caffeinated to decaffeinated coffee and tea to see what effect it would have on patient's symptoms. The first study reported an improvement in patients' symptoms but the two more recent studies reported no effect whatsoever.

One thing that is clear about both smoking and caffeine intake among individuals with schizophrenia is that more studies are needed to clarify the consequences of the behavior. Until they are done I would suggest the following:

1. Recognize the strength of these addictions in many individuals with schizophrenia. Obviously some reasonable maximum limits must be set, such as one pack of cigarettes and four cups of coffee or colas per day, but setting limits is different from trying to prohibit the behavior altogether. In my experience some mentally ill individuals who are strongly addicted to nicotine and caffeine will fight, sell their clothes, and even prostitute themselves to satisfy their addictions. Only masochists and martyrs pick fights they know they cannot win.

2. Be aware that smoking and drinking coffee are among life's most pleasurable activities for some individuals with schizophrenia. The fact that this is so is sad, but that does not change the reality. We should be careful about taking away such pleasures unless we are certain that the gains from doing so are worth it. The recent ban on smoking in hospitals by the Joint Commission on Health Care Organizations did not take into account the fact that for some individuals with schizophrenia these hospitals are their homes.

3. Demand that individuals with schizophrenia who smoke do so in a safe manner (e.g., not in bed) and only in specified places. Nonsmokers have the right to not be exposed to the known dangerous effects of second-hand smoke. Establish clear penalties for not adhering to such rules, and enforce them.

4. Since cigarettes and coffee are very important to many individuals with schizophrenia, they can be used to reinforce other important behaviors, such as taking prescribed medication, as discussed below. This was once called bribery but is now called positive reinforcement. It works.

ALCOHOL AND STREET DRUGS

Alcohol and street drug abuse among individuals with schizophrenia is a large and apparently growing problem. A community study done in the early 1980s reported that 34 percent of individuals with schizophrenia abused alcohol, 26 percent abused street drugs, and altogether 47 percent abused one or both of these. Studies of this problem done over the past 30 years strongly suggest that the incidence of substance abuse by individuals with schizophrenia has increased significantly. The severity of the problem may vary considerably, from an occasional episode of abuse to almost continuous abuse.

There are many reasons why individuals with schizophrenia abuse alcohol and drugs. Probably the most important one is the same reason why individuals who do *not* have schizophrenia abuse alcohol and drugs—it makes them feel good. Substance abuse is endemic in the general population and there is no reason why individuals with schizophrenia should be exempt. It is important to realize, therefore, that many individuals with schizophrenia who are abusing alcohol and street drugs would also be doing so if they had never become sick.

There are other reasons for alcohol and drug abuse that are specific to schizophrenia. Substance abuse provides a social network and something to do for individuals who are often socially isolated and bored. There is also evidence that some individuals with schizophrenia are self-medicating with the alcohol or street drugs, resulting in decreased anxiety, decreased depression, and increased energy. One recent study identified specific subjective effects of alcohol, marijuana, and cocaine on individuals with schizophrenia who had used the drugs. It is also possible that there is a genetic connection between having a predisposition to schizophrenia and a predisposition to alcoholism but the data on this question are not definitive.

Many of the consequences of alcohol and street drug abuse for individuals with schizophrenia are identical to the general population and include impaired family and interpersonal relations, job loss, loss of housing, financial debt, medical problems, and arrests and jailings. In addition it has been shown that individuals with schizophrenia who are substance abusers have many more symptoms, more frequent violent episodes, a higher use of emergency psychiatric services, lower compliance with antipsychotic medication, and twice as high a rate of rehospitalization compared to nonsubstance abusers. A large number of them end up among the homeless population.

The treatment of individuals with schizophrenia who also are severe substance abusers is quite unsatisfactory. Many are ping-ponged back and forth between the mental illness treatment system and the substance abuse treatment system, rejected on both sides. They are the patients nobody wants.

A limited number of model treatment programs have been created, usually referred to as MICA (Mentally Ill Chemical Abuser) programs; some of these are listed in chapter 8. Of special note are the

Continuous Treatment Teams to promote integrated services and continuity of care set up by New Hampshire, which have reported stable remissions from alcoholism in over half of the treated patients with schizophrenia.

A variety of treatment approaches have been tried. The Twelve-Step self-help methods of Alcoholics Anonymous (AA) and Narcotics Anonymous (NA) are effective for only a minority of individuals with schizophrenia, although some do better with a lower-key modified Six-Step program. A disadvantage of some such groups is that they encourage total abstinence from all drugs, sometimes interpreted as including antipsychotic medications as well. Individuals with schizophrenia also do not do well in the confrontational groups promoted by some AA and NA chapters.

In some cases it is necessary to utilize compulsory monitoring techniques to decrease alcohol and drug abuse in individuals with schizophrenia. This is especially true for those patients who become violent or otherwise get in trouble when abusing alcohol or street drugs. Urine testing can be used to ascertain street drug use, and skin patches are being developed that change color if alcohol is ingested. Alcohol abuse can sometimes be controlled by the use of disulfiram (Antabuse), which, if taken each day, makes the person physically ill if they then drink alcohol during the ensuing 24 hours. Disulfiram can be used in individuals with schizophrenia but it tends to decrease blood levels of antipsychotics, so the person may need to take a higher dose of the antipsychotic while on disulfiram.

Families of individuals with schizophrenia who are abusing alcohol or street drugs need to be aware of how common this problem is and learn to recognize it. A useful clue is the disappearance of large amounts of the person's money that cannot be accounted for. Making the substance abuser aware of the effects and consequences of their substance abuse, setting and adhering to clearly defined limits, and utilizing compulsory treatment modalities (often mandated by the courts for individuals who have pending charges) are all important parts of a comprehensive treatment plan.

Should an individual with schizophrenia be allowed to drink at all? Many clinicians say no. I would agree with this if the person has a history of violent behavior or if alcohol appears to exacerbate the symptoms of their illness. However, if these are not factors and the person has had no tendency to abuse alcohol, I know of no reason why someone with schizophrenia should not have an occasional social drink if that is something they enjoy doing and is part of their culture. Having a beer at the end of the day with friends or having a glass of wine with dinner is for many people a pleasurable part of life. People who have had the misfortune to have been afflicted with schizophrenia should not be further penalized or deprived of small pleasures that are available to other people unless there is a clear reason to do so. At the same time I personally tell patients and their families to set clear limits on any alcohol intake (e.g., two cans of beer or two glasses of wine or one ounce of alcohol per day) and to be constantly alert for any signs of alcohol abuse.

Street drug use by persons with schizophrenia can be summed up in one word. NO. For many patients, even marijuana may set off psychotic symptoms in an unpredictable way, and it may take days to recover from them fully. One young man I treated remained virtually symptom-free on medication except when he smoked marijuana; he then become floridly psychotic for several days. Not every person with schizophrenia reacts so dramatically, of course, but there is no way to predict which will do so. Stronger drugs, especially PCP and amphetamines ("speed"), are like poison for anyone with schizophrenia. Families should discourage their use in every way possible, and should not allow a family member with schizophrenia in the home if street drug use is suspected. This rule is absolutely mandatory if the person has a history of assaultive or violent behavior; many of the homicides committed by those afflicted with schizophrenia appear to occur following use of street drugs. Draconian measures to discourage street drug use are perfectly legitimate, including requiring the person with schizophrenia to periodically submit to urine testing for street drug use as a condition of living at home, receiving support from the family, or remaining out of the hospital.

SEX, PREGNANCY, AND AIDS

Sex is an important issue for most men and women and there is no reason to think that it should be any different for individuals with schizophrenia. Mentally ill individuals are commonly consigned to an asexual status in our imaginations but that is a mistake. Individuals with schizophrenia run a wide range, from having virtually no interest in sex to being preoccupied with it, the same range found in individuals who do not have schizophrenia.

Studies suggest that approximately two-thirds of individuals with schizophrenia are sexually active in any given year. One study of women outpatients reported that 73 percent of them were sexually active; another study of men and women outpatients reported that 62 percent were sexually active, including 42 percent of the men and 19 percent of the women who had had multiple sexual partners within the past year. A study of individuals in a psychiatric admissions unit similarly found that 66 percent had been sexually active within six months, whereas a survey of long-term patients in a state psychiatric hospital noted that "sexual activity was extensive and far-ranging at the hospital."

Sexual activity for individuals with schizophrenia, however, is more difficult than for individuals who do not have schizophrenia. Imagine how complex sex would seem if you had delusions that the person was trying to harm you, or you were hearing constant auditory hallucinations. Dr. M. B. Rosenbaum, in a sensitive article on the sexual problems of persons with schizophrenia, described one patient who "vividly described all the angels and devils in his bedroom telling him what and what not to do" while having intercourse. Dr. Rosenbaum concluded: "It is hard for most of us to 'get it together' sexually—how much harder for the schizophrenic with his or her many very real limitations!"

Antipsychotic medications may also interfere with the sex lives of individuals with schizophrenia. One study reported antipsychotic medication side effects affecting sexual function in 30 to 60 percent of individuals taking the medications. These effects included decreased libido, male impotence, orgasmic dysfunction, and female menstrual irregularities. Such side effects are a major reason why some patients discontinue taking their medications, although they usually do not verbalize this. A few individuals have had their sexual lives improved by antipsychotic medications; for example, one report described two heterosexual men who "would routinely engage in continuous sexual activity for two to six hours while taking the medication at a properly adjusted dose." Whenever sexual side effects are being evaluated, it is important to inquire about sexual dysfunction prior to the onset of their illness as well. Since sexual dysfunction is relatively common in the general population, some cases of sexual dysfunction reported by individuals taking antipsychotics are pre-existing and not connected to the antipsychotic.

Another problem is how to assess whether the patient is a consenting adult or is being taken advantage of in the sexual situation. This usually applies to women, although occasionally men will be taken advantage of by homosexuals. Questions which the family should ask itself include: Is she able to say no to men in nonsexual situations? Is her judgment reasonably good in other areas of her day-to-day functioning? Is she discreet, which suggests good judgment, in her sexual encounters? Is she trying to avoid men or is she seeking them out? Is she agreeing to sex primarily to obtain specific payment, most often cigarettes or food?

Consultation with the patient's psychiatrist and/or nursing staff at the halfway house or the psychiatric ward where the patient is known will often clarify the consent issue for the family. The family of one woman, for example, became upset when they found that she was having intercourse regularly at the halfway house and she told her parents she was being taken advantage of. Discussion with half-way house staff established that the woman was seeking out the sexual encounters, and her claim of being taken advantage of was designed to assuage the disapproval of her parents. If a woman really is being taken advantage of, however, increased supervision and restrictions in her activity may be indicated. Women who consent to intercourse merely to acquire cigarettes or food need a plan formulated by the families and psychiatric staff to provide these items reliably, so the person with schizophrenia will be less tempted to prostitute herself.

Protection against pregnancy is another problematic area for individuals with schizophrenia. According to one authority "the rate of children born to psychotic women is estimated to have tripled since deinstitutionalization first began in the United States." Condoms are the first choice for contraception because they provide protection against AIDS as well as against pregnancy; however, many men will not use them. Unplanned pregnancies are relatively common among women with schizophrenia; in one study 31 percent of the women had had induced abortions. Two methods of long-term contraception have been approved by the Food and Drug Administration and are now available for use by women. One is injections of medroxyprogesterone acetate (Depo-Provera), which need only be given every three months. The other is progestin implants beneath the skin (Norplant), which last for five years. Both methods can produce some menstrual irregularities but are highly effective and satisfactory contraceptives for many women.

Ethical aspects of contraception in women with schizophrenia can also pose major problems. Some women may not wish to use contraception for religious reasons. Others may not wish to do so because they want to become pregnant. It is easy to empathize with, for example, a 36-year-old woman who has just been released from the hospital after fifteen years and wants to have a baby before it is too late; it is also easy to empathize with the infant who is born into such a situation and who is totally dependent for care on its mother. The genetic facts on a baby born to two persons with schizophrenia are harsh—an estimated 46 percent of these children will eventually develop schizophrenia (see chapter 10). It is also true that most people with schizophrenia have enough difficulties looking after their own needs without the burden of a dependent infant. A study of 80 female "chronic psychiatric outpatients" reported that only one-third of the 75 children they had borne were being reared by the mothers. To assist in thinking through ethical issues regarding contraception in women with schizophrenia, some guidelines have been proposed by the Center for Ethics, Medicine and Public Issues at Baylor College of Medicine.

Once a baby has been conceived, the couple and their families are often caught between a rock and a hard place. Abortion and adoption should both be considered; responsible decisions frequently involve consultation with the psychiatrist, family physician, lawyer, religious adviser, and social worker. Often from such consultations a consensus will emerge on the best course of action, and this sharing of decision-making will alleviate the burden on both the patient and the patient's family.

It is known that women with schizophrenia are less likely to seek prenatal care or to follow instructions for it. Some studies have claimed that women with schizophrenia have an excess number of complications of pregnancy and birth, but an extensive review of these studies by Dr. Thomas F. McNeil, an acknowledged expert in this field, concluded that this is not so.

The major dilemma of pregnancy in women with schizophrenia is whether to take antipsychotic medications during the pregnancy. The safest advice regarding medications to give any pregnant woman is not to take anything. That may be impossible for women with schizophrenia. The antipsychotic drugs have been used by thousands of women while pregnant and appear to be safe compared to many other drugs used in medicine. Recent studies, however, have shown that these drugs occasionally cause malformations or congenital anomalies to the growing fetus, so they should not be considered completely safe and should be taken only when absolutely necessary. The most critical time for such damage appears to be the first three months of pregnancy.

Given what is currently known, a reasonable plan for pregnant women with schizophrenia is the following:

A. Stop antipsychotic medication for the first three months of pregnancy if she can do so without a serious relapse.

B. Remain off medication for as much of the pregnancy as possible beyond three months unless symptoms start to recur.

C. If it is necessary to restart the medication, use whichever medication she has responded to in the past. There is insufficient data yet to say that one type of antipsychotic medication is more dangerous than another during pregnancy.

D. Do not be heroic by avoiding medications at all costs. If the woman needs medication, use it. Having a pregnant woman who is acutely psychotic has risks of its own to both the woman and the fetus.

E. Discuss the issue of medication in detail before the pregnancy or as early in the pregnancy as possible. Be certain that the woman's family and all concerned understand the options. If the decision is made to stop medication, draw up a contract that specifies that the woman will resume medication if the doctor deems it advisable. The contract must be binding on the woman, even if she changes her mind because of her psychosis, so that she can be medicated involuntarily if necessary; this is sometimes referred to as a "Ulysses contract" after the Greek hero who ordered his sailors to tie him to the mast and not to change course even if he ordered them to do so in response to the Sirens' song.

Regarding the taking of antipsychotic drugs while breastfeeding, this should not be done. The drugs are transmitted in the breast milk in small amounts but because the baby's liver and kidneys are not mature the drugs may accumulate in the baby's body. Since a woman who needs medication has the option of bottle feeding, it seems an unnecessary risk to take.

AIDS is a new and important threat to the health of individuals with schizophrenia. Surveys of the HIV positivity rate among admissions to state psychiatric hospitals have ranged from 1.6 percent in

Texas to 5.5 percent in New York, but these surveys include patients with all diagnoses. The only survey done to date of HIV positivity of psychiatric admissions specifically with schizophrenia reported that 3.4 percent were positive in a university hospital in New York City.

Studies on individuals with schizophrenia regarding their knowledge about AIDS and its risk factors have reported a remarkably poor understanding. In one study of women with schizophrenia, 36 percent said that you can get AIDS by shaking hands, 58 percent said you can get it from a toilet seat, and 53 percent did not know that condoms help prevent AIDS. A 1993 study of condom use in the previous six months among individuals with schizophrenia found that condoms had been consistently used by only two of eight individuals who had had a single sexual partner and one of 15 individuals who had had multiple sexual partners. In another study, one-third of seriously mentally ill individuals had been treated for a sexually transmitted disease, a major risk factor for HIV transmission. Clearly we are just seeing the beginning of a major AIDS problem among individuals with schizophrenia and other major psychiatric illnesses.

What can patients and families do about the problems connected with AIDS? Open discussion, education, and the use of condoms are obvious needs and should be given high priority. An AIDS education program for patients with serious mental illnesses has been developed by Dr. Robert M. Goisman and his colleagues at the Massachusetts Mental Health Center. The AIDS epidemic is upon us and will not exempt individuals with schizophrenia.

MEDICATION NONCOMPLIANCE

Medication noncompliance by individuals with schizophrenia is a major source of frustration for families and the single biggest cause of relapse and rehospitalization. It is extremely common, with studies showing that approximately 70 percent of patients are noncompliant with medication by the end of the second year following hospitalization. It is also extremely costly; one research group estimated that medication noncompliance for schizophrenia costs approximately $136 million per year. Medication noncompliance is also found in other medical conditions, such as hypertension, heart disease, rheumatoid arthritis, and tuberculosis, but it appears to be of greater magnitude in schizophrenia.

There are three principle reasons for medication noncompliance in schizophrenia: lack of insight, medication side effects, and a poor doctor-patient relationship.

Lack of Insight

Impaired insight has been noted to be a symptom of schizophrenia for almost two centuries. In 1919, for example, Emil Kraepelin noted that "understanding of the disease disappears fairly rapidly as the malady progresses in an overwhelming majority of cases." One study of insight estimated that 81 percent of individuals with schizophrenia have significantly impaired insight, but two recent studies, carried out in New York and London, concluded that the percentage is approximately 50 percent. There is recent evidence that the impaired insight found in some individuals with schizophrenia is part of the disease process affecting the frontal lobes, i.e., the area of the brain we use for insight into ourselves is not functioning properly. There is also evidence that antipsychotic medications do not improve insight in most patients, even though other symptoms, such as delusions and hallucinations, may be improved.

One of the consequences of lack of insight is completely predictable—if a person does not believe he/she is sick, why take medication? In one study of schizophrenia, for example, the number of patients who were compliant with medication was twice as high among those with insight compared to those without insight. It is therefore not surprising that several studies have also reported an inverse correlation between insight and rehospitalization rates. Lack of insight produces medication noncompliance, which leads to relapse and rehospitalization.

Medication Side Effects

A second major reason for medication noncompliance among individuals with schizophrenia is the side effects of the medication. As expressed by Esso Leete who has schizophrenia: "Unfortunately the side effects of antipsychotic medications can often be more disabling than the illnesses themselves, and I have even experienced side effects from the pills I took to control the side effects of the antipsychotic medications."

Studies have shown that many psychiatrists are not clinically astute in their ability to diagnose side effects. In one study of psychiatrists, for example, "the major finding was a high rate of clinical under-recognition of all major extrapyramidal syndromes." Another study reported that "psychiatrists misjudged the bothersomeness to patients of 24 percent of side effects and 20 percent of symptoms." Among the most troubling side effects of antipsychotic medication are akathisia (feelings of restlessness), akinesia (decreased spontaneity), and sexual dysfunction. An early study of drug refusal by patients with schizophrenia found that "the reluctance to take antipsychotic medication was significantly associated with extrapyramidal symptoms—most notably a subtle akathisia." The author noted that the akathisia could change over time "so that a patient could be optimally medicated on one visit, and experience an akathisia or other EPI [extrapyramidal involvement] on the same dosage of phenothiazines two weeks later." Giving the patient an extra supply of antiparkinson drugs to take on an as-needed basis is a suggested solution. Akinesia is also especially difficult for clinicians to appreciate because it is primarily a subjective experience and may be confused with depression.

Poor Doctor-Patient Relationship

A third major cause of medication noncompliance in individuals with schizophrenia is a poor doctor-patient relationship. Arriving at the best antipsychotic medication and the right dose of that medication for any given individual should be a shared undertaking between the doctor and patient. Dr. Ronald Diamond, in a lucid paper on the subject, says that "it is still important to listen to what patients say and to take seriously their experience with their medication." Betty Blaska, writing from a consumer's point of view, makes the same point: "Many of the mistakes [of the psychiatrists] previously described come down to one thing: a refusal to see the consumer as an expert on his or her illness. The person with schizophrenia is *the* authority on *his* schizophrenia."

Instead, the norm for doctor-patient relationships in American psychiatry is complaints such as "I have this side effect but my doctor won't listen or take it seriously." One reason for this problem with doctor-patient relationships is that many of the psychiatrists in American public sector jobs were trained in other countries where the doctor is considered to be *the* authority and patients are not supposed to question his/her advice or judgment. Another reason is that the norm in many community mental health programs is for the psychiatrist to see the patient for 15 minutes every two or three months to check the medications; such a time frame precludes discussion of any except the most severe side effects.

There are other reasons for medication noncompliance in individuals with schizophrenia. Men especially do not like to take medication of any kind because it impugns their masculinity and elicits fears of dependency. Other patients may view medication noncompliance as exciting risk-taking behavior, like driving too fast or hang-gliding. Others do not take medication as a way to deny their illness; for them, taking a pill each night is a reminder of their misfortune and the parts of their lives that have been lost. Dorothy Minor illustrated such reasoning very nicely:

> I did not want to believe I was sick, falling to the false logic of medication. Instead of thinking, "I am sick; therefore I need medication," I thought, "I am taking medication; therefore I am sick, and if I stop taking medicine, I will be well."

Still other patients refuse to take medication because of their delusions, which may be either grandiose (e.g., a belief that you are all-powerful and therefore do not need the medication) or paranoid (e.g., a belief that people are using the medication to poison you).

What are the answers to medication noncompliance? It is important for families and mental illness professionals to recognize how common noncompliance is, including the high frequency of surreptitious noncompliance when others think the patient is taking his/her medicine. It is also important to ascertain the reasons for the noncompliance, because solutions to the problems of lack of insight, medication side effects, a poor doctor-patient relationship, and delusional thinking are quite different.

Better education of the patient should be helpful in most cases. One recent study of psychiatric patients' knowledge of their medication at the time of hospital discharge found that 37 percent of the patients did not know why they were supposed to take their medication and 47 percent did not know when to take it. Part of this is undoubtedly owing to the cognitive impairment of the person secondary to the illness. Using pill containers that have separate compartments for each day and using once daily dosing also simplifies medication taking. Using injectable depot fluphenazine (Prolixin) or haloperidol (Haldol), which only has to be given every one to four weeks, can also be very helpful when indicated.

The doctor-patient relationship can be improved if the psychiatrist is willing to accept the patient as a partner, not as an underling to carry out orders. Having the patient keep a daily diary of side effects and giving the patients some autonomy to increase or decrease medication dosage as needed can both be helpful. Medication should be approached as a joint venture with risks and benefits weighed against each other. The risks of medication noncompliance include rehospitalization, violence, jail, homelessness, and suicide, whereas the benefits include no side effects. The risks of medication compliance include side effects, whereas the benefits include living a more normal life and achieving a modified form of some of the person's original life goals.

For individuals who lack insight, none of the above may be effective in persuading them to take medication. Positive reinforcement is always worth trying and coffee and cigarettes may be sufficient. A higher stakes positive reinforcement is to have the clinic or case manager become the person's payee for his/her Supplemental Security Income (SSI) check and then to give the person his/her money when the individual comes to the clinic to get his/her fluphenazine or haloperidol injection or to give the individual an allowance upon taking his/her oral medication each day. Although this is not strictly legal in some states, it has become a very common practice and would probably be upheld by most courts. In 1988, for example, the U.S. Third Circuit Court of Appeals ruled that a man with borderline mental retardation and epilepsy was not entitled to receive his disability payments because he was noncompliant with the medication he needed to control his epilepsy.

For individuals who lack insight and in whom positive reinforcement is not effective, coercion is the only remaining option. Coercing an individual with schizophrenia can legally be done in one of three ways:

Conditional Release

When the person leaves the hospital following an involuntary admission he/she can be put on extended or conditional release in most states. Continuing to live outside the hospital becomes dependent on taking medication and following other treatment plans. Conditional release is used commonly for individuals who have legal charges against them, and is similar to being on parole. New Hampshire has used conditional release most extensively and most successfully, for individuals with serious mental illnesses.

Conservatorship or Guardianship

Conservators or guardians are court-appointed individuals who act on behalf of persons who are mentally disabled to protect their interests. They are used widely for individuals who are mentally retarded but, except for a few states, such as California, are used much less frequently for individuals who are mentally ill. In some states the conservator can order the mentally ill individual to take medication and arrange for hospitalization if the individual fails to comply. Studies of conservatorships for people with schizophrenia who lack insight have found it to be an effective mechanism in helping to stabilize the person.

Outpatient Commitment

Whereas a conditional release is an extension of an involuntary inpatient commitment, an outpatient commitment is a separate legal proceeding. The court in effect says that the mentally ill person can live in the community only as long as he/she complies with the treatment plan, which almost always includes taking medication. Two-thirds of all states have some provision for outpatient commitments, but it is only used frequently in 12 of those states (Arizona, Iowa, Kansas, Michigan, Nebraska, North Carolina, North Dakota, Rhode Island, Utah, Vermont, Washington, and Wisconsin) and the District of Columbia. Studies carried out in Arizona, North Carolina, and the District of Columbia have shown outpatient commitment to be highly effective in reducing the rehospitalization rate.

For individuals with schizophrenia who are being coerced to take medication because of their lack of insight, a common problem is how to monitor whether or not they are actually taking the medication. Using injectable depot fluphenazine (Prolixin) or haloperidol (Haldol) is the obvious solution for patients who respond to one of these medications. Many antipsychotics also come in liquid form that can be mixed with juice and the person can be observed swallowing it. Patients taking lithium pills can be monitored by taking blood samples and checking their lithium level. For individuals taking other kinds of pills or capsules, it is possible to mix substances such as riboflavin or isoniazid with the medication and then take urine samples to see whether the person is taking the medication. These measures have been used to assess medication compliance in other diseases, such as tuberculosis, but to date have not been used to routinely monitor medication compliance in individuals with schizophrenia.

For many mental illness professionals and other people, coercive treatment for individuals with schizophrenia is anathema. It contravenes our beliefs about civil liberties, the rights of individuals to privacy, and the freedom of speech and thought. The American Civil Liberties Union and the Mental Health Law Project in Washington, D.C., have staunchly opposed laws allowing coerced treatment and have obtained court rulings in some states that have made coerced treatment virtually impossible.

What these well-meaning but misguided advocates have failed to understand is that approximately half of all individuals with schizophrenia have impaired insight. When such individuals refuse medication they are doing so as part of illogical or irrational thought process. The right to be free of the symptoms of a brain disease must be weighed against the right to privacy. As articulated by one observer, psychiatric patients "will suffer if a liberty they cannot enjoy is made superior to a health that must sometimes be forced on them." The rights of the individual must also be weighed against the needs of the person's family and society as a whole, especially in those individuals who become assaultive or violent when not taking medications.

Underlying much of the debate over this issue is, many suspect, long-standing acrimony between the legal and the psychiatric professions. And since most judges are graduates of the former, the decisions to date have bent significantly toward the lawyers. This would be harmless enough if we were dealing only with a urinating contest among adolescent boys, but in fact many patients have been and are being hurt by legal decisions that ostensibly protect their rights but in reality do so at the expense of their health. As succinctly summarized by a prominent New York State legislator: "The state must begin now to reorder its priorities for the mentally ill; instead of first guaranteeing a client's right to refuse treatment, we must first guarantee his right to receive it."

I myself come down strongly on the side of giving patients medication against their will if they need it. Checks and balances should certainly be built into the system to protect the patient in the same way that involuntary hospitalization should be periodically reviewed. But the fact is that persons with schizophrenia are really sick, and to withhold medication usually hurts rather than helps them. I would urge those who advocate an elaborate court proceeding before involuntary medication can be given to spend a day on an acute psychiatric admission ward where the patients have not been medicated; it will be an unforgettable experience.

ASSAULTIVE AND VIOLENT BEHAVIOR

Assaultive and violent behavior by some individuals with schizophrenia has become an increasing problem in recent years. Studies have made clear that *most* individuals with schizophrenia are not assaultive or violent but that a small number of them are. The common denominators of those who are assaultive and violent are abuse of alcohol or drugs and noncompliance with antipsychotic medication.

Two studies of families who belong to the National Alliance for the Mentally Ill (NAMI) have demonstrated a high incidence of assaultive and violent behavior. In a 1986 survey 38 percent of the families "reported that their ill relative was assaultive and destructive in the home either sometimes or frequently." A 1990 NAMI survey of 1401 families reported that within the preceding year 10.6 percent of the seriously mentally ill individuals had physically harmed another person and another 12.2 percent had threatened harm.

These findings are consistent with other studies of assaultive and violent behavior among individuals with serious mental illnesses. Rabkin reviewed studies done in the 1960s and 1970s and reported that for patients discharged from public mental hospitals "arrest and conviction rates for the subcategory of violent crimes were found to exceed general population rates in every study in which they were measured." In another study, it was found that 15 of 20 individuals who were arrested for attempting to push people in front of subway trains in New York City had a diagnosis of schizophrenia. Steadman et al. also followed up patients discharged from mental hospitals and reported "that 27 percent of released male and female patients report at least one violent act within a mean of four months after discharge."

Other surveys of mentally ill individuals living in the community have reported similar findings. A methodologically excellent study by Link et al. in New York City found that former psychiatric patients were two to three times more likely than other community residents to have used a weapon or hurt someone badly and that most of the excess violence was committed by those individuals who were psychiatrically sickest and presumably not taking medication. Similarly, in the five-site Epidemiologic Catchment Area (ECA) study carried out by the National Institute of Mental Health, individuals with schizophrenia reported having used a weapon in a fight more than 20 times as often as individuals with no psychiatric disorder. There was also found to be a high correlation between violent behavior in schizophrenia and concurrent alcohol or drug abuse.

It should be emphasized that America is a violent society and, within this broad context, the contribution of individuals with schizophrenia to total violence is very small. It should also be reiterated that most individuals with schizophrenia are not assaultive or violent. However, a minority of individuals with schizophrenia are assaultive or violent and the problem will not go away simply by repeating outdated mantras to the contrary.

The three best predictors of assaultive and violent behavior in individuals with schizophrenia are concurrent alcohol or drug abuse, noncompliance with medication, and a past history of being assaultive or violent. Families that are faced with this problem must learn to recognize cues of impending violence and pay attention to them. If an individual with schizophrenia becomes assaultive or violent it is best to stay calm (listen mostly, but respond in a calm and sympathetic manner), keep physically distant from the person, and call for help and/or the police as necessary.

Most assaultive and violent behavior can be prevented with planning. If there have been one or more episodes in the past, the family should have safe-proofed the house (e.g., sharp knives are kept locked up), asked for a review of the person's medication, explored options for improving medication compliance (e.g., outpatient commitment), made an effort to reduce alcohol or drug abuse by controlling the person's funds, and conveyed very clearly to the person the precise consequences (e.g., the person will no longer be allowed to live at home) if assaultive or violent behavior recurs. If it does, then it is mandatory to carry out those consequences.

A family within which the patient has been assaultive or violent is particularly poignant and lives in a special circle of Hell. Its members are often afraid of the patient, yet at the same time feel sorry for him/her and recognize that the behavior was a product of abnormal brain function. The ambivalence inevitably felt by the family members is formidable; fear and love, avoidance and attraction rest uneasily side by side. Afterward, no matter how well the patient gets, no matter how much time elapses, the memory of the past assault or violence never fully recedes.

SUICIDE

The largest single contributor to the excess death rate in individuals with schizophrenia is suicide. A recent review of studies done on this subject concluded that "suicide is the number one cause of premature death among schizophrenics, with 10 to 13 percent killing themselves." This rate is just slightly lower than the 15–17 percent suicide rate reported in contemporary studies of manic-depressive disorder. Among individuals in the general population the suicide rate is approximately 1 percent.

Depression represents the single most important cause of suicide among persons with schizophrenia, just as it does among persons without schizophrenia. The majority of patients will experience significant depression at some point during the course of their illness; this realization should lead psychiatrists to remain alert for depression and to treat it more aggressively with antidepressant medication (see chapter 7). Depression may arise from the disease process itself (i.e., the schizophrenia affects the brain chemistry so as to cause depression), from the patients' realization of the severity of their illness (i.e., as a reaction to the disease), or occasionally as a side effect of medications used to treat schizophrenia. Depression must also be differentiated in schizophrenia from the slowed movements (akinesia) and slowed thought processes which may be symptoms of the disease.

Most persons with schizophrenia who commit suicide do so within the first ten years of their illness. As might be expected, approximately three-quarters of them are men. Those at highest risk have a remitting and relapsing course, good insight (i.e., they know they are sick), a poor response to medication, are socially isolated, hopeless about the future, and have a gross discrepancy between their earlier achievements in life and their current level of function. Any patient with these characteristics *and* associated depression should be considered a high risk for suicide. The most common time for suicide is during a remission of the illness immediately following a relapse.

Occasionally persons with schizophrenia will commit suicide accidentally in a stage of acute psychosis, e.g., they may jump off a building because they think they can fly or because voices tell them to do so. Most suicides in schizophrenia are intended, however, and are often carefully planned by the person. Like all clinicians who have taken care of large numbers of patients with schizophrenia, I have known several who eventually committed suicide, and such deaths evoke great sadness.

There are other suicides, however, which evoke not only sadness but anger. These are the preventable ones—the patient who is treated inadequately with medications and then told that nothing more can be done, or the patient who is doing nicely on medication until another doctor reduces it and begins insight-oriented psychotherapy. I wish I could say that these suicides were rare occurrences but they are not. The high suicide rate in schizophrenia is in part due to our inadequate care system (or, more accurately, nonsystem) on which these patients are forced to rely.

What can families and friends of individuals with schizophrenia do to minimize the risk of suicide? The most important thing is to be alert for it, especially in an individual who is depressed and who has recently recovered from a relapse. Past suicide gestures or attempts are an important predictor of future attempts. Expressions of guilt and worthlessness, hopelessness about the future, an unwillingness to make plans for the future, and putting one's affairs in order (e.g., giving away prized possessions or making a will) are all red flags that may indicate serious suicidal intent.

Families and friends should then *ask* and *act*. Ask the person if he/she is planning to commit suicide, e.g., "I know you have been depressed recently and I am very worried about you. Are you planning to harm yourself?" Some people are afraid to ask about suicide because they fear it will put the idea into the person's head. This is not true, and often the person is relieved to be able to talk about suicidal thoughts and plans. Most people who are planning to commit suicide have mixed feelings about it. Do not directly argue with the person about committing suicide but rather point out the reasons for not doing so. One excellent reason at this time is the promise of more effective medications with fewer side effects that are likely to become available in the next few years.

Act by taking away the person's planned modalities for committing suicide (e.g., a gun or pills) and similar weapons in the immediate environment. Act also by ensuring that the person's treating psychiatrist is aware of the person's suicidal intentions and urge him or her to aggressively treat the person's depression. If the psychiatrist is reluctant to act, put your advice and admonitions in a registered letter to the psychiatrist, if necessary, adding that you have consulted your lawyer about the case. The psychiatrist will get the message. In some cases involuntary commitment to a psychiatric unit may be necessary to ensure the person's safety until the antidepressant medication can take effect.

Despite the best efforts of family and friends, however, some individuals with schizophrenia will commit suicide. If family and friends have done what they can do to help, they should not feel guilty or blame themselves. Suicide in schizophrenia is the final and ultimate measure of the tragedy of this disease.

RECOMMENDED FURTHER READING

Caldwell, C. B., and I. I. Gottesman. "Schizophrenics Kill Themselves Too: A Review of Risk Factors for Suicide." *Schizophrenia Bulletin* 16 (1990): 571–89.

Cohen, J., and S. J. Levy. *The Mentally Ill Chemical Abuser: Whose Client?* New York: Lexington Books, 1992.

Corrigan, P. W., R. P. Liberman, and J. D. Engel. "From Noncompliance to Collaboration in the Treatment of Schizophrenia." *Hospital and Community Psychiatry* 41 (1990): 1203–11.

Diamond, Ronald. "Drugs and the Quality of Life: The Patient's Point of View." *Journal of Clinical Psychiatry* 46 (1985): 29–35.

Evans, K., and J. M. Sullivan. *Dual Diagnosis: Counseling for the Mentally Ill Substance Abuser.* New York: Guilford Press, 1990.

Hatfield, A. "Coping with Aggressive Behavior." National Alliance for the

Mentally Ill, 1992, pamphlet.

Hatfield, A. "Dual Diagnosis: Substance Abuse and Mental Illness." National Alliance for the Mentally Ill, 1992, pamphlet.

Goisman, R. M., A. B. Kent, E. C. Montgomery et al. "AIDS Education for Patients with Chronic Mental Illness." *Community Mental Health Journal* 27 (1991): 189–97.

Lehman, A. F., and L. D. Dixon. *Substance Abuse Among Persons with Chronic Mental Illness.* New York: Harwood Press, 1994.

Lohr, J. B., and K. Flynn. "Smoking and Schizophrenia." *Schizophrenia Research* 8 (1992): 93–02.

Minkoff, K., and R. E. Drake, eds. *Dual Diagnosis of Major Mental Illness and Substance Abuse.* San Francisco: Jossey-Bass, 1991.

Monahan, J. "Mental Disorder and Violent Behavior." *American Psychologist.* 47 (1992): 511–21.

Torrey, E. F. "Violent Behavior by Individuals with Serious Mental Illnesses." *Hospital and Community Psychiatry,* 45(1994): 653–62.

10

QUESTIONS ASKED BY CONSUMERS
AND FAMILIES

Lunacy, like the rain, falls upon the evil and the good; and although it must forever remain a fearful misfortune, yet there may be no more sin or shame in it than there is in an ague fit or a fever.

Inmate of the Glasgow Royal Asylum, 1860

Schizophrenia brings with it myriad practical problems. Other chronic diseases, such as polio, kidney failure, and cancer, may drain patients and families emotionally, physically, and sometimes financially. When the chronic disease affects the person's brain, however, then the management of the disease assumes herculean dimensions. Whatever one does and however hard one tries, there is always the lingering feeling that it is not quite enough. Managing schizophrenia is a task for Sisyphus, condemned forever to roll a huge stone uphill only to have it roll back down again.

DOES SCHIZOPHRENIA CHANGE
THE UNDERLYING PERSONALITY?

Does schizophrenia change a person's underlying personality? For many years I suspected that it did not, based both on my own experiences in observing my sister and in working with hundreds of people afflicted with the disease. I remember one young man whose symptoms I helped to get under control using a combination of antipsychotic medications. His family, however, kept complaining that it was impossible to get him up in the morning and urged me to try different medications. After doing this for several months without success, I inquired whether the family had had difficulty getting him up before he got sick. "Oh yes," they said, "he would never get up then either, just like he doesn't get up now." That ended my medication changes and taught me a most useful lesson.

Recently, an opportunity arose to ascertain whether schizophrenia changes the underlying personality. We utilized identical twins in which one had schizophrenia and the other was well. Since personality traits of identical twins are remarkably alike, by testing the personality traits of twins in which one is sick and one is well it should theoretically be possible to tell how much a person's personality has been changed by having schizophrenia. A total of 27 identical twin pairs discordant for schizophrenia were tested.

The results were clear and unequivocal. On personality scales that measure traits such as happiness, nervousness, and satisfaction with social relationships, the twins with schizophrenia scored significantly lower, as would be expected from having the disease. However, on the remainder of the scales of personality traits there were remarkably few differences and on many scales, such as adherence to traditional values or interest in risk-taking behavior, there were virtually no differences. A pair of quiet, pious women were both still quiet and pious even though one had severe schizophrenia. A pair of hell-raising, risk-taking young men were both still raising hell and taking risks, even though one had schizophrenia. The underlying, core personality of the person with schizophrenia had only been minimally altered.

The fact that schizophrenia alters a person's underlying personality relatively little has been noted by some observers. The mother of one of the most severely affected women I have treated expressed it as follows: "The daughter I would have had—were it not for this evil illness—exists in embryo in the daughter I do have." The disease and the person are not the same; they can, and should, be separated. Schizophrenia is an equal opportunity disease and randomly affects personality types from the most selfish and narcissistic to the most giving and altruistic. Once the person has schizophrenia, those underlying personality traits still are visible beneath the delusions, hallucinations, thinking disorders, and altered affect.

It is always tempting, of course, to attribute all undesirable personality traits in a person to the disease. I have known families who retrospectively idealized the personality of their family member before the person got schizophrenia when the facts were quite different. I have also known individuals with schizophrenia who used their disease as an excuse for all of their shortcomings and weaknesses when in fact they had the same shortcomings and weaknesses prior to getting sick.

It should be self-evident that schizophrenia also does not change the underlying personalities of mothers, fathers, brothers, or sisters. Family members come in all personality types and are not fundamentally changed by another family member having schizophrenia. Parents and siblings may be intrusive, helpful, rejecting, or loving, but such personality traits pre-exist the onset of schizophrenia in their family member. It was in fact the existence of undesirable personality traits in some parents of individuals with schizophrenia that formed the basis of family interaction theories of schizophrenia, reviewed in chapter 6; what these researchers failed to point out was that the undesirable personality traits in these families were neither more nor less common than they were in any other family. Schizophrenia is an equal opportunity disease for families as well as for individuals.

ARE PEOPLE WITH SCHIZOPHRENIA RESPONSIBLE FOR THEIR BEHAVIOR?

One of the most challenging problems for individuals with schizophrenia, their families, and mental illness professionals is to assess how much control a person with schizophrenia has over his/her symptoms and behavior. Most individuals have some control and can be held at least partly responsible, but the degree varies widely from individual to individual and, in a single individual, from week to week. Many patients, for example, can suppress with great effort their auditory hallucinations or bizarre behavior for brief periods but not for long periods. The dilemma of responsibility was expressed nicely by Dr. John Wing, a leading schizophrenia researcher in England:

> Part of the peculiar difficulty in managing schizophrenia is that it lies somewhere between conditions like blindness which, though severely handicapping, do not interfere with an individual's capacity to make independent judgments about his own future, and conditions like severe mental retardation, in which it is clear that the individual will never be able to make such independent judgments. There is frequently a fluctuating degree of insight and of severity.

What should be done, for example, when your son with schizophrenia insists on suddenly disrobing in front of visiting Aunt Agatha?
In some cases he may be responding to command hallucinations that
are telling him that if he does not do so the world will end and he will
be responsible. In other cases his disrobing may represent a complex
mixture of confused thinking and resentment against some real or
imagined slight by someone who looks like Aunt Agatha. In still other
cases his disrobing may represent a consciously hostile gesture toward
Aunt Agatha or toward his family. Some individuals with schizophrenia, just like some individuals who do not have schizophrenia, are very
skilled at using their symptoms to manipulate those around them to get
what they want. Some patients who are placed where they do not want
to live, for example, know exactly what to do behaviorally to ensure
that they will be returned to the hospital or wherever they were living
previously. And I have had many patients improve and tell me explicitly, "Doc, I'm a little better but I'm not well enough to go to work."

How can you tell how much responsibility the person with schizophrenia has for his or her behavior? Family members, friends, and
mental illness professionals who have known the person for a long
period of time are most capable of making such assessments because
they know the person's underlying personality traits. In the case cited
above, the family should sit down with the person after Aunt Agatha
has gone and calmly review what happened, why it happened, how it
might be prevented in the future, the consequences of such behavior
for the person's living at home, and the legal consequences for disrobing in public. It is often useful to include the patient's psychiatrist,
counselor, social worker, or case manager in such discussions.

The question of responsibility for behavior for persons with schizophrenia becomes even more convoluted when the person is charged
with a crime. In such cases the person may be declared incompetent to
stand trial and involuntarily committed to a mental hospital, or he/she
may be brought to trial. In such cases the insanity defense is often
invoked for persons with schizophrenia.

The insanity defense dates back to the thirteenth century, when it
was known as the "wild beast test" (insofar as persons are like wild
beasts they cannot be held accountable). In England in the nineteenth
century it was modified in the M'Naghten case to the "right or wrong
test" (insofar as persons do not know right from wrong they cannot be
held accountable). In the United States in recent years this has been
replaced in many states by the "product test" (insofar as their acts were

a product of mental disease persons cannot be held accountable) or by various modifications and compromises between the "right or wrong test" and the "product test." Most of these incorporate a volitional element, stating that the person acted on an "irresistible impulse."

Among the arguments urging the insanity defense for persons accused of crimes is the fact that it protects them from being simply convicted and punished as if they had been fully responsible. Thus, a person with schizophrenia who steals a car with the key in it because he thought it was his car or because voices told him to do so is not treated in the same way as a car thief who steals it to sell to others.

Arguments against use of the insanity defense are impressive, and many people have suggested that it be abolished. Deciding whether a person's behavior is a "product" of his or her mental illness is an exceedingly difficult and subjective task. As one observer has noted, "Almost all crimes, by definition, involve transgressions of societal norms that could be called insane." And in terms of an "irresistible impulse" it has been noted that "the line between an irresistible impulse and an impulse not resisted is probably no sharper than that between twilight and dusk." Such judgments are made even more difficult by the fact that they are retrospective. Who can really know what was in a person's mind when a criminal act was being committed months before he or she comes to trial?

Many proposals to change the insanity defense have included a two-part trial in which the issues of guilt for the crime and extenuating circumstances (including insanity) would be separated. In the first part the only question addressed would be whether or not the accused actually committed the crime. If the person was found guilty, *then* psychiatrists and other witnesses would be allowed to testify on the person's mental state and other extenuating circumstances; this testimony would be used to help decide where the person should be sent (prison or psychiatric hospital) and for how long.

If the second part of the trial specifically addressed the question of responsibility, such a system would be a definite improvement over the current legal quagmire engendered by the insanity defense. The insanity defense as currently practiced includes an assumption that persons are either responsible or not responsible for their actions. Sane persons are considered to be responsible, insane persons to be not responsible; it is an all-or-nothing determination. Such simplistic thinking, however, contradicts the experience of everyone who has ever lived with someone with schizophrenia. People with schizophrenia sometimes are fully responsible for their behavior and sometimes are not at all responsible; in the majority of cases, however, the truth is somewhere in between.

WHAT SHOULD BE THE RIGHT ATTITUDE TOWARD THE DISEASE?

Developing the right attitude is the single most important thing an individual or family can do to survive schizophrenia. The right attitude evolves naturally once there is resolution of the twin monsters of schizophrenia—blame and shame. These lie just beneath the surface of many families, impeding the family from moving forward, souring relations between family members, and threatening to explode in a frenzy of fingerpointing, accusations, and recriminations. Blame and shame are the Scylla and Charybdis of schizophrenia.

As should be clear from chapter 6, feelings of blame and shame are completely irrational. There is no evidence whatsoever that schizophrenia is caused by how people have been treated either as children or as adults; it is a biological disease of the brain, unrelated to interpersonal events of childhood or adulthood. But many people believe otherwise, and their feelings have often been based on what a mental health professional has said (or at least implied) to them. An excellent description of this process is recounted by Louise Wilson in *This Stranger, My Son:*

> Mother: "And so it is we who have made Tony what he is?" Psychiatrist: "Let me put it this way. Every child born, every mind, is a tabula rasa, an empty slate. What is written on it"—a stubby finger shot out, pointed at me—"you wrote there."

The consequences are predictable, with the mother lying awake at night remembering all the things she did that might have caused the schizophrenia.

> We had moved too often during his early years. . . . My tension during the prenatal period when his father was overseas . . . His father's preoccupation with his profession . . . No strong companionship and father image . . . A first child, and too many other children coming along too rapidly . . . Our expectations were too high . . . He had been robbed of his rightful

babyhood, had grown up too fast . . . Inconsistent handling . . . Too permissive . . . Too much discipline . . . Oedipal fixation . . .

There is, of course, not a mother, father, brother, or sister in the world who has not done things he or she regrets in past relationships with other family members. We are, after all, rather imperfect human beings, and it is not surprising that at times we all speak or act impulsively out of jealousy, anger, narcissism, or fatigue. But fortunately we have resilient psyches, capable of absorbing random blows without crumbling or being permanently damaged. People do not cause schizophrenia; they merely blame each other for doing so.

Moreover, not only do the well family members blame each other for causing the schizophrenia in the family, but the person with schizophrenia may also do so. James Wechsler's son, in *In a Darkness,* once turned to him and angrily exclaimed, "You know, Dad, I wasn't *born* this way." And in *This Stranger, My Son,* Louise Wilson recounts the following conversation with her son:

> "I read a book the other day," Tony said. "It was in the drugstore. I stood there and read it all the way through."
>
> We waited, alarmed by the severity of his expression.
>
> "It told what good parents ought to be. It said that people get . . . the way I am . . . because their parents weren't qualified to be parents."
>
> "Oh Tony," I began, but Jack's signal silenced me.
>
> "I'm a miserable wreck, because both of you are, too. You're queers and you never should have had a child."
>
> "In what way are we queer?" Jack asked quietly.
>
> "You never played ball with me. All you ever wanted to do was tramp around looking at birds or read. Or work in the damned hospital."
>
> "Well, maybe it would have been more fun for you if I'd been an athlete. I can see that. But I really don't see why that should make me such a terrible father."
>
> "Read the book!" Tony exclaimed.
>
> "Tony, there are a lot of things written in books, a lot of opinions that are inaccurate, distorted, or just plain wrong. Besides, I'm sure the book—"
>
> "Listen, even the doctor that I've got here agrees! He says nobody's born with problems like mine!"

The blaming of one another for the illness magnifies the tragedy of schizophrenia manyfold. By itself it is a chronic disease of the brain and a personal and family disaster of usually manageable proportions. But when family members add blame to its burden, the disease spreads its roots beneath the whole family structure and becomes a calamity of boundless dimensions. The pain that blame causes in such circumstances must be seen to be believed. One woman wrote to me:

> My mother died twelve years ago, tormented by my sister's illness. After reading every book and article published on the subject, she decided that she was to blame. My father, who is in his seventies, brought my sister home from the state hospital for five years following my mother's death, in memory of my mother, trying to prove that she wasn't sick. My sister was so sick he finally had to return her to the hospital.

Few members of the mental health profession have focused on the amount of harm that has been done by the idea that parents and families cause schizophrenia. Psychiatrists especially, as members of the medical profession, see themselves as unlikely to cause harm. We now know that this is not so, and it is likely that in the twentieth century psychiatrists as a group have done more harm than good to persons with schizophrenia. The harm has not been done maliciously; indeed I know of few psychiatrists who could be characterized as mean-spirited. Rather the harm has been done inadvertently because of prevailing psychodynamic and family interaction theories of the disease (see chapter 6). But it is harm nonetheless. William S. Appleton is one of the few professionals who have written about this, and he has analyzed the undesirable consequences that follow when professionals blame the families for causing the disease:

> Badly treated families retaliate in ways that are detrimental to the patient. They become less willing to tolerate the problems he causes, are less agreeable to changing their behavior toward him, do not give much information when interviewed, and pay few visits to the hospital.

Occasionally, families are reluctant to give up the blame and guilt they feel. This may occur, for example, in a family where there are still young children; if the parents believe themselves to be responsible for the schizophrenia in their older child, then by changing their behavior they can theoretically prevent it in the younger children. If, on the other hand, they believe that schizophrenia is a random biological happening, as all the evidence suggests, then they are helpless to prevent it. Guilt in such families provides an illusion of control. Another type of family sometimes encountered that resists giving up guilt is one in which guilt is the family's way of life. Usually one or more members of such families are in psychoanalysis and the family seems to thrive on guilt, wallowing in it and blaming each other as their principal pastime. In such families, as one mother explained to me, "guilt is the gift which keeps on giving." I encourage individuals with schizophrenia who come from such families to minimize time spent within the family setting because it is detrimental to progress and to getting on with life despite a handicap.

The obverse of blame is shame. Inevitably, if families believe that they have somehow caused the schizophrenia, they will try and hide the family member affected, deny the illness to their neighbors, and otherwise dissociate themselves from the victim in a multiplicity of ways. Persons with schizophrenia sense this and feel more isolated than ever. It is not unusual for the patient then to react angrily toward the family, retaliating by making less effort to control bizarre behavior, and perhaps disrobing in front of elderly Aunt Agatha. Such behavior generates more shame in the family, producing more isolation and anger in the patient, and the downward spiral of shame and anger continues.

Education may resolve the problem of blame and shame. When family members come to understand that they did not cause the disease, the blame and shame felt by them are usually markedly reduced and the living situation for the person with schizophrenia improved. The question of who is responsible for the disease should be asked of all family members, and the person with schizophrenia should participate in the discussion if possible. Once this is opened up, the beliefs and fears that will sometimes emerge in the ensuing discussion are extraordinary. And once the issue of blame and shame is resolved and put to rest, schizophrenia becomes much easier to live with. One parent expressed it this way:

> Once you have unloaded your guilt, laid upon you by well-meaning professionals, the next step is easier. If you have done nothing wrong and have been doing the best you can, then you have nothing to be ashamed of. You can *come out of the closet*. The relief experienced by this act gives you strength to go on, and support starts coming out of the woodwork.

Once blame and shame have been put aside, the right attitude naturally evolves. The right attitude has four elements and can be called a SAFE attitude: Sense of humor, Acceptance of the illness, Family balance, and Expectations which are realistic.

Sense of Humor

At first glance, a sense of humor seems antithetical to schizophrenia. How can the most tragic disease known to mankind elicit humor of any kind? And yet it is precisely because schizophrenia is such a tragic disease that a sense of humor is mandatory. Without humor the family burns out and loses its resiliency to handle the inevitable ups and downs inherent in the disease. The people I have seen that were most successful in coping with schizophrenia were those who had retained a sense of humor and an appreciation of the absurd.

What do I mean by a sense of humor? I certainly do not mean laughing *at* a person with this disease. Rather it is laughing *with* them. For example, one family in which the son relapsed each autumn and required rehospitalization had a standing family joke with the son that he always carved his pumpkins in the hospital. And when I sent my sister with schizophrenia a new suit as a gift she replied that "the suit looks ghastly on me and I gave it away." It is the kind of ingenuous reply which is often found in schizophrenia, a reply stripped of the social graces to which we have become accustomed, a reply which we would all like to make on occasion but usually do not. Being able to laugh with a person with schizophrenia on such occasions is good therapy for everyone; becoming indignant is not.

Perhaps the best example of the benign sense of humor so necessary in schizophrenia was told by researcher H. B. M. Murphy, while surveying a small Canadian village for individuals with schizophrenia:

One of our other informants learnt first of another case in a fashion which still less suggests shame or embarrassment. To use his own words, it happened that my wife had been making a social visit to them and she noticed a blanket over the parlour sofa as if some stuff had been covered up there. After a time, while they were having tea, it moved. She must have seemed a little startled, for they said: "Oh, that's just Hector. He always hides himself like that." Then they went on with tea!

Acceptance of the Illness

For both the patient and the family, this is the second important ingredient in the right attitude. Acceptance does not mean giving up, but
rather an acknowledgment that the disease is real, that it is not likely to
just go away, and that it will impose some limitations on the person's
abilities. It is acceptance of things as *they are,* not things as you wish
them to be.

Esso Leete, an articulate woman who has schizophrenia, described
the problems she has had in accepting her disease as follows: "I am
haunted by an evasive picture of what my life could have been, whom I
might have become, what I might have accomplished." Once acceptance has been achieved, however, the person is freed up from a huge
burden, as Judith Baum, another mentally ill woman described: "There
came the morning, sunny and bright and cold, when I accepted the fact
that I had a mental illness. It was a stormy, angry and tearful time. But
with acceptance came release."

Many individuals with schizophrenia and their families never
learn to accept the disease. They go on, year after year, denying it and
pretending it does not exist. When acceptance can be achieved it
becomes easier for everyone. One mother wrote about her sick daughter's reaction when the daughter fully realized her diagnosis and that
she had been the 1 in 100 to get the disease: "Well, I guess if it's per-
centage-wise it might as well be me. I have such a terrific family to
hold my hand, and since I've been tagged someone else has escaped."
Such an extraordinary attitude is an ideal to be striven for but rarely
achieved, because such insight and kindness are so unusual.

More common, unfortunately, is anger in both the patient and the
family. The anger may be directed at God for creating a world in which
schizophrenia exists, at fate for dealing a bad hand, at the patient for
becoming sick, or at each other for causing the illness. It varies from
being a mild resentment bubbling to the surface when social activities
must be curtailed because of the person with schizophrenia, to a more
virulent bitterness flowing beneath the surface of their daily activities
like a caustic acid. Occasionally the anger does not achieve overt
expression but rather turns inward; it is then seen as depression.

Whenever I encounter such families I wish I could send them to a
Buddhist monastery for a month. There they might learn the Oriental
acceptance of life as it is, an invaluable attitude in surviving this dis-

ease. Such acceptance puts schizophrenia into perspective as one of life's great tragedies but stops it from becoming a festering sore eating away at life's very core. As one mother told me, "You can't stop the bird of sorrow from flying over your head, but you can stop it from making a mess in your hair."

Family Balance

An important aspect of the right attitude in surviving schizophrenia is an ability to weigh the needs of the ill family member against those of others in the family. Families that selflessly sacrifice everything for the person with schizophrenia are usually doing so because they feel irrationally guilty about possibly having caused the disease. To provide care for a seriously disabled person living at home may be a job requiring 168 hours per week; furthermore, it is unpaid and offers few thanks. Who is to care for the caregiver, who more often than not is the mother? How are we to weigh the needs of other children? Or the needs of the parent or parents to get away periodically? It is important to weigh these conflicting needs calmly and rationally, recognizing that the person with schizophrenia does not always come first. It may be necessary, for example, to occasionally rehospitalize a person with schizophrenia for the needs of the family and not the needs of the patient; perceptive mental illness professionals recognize such dilemmas and support the family in such decisions.

Expectations Which Are Realistic

Modifying assumptions about a person's future is difficult to accomplish but important to attempt, for it often follows directly from acceptance of the disease. It is especially difficult if the person with schizophrenia had been unusually promising prior to becoming ill. Such families tend to hang on to the hope, year after year, that the person with schizophrenia will someday become normal again and resume his or her career. Grossly unrealistic plans are made, money is saved for college or a big wedding, and family members fool each other with the shared myth of "when he gets well again."

The problem with the myth is that the ill person knows it is a myth, and it puts him/her in a no-win situation. There is nothing the person can do to please the family except to get well, and that is beyond his or her control. Several observers have noted this problem and have urged families to lower their expectations for the person. If this is done, the families themselves become happier. Creer and Wing noted in their interviews with such families:

> Several relatives mentioned that giving up hope had paradoxically been the turning point for them in coming to terms with their unhappiness. "Once you give up hope," one mother said, "you start to perk up." "Once you realise he'll never be cured you start to relax." These relatives had lowered their expectations and aspirations for the patient, and had found that doing this had been the first step in cutting the problem down to manageable size.

Another parent said, "You've got to reach bedrock, to become depressed enough, before you are forced to accept the reality and the enormity of the problem. Having done that, you don't allow your hopes to become too high and thus leave yourself open to disappointment when they are not fulfilled."

This does not mean that families should have no expectations at all of the person with schizophrenia. H. Richard Lamb, one of the few psychiatrists who have worked assiduously on the rehabilitation of such patients, has said, "Recognizing that a person has limited capabilities should not mean that we expect nothing of him." Expectations must be realistic, however, and consonant with the capabilities of the person with schizophrenia. Just as the family of a polio victim should not expect the person's legs to return to complete normality, so too the family of a person with schizophrenia should not expect the person's brain to return to complete normality. Psychiatrist John Wing wrote:

> A neutral (not overemotional) expectation to perform up to *attainable* standards is the ideal. This rule, if difficult for the specialist to adopt, is a thousand times more difficult for relatives. Nevertheless, we should be humbled to recognize that a large portion of relatives, by trial and error, do come to adopt it, without any help from professionals.

The effect of lowering one's expectations is often to be able to enjoy and share things with the person for the first time in many years. Thus if someone who was an accomplished flutist prior to becoming ill takes up the flute again to play simple pieces, both the person and the family can enjoy that accomplishment. It no longer is going to be seen, implicitly or explicitly, in the light of when-you-are-well-you'll-be-able-to-give-concerts-again-dear. Similarly, if the person is able to ride a bus for the first time alone or go to the store by himself or ride a bicycle, these accomplishments can also be celebrated for what they are—often magnificent accomplishments for a person whose brain is not functioning properly. The person with schizophrenia and the family need to be able to find joy in such accomplishments just as a polio victim finds joy in relearning to walk. Oliver Sacks, in his book *The Man Who Mistook His Wife for a Hat,* expresses this attitude well in his story about brain-damaged and deformed Rebecca who could still see beauty in life:

> Superficially she *was* a mass of handicaps and incapacities . . . but at some deeper level there was no sense of handicap or incapacity, but a feeling of calm and completeness, of being fully alive, of being a soul, deep and high, and equal to all others. . . . We paid far too much attention to the defects of our patients, as Rebecca was the first to tell me, and far too little to what was intact or preserved.

HOW CAN RELAPSES BE REDUCED?

The threat of relapse is a shadow hanging over all individuals with schizophrenia and their families. Each minor deviation from the person's usual behavior is regarded as suspect. The question hangs in the air, often not expressed in words but rather as a sideways glance: "Is this the beginning of another episode?" "Should I/he/she take additional medicine?" "Should I say anything?"

As with all aspects of schizophrenia, the better informed consumers and families are, the better everyone will do. The best study of relapse in schizophrenia was done by Drs. Marvin Herz and Charles Melville. They questioned 145 patients who had relapsed and 80 family members. The following symptoms and signs were the most frequently reported:

Patients reported	Percent
being tense and nervous	80
eating less	72
trouble concentrating	70
trouble sleeping	67
enjoy things less	65
restlessness	63
not able to remember things	63
depression	61
being preoccupied with one or two things	60
seeing friends less	60
being laughed at, talked about	60

Families reported	Percent
being tense and nervous	83
restlessness	79
trouble concentrating	76
depression	76
talking in nonsensical way	76
loss of interest in things	76
trouble sleeping	69
enjoy things less	68
being preoccupied with one or two things	65
not able to remember things	60
hearing voices, seeing things	60

The remarkable thing about this study is the similarity of symptoms and signs reported by the patients and their families. In a later paper, Herz concluded that "it is extremely important to educate both patients and families" about the symptoms and signs of relapse, and that "family involvement is a crucial component in the treatment of schizophrenia."

In many cases the patient and/or family has learned over time which symptoms and signs herald relapse. One woman who had had multiple episodes of schizophrenia described to me the things she looks for: "My main prodromal symptoms are quick irritability and anger and, when out-of-doors, thinking that everyone I see looks familiar although I do not know *whom* they remind me of." Another woman described her relapse as occurring in four stages:

In the first stage, I feel just a bit estranged from myself. From my eyes the world seems brighter and more sharply defined, and my voice seems to echo a bit. I start to feel uncomfortable being around people, and also uncomfortable in sharing my changing feelings.

In the second stage, everything appears a bit clouded. This cloudiness increases as does my confusion and fear, especially fear of letting others know what is happening to me. I try to make logical excuses and to get control over the details of my life, and often make frantic efforts to organize everything; cleaning, cataloging, and self-involved activity is high. Songs on the radio begin to have greater meaning, and people seem to be looking at me strangely and laughing, giving me subtle messages I can't understand. I start to misinterpret people's actions toward me, which increases my fear of losing control.

In the third stage, I believe I am beginning to understand why terrible things are happening to me: others are the cause of it. This belief comes with a clearing of sight, an increasing level of sound, and an increasing sensitivity to the looks of others. I carry on an argument with myself as to whether these things are true: "Is the FBI or the devil causing this? . . . No, that's crazy thinking. I wonder why people are making me crazy."

In the fourth and last stage, I become chaotic and see, hear, and believe all manner of things. I no longer question my beliefs, but act on them.

Each person with schizophrenia has their own particular symptom pattern when relapsing, and that pattern tends to be similar from relapse to relapse. Personally, I find changes in the person's sleep pattern an especially useful indicator, and I ask about this frequently.

How can relapses be reduced? First, everyone with schizophrenia should keep their own relapse symptom list, and it should be familiar to their family and friends. Second, individuals with schizophrenia should try to identify those things that tend to exacerbate relapses (e.g., the stress of social situations) and avoid them when necessary. For example, it may be possible to attend the wedding of a friend when things are going well, but it may be best to call and say you cannot come if you think that you might be in the early stages of a relapse. Spending more time alone, reducing work hours, and getting more exercise are all examples of strategies used by some people with schizophrenia to reduce stress.

Third, always keep in mind that the single most common cause of relapse is not getting enough medication. This may be because the person stopped taking it, or because the doctor reduced the dosage, or simply because the person needs more medication at this point in their illness. And extra medication in the early stages of relapse will frequently abort it and get the person back to baseline. For this reason I give many patients an extra supply of medication and allow them to increase it on their own if they feel that they need it. Physicians do this all the time with diabetics who may need more insulin on some days and less on other days, and I find the same principle useful in schizophrenia.

Finally, remember that schizophrenia has ups and downs for no apparent reason, just as multiple sclerosis and Parkinson's disease do, and that most people have occasional relapses no matter how hard they try to avoid them. This is part of the disease process that must be accepted. For most people with schizophrenia, then, relapses can be reduced but they cannot be prevented altogether.

HOW CAN CONSUMERS SURVIVE SCHIZOPHRENIA?

For a person with schizophrenia, surviving the disease is often a major challenge. In recent years, however, a large number of suggestions have been put forward by individuals who are affected and by mental illness professionals. Such suggestions can make survival easier.

Most individuals with schizophrenia do better if they have a daily routine and a predictable schedule. This allows them to anticipate stresses and minimize surprises. One consumer, Esso Leete, believes that "a controlled environment is probably so important to me because my brain is not always manageable. Making lists organizes my thoughts."

Most individuals who successfully manage their schizophrenia also have specific plans for doing so. Identifying and coping with specific stressors is one aspect of this. For example, Leete describes her four-part approach as "recognizing when I am feeling stressed; identifying the stressor; remembering from past experience what action helped in the same situation or a similar one; and taking that action." Keeping a card in one's wallet or purse listing what to do when under stress may also be useful.

General coping strategies for surviving schizophrenia consist of activities such as exercise, good diet, and pursuing hobbies. Specific coping strategies are both varied and imaginative. For example, some individuals with auditory hallucinations find earplugs helpful to minimize the voices, sometimes in conjunction with a radio. Esso Leete minimizes her paranoia by always choosing "a seat where I can face the door, preferably with my back to the wall instead of to other people" and by "asking the people I am with questions like who they are calling, where they are going, or whatever."

Dr. Frederick Frese, a psychologist who has been hospitalized on multiple occasions for paranoid Schizophrenia, likens having schizophrenia to being a person in a foreign country where language, customs, and assumptions are alien. As such he recommends studying the "chronically normal persons," or CNPs, as he calls them, in order to become more aware of how their behavior differs. He says, for example, that CNPs usually look directly at persons to whom they are talking but "we are more easily distracted and if we look at others while we are talking we will see their facial reactions, making it more difficult to focus on what we are saying." Dr. Frese offers many practical suggestions, such as "don't talk with your voices where CNPs can see or hear you because it makes them very uncomfortable."

One of the most important things that individuals with schizophrenia can do to survive is to join self-help groups. These go under a variety of names such as Recovery Inc., Schizophrenics Anonymous, Project SHARE, On Our Own, and Psychosis Free. All such groups provide support and education and a place where, as one patient put it, "I can just be myself." Many groups also include advocacy efforts to decrease stigma and promote improvements such as better low-cost housing for mentally ill individuals. An increasing number of consumers have become affiliated with the National Alliance for the Mentally Ill (NAMI), and in 1990 a consumer, Thomas Posey, was elected President of NAMI's Board of Directors. Many consumers have also joined state consumer organizations and the National Mental Health Consumer's Association.

Such responsible consumer groups should not be confused with the much smaller group of "psychiatric survivors," as they call themselves, who are militantly opposed to psychiatry in general and to involuntary hospitalization and medication in particular. This antipsychiatry group denies the overwhelming evidence that schizophrenia is a brain disease and in general has adopted the positions of Drs. Szasz and Laing (see chapter 6). A more recent guru of this group has been Dr. Peter Breggin, a psychiatrist who has acknowledged receiving "extensive help from reform-minded allies in the world-wide Church of Scientology" and who in 1987 was investigated by a state medical board for "a complaint of professional irresponsibility." The antipsychiatry consumers, although small in numbers, have had a disproportionate amount of publicity because of funding support they have received through the National Institute of Mental Health (NIMH). Strange as it seems, the federal agency that is in charge of research on schizophrenia has at the same time been the main benefactor of the antipsychiatrists.

One of the most exciting recent developments among individuals with schizophrenia is the increasing role they are playing in providing mental illness services. In many communities they run drop-in centers for mentally ill persons. In San Francisco, consumers have been trained and hired as "peer counselors" on locked psychiatric inpatient units. And in San Mateo County, California, consumer "peer counselors" have been hired to do AIDs education and to provide support for other consumers who are being moved from psychiatric hospitals to apartment living. In Denver, consumers since 1986 have been trained in a six-month training program as case management aides and are playing an increasingly important role in the state's Community Mental Health Centers. The Denver consumer provider program has been replicated in Texas, Washington, and Massachusetts (see Appendix C) and logically should represent a wave for the future of mental illness services.

HOW CAN FAMILIES SURVIVE SCHIZOPHRENIA?

Families of individuals with schizophrenia face many problems in addition to those discussed in chapter 9. Family members, especially mothers, are often asked to simultaneously be the person's case manager, psychotherapist, nurse, landlord, cook, janitor, banker, disciplinarian, and best friend. This impossible array of family tasks is relatively new, since, prior to the 1960s, the majority of people with schizophrenia were hospitalized at least intermittently.

One question that frequently comes up is how should family members behave toward someone with schizophrenia? In general, people who get along best with individuals with schizophrenia are those who treat them most naturally. This can be verified by watching the nursing

staff in any psychiatric hospital. The staff who are most respected by
both professionals and patients treat the patients with dignity and as
human beings, albeit with a brain disease. The staff who are least
respected treat the patients in a condescending manner, frequently
reminding them of their inferior status. Often this is because the staff
person does not understand schizophrenia or is afraid of it. The simple
answer, then, to the question "How should I behave toward a person
with schizophrenia?" is, Kindly.

Beyond this, however, there are certain aspects of schizophrenia as
a disease which do modify to some degree one's behavior toward a
person who has it. These modifications arise directly and predictably
out of the nature of the brain damage and the symptoms of the disease
as described in chapter 2. Persons with schizophrenia have great difficulty in processing sensory input of all kinds, especially two or more
simultaneous sensory stimuli. If this is kept in mind, then determining
how to behave toward the person becomes much easier.

Make communications, for example, brief, concise, and unam-
biguous. As explained by one family member: "Look at the person.
Talk in short, concise, adult statements . . . be clear and practical . . .
give one set of directions at a time with no options."

Another mother described how she communicates with her adult
son with schizophrenia:

> My son seemed to have difficulty dealing with all the stimuli around
> him. He responded slowly and said that he had difficulty with "everything
> coming at me." At those times it was important for me to speak in simple,
> slow sentences. Requests were made for one thing at a time. Keeping
> down complexity was very important. Strong emotion increased his diffi-
> culty in processing what I was saying. However much in a hurry I felt,
> there was no way to hurry him. Patience was absolutely necessary.
>
> I learned finally the futility of arguments. When S. was in more acute
> stages, it was easy to get into impossible rounds of arguments. Often he
> could not be reasoned with, but I didn't know how to back off. I learned
> to choose carefully what had to be done, plan ahead how I would handle
> the situation, and not respond to all the objections. For example, I might
> say in a clear, firm, simple statement, "You must be ready to leave at 8:00
> o'clock." Then I stood expectantly, even handing him his coat, and open-
> ing the door.

Sometimes leaving requests by way of memo or over the telephone seemed to work better than face to face—I am not sure why—sometimes he seemed to be overstimulated by my presence.

Ask the person with schizophrenia one question at a time. "Did you have a nice time, dear? Who went with you?" may seem like a straightforward two-part question for a normal person, but for a person with schizophrenia it may be overwhelming.

It is also counterproductive to try to argue people with schizophrenia out of their delusional beliefs. Attempts to do so often result in misunderstanding and anger, as described by John Wing:

Patients tended to develop sudden irrational fears. They might, for instance, become fearful of a particular room in the house. Maybe they would tell the family the reason for their fear. "There's a poisonous gas leaking into that room" or "There are snakes under the bed in that room." At first relatives are baffled by this. Some admitted they had grown frustrated with a patient's absolute refusal to abandon some idea, despite all their attempts to reason with him, and had lost their temper. But they found this only resulted in the patient becoming very upset, and in any case the idea continued to be held with as much conviction as ever.

Rather than arguing with the patient, simply make a statement of disagreement; this can be done without challenging or provoking him or her. Thus a reasonable response to "There are snakes under the bed in that room" is "I know you believe there are snakes there, but I don't see any and I doubt that there are," rather than a peremptory "There are *no* snakes in that room." The patient has some reason for believing that there are snakes there—perhaps he/she heard them or even saw them. It is often useful for the family member to acknowledge the validity of the patient's sensory experiences without accepting the person's interpretation of the experiences. Such a statement might be "I know you have some reason to believe there are snakes there, but I think that the reason has to do with the fact that your brain is playing tricks on you because of your illness."

Family members and friends of patients are often tempted to deal with the patient's delusional beliefs in a sarcastic or humorous manner. The statement about snakes, for example, might be responded to as follows: "Oh yes, I saw them there too. And did you see the rattlesnakes in the kitchen as well?" Such statements are never useful and are often very confusing for the patient. It also reinforces their delusional belief and makes it more difficult for them to separate their personal experiences from reality. One patient, who believed he had a rat in his throat and asked the doctors to look at it, was told sardonically by the doctors that the rat was too far down to see. When the patient recovered he recalled that "I would have been grateful if they had stated quite plainly that they did not believe that there was a rat in my throat." This is good advice.

Another useful way to handle the delusional thinking of people with schizophrenia is to encourage them to express such thinking only in private. Talking about snakes being under the bed is not harmful within the context of family and friends, but if said in a crowded elevator or announced to the saleslady in a store, it can be embarrassing for everyone concerned. Discuss this frankly and straightforwardly with the patient and it will often be appreciated. As Creer and Wing point out: "A more realistic aim is to try to limit the effect of such ideas upon the patient's public behavior. Many patients were well able to understand this and to limit odd behavior, such as talking to themselves, and the expression of odd ideas, to private occasions."

An impediment to communicating with persons with schizophrenia is their frequent inability to participate in normal back-and-forth conversation. "One patient returned home each evening from the day center, ate in complete silence the meal her aunt provided, and then went straight to her room. . . . Her aunt, who was lonely and elderly, would have been very glad for a chat in the evenings. She was puzzled by the patient's almost total lack of communication." Such patients often are aware of conversations around them but are unable to participate. "One young man generally sat in silence, or muttering to himself, while his parents were conversing about family matters. Later, however, they learned that he had quite often spoken to a nurse at the hospital about such topics of conversation at home and had clearly been taking in what was said despite all appearances to the contrary." Many such patients like to have other people around them but do not like to interact with them directly. "One lady said she had been surprised to hear from a friend that her nephew suffering from the disease liked to come and visit her. 'I would never have guessed it because when he comes he just sits in a chair and says absolutely nothing.'"

An analogous problem families have in their efforts to relate to persons with schizophrenia is their impaired ability to express emotions. Frequently the patient will relate to even close family members in what appears to be a cold and distant way. This emotional aloofness is quite normal for many persons with this disease and should be respected. Difficult though this coldness may be, do not take it personally. The patient may find it easier to express emotion or verbal affection toward a family pet, and it is often a good idea to provide the person with a cat or dog for this purpose.

A common problem is how the family should behave toward a person with schizophrenia when he/she is withdrawn. It is important to recognize the need of many persons with this disease to withdraw. One mother wrote me that while chatting with her ill daughter as they were doing the dishes, the daughter turned and said: "Leave me alone now, Mom, so I can enjoy my own world." Sometimes the withdrawal can be pronounced. I once had a patient who remained in her room at home for weeks at a time, coming out only during the night to eat.

It can be puzzling to know what to do in these cases of social withdrawal. Should you insist that the person emerge from the bedroom and interact socially, or should you leave him or her alone? The answer is, as a general rule, to leave the person alone. If the withdrawal seems excessive or too persistent, it is possible it may herald the recurrence of more severe symptoms and will require evaluation by the patient's psychiatrist. But in most cases the withdrawal is being used as a means for coping with the internal chaos in the patient's brain and is an appropriate response. Family members should remind themselves not to take such withdrawal as a personal rejection but should keep themselves available. As described usefully by one mother: "When our son was acutely ill we managed best by not being too intrusive, by not trying too hard to draw him out of his world and into ours, but by always being available at the times when he needed our support and tried to communicate."

In social situations it is important not to expect too much from persons with schizophrenia. Remember that they may be having problems assimilating sensory input or understanding what is being said. Minimize the number and scale of social events in the house in order to relieve pressure on the person. Patients can often handle one visitor at a time, but groups are usually overwhelming to them. Similarly, taking the person to group gatherings or parties outside the home is often a difficult and confusing experience for the person.

Experiment to find leisure time activities which are enjoyable. Those with a single (or dominant) sensory input are usually most successful. Thus a person with schizophrenia will often enjoy cartoons or a travelogue on TV but will not be able to understand a show with a plot. A boxing match may be preferable to a baseball game. Visual spectacles, such as a circus or ice show, are often very enjoyable, while a play is usually a total failure. Individuals are, of course, different in this regard, and it is necessary to explore different possibilities. The fact that people enjoyed something before they became ill does not mean that they necessarily will enjoy it after they become ill.

A common trap that families frequently fall into is to blame *all* the person's undesirable or unwanted behavior on the disease. It should be called "the disease trap." Every little shortcoming, including the person's failure to pick up dirty socks or replace the cap on the tube of toothpaste, is blamed on schizophrenia. Families need to remind themselves that human beings come with peccadilloes built in and that there are few around who have achieved perfection. Resist the temptation to blame everything on schizophrenia and ask how many mistakes *you* made in the last week. Along the same line, allow individuals with schizophrenia to have a bad day now and then, just as we allow those of us without schizophrenia to have a bad day. We all need such days since our neurochemical and neurophysiological machinery does not work perfectly all the time; extending the privilege of a bad day to individuals with schizophrenia is both common sense and common courtesy.

Above all, cultivate the art of being unflappable. Radiate quiet confidence that you can handle any idea, however strange, that your relative may come up with. If the person's auditory hallucinations are worse that morning, simply comment on it matter-of-factly, just as if you noticed that a person's arthritis is worse: "I'm sorry to see that the voices are bothering you more today." One parent said, "The most remarkable lesson I have learned about managing a schizophrenic person at home is to try to stay as calm as possible. The upsets and delusions have not been caused by me, and being calm keeps my son that way also. I might be heaving inside but my behavior on the outside is controlled."

If the family member with schizophrenia lives at home, two things are essential—solitude and structure. A person with schizophrenia needs his or her own room, a quiet place that can be used for withdrawing. Families solve this problem in a variety of ways, including putting a small house trailer in the backyard. Structure is also helpful for most persons with schizophrenia, and they function better with regular meal hours, chores, and a predictable daily and weekly routine. One mother said:

> I found structure was very important during the more difficult days. Things were done similarly each day and at designated times, and every day of the week had its individual character which was kept as consistent as possible. This seemed to give him a sense of order, that life was predictable, and also established a sense of time.

At the same time that routines are established, realize that the person with schizophrenia may deviate from them for no apparent reason. This is especially true of sleeping and eating routines. One father complained about his son, "My wife will cook a meal, and then he doesn't want it. Then two hours later he suddenly decides he does." An admirable solution to this kind of problem was outlined by this mother:

> The second practical suggestion concerns the schizophrenic's need for a sudden intake of food. At least in the case of our son, available wholesome snacks are very important. I've learned to keep yogurt, cheese, cold meat, etc., in the refrigerator; fruit on the table; and quick canned meals on the shelves. All this has seemed more important than a regular schedule of meals, although three good meals a day helps, too. The strict time doesn't matter. If Jim fixes himself a can of stew at four in the afternoon, I simply leave his dinner ready for him to heat up when he's ready.

Another thing needed for a family member with schizophrenia whether he/she is living at home or just visiting is a set of clearly defined limits regarding which behaviors are not acceptable. A failure to bathe for several weeks has consequences that affect all family members. No family should tolerate assaultive or dangerous (e.g., smoking in bed) behaviors, and this message must be conveyed clearly and unambiguously. The consequences for such behaviors should also be spelled out in advance and the family must be willing to follow through on the consequences if it becomes necessary to do so.

Another problem that perplexes many families is the amount of independence and autonomy that can be given to a person with schizophrenia. The problem is similar to that faced by parents of adolescent children. As a general rule, persons should be given as much autonomy and independence as they can handle, and this should be done in a graduated series of steps. For example, a person who believes he or she should be able to travel alone to a concert and stay out late should be given the opportunity to demonstrate readiness by successfully going to the store regularly, traveling alone to the halfway house during the day, avoiding street drugs, and not getting into trouble in public because of bizarre behavior. I have known families who discreetly followed their family member on initial forays into the community to ensure that no harm befell the patient. When the patient asks for more autonomy, the family should set up a series of conditions which must be met before the autonomy can be granted; for example, a patient who asks to travel home alone from the halfway house might be told that this can be tried once the patient has demonstrated familiarity with the bus route and has successfully gone for two weeks without forgetting to lock the door of the house.

Chores are another means by which persons with schizophrenia may demonstrate their readiness for more independence. Sweeping, cleaning, doing the dishes, taking out the garbage, feeding the dog, and weeding are all examples of chores which may be appropriate to assign to the ill family member. Families are sometimes reluctant to assign such chores, fearing that any stress will cause a recurrence of the patient's symptoms. Patients who are lazy may encourage such fears, pleading illness whenever there is work to be done. One mother described the resentment which is an inevitable consequence of this situation: "It's so annoying when you've got lots of housework to do, and there he is, a fine healthy-looking young man, and he just *sits* there doing absolutely nothing." Doing chores will not cause a patient to become sicker, and such chores are used extensively in halfway house settings and clubhouse programs. They are an ideal way for patients to assume more independence and they increase the person's self-esteem at the same time. I have seen some extremely psychotic patients doing chores quite nicely and feeling better for having done so.

The management of the patient's money may cause the most difficulty of all. Many patients know that a portion of their SSI check is earmarked for their personal needs, and they believe they should have the right to spend it however they please. They should be reminded, however, that the personal portion of the check is intended to cover necessities, such as clothes, as well as cigarettes and sodas.

Occasionally persons with schizophrenia can take total responsibility for their money and can manage it with minimal difficulties. I know one woman severely affected with paranoid schizophrenia, for example, who is very delusional much of the time but is able to take monthly trips to the bank and manage her funds. Predictably, she will not tell the doctors or nurses how much money she has. More common, however, is the person who cannot manage money at all; some patients, for example, will repeatedly give away any money they have to the first person who asks for it. For such persons it may be useful to link autonomy in money management to other behavior indicating independence. For example, if patients have difficulty with personal hygiene and grooming, it may be appropriate to agree to give them more money to spend as they wish every week that they successfully take a shower without being told. The successful performance of chores is another way that patients can demonstrate that they are ready for greater financial responsibility.

Issues of independence and money management may also cause problems for families because of the family's inability to understand that their family member is getting better. When one has lived with a severely psychotic individual who may have even needed help in dressing himself, it is often difficult to recognize a few weeks later that the person is now able to travel by bus alone and manage a weekly allowance. Families have often been both scared and scarred, and their ability to respond and adapt sometimes becomes constricted.

Three other factors that help families survive schizophrenia are family support groups, education, and respite care. Family support groups are available in over one thousand locations in the United States under the auspices of the National Alliance for the Mentally Ill (a contact in each state is listed in Appendix D) and in Canada under the Canadian Schizophrenia Society. Joining the local support group is for many families the single most important step they can take to survive schizophrenia.

Formal educational courses to assist families in understanding and coping with schizophrenia have been set up by several individuals and can be very helpful. Many of these are listed in Appendix C.

For families who have their ill family member living at home, it is essential to periodically have some time off. One way to accomplish this is by respite care. For example the Palo Alto Veterans Administration Medical Center in California has a program whereby people with schizophrenia who are living at home can be readmitted to the hospital for two to seven days every two months to provide the family some respite. In South Carolina the Alliance for the Mentally Ill, in conjunction with the South Carolina Department of Mental Health, began in 1990 a one-week summer camp respite program for individuals with serious mental illnesses to give the families a week off from their usual caregiving responsibilities.

IS EE EXPRESSED EMOTION OR ERUDITE ERUCTATIONS?

One form of family education on schizophrenia that has received much publicity in recent years is expressed emotion. It originated in England in the 1960s, when it was observed that some patients with schizophrenia relapsed when they returned home to live with their families. Out of this observation came a series of studies attempting to identify the family characteristics which were likely to produce relapse. These characteristics included being overly critical, hostile, overinvolved and overidentified with the ill family member, intrusive, and highly expressive of emotions. The mother in a high expressed-emotion (high EE) family says things like: "John, you look like a dirty slob. Why can't you ever change your clothes? It's very embarrassing to me." By contrast, the mother in a low EE family handles the same situation by saying things like: "John, you would probably feel much better if you put on some clean clothes."

The corollary which follows from high EE research is that families exhibiting such characteristics can be educated to be less critical, less involved, etc., and that when this occurs the family member with schizophrenia is less likely to relapse. As described by one of the major researchers in this field, the relapse rate can be lowered "by teaching the patients and their families better methods of coping with stressful events and by changing the attitudes of key family members in the direction of greater support, less destructive criticism, and less emotional overinvolvement."

At first glance, research on expressed emotion seems reasonable enough. On closer inspection, however, this research elicits from me personally some expressed emotions which can be summarized as follows:

Surprise

Given what is known about the difficulties people with schizophrenia have in sorting sensory stimuli and messages (see chapter 2), it would be surprising to find that they were not affected by overtly expressed criticisms, hostility, or overinvolvement by family members. The main thesis of EE research appears to be, in short, self-evident. It is therefore surprising to find so much attention and research resources devoted to demonstrating the obvious. In 1985 alone, for example, NIMH awarded grants totaling $687,000 for EE research, and during the year four new books deriving from this work were published with such titles as *Expressed Emotion in Families, Working with Families of the Mentally Ill, The Family and Schizophrenia,* and *Family Management of Schizophrenia.*

Skepticism

Given the manpower and hours devoted to working with high EE families, teaching them to become more tolerant, etc., it is difficult to imagine that the findings of these studies will ever be of more than academic interest. Compliance with medication-taking remains by far the single most important factor determining relapse rates; if half the energy devoted to educating families about high EE was devoted instead to ensuring compliance with medications, the relapse rate of the patients would decrease much more dramatically than anything demonstrated by EE. There remain many methodological problems with EE research which elicit skepticism of its importance; included are the well-known Hawthorn effect (things will change just because they are being closely studied) and the apparent confusion between cause and effect in many of the research projects (e.g., did the family's high expressed emotion cause the relapse or did the characteristics of the patient elicit the expressed emotion?).

Suspicion

Although most of the EE researchers seem genuinely convinced that families do not *cause* schizophrenia in their family member, that is not true of all of them. Dr. Michael J. Goldstein of the University of

California, Los Angeles, one of the more prominent researchers in the EE field, has carried out research on disturbed adolescent boys which he claims "provides evidence that family attributes measured during adolescence are associated with the *subsequent* presence of schizophrenia or schizophrenia-related disorders in the offspring once they entered young adulthood." In other words, the family causes schizophrenia. In *The New York Times,* Goldstein was quoted as claiming that "the parents of these kids engaged in character assassinations." Such assertions make families of people with schizophrenia justifiably suspicious of EE research. Is EE research merely the offspring of Gregory Bateson's double-bind?

What, then, is the role of EE in schizophrenia? People with schizophrenia do best in situations where people are calm and communicate clearly and directly. The attributes of the right attitude discussed above (sense of humor, acceptance of the illness, family balance, and expectations which are realistic) are the antithesis of high expressed emotions; insofar as families are striving to achieve these, they should not worry about expressed emotion.

What about counseling or family "therapy" to help the family learn to live with the disease? If families wish to seek help from a mental health professional, that may be useful in some instances. Be very careful, however, that the mental health professional has an educational approach and will help you learn ways to manage the family situation, not a psychoanalytic approach that will merely produce guilt and blame. Families with mentally ill family members need to be educated, not "treated," and to do everything they can to learn how to live with a difficult situation. This is precisely the same for families with members affected by multiple sclerosis, polio, severe diabetes, renal disease, or any other long-term disabling disease.

WHAT IS THE EFFECT OF SCHIZOPHRENIA ON SIBLINGS, CHILDREN, AND SPOUSES?

Although most accounts of schizophrenia focus on the effects of the disease on mothers and fathers of ill individuals, schizophrenia is a problem for other family members as well. Brothers, sisters, sons, daughters, husbands, wives, uncles, aunts, grandfathers, and grandmothers may all be profoundly involved in the care of family members with schizophrenia. As such they have all of the same problems described in this and preceding chapters. There are certain problems, however, that these other family members confront frequently.

Shame and Embarrassment

Family members may be profoundly embarrassed by the psychotic behavior of their ill relative. Roxanne Lanquetot, whose mother had schizophrenia, recalls being "convinced that I would have been better off an orphan, I tried to hide my mother and deny her existence by pretending she didn't exist." Kathleen Gordon's ill mother would take her children "and sit us down on the side of a busy street and count trucks for hours on end. And write down the names of all the trucks that went by." One young woman I know almost literally stumbled over her mother, homeless and psychotic, in an airport as she was returning to college. And Meg Livergood, stopped for a red light in Miami, saw her homeless sister with schizophrenia shuffle across the street in front of her car but was too embarrassed to call out to her. One common reaction to such shame and embarrassment is to move as far away from the family home as possible.

Anger, Jealousy, and Resentment

Individuals with schizophrenia frequently occupy an inordinate amount of their family's energy and time, leaving little for other family members. Wendy Kelley recalled that when her sister developed schizophrenia "suddenly both my brother and I felt there was no time for us; everyone was consumed by what was going on with my sister." Jody Mozham, whose father had schizophrenia, remembers being "envious watching my friends have regular conversations with their fathers. . . . I had a father, yet I didn't." Anger and resentment may become exacerbated if large amounts of the family's financial resources, such as money set aside for college, must be used to pay for the ill person's treatment.

Depression and Guilt

When a person develops schizophrenia, other family members may lose a relationship. Ami Brodoff expressed this loss poignantly:

> That day, many days before it, and many days since, I've missed my older brother with the persistent ache and longing usually reserved for a loved one lost through death. Although grieving for someone who has died is painful, some sense of peace and acceptance is ultimately possible. However, mourning for a loved one who is alive—in your very presence and yet in vital ways inaccessible to you—has a lonely, unreal quality that is extraordinary painful.

The family members who did not develop schizophrenia may also develop survivor guilt, a common phenomenon in airplane accidents and other random tragedies. Paul Aronowitz described this when he announced to his brother, who was affected with schizophrenia, that he was getting married: "'It's funny,' his brother answered matter-of-factly. 'You're getting married, and I've never even had a girlfriend.'"

Pressure to Succeed

The siblings or children of individuals with schizophrenia often try to compensate for their ill family member by being as perfect as possible. In a study of the children of mentally ill parents, Kauffman et al. labeled the extremely competent offspring as "superkids."

Fear of Becoming Sick

Most siblings and children of individuals with schizophrenia are themselves haunted by a fear that they too will develop the disease. As Roxanne Lanquetot recalls: "Growing up with a mentally ill mother was oppressive and worrisome and it interfered with the development of my sense of self. I was terrified that I was like my mother and therefore had something wrong with me."

Forced to Play Unwanted Roles

Schizophrenia changes family relationships, often profoundly. Margaret Moorman in *My Sister's Keeper* described how difficult it was to change from being a younger sister to being, in essence, a mother for her older sister. Husbands and wives whose spouse becomes ill often must become their spouse's parent. Jody Mozham described the effect of her father's illness on her mother: "She once knew this dream man that turned into an invalid. No longer did she have the role of being a wife, she was his guardian." Kathleen Gordon, both of whose parents had schizophrenia, even at age four "was aware that I could not trust my parents in what they told me to do or in their behavior" and by age nine was the "virtual head of her household."

There are many things that family members can do to alleviate some of the burden of having a relative with schizophrenia. Education is most important, and this should always include even small children in the family whose ability to understand is much greater than most adults assume. Support groups can be extremely helpful, including the Siblings and Adult Children Network of the National Alliance for the Mentally Ill (NAMI). Julie Johnson, whose brother has schizophrenia, developed an eight-stage healing process for siblings as outlined in her book *Hidden Victims*. Acceptance of the inevitable role shifts comes slowly but is very helpful, including the fact that siblings will ultimately end up with at least some responsibility for their ill brother or sister once their parents have died.

Finally, many brothers, sisters, husbands, wives, sons, and daughters are learning to cope with schizophrenia by becoming advocates for better services and more research, working actively within their local NAMI chapters. A corollary of this is that many schizophrenia researchers, including myself, began working in this field primarily because we had a family member affected with the disease. I also know many clinical psychiatrists, psychologists, psychiatric social workers, and psychiatric nurses whose work is also motivated by the fact that someone in their family has schizophrenia. They tend to be among the best professionals.

SHOULD PEOPLE WITH SCHIZOPHRENIA
DRIVE MOTOR VEHICLES?

Remarkably little has been written about whether individuals with schizophrenia should drive motor vehicles, despite the fact that patients, their families, and insurance companies face this problem regularly. In a 1989 study of this problem it was reported that only 68 percent of outpatients with schizophrenia drive compared to 99 percent of nonpsychiatrically ill controls. Even those patients who did drive did so far less than the controls. Most importantly, mile for mile, the drivers with schizophrenia had an accident rate that was twice as high as the controls. Two earlier studies had not found a higher accident rate among drivers with schizophrenia.

Should individuals with schizophrenia drive motor vehicles? Driving a vehicle utilizes three separate skills: 1) planning trips and making decisions about crowded roads and darkness; 2) tactical decisions involving judgment and paying attention, such as knowing when to pass another vehicle; and 3) operational coordination such as quickly putting on the brakes. Individuals with schizophrenia are least likely to have problems with operational coordination, although some slowing of movements may be a side effect of antipsychotic drugs. However, some individuals with schizophrenia are clearly impaired in their planning and/or tactical decisions, and this should be self-evident from their planning, judgment, and ability to pay attention in other areas of their lives.

In summary, the majority of individuals with schizophrenia can and do drive. However, those whose planning and/or tactical decisions are clearly impaired should not drive. For some patients whose ability to drive is dependent on taking antipsychotic medication, it would seem reasonable to make their driving license conditional on taking medication, much as is done for some people with epilepsy.

WHAT ABOUT SAFETY ISSUES?

Individuals with schizophrenia are victimized much more often than is generally acknowledged. This victimization has increased as progressively more severely impaired individuals have been deinstitutionalized from state psychiatric hospitals. In one study of 114 people with schizophrenia living in a board-and-care home in Los Angeles, during the preceding year 25 of them (22 percent) had been robbed and 34 of them (30 percent) had been "beaten up, assaulted or raped." For people with schizophrenia who are living in public shelters or on the streets, the number who are robbed or assaulted is even higher. When people with schizophrenia call the police or attempt to bring charges, they may be hampered by their inability to explain to the police what happened, skepticism on the part of the police, and the reality that if the case should go to court the patient would be a very poor witness. Most released patients learn these facts of life soon after leaving the hospital and are forced to accept assaults as a part of life if they wish to remain in the community. Many cite this as a major reason for wishing to return to the hospital, the "asylum," where they feel safer.

Several steps can be taken to improve the safety of individuals with schizophrenia. Most important is not placing group homes or other living facilities in high crime neighborhoods. For individuals with schizophrenia who are living on their own, partially subsidized housing is needed because in many cities the only housing units that are affordable on SSI or SSDI are in high crime areas. This is also a major reason why many people with schizophrenia have a better quality of life living in a small town rather than in a large city.

Another step which will improve the safety of individuals with schizophrenia is organized training sessions on self-defense, how to avoid being victimized, and how to report a crime to the police. Bringing members of the local police force to the group home, day program, clubhouse, or other gathering place would make such training sessions more effective as well as making both the police and the patients more comfortable with each other.

HOW DO RELIGIOUS ISSUES AFFECT PEOPLE WITH SCHIZOPHRENIA?

Like all human beings, persons with schizophrenia have a need to relate to a god or philosophical worldview which allows them to place themselves and their lives within a larger context. For persons with schizophrenia this can be particularly problematical for many reasons. For one thing, the onset of the disease often occurs during the same period of life when religious and philosophical beliefs are in great flux, thus making resolution extremely difficult. Another complicating factor is that many persons with this disease undergo intense heightened awareness, or "peak experiences" (as described in chapter 2), during the early stages of their illness and conclude that they have been specially chosen by God. When auditory hallucinations are experienced, these usually reinforce such a belief. Still another impediment to resolution of religious concerns is the person's inability to think metaphorically and in symbols, which most formalized religious belief systems require.

It is therefore not surprising that religious concerns continue to be important for many persons with this disease throughout the course of their illness.

Delusions of a religious nature are extremely common, and can be found in almost half of all people with schizophrenia. It is also known that members of the clergy are frequently consulted by individuals with schizophrenia; in one study it was found that "the clergy are as likely as mental health professionals to be sought out by individuals from the community who have serious psychiatric disorders." Many clergy are knowledgeable and helpful in such situations. Unfortunately, however, many others are not current regarding what is known about serious mental illnesses and erroneously tell mentally ill persons or their families that the illness has been caused by sin. Such a message can, of course, be very destructive and make an already bad situation much worse. Various efforts are under way to educate the clergy about mental illness, including groups such as the Religious Outreach Network and Pathways to Promise, organized under the National Alliance for the Mentally Ill (see Appendix C).

Occasionally individuals with schizophrenia resolve their religious concerns by joining a religious cult of one kind or another. The variety of available cults is wide and includes the Unification Church ("Moonies"), Hare Krishna, Divine Light Mission, Jesus People, Scientology, and many smaller groups. A study reported that 6 percent of members from the Unification Church and 9 percent of members from the Divine Light Mission had been previously hospitalized for psychiatric problems. However, psychiatrists who have studied such groups believe that most of these previously hospitalized members were severely neurotic. The groups themselves tend to exclude seriously disturbed individuals as too disruptive to the closely cooperative living and working conditions demanded by the groups.

For individuals with schizophrenia who are accepted into these cults there may be some advantages. A highly structured belief system and life style are inherent in such groups, as is also a sense of belongingness and community. These in turn lead to increased self-esteem in the member. Some cults also value unusual religious experiences, and in such settings a person with schizophrenia may feel more comfortable with his/her "peak experiences" or auditory hallucinations.

The cults also pose additional potential dangers, however. Many such groups emphasize the desirability of not taking any drugs; patients who are doing nicely on maintenance fluphenazine or haloperidol may be encouraged to stop the drug, with resultant relapse. The groups may also encourage the person to deny the reality of his or her illness, casting problems such as delusional thinking and auditory hallucinations into the mold of spiritual shortcomings rather than acknowledging that they are products of a brain disease. Some groups may also encourage paranoid thinking in persons who are already inclined in that direction, as there is often a siege mentality in the cults, a "we-they" feeling that the world is out to persecute them as a group. Finally, a few religious cults may exploit the money or property of members with schizophrenia, as they sometimes do of other members as well.

WHY IS CONFIDENTIALITY A PROBLEM?

The need for confidentiality of communications between persons with schizophrenia and mental illness professionals, including the confidentiality of their records, periodically raises ethical problems for both professionals and the families of patients. For example when a person with schizophrenia (or any other mental disorder) confides to a mental illness professional a wish or plan to harm another person, in the past such communications were considered to be confidential and legally exempted from disclosure under physician-patient confidentiality. In 1976, however, courts in California ruled that mental illness professionals have a duty to warn the potential victim in such situations. This ruling, generally referred to as the Tarasoff decision, has been extended to many other states.

The biggest problem of confidentiality for patients' families is the reluctance of mental illness professionals to share information about the family member's illness because of the fear of breaking confidentiality. State laws vary in this regard but such confidentiality has been invoked to an absurd degree by professionals in many states. The following, for example, is an account of a mother's attempts to get information about her son during the six months he was committed to a psychiatric hospital in Boston:

> I was never told how he was doing. I was in complete darkness about his prognosis, whether positive or negative. Each time I questioned the social worker assigned to his case, which was almost daily, the answer would be, "Danny would not give us permission today to tell you how he was doing."
>
> This was the reply I received for the first month or so. Then one day, moved by pity because of the state of anxiety I was in, she replied to my inquiry, "Danny would not give us permission today to tell you how he was doing but the patients on the ward are doing well today."
>
> I grasped at her coded message with much relief. But after hearing that same coded message and only that for the remainder of his commitment, it became quite evident to me that the system was as ill as my son and needed much help.

This is a travesty of confidentiality. More often than not, such reluctance to share information under the guise of confidentiality simply reflects the disinterest of the mental illness professionals in having anything to do with the families. It may also represent the lingering psychoanalytic orientation of the professionals with an implicit message: "You the family caused this disease, so now as punishment you have no right to know what is going on."

What can the family do? Become knowledgeable about the state laws regarding confidentiality. Get the laws changed if they appear to be too restrictive. On individual cases complain to the professional's supervisors and act in concert with other organizational consumers as outlined in chapter 11. Do not accept any less information than you would expect to be forthcoming from professionals if your family member had another brain disease, such as multiple sclerosis or Alzheimer's disease.

SHOULD YOU TELL PEOPLE
THAT YOU HAVE SCHIZOPHRENIA?

The question of whether or not to tell people that you have schizophrenia is a difficult one, especially when the person is a prospective date or employer. Increasingly frequently, however, the answer is "yes."

Some issues to consider in thinking about the problem are: Is the person likely to find out anyway? How sophisticated is the person likely to be about mental illness? If I withhold this information, will the person be able to trust me on other issues? How difficult is it for me to interact with the person knowing that I have not told him/her?

Since the early 1980s there has been a dramatic increase in open discussion of schizophrenia by both consumers and their families. The Americans with Disabilities Act affords some theoretical protection against discrimination by employers, but how effective this will be in actuality remains to be seen. There are still occasions, however, when it is better not to disclose the fact that you have schizophrenia. On such occasions Dr. Frederick Frese, a psychologist who has schizophrenia, suggests "that you respond by saying you are a writer, an artist, a (mental health) consultant, or perhaps that you freelance, depending on how you have been spending your time. None of these responses are lies, per se, but they leave considerable latitude for interpretation and they do not require that you have a specific employer or work location."

GENETIC COUNSELING: WHAT ARE THE CHANCES OF GETTING SCHIZOPHRENIA?

Almost every brother, sister, son, daughter, nephew, or niece of a person with schizophrenia has at one time or another wondered about the chances of themselves or their children developing schizophrenia. Furthermore, with most individuals with schizophrenia now living in the community, it is inevitable that increasing numbers of them are marrying and having children of their own.

One might suppose that information on the risk of developing schizophrenia in relatives of affected individuals would be accurate, widely available, and generally agreed upon by the experts. One would be wrong. As discussed in chapter 6, opinions regarding the relative importance of genetic factors in the causation of schizophrenia vary widely and these opinions in turn inevitably color genetic counseling. A researcher who believes that genetic factors are the most important antecedents of schizophrenia will give comparatively conservative advice regarding reproduction among relatives, while a researcher who believes that genetic factors are comparatively unimportant will be likely to give less conservative advice.

The most widely utilized lifetime risk figures for developing schizophrenia have been compiled by Dr. Irving I. Gottesman, one of the foremost researchers on the genetics of schizophrenia. They are as follows:

Risk for any random individual	1.5 percent
Risk for brother or sister when one sibling is affected	9.6 percent
Risk for half-brother or sister when one sibling is affected	4.2 percent
Risk for child when one parent is affected	12.8 percent
Risk for child when both parents are affected	46.3 percent
Risk for nephews and nieces of affected person	3.0 percent
Risk for grandchildren of affected person	3.7 percent

The bottom line of these risk figures is that genetics *do* play some role in the causation of schizophrenia and that having a relative with schizophrenia *does* increase a relative's risk for also developing the disease. In addition to this conclusion, however, there are several additional points which should be noted:

1. There are suggestions that the risk figures cited above are worst-case scenarios and that the true risks may not be as high. This is because many of the studies on which these risk figures are based were done many years ago using less sophisticated research methodology (e.g., no control groups, diagnostic criteria not standardized, relatives not personally examined, researcher nonblind regarding subjects' relationships). For example, two more recent studies of the risk of schizophrenia in the children of two parents with the disease reported definite schizophrenia in only 28 and 29 percent of them. Similarly it is generally stated in textbooks that the risk of developing schizophrenia is 50 percent in the second twin when one identical twin develops the disease. A recent reanalysis of the studies on which this figure was based concluded that a more accurate risk figure was only 28 percent.

2. It is clearly established that an increased number of relatives

with schizophrenia substantially increases the risk of developing the disease. From a practical point of view this means that if your sister is your only close relative with schizophrenia, your own risk is very low. If, on the other hand, your uncle and sister both have schizophrenia, then your risk is higher. And if you are unfortunate enough to come from one of the relatively rare families which are heavily loaded with the disorder (e.g., mother, aunt, grandfather, and two siblings affected), then your own risk is substantially higher and you should give serious consideration to the question of having children.

3. The risk of having a child who will develop schizophrenia obviously increases with the number of children one has. If you come from a family with several members affected with schizophrenia, your chances of having a child with schizophrenia are four times greater if you have eight children rather than two.

4. The risks of developing schizophrenia can be viewed as a glass half empty or half full. For a brother or sister of an affected sibling the probability of developing schizophrenia is 9.6 percent, but the risk of *not* developing it is 90.4 percent. For a child when one parent is affected, the risk of developing schizophrenia is 12.8 percent but the probability of *not* developing it is 87.2 percent. Even for identical twins the probability of the second twin *not* developing schizophrenia is 72 percent.

5. Schizophrenia is only one of many disorders for which there is some genetic risk. Creating life is, and always has been, a genetic lottery. Knowing the odds in the game will not make the decision for you but will allow you to choose more intelligently.

WHAT WILL HAPPEN WHEN THE PARENTS DIE?

One of the most troubling problems for families with a family member with schizophrenia is what will happen after the family members who are providing the care die. Typically it is a mother and father who provide much of the care needed by an ill son or daughter, although in other cases the same problem may arise for an aging or sick person who is providing care for an ill sibling. In the old days such care was transferred to the extended family or the state hospital. Now, however, the extended family has disappeared and the state hospital will simply discharge the person with schizophrenia to live in the community. The specter of their family member ending up living in public shelters and on the streets haunts many families.

Guardianship is one mechanism used by families to ensure care for the family member and safeguard his or her assets after the death of the well family members. The guardian may be either a relative or friend of the patient or, if none is available or appropriate, another person selected by the judge. The appointment of a guardian occurs most frequently when the patient owns large amounts of money or property or is likely to inherit some. Guardianship is a legal relationship authorizing one person to make decisions for another and is based upon the same *parens patriae* tenet of English law which permits involuntary hospitalization. When the guardian has jurisdiction only over the property of the patient, it is frequently referred to as a conservatorship. When both property and personal decisions are involved it is called a guardianship.

Guardianship (and conservatorship) laws are remarkably outmoded in most states. In many instances no distinction is made between personal and property decisions, and a guardian automatically is granted decision-making permission for both. Personal decisions affected by a guardianship may include where the patient may reside, the right to travel freely, and the right to consent to medical or psychiatric treatment; property decisions may include the right to sign checks or withdraw money from a bank account. Most guardianship laws are all-or-nothing affairs and fail to take into account the ability of patients to manage some areas of their lives but not others. The laws are often extremely vague: the law in California, until recently changed, said that a guardian could be appointed for any "incompetent person . . . whether insane or not . . . , who is likely to be deceived or imposed upon by artful and designing persons." This could include most of us! The actual appointment of a guardian is usually done without legal due process and without the patient present; nor is there periodic review to determine whether the guardianship is still necessary.

Another mechanism used by some families to plan for the future are nonprofit organizations founded by groups of families. These organizations will accept responsibility for the ill family member after the death of the well family members. For many years, such organizations have been utilized by families with mentally retarded members; recently groups under the National Alliance for the Mentally Ill have been setting them up on a local level. For example, in Virginia and Maryland there is the Planned Life Assistance Network (PLAN), with family members serving on the organization's board of directors. A person who joins pays a membership fee and annual dues, then develops a plan of care for the family member with schizophrenia to be activated after the death of other family members. At that time the professional staff and volunteers of PLAN will assume the responsibilities previously provided by the family, including visiting the person regularly, maintaining contact with the person's doctor or case manager, paying the person's bills, acting as payee for SSI payments, and assuming other fiscal or supervisory functions as needed.

RECOMMENDED FURTHER READING

Backlar, P. *The Family Face of Schizophrenia: Practical Counsel from America's Leading Experts.* New York: G. P. Putnam, 1994.

Bernheim, K. F., and A. F. Lehman. *Working with Families of the Mentally Ill.* New York: W. W. Norton, 1985.

Bernheim, K. F., R. R. J. Lewine, and C. T. Beale. *The Caring Family: Living with Chronic Mental Illness.* New York: Random House, 1982.

Busick, B. S., and M. Gorman. *Ill Not Insane.* Boulder, CO: New Idea Press, 1986.

Creer, C., and J, Wing. *Schizophrenia at Home.* London: Institute of Psychiatry, 1974.

Dearth, N. S., B. J. Labenski, M. E. Mott, et al. *Families Helping Families.* New York: W. W. Norton, 1986.

Deveson, A. *Tell Me I'm Here.* New York: Penguin, 1992.

Esser, A. H., and S. D. Lacey. *Mental Illness: A Homecare Guide.* New York: John Wiley, 1989.

Flach, F. *Rickie.* New York: Fawcett Columbine, 1990.

Garson, S. *Out of Our Minds.* Buffalo: Prometheus Books, 1986.

Gottesman, I. I. *Schizophrenia Genesis: The Origins of Madness.* New York: W. H. Freeman, 1991.

Hatfield, A. B., ed. *Families of the Mentally Ill: Meeting the Challenge.* San Francisco: Jossey-Bass, 1987.

Hatfield, A. B. *Family Education in Mental Illness.* New York: Guilford Press, 1990.

Hatfield, A. B., and H. P. Lefley, eds. *Families of the Mentally Ill: Coping and Adaptation.* New York, Guilford Press, 1987.

Hatfield, A. B., and H. P. Lefley. *Surviving Mental Illness: Stress, Coping and Adaptation.* New York: Guilford Press, 1993.

Hinckley, J., and J. A. Hinckley. *Breaking Points.* Grand Rapids, MI: Chosen Books, 1985.

Howells, J. G., and W. R. Guirguis. *The Family and Schizophrenia.* New York: International Universities Press, 1985.

Hyland, B. *The Girl with the Crazy Brother.* New York: Franklin Watts, 1987.

Jeffries, J. J., E. Plummer, M. V. Seeman, and J. F. Thornton. *Living and Working with Schizophrenia.* Toronto: University of Toronto Press, 1990. (This is a revised edition of the book by M. V. Seeman et al.)

Johnson, J. *Hidden Victims.* New York: Doubleday, 1988.

Johnson, J. *Understanding Mental Illness.* Minneapolis: Lerner, 1989.

Keefe, R. and P. Harvey. *Understanding Schizophrenia.* New York: The Free Press, 1994.

Lamb, H. R. *Treating the Long-Term Mentally Ill.* San Francisco: Jossey-Bass, 1982.

Lefley, H. P., and D. L. Johnson, eds. *Families as Allies in Treatment of the Mentally Ill.* Washington: American Psychiatric Press, 1990.

Marsh, D. T. *Families and Mental Illness: New Directions in Professional Practice.* New York: Prager, 1992.

McElroy, E., ed. *Children and Adolescents with Mental Illness: A Parents Guide.* Kensington, MD: Woodbine House, 1988.

Mendel, W. *Treating Schizophrenia.* San Francisco: Jossey-Bass, 1989.

Moorman, M. *My Sister's Keeper.* New York: W. W. Norton, 1992.

Olson, L.S. *He Was Still My Daddy.* Portland: Ogden Howe, 1994.

Peschel, E., R. Peschel, C. W. Howe, and J. W. Howe. *Neurobiological Disorders in Children and Adolescents.* San Francisco: Jossey-Bass, 1992.

Riley, J. *Crazy Quilt.* New York: William Morrow, 1984.

Riley, J. *Only My Mouth Is Smiling.* New York: William Morrow, 1982.

Rollin, Henry, ed. *Coping with Schizophrenia.* National Schizophrenia Fellowship. London: Burnett Books, 1980.

Russell, L. M., A. E. Grant, S. M. Joseph et al. *Planning for the Future: Providing a Meaningful Life for a Child with a Disability After Your Death.* Evanston, IL: American Publishing Company, 1994 and updated annually.

Vine, P. *Families in Pain: Children, Siblings, Spouses, and Parents of the Mentally Ill Speak Out.* New York: Pantheon, 1982.

Walsh, M. *Schizophrenia: Straight Talk for Family and Friends.* New York: William Morrow, 1985.

Wasow, M. *Coping with Schizophrenia: A Survival Manual for Parents, Relatives and Friends.* Palo Alto: Science and Behavior Books, 1982.

Wechsler, J. *In a Darkness.* Miami: Pickering, 1988. Originally published in 1972.

Wilson, L. *This Stranger My Son.* New York: New American Library, 1968.

Woolis, R. *When Someone You Love Has a Mental Illness.* New York: Jeremy P. Tharcher/Perigee Books, 1992.

11

HOW TO BE AN ADVOCATE

They say, "Nothing can be done here!"
I reply, "I know no such word in the vocabulary I adopt!"

Dorothea Dix, 1848

Dorothea Dix was an extremely effective advocate for persons with serious mental illnesses. She went into the poorhouses and jails to witness the atrocious conditions. She emphasized that mentally ill persons are not hopeless cases but rather can function much better if given adequate care and humane living conditions. She testified before innumerable state legislatures and investigatory commissions, always emphasizing the consequences of poor psychiatric care for individuals. She confronted and embarrassed officials, from local clerks to governors, publicly accusing them of not doing their jobs. Most important, she never took "no" for an answer.

Dorothea Dix has much to teach us today. Although not every consumer and family member can achieve her stature as an advocate, we all can do some work to improve the lives of people with diseases like schizophrenia. In doing so it is useful to keep in mind four general principles:

1. Master the facts of the situation. Credibility comes from facts, not merely from emotions.
2. Consumers make excellent advocates. There is no substitute for the credibility that comes from having schizophrenia or other serious mental illness.
3. Put everything in writing, including your summary of meetings with officials. Send copies to everyone concerned. Officials can deny ever hearing you say something, but it is much more diffi-

cult for them to deny having received your letter when you have
a copy of it.
4. Be careful of being co-opted. Politicians are experts at verbally
agreeing with people and then doing nothing. Judge public officials by what they do, not what they say. Don't accept crumbs
when what is needed is a seven-course meal.

THE POLITICS OF NEGLECT

Why, one might ask, was it necessary for families and consumers to
organize in the 1980s before public attention was turned to schizophrenia? Why had not the American Psychiatric Association, the National
Institute of Mental Health, or the National Mental Health Association
provided leadership on this disease?

The American Psychiatric Association (APA) was an especially
good candidate for such leadership. It had been begun in the 1840s as
an association of superintendents of state hospitals and, until World
War II, its major area of interest was the seriously mentally ill. With
the ascendance of psychoanalysis in the United States and the 1930s
influx of psychoanalysts from prewar Europe, however, the prestige
and dominant interest of American psychiatry shifted sharply to private
psychotherapy for the worried well. Patients with serious mental disorders were no longer viewed as interesting or desirable, and in fact the
more prestigious a psychiatrist you were considered to be, the less
chance that any of your patients would have schizophrenia.

Lack of APA interest in the seriously mentally ill was clearly
demonstrated in the 1970s when Dr. John Spiegel, then president of the
organization, toured the country to discuss with groups of psychiatrists
the ten most important problems facing American psychiatry. The last
problem on the list was that of the chronic mental patient. Dr. Spiegel
noted that "although audiences tended to respond to the other points
vigorously, on this issue, except for a rare complaint that something
ought to be done about it by the leaders of psychiatry, there was a
numbing silence." A study at that time showed that only 11 percent of
patients seen by psychiatrists in private practice were diagnosed with
schizophrenia, despite the fact that schizophrenia was by far the most
serious problem facing America's psychiatrists.

By the mid-1980s the APA had evolved into being merely a union
to protect the vested interests of the nation's private psychiatrists. The

energy and resources of the organization were devoted to lobbying for insurance coverage to pay psychotherapy fees for the worried well and to keeping psychologists and psychiatric social workers from taking away private patients. Some individual psychiatrists have done, and are continuing to do, outstanding jobs in providing competent and humane care to individuals with schizophrenia. The National Alliance for the Mentally Ill has recognized this fact by publicly commending such psychiatrists at the APA's annual meeting. And a few APA leaders, such as Drs. John Talbott and Richard Lamb, have exhorted their colleagues to take more interest in patients with schizophrenia. These exhortations produce occasional spasms of institutional guilt resulting in study groups or conferences, but little else. Most of the time the APA continues to act simply as a union for the nation's privately practicing psychiatrists. As such it is no more likely to provide leadership for patients with serious mental disorders than is the Brotherhood of Teamsters or the AFL-CIO.

The National Institute of Mental Health (NIMH), created in the late 1940s as a research institute for serious mental illnesses, also seemed a logical candidate to provide leadership on the seriously mentally ill. However, NIMH was not interested in these patients. Instead it strove to become an Institute of human behavior with tentacles extending to all problems of society, from poverty and racism to campus unrest, urban blight, child-rearing practices, and divorce. Its name, the National Institute of Mental Health rather than the National Institute of Mental Illness, was used to condone an interest in virtually every social problem in America *except* the problem of the seriously mentally ill. Whereas the problem of the seriously mentally ill should have been the primary focus of NIMH, it instead became a minor issue relegated to the back corridors and trotted out ceremonially for official occasions such as budget hearings. In such an atmosphere NIMH was about as likely to provide leadership for the seriously mentally ill as was the Smithsonian Institution.

The National Mental Health Association (NMHA), an advocate group for the mentally ill, should theoretically have been another candidate to provide leadership for the seriously mentally ill. It had been, after all, founded in 1909 by Clifford Beers (who had himself been hospitalized with manic-depressive psychosis) with the express purpose of reforming care in state mental hospitals. By World War II, however, the Mental Health Association, like American psychiatry generally, had lost interest in the seriously mentally ill. It had instead supported the private practice, problems-of-living model of American psychiatry, acting as a handmaiden for psychiatrists and other mental health professionals and strongly supporting NIMH. On issues such as the coverage of individual psychotherapy under health insurance, the Mental Health Association became very active, mobilizing volunteers to visit and write their congressmen and otherwise lobbying for the rights of the worried well. Much of its rhetoric has focused on the need for good mental health, a concept as nebulous as it is all-inclusive. "Have you hugged your kid today?" Mental Health Association posters asked. Like motherhood and apple pie, it is difficult to be against hugging your kid, but if most of an organization's energy goes into hugging kids there is little energy left over to promote better services for the truly mentally ill.

At the local level in cities such as Pittsburgh, Philadelphia, and Honolulu, the Mental Health Association has worked hard on behalf of the seriously mentally ill. At the national level, however, it has continued to champion the ephemeral concept of "mental health" and shown little interest in the mentally ill. In 1977, in fact, the organization gave its annual research award to two researchers whose work was based on the thesis that families cause schizophrenia. In terms of the politics of mental illness, the National Mental Health Association is quietly slipping into oblivion, a relic of the past.

Effective public leadership for individuals with schizophrenia and other serious mental illness had to await the birth of the National Alliance for the Mentally Ill (NAMI). Begun in 1979 by 200 families, NAMI has grown to 140,000 members and over 1000 local chapters that provide education, support, and advocacy. Consumers are playing an increasingly influential role in this organization, and in 1990 a consumer, Thomas Posey, was the President of NAMI's Board of Directors. One of the most important things a consumer or family that has been afflicted with schizophrenia can do is to join NAMI. A NAMI contact in each state is listed in Appendix D.

HOW TO DECREASE STIGMA

People with schizophrenia and their families have to live with an extraordinary amount of stigma. Schizophrenia is the modern-day equivalent of leprosy, and in the general population the level of ignorance about schizophrenia is appalling. A survey among college freshmen found that almost two-thirds mistakenly believed that "multiple personalities" are a common symptom of schizophrenia, whereas less than half were aware that hallucinations are a common symptom. One poll found that 55 percent of the public does not believe that mental illness exists, and only 1 percent realizes that mental illness is a major health problem. On television, persons with schizophrenia are portrayed as aggressive, dangerous, and homicidal; in one study 73 percent of psychiatric patients on television were characterized as violent and 23 percent were homicidal maniacs. There is no other disease in the western world which confers such social ostracism on the people afflicted and on their families.

It is feasible to change the public perception of schizophrenia and to decrease the stigma associated with the disease. For other conditions the National Association for Retarded Citizens and the Epilepsy Foundation have demonstrated that progress can be made, and the Alzheimer's Disease and Related Disorders Association is presently making some. Advocacy groups have successfully organized fights for diseases far rarer than schizophrenia. Take muscular dystrophy, for example, with its Jerry Lewis telethons and massive media blitz each September. In viewing such a drive next Labor Day, remember that for every patient with muscular dystrophy there are sixty patients with schizophrenia.

The following activities will help educate people about schizophrenia and thereby decrease stigma.

- Develop a speakers bureau and offer to talk to community service organizations (e.g., Kiwanis, Lions, Rotary), school assemblies, and local companies. Mr. and Ms. Ron Norris in Wilmington, Delaware, persuaded the Du Pont Corporation to fund the making of a film that can be used for such presentations. It is called "When the Music Stops" and is 20 minutes long.

- Schools are an especially fertile ground for decreasing stigma. Several state AMIs have developed working groups which target the schools. For example, in 1993 AMI of New York State developed a lesson plan on mental illness for grades 4–6, 7–8, and 9–12, then sent it to the Health Coordinators in every school district in the state and urged local AMI members to encourage the Health Coordinator to use it.

- There are 344,000 churches, synagogues, and mosques in the United States. The clergy are often the first people consulted by individuals with schizophrenia and their families, so the clergy are natural allies. Offer to give a talk on schizophrenia to the congregation; Mental Illness Awareness Week is a good time to do so. AMI of Maine developed a Religious Outreach Committee to educate all clergy in the state. Pathways to Promise, which started as part of the AMI group in St. Louis, is attempting to educate clergy on a national level. In some areas clergy still teach that mental illness is a sign of sin. Religious groups are the main providers of care for the homeless mentally ill, since these groups operate most public shelters; they are therefore aware of the vast numbers of untreated individuals with schizophrenia.

• Become a stigma-spotter. Be alert for evidence of prejudice against the seriously mentally ill in the media. Ask patients with these disorders about discrimination they encounter in housing and jobs. Establish a coalition of consumers and family members to combat stigma by letters, telephone calls, and public education. The National Stigma Clearinghouse (see Appendix C), originally organized under the New York State Alliance for the Mentally Ill, has done an outstanding job of this.

• Establish contact with officials of local newspapers and radio and television stations. Encourage them to consider more coverage of the problems of the seriously mentally ill, e.g., an exposé of a rundown boarding house. Educate them about schizophrenia and manic-depressive illness. Ask them to speak at a meeting of your support group. Utilize the NAMI publication *Anti-Stigma: Improving Public Understanding of Mental Illness.*

• Organize a local advertising campaign to combat stigma. For example, the Ontario Friends of Schizophrenics and the New York State AMI funded a series of billboards and posters (e.g., on city buses), explaining what schizophrenia is and how widespread it is. An AMI group in Ohio persuaded a local grocery chain to put on the grocery bags: "The brain is part of the body. It too can become ill. Schizophrenia and depressive disorder are *no fault* brain illnesses."

• Educate mental health professionals in training by offering to make presentations to local nursing schools, schools of social work, university departments of psychology, schools of medicine, and psychiatric residency training programs.

• Initiate a dialogue between your group and the local psychiatric society. Ask them to make a presentation to your group and ask to make one to their group. Both sides will emerge with a better understanding of each other's problems and with ideas on how you can be helpful to each other. The Northeast Ohio Alliance for the Mentally Ill in Cleveland has done this very effectively.

• Educate lawyers and judges about schizophrenia. Request time to make a presentation to the monthly meeting of the local Bar Association and offer to teach a class at the law school.

• Offer to give a lecture to police trainees. Police officers come into frequent contact with individuals with schizophrenia on the street; the more education they have, the more humane services they will render.

In summary, stigma regarding schizophrenia can and will be reduced. A good example of where we are headed is illustrated by the following "Rex Morgan, M.D." comic strip, which appeared in 1990:

Rex Morgan, M.D. By Nick Dallis and Tony DiPreta

Rex Morgan, M.D., educates the public about schizophrenia. This kind of education is the most effective way to decrease stigma. Reprinted with special permission of North America Syndicate, copyright 1990.

HOW TO ADVOCATE FOR MORE RESEARCH

As detailed in chapter 6, support and funding for schizophrenia research was until recently remarkably deficient. It has been primarily through the leadership of the National Alliance for the Mentally Ill and its friends in Congress that the situation been turned around. Consumers and families can continue to increase research resources by doing the following.
- Raise research funds for the National Alliance for Research on Schizophrenia and Depression (NARSAD). Many NAMI members sell holiday greeting cards for NARSAD and contribute directly to their fund-raising campaigns.
- Support efforts of researchers to maintain brain banks in which brains of persons who had serious mental illnesses are collected after death. These are exceedingly useful for research.

- Support animal research. Animals are essential both for understanding the causes of schizophrenia as well as for developing better treatments. In recent years some animal rights activists have lobbied to ban the use of animals for medical research. The public must be educated to realize that such a ban would seriously impair research efforts.
- Pressure the National Institute of Mental Health (NIMH) to allocate more research resources to schizophrenia and other serious mental diseases. NIMH still spends an extraordinary amount of its funds on frivolous research projects. Let your congressperson and senator know what you think about that. Your elected representatives are ultimately responsible for NIMH's budget and they can, if we encourage them, hold NIMH to its original and most important task.

HOW TO IMPROVE SERVICES

The history of schizophrenia in twentieth-century America is a history of unprecedented neglect. Here is a disease which affects one out of every one hundred individuals, which is bringing chaos and tragedy to 1.8 million individual Americans and their families on any given day, which costs state and federal governments billions of dollars each year. Yet what do we offer the sufferers of this disease? Frequently, mediocre psychiatric care in state hospitals. Eviction from the hospital to live in vermin-infested boarding houses and fear-infested back alleys. Minimal psychiatric and medical follow-up. Virtually no sheltered workshops or opportunities for partial employment. In terms of services for schizophrenia it has been said that patients with this disease "are not falling between the cracks—they are lost in the ravines."

The following activities will improve services for individuals with schizophrenia.

- Publish a resource book describing local resources for persons with schizophrenia and manic-depressive psychosis. Several AMI groups that have done this can be used as models (e.g., AMI of Dupage County, Illinois, Washington AMI, Colorado AMI, Missouri AMI).
- Become an expert on low-cost housing. Visit existing units being used by persons with schizophrenia living in your community, take pictures, and show them to the county council, etc. Visit model housing projects and make people in your community aware of what can be done.
- Encourage the setting up of group homes by working against restrictive zoning ordinances.
- If there is a great lack of halfway houses in your community, work with

the local agencies to set one up yourself. The Main Line Mental Health Group outside Philadelphia successfully did this, renovating a mansion adjacent to Haverford State Hospital into what is almost certainly the most elegant and comfortable halfway house in the United States.

- Become an expert on vocational training for the seriously mentally ill. Visit model programs. Meet with state vocational training officials and explore possibilities. Go to the state legislature if necessary.

- Visit the nearest state-sheltered workshop. Ask the director why more persons with schizophrenia are not included. If, as in most such workshops, they are few and far between, organize a letter and telephone blitz of the state legislature to get the policy changed. Look at model workshops.

- Organize part-time jobs with local business and industry to be filled by persons with schizophrenia and manic-depressive psychosis.

- Organize a local clubhouse for the seriously mentally ill, using the Fountain House model in New York City. Encourage the state to fund such programs.

- Become an expert on SSI and SSDI regulations. Do a brief survey to ascertain how many people with schizophrenia and/or manic-depressive psychosis are eligible for but are not in fact receiving their benefits. Meet with the local officials in charge of these programs. Ask consumer and families to bring to your attention instances where persons with these diseases have been rejected or cut off from benefits.

- Lobby for the amending of Medicaid and Medicare so that they do not discriminate against persons with schizophrenia. A step in this direction took place in 1986, when Congress liberalized Medicaid coverage for the chronically mentally ill.

- Work to get consumer and representatives of family support groups on all city, county, and state mental health boards and advisory commissions, as well as the boards of directors of CMHCs.

- Become politically aware. Identify the legislators in your county and state who support the concerns of the mentally ill. Let these legislators know that you back them because of their stand. Organize political support for them in elections.

- Become expert on the county and state mental health budget. Where is the money going? Who is getting services? Who is *not?* Attend the key subcommittee meetings. Offer to testify as a consumer or family member.

- Meet regularly with the director of the local CMHC. Push to raise the seriously mentally ill to top priority for clinic services.

- Lobby the state legislature to mandate the seriously mentally ill as prime candidates for expenditure of state mental health dollars. Accomplishing this in some states (e.g., Colorado and Oregon) has proved very helpful.

- Arrange for introduction of legislation in your state to change the name of the state Department of Mental Health to the Department of Mental Illness. It will help people to focus on the real problems. The

Massachusetts AMI has attempted to do this.

- Lobby for establishment of a bill of rights guaranteeing minimum standards of service for the seriously mentally ill. For a model of such a bill, write to Deputy Commissioner for Mental Health, Iowa Department of Human Services, Des Moines, IA 50319.
- Set up a system of respite care among a group of families, with families covering for each other so they can get away on vacations. AMI of South Carolina did this. Suggest to local authorities that they support such services and provide some of the necessary manpower.
- Organize a plan for providing continuing care for the seriously mentally ill after the well family members have died (e.g., Planned Lifetime Assistance Network (PLAN), described in chapter 9).
- Educate insurance companies about the necessity of covering schizophrenia and manic-depressive illness in exactly the same way multiple sclerosis is covered. They should be encouraged to differentiate these brain diseases from problems of living, for which insurance coverage is not practical since there is no logical cutoff to the need. Take an insurance executive to lunch, or have your AMI group make a formal presentation to the company staff so that they will better understand the disease.
- Change state insurance laws to require insurance companies to cover schizophrenia and other serious mental illnesses in the same way as they cover serious physical illnesses. Maine successfully did this.
- Publish a booklet outlining commitment laws and procedures in your state, including the major impediments to hospitalizing seriously mentally ill individuals.
- Combat the negligent release of patients by state hospital or other psychiatric inpatient units. If the patient scheduled to be released is known to be a danger to himself or others, send a letter such as the following by registered mail:

Dear _____,

You have under your care John Doe. I am informed that you intend to release John Doe. You should not do so. I know John Doe to be a danger to himself and to others. You already have information which puts you on notice of this fact. If there is any doubt, I now put you on notice.

If in spite of this information you release John Doe and he causes injury to himself or to others, you will be responsible because you were on notice that your release of John Doe will be the substantial factor in causing either harm to him or to others or to both.

Better yet, have a lawyer send it.

- Sue mental illness professionals who endanger patients by negligently reducing medication to levels known to be too low, or who release patients from the hospital when it is clear that the patients cannot care for themselves.

- If laws in your state have tilted too far toward the patient's right to refuse treatment, begin a campaign to restore muscle to the laws, so that patients who need treatment will be treated. Open a public dialogue with lawyers and judges. Make it a political issue. Form an alliance with mental illness professionals working for the same goal.
- Advocate wider use of outpatient commitment laws, which permit patients to live in the community only so long as they continue to take medication.
- Work with the State Commissioner of Mental Health to set up quarterly meetings between consumers, family groups, and mental illness professionals to discuss problems. In Maine such a program has proved to be very successful.
- Work with state mental health officials to devise innovative ways to recruit good mental illness professionals into the state system, such as Maryland has done. Let good mental illness professionals know that the families appreciate them.
- Establish public awards at the local and state levels for outstanding employees of the mental illness system. Civil service systems do not reward excellence so support groups must. Create a coalition with other community groups (e.g., Kiwanis, Rotarians, Elks, etc.) to form annual awards presentation ceremonies.
- If necessary, bring legal suits against city and state governments, insisting that they provide psychiatric aftercare and shelter for released mental patients.
- Ascertain how many seriously mentally ill children are being sent to other states for inpatient treatment. Publicize the fact. Ask officials why they cannot be treated in your state.
- Ascertain whether families of seriously mentally ill children in your state are being asked to give up custody of their children as a condition for receiving services. If so, go to the media and ask them to publicize this medieval practice.
- Advocate a mandatory service pay-back system in public facilities for all psychiatrists, psychologists, and psychiatric social workers who are trained with state funds.
- Advocate for changing state licensing laws to require, as a condition of licensure, two hours a week of *pro bono* services in public facilities (e.g., mental health centers, jails, shelters) for all psychiatrists, psychologists, and psychiatric social workers.
- Visit local nursing homes and get to know the administrators. Explore with them and with local officials how psychiatric care can be improved for the many persons with serious mental illnesses who are confined to nursing homes. Ask the administrator to make a presentation to your support group. Encourage the establishment of in-service education about

serious mental illnesses to the nursing home staffs.

- Organize regular unannounced inspections of public psychiatric inpatient units. Several states AMIs have successfully done this.
- Work with the psychiatric staff of the local Veterans Administration (VA) Hospital. In Largo, FL, an AMI group called the Suncoast Community Support Auxiliary works closely with the Bay Pines VA Hospital to provide support, advocacy, and services through its Community Support Group. In Maine an AMI group formed a wives' support group at the Togus VA Hospital. The VA Hospital in West Haven, CT, has a continuous treatment team (PACT model); ask why your VA doesn't have one too. The VA Hospital in Denver has an exemplary rehabilitation program (Bayaud Industries); ask why your VA doesn't have one too.
- If the inpatient psychiatric unit in your local hospital is deficient, notify the Joint Commission on Accreditation of Healthcare Organizations (JCAHO) at 1 Renaissance Boulevard, Oak Brook Terrace, IL 60181 (telephone 708-916-5600). JCAHO inspects most such facilities every three years. You can ask to meet with the JCAHO accreditation team to make your concerns known when they next visit the hospital. Be sure to also send your concerns to JCAHO by registered letter.
- If the hospital flagrantly disregards the rights of patients, ask for an investigation by the Civil Rights Division, U.S. Department of Justice, Washington, D.C. 20530.
- Another means of safeguarding the rights of hospitalized mentally ill persons is through the 1986 Protection and Advocacy Law, which mandates that each state must have a patient protection and advocacy agency. Become familiar with how it can be used. Educate other families.
- In larger states, do a ranking of state hospitals and/or CMHCs on the quality of care they provide for the seriously mentally ill. Publicize the rankings. The AMIs of North Carolina and Alabama have done this.

HOW TO ORGANIZE FOR ADVOCACY

Your advocacy efforts will only be effective if you have a well-organized and strong group. Numbers of members help, but in fact effective advocacy in most organizations is usually accomplished by a small number of its members. Consumers, siblings, children of mentally ill individuals, spouses, parents, grandparents, friends, and mental illness professionals who are interested can all play important roles. Considering the fact that there are 1.8 million persons with schizophrenia today in the United States, a coalition of them, their families, and friends should theoretically be able to accomplish almost anything. To do so, however, it is necessary to get more of them out of the closets and into the streets. Some suggestions for doing so are the following.

- Increase membership in your local support group. Leave brochures for your group with all local mental illness professionals. Give brochures to drug salesmen who visit physicians. Leave leaflets on the windows of cars parked in the visitors lot of the state hospital. Put notices on community bulletin boards, in church bulletins, company and local newspapers. One AMI group persuaded a grocery chain to print their name and telephone number on milk cartons. Another persuaded the telephone company to include information on their group with telephone bills.
- Organize special support groups for siblings, children of mentally ill individuals, wives and husbands, the parents of seriously mentally ill children, and individuals using the VA system. All these have been started by some AMI groups.
- Enlist the help of the individuals who run the local homeless shelter and your local law enforcement officials. These people are acutely aware of the failure of public services for individuals with serious mental illnesses. They are potentially good allies.
- Enlist the assistance of local civic groups that are also concerned about problems of seriously mentally ill individuals. For example, some Kiwanis Clubs have been helpful, and the League of Women Voters in Illinois undertook a major survey of services for mentally ill individuals.
- If *none* of the above suits your aptitudes or abilities and you still want to help, there is one thing left. As advocated in the movie *Network,* when fed up with existing conditions you should lean out your window and yell loudly: "I'm mad as hell and I'm not going to take it anymore!" After doing this you will be forced to explain to your neighbors what is going on, and several more families will thereby become educated about schizophrenia.

Services for individuals with serious mental illnesses are not likely to improve until enough individuals become angry and get organized. Persons with schizophrenia will continue to be fourth-class citizens, leading twilight lives, often shunned, ignored, and neglected. They will continue to be, in the words of President Carter's Commission on Mental Health, "a minority within minorities. They are the most stigmatized of the mentally ill. They are politically and economically powerless and rarely speak for themselves. . . . They are the totally disenfranchised among us." The mad will become liberated only when those of us fortunate enough to have escaped the illness show how mad we really are.

A

READINGS ON SCHIZOPHRENIA: THE 15 BEST AND THE 15 WORST

The following are my nominations for the 15 best and 15 worst readings on schizophrenia. Since the previous edition of this book the "best" list has become much more competitive because of many fine new books being published on schizophrenia. By contrast, it is becoming increasingly difficult to find new books for the "worst" list and many of those listed here are quite old; surely this is a sign of progress. The "best" books should be in the libraries of every NAMI chapter. The "worst" ones should be appreciated for what they are—fossils of the Freudian Age and other follies.

THE FIFTEEN BEST

Andreasen, Nancy C. *The Broken Brain: The Biological Revolution in Psychiatry.* New York: Harper and Row, 1984. Although it is now somewhat dated, this is still one of the best accounts of brain research. Its especially clear description of the structure and function of the brain provides lay readers with everything they need to know to follow the current neuroscience revolution. It covers not only schizophrenia but manic-depressive psychosis, Alzheimer's disease, and anxiety disorders as well.

Deutsch, Albert. *The Shame of the States.* New York: Harcourt, Brace and Company, 1948. Deutsch was a crusading New York journalist who undertook a twelve-state examination of public mental hospitals. His shocking descriptions of the conditions he found are matched in the photographs by a cameraman who accompanied him. The book stands as a monument to our past inhumanity to the seriously mentally ill, and a warning of what can happen to defenseless people who have no organized lobby to speak for them. "Could a truly civilized community permit humans to be reduced to such animal-like level?" Deutsch asked.

Deveson, Anne. *Tell Me I'm Here.* New York: Penguin Books, 1992. This is a superb, powerfully written account of a son's schizophrenia as seen through his mother's eyes. Deveson is a broadcaster and film maker, well-known to the Australian public, and her account of her son's illness has enabled many Australian families with a seriously mentally ill family member to come out of the closet. Her story is much more terrifying than the worst fictional horror story because it is real. Deveson skillfully captures the various shades and nuances of the tragedy we call schizophrenia.

Gottesman, Irving I. *Schizophrenia Genesis: The Origin of Madness.* New York: W.H. Freeman, 1991. Gottesman is one of the leading researchers on the genetics of schizophrenia, and in this book he summarizes the pertinent studies. He also weaves into the text personal accounts of having schizophrenia, which makes the research data both more pertinent and more interesting.

Hatfield, Agnes B., and Harriet P. Lefley. *Surviving Mental Illness: Stress, Coping and Adaptation.* New York: Guilford Press, 1993. Eminently practical and well-written, this book will be useful for families trying to sort out the myriad problems confronting them when a family member becomes seriously mentally ill. Emphasis is put on the importance of understanding what the sick person is experiencing, so the book includes some very useful personal accounts by Dr. Frederick Frese, Esso Leete, and Daniel Link.

Isaac, Rael Jean, and Virginia C. Armat. *Madness in the Streets.* New York: The Free Press, 1990. This is a useful history of the "mental health" movement and how so many individuals with serious mental illnesses have ended up homeless and on the streets. There is enough blame to go around for just about everyone involved in the "mental health" scene, but the lawyers with the American Civil Liberties Union and the Mental Health Law Project collect (and deserve) the largest share. It is a well-written and depressing history, and essential to understand if we expect to improve things.

Marsh, Diane T. *Families and Mental Illness: New Directions on Professional Practice.* New York: Praeger, 1992. This is the best of several recently published books regarding the family's role as caregiver for their mentally ill relative and how mental illness professionals can enhance that role. It is aimed primarily at professionals and would make a nice gift for any psychiatrist, psychologist, psychiatric social worker, or psychiatric nurse. It is especially important to get books such as this into the hands of mental illness trainees before they have become misinformed by some of their out-of-date teachers. Another worthy book in this genre is Harriet P. Lefley and Dale L. Johnson, eds., *Families as Allies in Treatment of the Mentally Ill* (Washington: American Psychiatric Press, 1990).

Mendel, Werner. *Treating Schizophrenia.* San Francisco: Jossey-Bass, 1989. This was the late Dr. Mendel's last book and is a tribute to his remarkable work. He followed 497 patients with schizophrenia for up to 35 years. The book is unusual in its longitudinal perspective on the disease and in emphasizing the importance of the relationship between the psychiatrist and the individual with schizophrenia in helping the latter to cope. At the time of his death Dr. Mendel had retired from private practice and was working in a state psychiatric hospital. Oh that we had more such doctors!

Moorman, Margaret. *My Sister's Keeper.* New York: W.W. Norton, 1992. The effect on siblings of having a seriously mentally ill brother or sister has been little studied or written about. Moorman's account of her older sister's schizophrenia goes a long way toward filling that gap. She is especially articulate about the problems of role reversal as a younger sister who had to, in effect, become an older sister to her older sister. Part of the book was originally in the *New York Times,* and Moorman also did a show on this subject on "Oprah."

North, Carol. *Welcome, Silence: My Triumph Over Schizophrenia.* New York: Simon and Schuster, 1987. This is the personal account of a young woman's fight against the symptoms of schizophrenia. Although her case is quite atypical in many ways, the book includes excellent descriptions of what it is like to experience auditory hallucinations and to fight the symptoms of the disease. North was one of the few patients who responded dramatically to renal dialysis as an experimental treatment, and she is today a fully trained psychiatrist who specializes in serious mental illness.

Riley, Jocelyn. *Crazy Quilt.* New York: William Morrow, 1984. An unusual children's book, the fictional account of a thirteen-year-old girl whose mother has schizophrenia. It is a poignant reminder of the effects of this disease on other family members and the fact that children need education and support just as siblings and parents need them. We need many more such books so that children, too, may understand. An earlier book by the same author, *Only My Mouth Is Smiling* (1982), is also good. Another worthy children's book is Betty Hyland's *The Girl with the Crazy Brother* (New York: Watts, 1987), in which a sixteen-year-old girl has to cope with the onset of schizophrenia in her brother.

Sheehan, Susan. *Is There No Place on Earth for Me?* Boston: Houghton, Mifflin, 1982. Susan Sheehan's superb study originally appeared in *The New Yorker* magazine. It provides the best available description of the course of a chronic schizophrenic illness, the difficulties encountered by a person with the disease, the frustrations for the family, and the mediocre care available at the state hospital. It is searingly accurate and mandatory reading for anyone who wants to understand the tragedy of this disease. The patient described has the schizoaffective subtype.

Walsh, Maryellen. *Schizophrenia: Straight Talk for Families and Friends.* New York: William Morrow, 1985. This is one of the best accounts of schizophrenia from the point of view of the parent of a person afflicted. Articulate and angry, yet able to maintain a sense of humor, Ms. Walsh describes confrontations with the ignorance and the indignities faced by families. There is familiarity and comfort in sharing her ordeals, and hope in joining her fight to change the system.

Wechsler, James. *In a Darkness.* New York: Norton, 1972. Republished in Miami by Pickering Press, 1988. A product of the dark 1960s, when most families were told that they had caused the disease, this is an account of a son's schizophrenia written by his father, a distinguished journalist. It is an articulate and poignant account of 10 years of searching for a good psychiatrist and a cure, and of the family chaos caused by the illness. The family's agony of not knowing what to do is exceeded only by the pain of the son's eventual suicide.

Woolis, Rebecca. *When Someone You Love Has a Mental Illness: A Handbook for Family, Friends, and Caregivers.* New York: Jeremy P. Tarcher/Perigee Books, 1992. This is a handy book to have around because of its numerous "Quick Reference Guides" for such subjects as "Handling Your Relative's Anger," "Dealing with Bizarre Behavior," "Preventing Suicide," and "Rules for Living at Home or Visiting." It does not provide long discourses on the various subjects but tells you what to *do.* It is a practical book par excellence.

THE FIFTEEN WORST

Barnes, Mary, and Joseph Berke. *Mary Barnes: Two Accounts of a Journey Through Madness.* New York: Ballantine Books, 1973. This is the book that made Ronald Laing's approach to schizophrenia widely known. Schizophrenia, it says, is a "career" that is "launched with the aid and encouragement of one's immediate family." The family member with schizophrenia is often "the least disturbed member of the entire group." This assertion is preposterous in any context, but it becomes completely bizarre when one realizes that Laing's own daughter was diagnosed with schizophrenia. Moreover, the authors claim that suffering from schizophrenia can be a growth experience—"psychosis may be a state of reality, cyclic in nature, by which the self renews itself." There is no end to such absurd drivel in this book.

Bateson, Gregory, Don D. Jackson, Jay Haley, and John Weakland. "Toward a Theory of Schizophrenia." *Behavioral Science* 1 (1956): 251–64 and reprinted in several books, including *Beyond the Double Bind,* edited by Milton M. Berger, New York: Brunner Mazel, 1978. This paper gave birth to the double-bind, the heads-I-win-tails-you-lose method of family communication which the authors "hypothesize goes on steadily from infantile beginnings in the family situation of individuals who become schizophrenic." The authors admitted that "this hypothesis has not been statistically tested" and in fact it never was; nevertheless, it was adopted as fact by two generations of mental health professionals who proceeded to blame the family (especially the mother) for causing the disease. Schizophrenia, say the authors, is "a way of dealing with double-bind situations to overcome their inhibiting and controlling effect." What seems incredible in retrospect is that theoretically intelligent people could postulate the symptoms of schizophrenia as the product of such relatively innocuous family communications. The fact that psychiatrists, psychologists, and social workers bought it—untested—is a scathing indictment of their intelligence quotient.

Breggin, Peter R. *Toxic Psychiatry.* New York: St. Martin's Press, 1991. It would have been difficult to imagine that Dr. Breggin could have written a worse book than his previous one, *Psychiatric Drugs: Hazards to the Brain,* but he has accomplished this considerable feat. Schizophrenia, Breggin tells us, is "a psychospiritual overwhelm," which is caused by child abuse and/or by the drugs used to treat it. His style is a disjointed hysteria in which he grossly exaggerates the negatives and ignores the positives. For example, his opinion of antipsychotic drugs has not improved since 1986, when he wrote: "Psychiatry has unleashed a plague on the world with millions upon millions of permanently damaged patients. It's the worst doctor-induced catastrophe in the history of medicine." Rather than antipsychotic drugs, Breggin recommends psychotherapy, love, and empathy as the treatments of choice for schizophrenia. The book is truly a "psychospiritual" underwhelm, and St. Martin's Press should be ashamed to have its name on it.

Cooper, David. *Psychiatry and Anti-Psychiatry.* New York: Ballantine Books, 1967. Another confused protege of R.D. Laing, Cooper in this book romanticized the individual with schizophrenia as merely expressing the pathology of the family. Specifically he speculated that "in the 'psychotic' families the indentified schizophrenic patient member by his psychotic episode is trying to break free of an alienated system and is, therefore, in some sense less 'ill' or at least less alienated than the 'normal' offspring of the 'normal' families." This is pure British bunkum.

Goffman, Erving. *Asylums: Essays on the Social Situation of Mental Patients and Other Inmates.* Garden City, NY: Anchor Books, 1961. Supported by funds from the National Institute of Mental Health, sociologist Goffman spent a year at St. Elizabeths Hospital in Washington, D.C., observing the patients. He concluded that most of the patients' behavior was a reaction to being hospitalized, not a result of their illnesses. The logical corollary is that one only needed to open the gates of the hospital and let the patients go free, no strings (or medication) attached, and they would live happily after. *Asylums* was widely read and an important influence on mental health administrators who decided to do exactly that. One only wishes today that Goffman could be given a mattress under a bridge or freeway in any American city so that he could observe how the experiment turned out.

Green, Hannah. *I Never Promised You a Rose Garden.* New York: Holt, Rinehart and Winston, 1964. If a prize were to be given to the book which has produced the most confusion about schizophrenia over the past 30 years, this book would win going away. The young woman with schizophrenia (in fact her symptoms are much more characteristic of hysteria) is helped to become well by psychoanalytic psychotherapy. Such therapy is about as likely to cure schizophrenia as it is likely to cure multiple sclerosis. The book belongs in the Kingdom of Ur with the young woman's fantasies.

Kesey, Ken. *One Flew Over the Cuckoo's Nest.* New York: Signet Books, 1962. Made into a popular movie, this is a fictional version of the idea promoted by Erving Goffman in *Asylums* and by the movie "King of Hearts." Randle McMurphy tries to mobilize the patients in the state hospital to challenge Big Nurse Ratched and the evil psychiatrists who work there. The patients are depicted as oppressed, not sick, and in the end Chief Broom escapes from the hospital to live happily ever after. In reality Chief Broom probably joined the legion of homeless mentally ill individuals living under some bridge, ended up in jail, was beaten up, or all of the above. Kesey was a guru of psychedelic drugs at the time, and his story also has an hallucinatory ring to it.

Lidz, Theodore. *The Relevance of the Family to Psychoanalytic Theory.* Madison, CT: International Universities Press, 1992. This book completes 45 years of pumpkin-headed publications by Dr. Lidz, Professor of Psychiatry at Yale University. His career started in 1949 with "Psychiatric Problems in the Thyroid Clinic," which asserted that individuals with hyperthyroidism "had in childhood felt less wanted than a sibling." He then moved on to his study of 16 families in which one member had schizophrenia: "In each family at least one parent suffered from serious and crippling psychopathology, and in many both were markedly disturbed ... the father appeared to be seriously disturbed just as often as the mother." Over the years Lidz and his colleagues evolved a two-part classification of families with a member with schizophrenia into "skewed" or "schismatic," and said that "they both revolve around the egocentricity of one or both parents." In his 1992 book Lidz still claims that "by now numerous investigators have found serious disorders of communication in all families of schizophrenia patients." It is the distant cry of the Yaleosaurus, thought to have been long extinct! It is doubtful if ever in the history of medicine so many papers and books have been published on so few patients in studies of such doubtful scientific merit.

Menninger, Karl. "Parents Against Children" and "Men, Women, and Hate." *Atlantic Monthly* 163 (1939): 158–168 and 164 (1939): 163–175. These little-known articles by Karl Menninger are classic, blame-the-mother, psychoanalytic poppycock. For example, he wrote: "On the day I write this I have just talked with a mother whose boundless but unrecognized hate for her son drove him into a state of hopeless mental illness." Menninger's view of women provided a new standard for misogyny. He deplored "the subtle cruelties inflicted by unconsciously resentful mothers upon their defenseless children"; however, he failed to realize the overt cruelties inflicted by incomprehensively ignorant psychoanalysts upon their defenseless patients and families. If these articles ever circulate widely, there will probably be a women's march on Topeka.

Modrow, John. *How to Become a Schizophrenic: The Case Against Biological Psychiatry.* Everett, WA: Apollylon Press, 1992. This is a pathetic book by a man who was once diagnosed with schizophrenia. "My fate had been sealed not by my genes, but by the attitudes, beliefs, and expectations of my parents [who] had serious psychological problems of their own." His symptoms, says Modrow, were merely the consequence of the stress his mother and father subjected him to. In one chapter he claims that "schizophrenia is largely caused by feeling of intense self-loathing." Elsewhere he reassures us that "there is no vast difference between schizophrenia and normalcy." "Psychiatry," says the author, "can be compared to the Ku Klux Klan and other racist or white supremacist organizations." One can sympathize, to some extent, with anyone with schizophrenia who is trying to make sense of this terrible affliction. It is much less easy to sympathize with the muddleheadedness of Drs. Thomas Szasz ("an impressive piece of work"), Theodore Lidz ("a very important contribution"), and Peter Breggin ("one of the best things I've read on the subject"), who provided cover endorsements for this sad tome.

Mosher, Loren R., and Lorenzo Burti. *Community Mental Health.* New York: W.W. Norton, 1989. If you have ever wondered why the National Institute of Mental Health (NIMH) exerted so little leadership for individuals with serious mental illnesses for so many years, this book may provide you with an answer. Dr. Loren Mosher was, for over a decade, the Chief of NIMH's Center for Studies of Schizophrenia. Incredibly, he believes that schizophrenia is merely "disturbed and disturbing behavior," not a disease. He is staunchly anti-medication "because many psychotropics separate persons from their experience of themselves" and adds that "we do not believe in routine maintenance neuroleptic drug treatment for persons labeled schizophrenic." Instead he believes "that madness is all too understandable, and that it can be effectively treated by psychosocial methods," mostly love, understanding, and a soft teddy bear. In the context of 1990s psychiatry, the book is a relic from the distant past. Dr. Mosher is now in charge of psychiatric services for Montgomery County, Maryland; I would advise individuals with schizophrenia to avoid that county.

Robbins, Michael. *Experiences of Schizophrenia.* New York: Guilford Press, 1993. This book may well become a collector's item as one of the last books written in which psychoanalysis and other forms of insight-oriented psychotherapy are recommended as the treatment of choice for schizophrenia. As such, it follows in the tradition of Boyer and Giovacchini's *Psychoanalytic Treatment of Schizophrenic, Borderline and Characterological Disorders* (1980) and Karon and Van den Bos' *Psychotherapy of Schizophrenia: Treatment of Choice* (1981). Robbins describes selected cases of schizophrenia that he treated with psychoanalysis for up to seven years. Like most psychoanalysts Robbins blames families for causing schizophrenia, describing them as "quietly totalitarian and controlling, suppressive of the autonomy and potential for separation of individual members." Psychoanalysis is not the treatment of choice for schizophrenia; on the contrary, since it often makes the patient worse, it can be said to be the nontreatment of choice.

Rubin, Theodore I. *Lisa and David.* New York: Macmillan, 1961. This book is included because it became a movie (*David and Lisa*) and thus influenced a generation of thinking about schizophrenia. Lisa, a thirteen-year-old girl with "hebephrenic schizophrenia," and David, a fifteen-year-old boy with "pseudoneurotic schizophrenia," are eloquently described in their daily activities in a residential treatment center in 1959 and 1960. Unfortunately, the author is a psychoanalyst whose only plan for treatment for the two is continued psychotherapy until they can "become involved in problems of . . . neurotic defenses, sexuality, and family relations." The two case histories cry out for antipsychotic drug therapy, which was available in 1959 and 1960, but is nowhere to be seen. One only hopes that in the intervening years the families of Lisa and David have taken them out of such an anachronistic treatment facility and found them more up-to-date treatment.

Szasz, Thomas. *Schizophrenia: The Sacred Symbol of Psychiatry.* New York: Basic Books, 1976. Starting with *The Myth of Mental Illness* in 1961 and continuing with *The Manufacture of Madness* (1970), *Schizophrenia: The Sacred Symbol of Psychiatry* (1976) and

Psychiatric Slavery (1977), Szasz has produced more erudite nonsense on the subject of serious mental illness than any writer alive. As a historian Szasz is first class, but as a psychiatrist he never moved beyond a strictly psychoanalytic approach to treating schizophrenia. He argues, for example, that schizophrenia is merely a creation of psychiatry and "if there is no psychiatry there can be no schizophrenics." What wonderful simplicity! One wonders whether he has *ever* seen a patient with this disease.

Tietze, Trude. "A Study of Mothers of Schizophrenic Patients." *Psychiatry* 12 (1949): 55–65. Although Frieda Fromm-Reichmann used the term "schizophrenogenic mother" in a paper one year prior to Tietze's paper, this study was usually referenced to justify the concept. Tietze interviewed twenty-five mothers of schizophrenic patients and freely admits that "in order to arrive at valid conclusions it would be necessary to compare the twenty-five mothers of this series with a control group of mothers who have never produced a schizophrenic child." Alas, she says, she could not find any controls. Furthermore the twenty-five mothers were "hostile and resented the psychiatrist" [Dr. Tietze] for blaming them for causing their children's illness. Dr. Tietze is not discouraged by these minor methodological problems, and proceeds to draw conclusions which must qualify as true hallucinations. Should be read only on days when one wishes to froth at the mouth.

B

USEFUL VIDEOTAPES

(Prepared by Mrs. Katie Petray, Alliance for the Mentally Ill of Fox Valley, IL)

The following is a selected list of useful videotapes on schizophrenia and serious mental illnessess. Many of them have been produced by Alliance for the Mentally Ill (AMI) family groups, mental health professionals, and professional filmmakers for public television to illustrate the symptoms of the major mental illnesses, to increase understanding, and to enhance coping skills. Some of the videos highlighted at the 1993 NAMI Convention are also listed here.

At the top of the list of "eye opening" videos produced about schizophrenia is a two-part video: "Schizophrenia: Surviving in the World of Normals" (1991) in which psychologist and mental health consumer Fred Frese, Ph.D., shares his insights into schizophrenia, and "A Love Story: Living with Someone with Schizophrenia," in which his wife, Penny Frese, Ph.D., relates her experiences from the perspective of a spouse. "Schizophrenia: A Major Forum" (1993), a three-part series shown on Lifetime TV, presents stimulating panel discussions on the issues of "Increasing Compliance Via an Alternative to Oral Medication" and "Relapse." "Broken Minds" (1990) features a report on the twin study project researching schizophrenia conducted by Dr. Torrey. "Madness," from Part 7 of the 1984 series on the brain produced by PBS, and "Out of Darkness," the 1994 ABC television movie starring Diana Ross, are both excellent introductions to schizophrenia. Facts about mental illness are presented in "News From Medicine: Peace of Mind" (1988), a video in which Lionel Aldridge relates the story of his struggles with schizophrenia. "Living with Schizophrenia: A Video Manual for Families" (1990) provides low-key and nontechnical explanations about schizophrenia and the difficulties families face.

Psychiatrists present down-to-earth explanations about treatment issues and the use of medications to treat schizophrenia in "Anti-Psychotic Medications for Schizophrenia" (1993).

Three skillfully presented videos produced about manic-depressive disorders and major depression are "Depression: The Storm Within" (1991), Mary Ellen Copeland's "Wellness Workshop: Depression" (1991), and "Depressive Illness on Campus: The NAMI Teleconference" (1991). In these videos, consumers share insights into gaining power over their illnesses.

AMI groups nationwide have produced many outstanding videos. A consumer describes her illness and highlights AMI supports, a group home, and consumer-run business in "AMI: Bringing Hope to the Mentally Ill" (AMI-DuPage Co, Illinois-1993). Family members relate the rewards of fighting stigma in "Silent No More" (AMI-Minnesota-1990). Accentuating the positive in rehabilitation is the focus of "Until There's a Cure: Hope and Progress Today" (AMI-Illinois-1992). Perspectives on the effects of mental illness on marriage are presented in "When Mental Illness Invades a Marriage" (AMI-Alabama-1993). "A Respite Program: Everyone Wins" (South Carolina AMI-1993) describes a unique camp program that provides vacation opportunities for consumers and their families. Three videos that reach out to minority groups, available in English and/or Spanish, are "When Mental Illness Invades the Minority Family" (AMI-Alabama-1991), "Spanish-Speaking Support Group for Families of the Seriously Mentally Ill" (AMI-San Diego, California-1992), and "Out of the Shadow and Into the Light: From Stigma to Unity" (AMI of New York-1991). "Mental Illness and the People Who Are Affected by Them" (AMI-Rhode Island-1993) is utilized as an instrument in training law enforcement officers.

Several wonderfully informative videos have been developed by mental health professionals. Mary Moller, R.N., has produced a series of three workshops, with study guides included: "Understanding and Communicating with a Person Who Is Hallucinating" (1989), "Understanding and Communicating with a Person Who Is Experiencing Mania" (1990), and "Understanding Relapse: Managing the Symptoms of Schizophrenia" (1991). Chris Amenson, Ph.D., explores coping skills in "Family Strategies" (1991). Robert Maseroni, M.D., produced "M.I., The Double Scarlet Letter" (1992), a play that features consumers as they confront difficult issues in their recovery.

Diane Marsh, Ph.D., focuses on building relationships between professionals and families in "Shattered Dreams" (1993).

Discussions among children, teens, and siblings reveal touching stories about mental illness. "KID TV" (Maine Department of Mental Health-1992) is an upbeat video designed to educate junior high school students. "After the Tears: Teens Talk about Mental Illness" (United Mental Health-1986) is heartwarming. "Promise" (Hallmark Playhouse-1987) tells the compelling story of a young man struggling with mental illness and his care-giving brother.

Many thought-provoking videos deal with the stigma associated with mental illness. A panel of experts explore the origin of stigma in a symposium "Mental Illness: Unraveling the Myths" (Rutgers University, New Jersey-1990), a powerful video first shown on WNET. "When the Music Stops" (DuPont-1987) continues to be widely enjoyed and used effectively by AMI affiliates as an introduction to mental illnesses and the NAMI family movement. "A Place To Come Back To" (Pathways to Promise-St. Louis, Missouri-1987) is designed to inform religious congregations about the needs of persons with mental illness. "Mental Illness in America: A Series of Public Hearings" (NIMH-1992) addresses a wide range of issues, including the need for improved services and discrimination in health insurance for people with mental illness.

- "Schizophrenia: Surviving in the World of Normals," and "A Love Story: Living with Someone with Schizophrenia." 1991.
  Wellness Reproductions, 23945 Mercantile Rd., Beachwood, OH 44122-5924. 216-831-9209; 800-669-9208.
  Two 58-min. presentations, videotape $69.95, shipping $7.00.
- "Schizophrenia: A Major Forum." 1993.
  KPR InforMedia, 333 East 38th St., New York, NY 10015.
  Three 30-min. videotapes, each $5.00, transcript $3.00.
- "Broken Minds." 1990.
  PBS Videos, P.O. Box 791, Alexandria, VA 22313. 703-739-5380.
  60-min. videotape $99.95 plus $8.50 shipping.
- "Madness," Part 7 of the PBS series on the brain. 1984.
  Annenberg CPB Project, P.O. Box 2345, South Burlington, VT 05407.
  60-min. videotape $29.95 plus $2.40 shipping.
- "Out of Darkness," ABC movie starring Diana Ross. 1994.
  Many AMI groups have loan copies.

- "News from Medicine: Peace of Mind." 1988.
  Cable News Network.
  NAMI, 2101 Wilson Blvd., #302, Arlington, VA 22201.
  703-524-7600.
  60-min. videotape $15.00.
- "Living with Schizophrenia: A Video Manual for Families." 1990.
  David Katz, Box 1196, Washington University, One Brookings
  Drive, St. Louis, MO 63116. 314-935-6683.
  41-min. videotape $55.00 plus $2.50 postage; rental $10.00.
- "Anti-Psychotic Medications for Schizophrenia." 1993.
  David Katz, Box 1196, Washington University, One Brookings
  Drive, St. Louis, MO 63116. 314-935-6683.
  26-min. videotape $35.00 plus $2.50 postage; rental $10.00.
- "Depression: The Storm Within." 1991.
  3rd in series "Let's Talk about Mental Illness."
  American Psychiatric Assn., Public Affairs, 1400 K St., NW,
  Washington, DC 20005. 202-682-6394.
  29-min. videotape $100.00, w/educational kit and user's guide
  (avail. 16mm film). For free loan, call 800-243-6877.
- "Wellness Workshop Depression." 1991.
  Hood/Copeland Video, 410 S. Michigan Ave., #826, Chicago, IL
  60605. 800-258-9181, 312-663-0600.
  60-min. videotape, $29.95 plus $2.00 shipping.
- "Depressive Illness on Campus: The NAMI Teleconference."
  1990. (Edited version).
  NAMI, 2101 Wilson Blvd., #302, Arlington, VA 22201.
  703-524-7600. 35-min. videotape $25.00.
- "AMI: Bringing Hope to the Mentally Ill." 1993.
  Nalco Chemical Co. for AMI-DuPage County, 1403 N. Main St.,
  Suite #209, Wheaton, IL 60187. 708-752-0066.
  18-min. videotape $15.00.
- "Silent No More." 1990.
  AMI of Minnesota, 970 Raymond Ave., #105, St. Paul, MN
  55114-1146. 612-645-2948.
  20-min. videotape $35.00; rental $20.00.
- "Until There's a Cure . . . Hope and Progress Today." 1993.
  AMI of Lake Country, 2025 Washington St., Waukegan, IL 60085.
  708-249-1515.
  20-min. videotape $20.00.

- "When Mental Illness Invades a Marriage." 1993.
  AMI of Alabama, 6900 6th Ave. South, Suite B, Birmingham, AL
  35212. 205-833-8336.
  40-min. videotape $15.00.
- "A Respite Program: Everyone Wins." 1993.
  South Carolina AMI, P.O. Box 2538, Columbia, SC 29202.
  803-779-7849.
  15-min. videotape $25.00.
- "When Mental Illness Invades the Minority Family." 1991.
  AMI of Alabama, 6900 6th Ave. South, Suite B, Birmingham, AL
  35212. 205-833-8336.
  29-min. videotape (English or Spanish) $45.00; preview $15.00.
- "Spanish-Speaking Support Group for Families of the Seriously
  Mentally Ill." 1992.
  AMI of San Diego, CA, San Diego State University, Attn: Dr.
  Maria Zuniga, School of Social Work, San Diego, CA 92115. 619-
  594-6865.
  55-min. videotape in Spanish $25.00.
- "Out of the Shadow and Into the Light: From Stigma to Unity." 1991.
  AMI of New York, 260 Washington Ave., Albany, NY 12210. 518-
  462-2000.
  29-min. videotape (English or Spanish) $20.00.
- "Mental Illnesses and People Who Are Affected by Them: For
  Law Enforcement Officers." 1992.
  AMI-Rhode Island, P.O. Box 28411, Providence, RI 02908.
  401-464-3060.
  50-min. videotape $25.00.
- "Understanding and Communicating with a Person Who Is
  Hallucinating." 1989.
  NurSeminars, Inc., W. 13523 Shore Rd., Nine Mile Falls, WA
  99026. 509-468-9673.
  63-min. videotape $89.95; preview $50.00; audiocassette/guide
  $18.00.
- "Understanding and Communicating with a Person Who Is
  Experiencing Mania." 1990.
  NurSeminars, Inc., W. 13523 Shore Rd., Nine Mile Falls, WA
  99026. 509-468-9673.
  60-min. videotape $89.95; preview $50.00; audiocassette/guide
  $18.00.

- "Understanding Relapse: Managing the Symptoms of Schizophrenia." 1991.
  NurSeminars, Inc., W. 13523 Shore Rd., Nine Mile Falls, WA 99026. 509-468-9673.
  $89.95 plus $5.00 shipping.
- "Family Strategies." 1991.
  California AMI (CAMI), 1111 Howe Ave. #475, Sacramento, CA 95825. 916-567-0163.
  29-min. videotape $35.00.
- "M.I., The Double Scarlet Letter." 1990.
  Center for Community Development, 9171 Central Ave., Suite #315, Capitol Heights, MD 20743. 301-808-2360.
  28-min. videotape $20.00.
- "Shattered Dreams." 1993.
  AMI-PA, 2149 N. 2nd St., Harrisburg, PA 17110. 717-238-1514.
  23-min. $39.95 plus $4.00 shipping/handling.
- "Kid TV." 1992.
  DMHMR: Division Public Education, State House Station 80, Augusta, ME 04333. 207-287-8576.
  17-min. videotape $25.00.
- "After the Tears: Teens Talk about Mental Illness." 1986.
  United Mental Health, Inc., 1945 5th Ave., Pittsburgh, PA 15219. 412-391-3820. 22-min. videotape $50.00.
- "Promise." Award-winning CBS movie. 1987.
  Some AMI groups have loan copies.
- "Mental Illness: Unraveling the Myths." 1990.
  Office of Television and Radio, Rutgers Univ., P.O. Box 10477, New Brunswick, NJ 08906-0477. 908-445-4194, ext. 105.
  60-min. videotape $35.00; transcript $5.00.
- "When the Music Stops: The Reality of Mental Illness." 1987.
  NAMI, 2101 Wilson Blvd., #302, Arlington, VA 22201. 703-524-7600.
  20-min. videotape $20.00.
- "A Place To Come Back To." 1987.
  Pathways to Promise, 5400 Arsenal St., St. Louis, MO 63139. 314-664-8400. 30-min. videotape $15.00.
- "Mental Illness in America: A Series of Public Hearings." 1992.
  NAMI, 2101 Wilson Blvd., #302, Arlington, VA 22201. 703-524-7600.
  15-min. videotape $10.00; 32-page report $4.00.

APPENDIX

C

USEFUL RESOURCES ON SCHIZOPHRENIA

LISTING OF THE BEST JOURNALS TO READ TO KEEP UP WITH WHAT IS GOING ON

- *Schizophrenia Bulletin*, a quarterly publication of the Schizophrenia Research Branch of NIMH, contains excellent summaries of evolving research. Cost is $17 per year. Orders to Superintendent of Documents, New Orders, P.O. Box 371954, Pittsburgh, PA 15250-7954.
- *Schizophrenia Research,* published nine times each year, contains current research and the abstracts from the two most important schizophrenia research meetings. Cost is $78 per year. Orders to Elsevier Science Publishers, Journal Dept., P.O. Box 211, 1000 AE Amsterdam, Netherlands.
- *Hospital and Community Psychiatry,* a monthly publication of the American Psychiatric Association, is the best single source of information on services and treatment. Cost is $60 per year. Orders to APA, 1400 K St., NW, Washington, DC 20077-1676.
- *Innovations and Research,* published quarterly by Boston University Center for Psychiatric Rehabilitation and NAMI. Cost is $35 per year. Orders to 730 Commonwealth Ave., Boston, MA 02215.
- *The Journal of the California Alliance for the Mentally Ill,* published quarterly by CAMI. Cost is $25 per year. Orders to CAMI, 1111 Howe Ave. #475, Sacramento, CA 95825.
- *NAMI Advocate,* published bimonthly by NAMI. Cost is $25 per year and it is free to NAMI members. Orders to NAMI, 2101 Wilson Blvd. #302, Arlington, VA 22201.

- *New Directions for Mental Health Services,* published quarterly by Jossey-Bass Publishers. Cost is $52 per year. Orders to Jossey-Bass Publishers, 350 Sansome St., San Francisco, CA 94104-1310.
- *Schizophrenia: Special Report 1993.* This publication is published by NIMH every 5 years. Single copies are available at no cost from the Public Inquiries Branch, NIMH 7-C-02, 5600 Fishers Lane, Rockville, MD 20857.

HOW TO GET INFORMATION ON SPECIFIC INTEREST GROUPS AND ACTIVITIES: NAMI HELPLINE 800-950-NAMI

- Family and consumer groups:
  National Alliance for the Mentally Ill (NAMI)
  2101 Wilson Blvd. #302
  Arlington, VA 22201
  (see also Appendix D)
- Siblings and adult children of persons with schizophrenia:
  NAMI SAC Network
- Families of children with schizophrenia:
  NAMI CAN Council
- Families of veterans with schizophrenia:
  NAMI Veterans Network
- Homeless or missing persons with schizophrenia:
  NAMI Homeless and Missing Persons Network
- Individuals with schizophrenia in jails and prisons:
  NAMI Forensic Network
- Improving the training of mental illness professionals:
  NAMI Curriculum and Training Committee
- Educating clergy about schizophrenia:
  NAMI Religious Outreach, NAMI; and also
  Pathways to Promise
  St. Louis State Hospital
  5400 Arsenal St.
  St. Louis, MO 63139
- Consumer groups: NAMI Consumer Council; and also
  National Mental Health Consumers' Association
  311 South Juniper St. #902
  Philadelphia, PA 19107

- Individuals with both schizophrenia and mental retardation:
  National Association for the Dually Diagnosed
  110 Prince St.
  Kingston, NY 12401
- Manic-depressive illness
  National Depressive and Manic Depressive Assn.
  Box 3395
  Chicago, IL 60654
- Support for research:
  National Alliance for Research on Schizophrenia and Depression
  (NARSAD)
  60 Cutter Mill Rd. #200
  Great Neck, NY 11021
- Fighting stigma:
  National Stigma Clearinghouse
  275 7th Ave. 16th Floor
  New York, NY 10001
- The accreditation status of a psychiatric hospital:
  Joint Commission on Accreditation of Healthcare Organizations
  1 Renaissance Blvd.
  Oak Brook Terr., IL 60181
- Clubhouses: Fountain House
  425 West 47th St.
  New York, NY 10036
- Continuous Treatment Teams: PACT model
  PACT Program
  108 S. Webster
  Madison, WI 53703
- Compeer:
  Compeer Inc.
  259 Monroe Ave. #B-1
  Rochester, NY 14607
- Fairweather Lodges:
  Coalition for Community Living
  2658 Roseland Ave.
  East Lansing, MI 48823
- Housing:
  Center for Community Change
  Trinity College of Vermont
  208 Colchester Ave.

Burlington, VT 05401
- Rehabilitation:
Center for Psychiatric Rehabilitation
Boston University
730 Commonwealth Ave.
Boston, MA 02215;
also
Thresholds
2700 N. Lakeview
Chicago, IL 60614

COURSES FOR EDUCATION ON SCHIZOPHRENIA

In recent years there have been a variety of courses and curriculums developed to educate people about schizophrenia. Some of these are targeted more at the families, some at consumers, and many can be used by both.
- NurSeminars by Mary D. Moller, MSN, RN
Center for Patient and Family Mental Health Education
W. 13523 Shore Rd.
Nine Mile Falls, WA 99026
- Journey of Hope Family Education and Support Program by Joyce C. Burland, Ph.D., Donna M. Mayeux, and Diane Gill
P.O. Box 2547
Baton Rouge, LA 70821
- Supportive Family Training by Ms. Sheila LeGacy
Family Support and Education Center
Transitional Living Services
239 West Fayette St.
Syracuse, NY 13202
- Maryland Family Education Program by Agnes B. Hatfield, Ph.D.
8351 Canning Terrace
Greenbelt, MD 20770
- UCLA Skills Training Modules
Psychiatric and Rehabilitation Consultants
P.O. Box 6022
Camarillo, CA 93011
- Bridges: People Helping People
Oregon AMI

161 High St., S.E., #212
Salem, OR 97310
- Coping Skills for Families
Training and Education Center
Mental Health Association of Southeastern PA
311 S. Juniper St., #902
Philadelphia, PA 19107
- How To Survive and Thrive with a Mentally Ill Relative by Chris Amensen, Ph.D.
San Gabriel Valley AMI
909 S. Fair Oaks
Pasadena, CA 91105
- Patient and Family Education by Kay McCrary, Ed.D., and Cynthia Bisbee, Ph.D.
Bryan Psychiatric Hospital
220 Faison Drive
Columbia, SC 29203
- Information on other programs can be found in T.E. Backer, R.B. King, and D.M. Callahan, *Innovation Directory: Family Involvement,* available for $10 from the Human Interaction Research Institute, 1849 Sawtelle Boulevard, #102, Los Angeles, CA 90025.

ADDRESSES OF CONSUMER PROVIDER TRAINING PROGRAMS

Consumer providers, also called consumer case managers and consumer case aides, are a new and promising type of mental illness worker. Individuals who have been affected with schizophrenia or other severe mental illness are selected and trained to work with other severely mentally ill individuals in mental health centers, housing programs, or rehabilitation programs. Information on programs training these workers is available from:
- Regional Assessment and Training Center
3520 West Oxford Ave.
Denver, CO 80236
Since 1987 has trained 10 classes.
- Consumer Provider Program
Mental Health Division
c/o Mr. James Dallas

Dept. of Social and Health Services
P.O. Box 45320
Olympia, WA 98504
First class of trainees graduated in 1994.
- Consumer Provider Program
CASCAP Inc.
678 Massachusetts Ave.
Cambridge, MA 02139
First class of trainees graduated in 1994.
- Consumer Education Program
MHMRA of Harris County
2850 Fannin
Houston, TX 77002
In 1994 was training its fifth class.

ADDRESSES OF EXEMPLARY CLUBHOUSES
(FOUNTAIN HOUSE MODEL)

Clubhouses provide individuals who have serious mental illnesses with social, recreational, educational, vocational, and housing opportunities. The original clubhouse, Fountain House, began in New York City in 1948. There are now more than 200 clubhouses in operation patterned after Fountain House. The following are some of the more exemplary clubhouses currently in operation. The map in chapter 8 shows their locations.

- Crossroads at the Larches
11 Williams St.
Hopedale, MA 01747
- Genesis Club, Inc.
274 Lincoln St.
Worcester, MA 01605
- Pioneer House
34 St. Peter St.
Salem, MA 01970
- Prime Time
41 East Maine St.
Torrington, CT 06790

- Fountain House
425 West 47th Street
New York, NY 10036
- Venture House
89-25 Parsons Blvd.
Jamaica, NY 10301
- Bridges
212 Williams St.
Watertown, NY 13601
- Harbor House
703 Main Street
Paterson, NJ 07503

- Chestnut Place Clubhouse
  4042 Chestnut St.
  Philadelphia, PA 19104
- Green Door
  1623 16th St., NW
  Washington, DC 20009
- Beach House
  Virginia Beach, VA 23456
- Clarendon House
  3141 North 10th St.
  Arlington, VA 22201
- Lakeside House
  5623 Lakeside Avenue
  Richmond, VA 23228
- Adventure House
  924 North Lafayette St.
  Shelby, NC 28150
- Sixth Avenue West
  714 6th Avenue West
  Hendersonville, NC 28739
- Gateway House
  P.O. Box 4241
  Greenville, SC 29608
- New Day Clubhouse
  P.O. Box 5396
  189 S. Converse St.
  Spartanburg, SC 29304
- Fellowship House
  5711 S.W. Dixie Highway
  Miami, FL 33143
- Thresholds
  2700 N. Lakeview
  Chicago, IL 60614

- Yahara House
  148 East Johnson St.
  Madison, WI 53703
- Independence Center
  4380 West Pine Blvd.
  St. Louis, MO 63108
- Breakthrough Club
  233 South St. Francis
  Wichita, KS 67202
- Cirrus House
  1509 First Ave.
  Scottsbluff, NE 69361
- Liberty Center
  112 South Birch
  Norfolk, NE 68701
- Cowlitz River Club
  537 14th Ave.
  Longview, WA 98632
- New Frontier Club
  2719 Rockefeller Ave.
  Everett, WA 98201
- Wilson House
  224 North 7th St.
  Pasco, WA 99301
- Alliance House
  1724 South Main St.
  Salt Lake City, UT 84115
- Rainbow Club
  P.O. Box 553
  Brigham City, UT 84302

ADDRESSES OF EXEMPLARY CONTINUOUS TREATMENT TEAMS
(PACT MODEL)

As described in chapter 8, one of the most effective models for providing treatment and rehabilitation services for individuals with serious mental illnesses is the PACT (Program of Assertive Community Treatment) model, which originated in Madison, WI. Continuous treatment teams based on this model are now widely used in many states. The following are some of the more exemplary continuous treatment teams currently in operation. The map in chapter 8 shows their locations.

- Greater Bridgeport CMHC
  1635 Central Ave.
  Bridgeport, CT 06610
- River Valley Services
  Connecticut Valley Hospital
  Middletown, CT 06457
- The Responsive Service
  Program
  Danbury Hospital
  Danbury, CT 06810
- First ACT Program
  Norwich Hospital
  Norwich, CT 06360
- Community Support/116A6
  VA Medical Center
  950 Campbell Ave.
  West Haven, CT 06516
- Community Counseling
  Center, Inc.
  Mobile Treatment Team
  101 Bacon St.
  Pawtucket, RI 02860
- South Shore Mental Health
  Center, Inc.
  Mobile Treatment Team
  55 Cherry Lane
  Wakefield, RI 02879
- Riverwood Rehabilitation
  Services, Inc.
  Mobile Support Team
  80 Cutler St.
  Warren, RI 02885
- Fernhook Community Mental

Health Center
14 Central Ave.
New Castle, DE 19720
- Connections
  601 Delaware Ave.
  Wilmington, DE 19801
- PROACT (Delaware State
  Hospital)
  1956 Maryland Ave.
  Wilmington, DE 19805
- ACT Team
  1222 W. Baltimore St.
  Baltimore, MD 21223
- Costar
  Department of Psychiatry
  Johns Hopkins University
  624 North Broadway
  Baltimore, MD 21205
- Palmetto Pathways Outreach
  1 Carriage Lane
  Charleston, SC 29403
- On-Site, Charleston-
  Dorchester Mental Health
  Center
  1565 Sam Rittenberg,
  Suite 100
  Charleston, SC 29407
- Roads, Charleston-Dorchester
  Mental Health Center
  300 N. Cedar Street, Suite A2
  Summerville, SC 29483
- Mental Health Cooperative
  Continuous Treatment Team

275 Cumberland Bend
Nashville, TN 37228
- Columbus Area Mental Health
  Center Extended Care Team
  1515 E. Broad St.
  Columbus, OH 43205
- The Bridge
  2835 N. Sheffield, Suite 411
  Chicago, IL 60657
- Harbinger
  1155 Front St., NW
  Grand Rapids, MI 49504
- ACT
  Kalamazoo County
  610 Burdick
  Kalamazoo, MI 49007
- Program of Assertive
  Community Treatment
  108 S. Webster
  Madison, WI 53703
- Green County Community
  Support Program

P.O. Box 216
Monroe, WI 53566
- Region I Mental Health Center
  2195 Ironwood Ct.
  Coeur d'Alene, ID 83814
- Region IV Mental Health
  Center
  1720 Westgate
  Boise, ID 83704
- The Virginia Street Project
  Santa Clara County Bureau of
  Mental Health
  1150 South Bascom Ave.,
  Suite 22
  San Jose, CA 95128
- Village Integrated Services
  Agency
  456 Elm Ave.
  Long Beach, CA 90802

There are also exemplary continuous treatment teams in Ontario, Canada, in Brockville (Assertive Community Rehabilitation Program), Scarborough (New Dimensions in Community Living), and Kingston (Community Integration Program).

D

CONTACTS FOR THE ALLIANCE FOR THE MENTALLY ILL BY STATE

For information, support, and advocacy, individuals with schizophrenia and their families should join the local chapter of the National Alliance for the Mentally Ill (NAMI). There are over 1000 AMI chapters in the United States. The following is a list of state AMI offices for individuals who wish to locate the nearest chapter in their state.

The national NAMI office is located at 2101 Wilson Boulevard, Arlington, VA 22201; telephone 800-950-NAMI. In Canada the national office for the Schizophrenia Society of Canada is located at 75 The Donway West, Suite 814, Don Mills, Ontario M3C-2E9;

telephone 416-445-8204.

Alabama AMI
6900 6th Ave. South, Suite B
Birmingham, AL 35212
205-833-8336

Alaska AMI
110 W. 15th Ave.
Suite B
Anchorage, AK 99501
907-277-1300
800-478-4462

Arizona AMI
2441 E. Fillmore St.
Phoenix, AZ 85008

602-244-8166

Arkansas AMI
4313 W. Markham
Hendrix Hall, Rm. 233
Little Rock, AR 72205
501-661-1548
800-844-0381

California AMI
1111 Howe Ave., Suite 475
Sacramento, CA 95825
916-567-0163

Colorado AMI
1100 Fillmore St.
Denver, CO 80206-3334

303-321-3104
Connecticut AMI
151 New Park Ave.
Hartford, CT 06106
203-586-2319

AMI of Delaware
2500 W 4th St., 4th St. Plaza,
Suite 12
Wilmington, DE 19805
302-427-0787

AMI District of Columbia—
Thresholds
422 8th St., SE
Washington, DC 20003
202-546-0646

Florida AMI
304 N. Meridian St.
Suite 2
Tallahassee, FL 32301
904-222-3400

Georgia AMI
1256 Briarcliff Rd., NE,
Rm. 412-S
Atlanta, GA 30306
404-894-8860

Hawaii AMI
1126 12th Ave., Suite 205
Honolulu, HI 96816
808-737-2778

Idaho AMI
313 N. Allumbaugh
Boise, ID 83704
208-376-4304

AMI Illinois State Coalition
730 E. Vine St., Rm.209
Springfield, IL 62703
217-522-1403

Indiana AMI
P.O. Box 22697
Indianapolis, IN 46222-0697
317-236-0056

AMI of Iowa
5911 Meredith Dr., Suite C-1
Des Moines, IA 50322
515-254-0417

Kansas AMI
112 SW 6th
P.O. Box 675
Topeka, KS 66601
913-233-0755
800-539-2660

Kentucky AMI
10510 La Grange Rd., Bldg. 103
Louisville, KY 40223
502-245-5284

Louisiana AMI
P.O. Box 2547
Baton Rouge, LA 70821
504-343-6928

AMI of Maine
Box 222
Augusta, ME 04332
207-622-5767 or 207-464-
5767
800-464-5767

AMI of Maryland
711 W. 40th St., Suite 451.
Baltimore, MD 21211
410-467-7100
800-467-0075

AMI of Massachusetts
295 Devonshire St., 4th Floor
Boston, MA 02210
617-426-2299

AMI of Michigan
24133 Northwestern
Hwy., #103
Southfield, MI 48075
313-355-0010
800-331-4AMI

AMI of Minnesota
970 Raymond Ave.,
Suite 105
St. Paul, MN 55114
612-645-2948

Mississippi AMI
603 Duling, Box 3
Jackson, MS 39216
601-922-1227

Missouri Coalition of AMI
204 E. High St.
Jefferson City, MO 65101
800-374-2138

Montana AMI
P.O. Box 1021
Helena, MT 59624
406-443-7871

Nebraska AMI
814 Lyncrest Drive
Lincoln, NE 68510
402-489-6239

AMI of New Hampshire
10 Ferry St., Unit 314
Concord, NH 03301
603-225-5359
800-242-6264

New Jersey AMI
200 W. State St., 3rd Floor
Trenton, NJ 08608-1102
609-695-4554

AMI of Nevada
1027 S. Rainbow Blvd., #172
Las Vegas, NV 89128
702-254-2666

AMI New Mexico
1720 Lousisana Blvd. NE
Suite 214
Albuquerque, NM 87110
505-254-0643

AMI of New York State
260 Washington Ave.
Albany, NY 12210
518-462-2000
800-950-3228

North Carolina AMI
4904 Waters Edge Dr., #152
Raleigh, NC 27606
919-851-0063
800-451-9682

North Dakota AMI
401 S. Main
Minot, ND 58701
701-852-5324
800-338-6646

AMI of Ohio
979 S. High St.
Columbus, OH 43206
614-444-2646
800-686-2646

Oklahoma AMI
1140 N. Hudson
Oklahoma City, OK 73103
405-239-6264
800-583-1264

Oregon Alliance of AMI
161 High St., SE, Suite 212
Salem, OR 97301
503-370-7774

AMI of Pennsylvania
2149 N. 2nd St.
Harrisburg, PA 17110-1005
717-238-1514
800-223-0500

AMI of Rhode Island
P.O. Box 28411
Providence, RI 02908
401-464-3060

South Carolina AMI
P.O. Box 2538
Columbia, SC 29202
803-779-7849

South Dakota AMI

P.O. Box 221
Brookings, SD 57006
605-697-7210
800-551-2531

Tennessee AMI
1900 N. Winston Rd., #511
Knoxville, TN 37919
615-531-8264

TEXAMI
100 E. 7th St., Suite 208
Austin, TX 78702
512-474-2225

Utah AMI
P.O. Box 58047
Salt Lake City, UT 84158
801-584-2023

AMI of Vermont
230 Main St., Suite 203
Municipal Center
Brattleboro, VT 05301
802-257-5546

Virginia AMI
P.O. Box 1903
Richmond, VA 23215
804-225-8264

AMI of Washington State
4305 Lacey Blvd. SE, Suite 11
Lacey, WA 98503
206-438-0211

West Virginia AMI
P.O. Box 2706
Charleston, WV 25330
304-342-0497

800-598-5653

AMI of Wisconsin
1245 E. Washington Ave.,
Suite 290
Madison, WI 53703
608-257-5888
800-236-2988

Wyoming AMI
1949 E. "A" St.
Casper, WY 82601
307-234-0440

NOTES

To include complete references to everything discussed in the book would result in a Notes section almost as long as the book. I have therefore been selective and included recent summary articles as well as references that are less likely to be known to readers.

EPIGRAPHS

Van Gogh letter quoted by J. Rewald, *Post-Impressionism: From van Gogh to Gauguin* (New York: Museum of Modern Art, 1962), p. 321. "To Winifred, With Love," a poem by Bill Hensleigh, Kalispell, MT., published in the "Lamplighter News," 1992, quoted with permission.

CHAPTER 1: DIMENSIONS OF THE DISASTER

"Schizophrenia is": W. Hall, G. Andrews, and G. Goldstein, "The Costs of Schizophrenia," *Australian and New Zealand Journal of Psychiatry* 19 (1985): 3–5. **"one of**

the most sinister": L. Wilson, *This Stranger, My son* (New York: Putnam, 1968), p. 174. **studies of homeless:** E. F. Torrey, *Nowhere To Go: The Tragic Odyssey of the Homeless Mentally Ill* (New York: Harper and Row, 1988). **survey of American jails:** E. F. Torrey, J. Stieber, J. Ezekiel et al., *Criminalizing the Seriously Mentally Ill* (Washington, D.C.: National Alliance for the Mentally Ill and Public Citizen Health Research Group, 1992). **"thought disorder":** R. Jemelka, E. Trupin, and J. A. Chiles, "The Mentally Ill in Prisons: A Review," *Hospital and Community Psychiatry* 40 (1989): 481–85. **episodes of violence:** See E. F. Torrey, "Violent Behavior by Individuals with Serious Mental

Illnesses," *Hospital and Community Psychiatry,* in press. **"The street people":** "A Ferocious Crime Against the Helpless," *Cape Cod Times,* July 22, 1984. **In California:** "A California Jury Ponders 9 Deaths," *New York Times,* August 8, 1993, p. 27. **the police removed:** "21 Ex-Mental Patients Taken from 4 Private Homes," *New York Times,* August 5, 1979, p. A-33. **in 1990:** S. Raab, "Mental Homes Are Wretched, A Panel Says," *New York Times,* August 6, 1990. **in Mississippi:** "9 Ex-Patients Kept in Primitive Shed," *New York Times,* October 21, 1982, p. A-21. **In Illinois:** R. Davidson, "A Mental Health Crisis in Illinois," *Chicago Tribune,* December 9, 1991. **In New York:** C. F. Muller and C. L. M. Caton, "Economic Costs of Schizophrenia: A Postdischarge Study," *Medical Care* 21 (1983): 92–104. **A study of readmissions:** J. L. Geller, "A Report on the 'Worst' State Hospital Recidivists in the U.S.," *Hospital and Community Psychiatry* 43 (1992): 904–08. **a 1993 study:** J. R. Husted and R. Charter, "Mental Illness Training for Law Enforcement," California Alliance for the Mentally Ill, 1993, mimeo. **only 3 percent:** M. Olfson, H. A. Pincus, and T. H. Dial, "Professional Practice Patterns of U.S. Psychiatrists," *American Journal of Psychiatry* 151 (1994): 89–95. **only 60 percent:** D. A. Regier, W. E. Narrow, D. S. Rae, et al., "The De Facto U.S. Mental and Addictive Disorders Service System," *Archives of General Psychiatry* 50 (1993): 85–94. **survey in Baltimore:** M. Von Korff, G. Nestadt, A.

Romanoski et al., "Prevalence of Untreated DSM-III Schizophrenia," *Journal of Nervous and Mental Disease* 173 (1985): 577–81. **in Wisconsin:** D. A. Treffert, "The Obviously Ill Patient in Need of Treatment," *Hospital and Community Psychiatry* 36 (1985): 259–64. **1.8 million:** Prevalence figures for schizophrenia in the United States were derived from the many publications of the ECA study, especially M. A. Burnam, R. L. Hough, J. I. Escobar et al., "Six-Month Prevalence of Specific Psychiatric Disorders Among Mexican Americans and Non-Hispanic Whites in Los Angeles," *Archives of General Psychiatry* 44 (1987): 687–94. **study of Mexican-Americans:** E. G. Jaco, *The Social Epidemiology of Mental Disorders: A Psychiatric Survey of Texas* (New York: Russell Sage Foundation, 1960). **Hutterites:** J. W. Eaton and R. J. Weil, *Culture and Mental Disorders: A Comparative Study of the Hutterites and Other Populations* (Glencoe: Free Press, 1955). **higher prevalence in urban:** E. F. Torrey and A. Bowler, "Geographical Distribution of Insanity in America: Evidence for an Urban Factor," *Schizophrenia Bulletin* 16 (1990): 591–604. **study in Stockholm:** G. Lewis, A. David, S. Andreasson, et al., "Schizophrenia and City Life," *Lancet* 340 (1992): 137–40. **study in North Carolina:** D. Blazer, L. K. George, R. Landerman, et al., "Psychiatric Disorders: A Rural/Urban Comparison," *Archives of General Psychiatry* 42 (1985): 651–56. **lowest**

socioeconomic class: M. L. Kohn, "Social Class and Schizophrenia: A Review," *Journal of Psychiatric Research* 6 (1968): 155–73; and M. L. Kohn, "Social Class and Schizophrenia: A Critical Review and a Reformulation," *Schizophrenia Bulletin* 7 (1973): 60–79. **Five separate studies:** See M. Kramer, B. M. Rosen, and E. M. Willis, "Definitions and Distribution of Mental Disorders in a Racist Society," in C. V. Willie, B. M. Kramer, and B. S. Brown, eds., *Racism and Mental Health* (Pittsburgh: University of Pittsburgh Press, 1973); and M. Kramer, "Population Changes and Schizophrenia, 1970–1985," in L. Wynne et al., eds., *The Nature of Schizophrenia* (New York: Wiley, 1978). **careful study in Rochester:** *Report of the President's Commission on Mental Health* (Washington, D.C.: U.S. Government Printing Office, 1978). **in Texas and in Louisiana:** Kramer, Rosen, Willis. **Director of NIMH, testifying:** Testimony of Dr. Shervert H. Frazier before Committee on Appropriations, U.S. Senate, November 20, 1986. **1986 survey:** R. W. Manderscheid and M. A. Sonnenschein, *Mental Health, United States, 1992* (Washington, D.C.: Government Printing Office, 1992), p. 287. **A 1988 survey:** B. J. Burns and D. B. Kamerow, "Psychotropic Drug Prescriptions for Nursing Home Residents," *Journal of Family Practice* 26 (1988): 155–60. **A 1993 random:** P. N. Tariot, C. A. Podgorski, L. Blazina, et al., "Mental Disorders in the Nursing Home: Another Perspective," *American Journal of Psychiatry* 150 (1993): 1063–69. **"chronic mental patients":** B. W. Rosner and P. V. Rabins, "Mental Illness Among Nursing Home Patients," *Hospital and Community Psychiatry* 36 (1985): 119–28. **recent survey of members:** D. M. Steinwachs, J. D. Kasper, and E. A. Skinner, "Family Perspectives on Meeting the Needs for Care of Severely Mentally Ill Relatives: A National Survey," Johns Hopkins University School of Hygiene and Public Health, 1992. **Schizophrenia Elsewhere in the World:** Unless otherwise indicated, all studies mentioned in this section are reviewed in E. F. Torrey, *Schizophrenia and Civilization* (New York: Jason Aronson, 1980); and E. F. Torrey, "Prevalence Studies in Schizophrenia," *British Journal of Psychiatry* 150 (1987): 598–608. **Dominica:** R. W. Kay, "Prevalence and Incidence of Schizophrenia in Afro-Caribbeans," *British Journal of Psychiatry* 160 (1992): 421. **Micronesia:** F. X. Hezel and A. M. Wylie, "Schizophrenia and Chronic Mental Illness in Micronesia: An Epidemiological Survey," *ISLA: A Journal of Micronesian Studies* 1 (1992): 329–54. **"insanity is a disease":** A. Halliday, *Remarks on the Present State of the Lunatic Asylums in Ireland* (London: John Murray, 1808). **Caribbean immigrants:** S. Wessely, D. Castle, G. Der, et al., "Schizophrenia and Afro-Caribbeans," *British Journal of Psychiatry* 159 (1991): 795–801. **Since 1985 similar:** R. E. Kendell, D. E. Malcolm, and W. Adams, "The

Problem of Detecting Changes in the Incidence of Schizophrenia," *British Journal of Psychiatry* 162 (1993): 212–18. **In Baltimore:** P. Lemkau, C. Tietze, and M. Cooper, "Mental-Hygiene Problems in an Urban District," *Mental Hygiene* 25 (1941): 624–46; and 26 (1942): 100–19. **in New Haven:** A. B. Hollingshead and F. C. Redlich, *Social Class and Mental Illness* (New York: John Wiley, 1958). **high incidence of *new* cases:** A. Y. Tien and W. W. Eaton, "Psychopathologic Precursors and Sociodemographic Risk Factors for the Schizophrenia Syndrome," *Archives of General Psychiatry* 49 (1992): 37–46. **$636,000:** A. E. Moran, R. I. Freedman, S. S. Sharfstein, "The Journey of Sylvia Frumkin: A Case Study for Policymakers," *Hospital and Community Psychiatry* 35 (1984): 887–93. **One study:** D. P. Rice and L. S. Miller, "The Economic Burden of Schizophrenia," Sixth Biennial Conference on the Economics of Mental Health, Bethesda, Md., September 21–22, 1992. **other study:** R. J. Wyatt, I. de Saint Ghislain, M. C. Leary, et al., "An Economic Evaluation of Schizophrenia—1991," *British Journal of Psychiatry* Supplement, in press. **In Australia:** G. Andrews, W. Hall, G. Goldstein, et al., "The Economic Costs of Schizophrenia," *Archives of General Psychiatry* 42 (1985): 537–43. **$180 billion:** R. J. Wyatt, "Science and Psychiatry," in J. T. Kaplan, B. J. Sadock, eds., *Comprehensive Textbook of Psychiatry,* 4th ed. (Baltimore: Williams & Wilkins,

1984), chapter 53, p. 2027. **"In whatever":** E. Jarvis, "Insanity and Idiocy in Massachusetts: Report of the Commission on Lunacy, 1855" (Cambridge: Harvard University Press, 1971), p. 104. **"schizophrenia has existed":** D. V. Jeste, R. del Carmen, J. B. Lohr, et al., "Did Schizophrenia Exist Before the Eighteenth Century?" *Comprehensive Psychiatry* 26 (1985): 493–503; see also N. M. Bark, "On the History of Schizophrenia," *New York State Journal of Medicine* 88 (1988): 374–83. **The other side:** E. F. Torrey, *Schizophrenia and Civilization* (New York: Jason Aronson, 1980). **Poor Mad Tom:** N. M. Bark, "Did Shakespeare Know Schizophrenia? The Case of Poor Mad Tom in King Lear," *British Journal of Psychiatry* 146 (1985): 436–38. **George Trosse:** Jeste et al., and F. Hare, "Schizophrenia Before 1800? The case of the Revd George Trosse," *Psychological Medicine* 18 (1988): 279–85. **insanity was increasing:** Torrey, *Schizophrenia and Civilization* and E. Hare, "Was Insanity on the Increase?" *British Journal of Psychiatry* 142 (1983): 439–55. **Figure 1.2:** Data is from A. L. Stroup and R. W. Manderscheid, "The Development of the State Mental Hospital System in the United States: 1840–1980," *Journal of the Washington Academy of Sciences* 78 (1988): 59–68. **"insanity is increasing":** E. Jarvis, "On the Supposed Increase in Insanity," *American Journal of Insanity* 8 (1852): 333. **"The successive reports":** Quoted in W. J. Corbet, "On the Increase of

Insanity," *American Journal of Insanity* 50 (1893): 224–38. **"the insane have increased":** F. B. Sanborn, "Is American Insanity Increasing? A Study," *Journal of Mental Science* 40 (1894): 214–19. **Deinstitutionalization:** Most of the material in this section is from Torrey, *Nowhere To Go.* **"no convictions were had":** Hearings on the National Neuropsychiatric Institute, Subcommittee on Health and Education, United States Senate, March 6–8, 1946, pp. 167 and 169. **"in some of the wards":** A. Deutsch, *The Shame of the States* (New York: Harcourt Brace, 1948), p. 28. **Kennedy's younger sister:** See Torrey, *Nowhere to Go,* pp. 102–06. **"it has been demonstrated":** President Kennedy's 1963 special message to Congress, reprinted in H. A. Foley and S. S. Sharfstein, *Madness and Government* (Washington, D.C.: American Psychiatric Press, 1983). **federal CMHC program:** E. F. Torrey, S. M. Wolfe, and L. M. Flynn, "Fiscal Misappropriations in Programs for the Mentally Ill: A Report on Illegality and Failure of the Federal Construction Grant Program for Community Mental Health Centers" (Washington, D.C.: Public Citizen Health Research Group and National Alliance for the Mentally Ill, 1990). **number of lawyers:** L. Caplan, "The Lawyers Race to the Bottom," *Washington Post,* August 6, 1993, A-24. **A 1980 survey:** C. A. Taube, B. J. Burns, and L. Kessler, "Patients of Psychiatrists and Psychologists in Office-Based Practice: 1980,"

American Psychologist 39 (1984): 1435–47.

CHAPTER 2: THE INNER WORLD OF MADNESS: VIEW FROM THE INSIDE

"What then does": H. R. Rollin, *Coping with Schizophrenia* (London: Burnett Books, 1980), p. 162. **R. W. Emerson,** *Journals* (1836). **I Never Promised You a Rose Garden:** See C. North and R. Cadoret, "Diagnostic Discrepancy in Personal Accounts of Patients with 'Schizophrenia,'" *Archives of General Psychiatry* 38 (1981): 133–37. **"Perceptual dysfunction":** J. Cutting and F. Dunne, "Subjective Experience of Schizophrenia," *Schizophrenia Bulletin* 15 (1989): 217–31. **"During the last":** A. McGhie and J. Chapman, "Disorders of Attention and Perception in Early Schizophrenia," *British Journal of Medical Psychology* 34 (1961): 103–16. **"Colours seem":** Ibid. **"Everything looked vibrant":** Cutting and Dunne. **"Lots of things":** Ibid. **"People looked deformed":** Ibid. **"I saw everything":** G. Burns, "An Account of My Madness," mimeo, 1983. **"These crises":** M. Sechehaye, *Autobiography of a Schizophrenic Girl* (New York: Grune & Stratton, 1951), p. 22. **"Everything seems":** McGhie and Chapman. **"Occasionally during":** Anonymous, "An Autobiography of a Schizophrenic Experience," *Journal of Abnormal and Social Psychology* 51 (1955): 677–89. **"I can proba-**

bly": M. Vonnegut, *The Eden Express* (New York: Praeger, 1975), p. 107. **"An outsider"**: E. Leete, "Mental Illness: An Insider's View," presented at annual meeting of National Alliance of the Mentally Ill, New Orleans, 1985. **In one study:** Cutting and Dunne. **"Sometimes when people"**: McGhie and Chapman. **"it was terrible"**: M. Barnes and J. Berke, *Mary Barnes: Two Accounts of a Journey Through Madness* (New York: Ballantine, 1973), p. 44. **"touching any patient"**: P. S. Wagner, "Life in the Closet," *Hartford Courant,* August 26, 1993. **"decay in my"**: Rollin, p. 150. **"a genital sexual"**: Ibid. p. 150 **One psychiatrist:** See M. B. Bowers, *Retreat from Sanity: The Structure of Emerging Psychosis* (Baltimore: Penguin, 1974). **"My trouble is" and "My concentration is"**: McGhie and Chapman. **"Childhood feelings"**: Bowers, p. 152. **"All sorts of"**: W. Mayer-Gross, E. Slater, and M. Roth, *Clinical Psychiatry* (Baltimore: Williams & Wilkins, 1969), p. 268. **"In College"**: Wagner. **"I was invited"**: A. Boisen, *Out of the Depths* 1960. Quoted in B. Kaplan, ed., *The Inner World of Mental Illness* (New York: Harper & Row, 1964), p. 118. **"Fear made me"**: Sechehaye, p. 26. **"It was evening"**: E. Leete, "The Interpersonal Environment," in A. B. Hatfield and H. P. Lefley, *Surviving Mental Illness* (New York: Guilford Press, 1993), p. 117. **"Suddenly my whole"**: M. Coate, *Beyond All Reason* (Philadelphia: J. B. Lippincott, 1965), p. 21. **"Before last week"**: Bowers,

p. 27. **"as if a heavy"**: B. J. Freedman, "The Subjective Experience of Perceptual and Cognitive Disturbances in Schizophrenia," *Archives of General Psychiatry* 30 (1974): 333–40. **"However hard"**: Rollin, p. 150. **Decreased pain perception:** See E. F. Torrey, "Headaches After Lumbar Puncture and Insensitivity to Pain in Psychiatric Patients," *New England Journal of Medicine* 301 (1979): 110; G. D. Watson, P. C. Chandarana, and H. Merskey, "Relationship Between Pain and Schizophrenia," *British Journal of Psychiatry* 138 (1981): 33–36; and L. K. Bickerstaff, S. C. Harris, R. S. Leggett, et al., "Pain Insensitivity in Schizophrenic Patients," *Archives of Surgery* 123 (1988): 49–51. **"At first it"**: N. McDonald, "Living with Schizophrenia," *Canadian Medical Association Journal* 82 (1960): 218-21, 678-81. **"When people are"**: McGhie and Chapman. **"I can concentrate"**: Ibid. **"I used to get"**: Cutting and Dunne. **"I have to"**: J. Chapman, "The Early Symptoms of Schizophrenia," *British Journal of Psychiatry* 112 (1966): 225–51. **"Everything is in"**: McGhie and Chapman. **"the teeth, then"**: Sechehaye, foreword. **"This morning"**: S. Sheehan, *Is There No Place on Earth for Me?* (Boston: Houghton Mifflin, 1982), p. 69. **"I can't concentrate"**: McGhie and Chapman. **"I tried sitting"**: B. O'Brien, *Operators and Things: The Inner Life of a Schizophrenic* (New York: Signet, 1976), pp. 97–98. **"During the visit"**: Sechehaye, p. 28. **"If I do"**:

Chapman. **"My thoughts get"**: McGhie and Chapman. **"I am not"**: Nijinsky, quoted in Kaplan, p. 424. **"How could a"**: O'Brien, p. 100. **"I was extremely"**: Sechehaye, pp. 66–67. **"The worst thing"**: Chapman. **"I feel that"**: Mayer-Gross, Slater, and Roth, pp. 281, 267. **"For instance, I"**: G. Bateson, ed., *Perceval's Narrative: A Patient's Account of His Psychosis 1830–1832* (1838, 1840) (New York: Morrow, 1974), p. 269. **"I may be"**: McGhie and Chapman. **"If I am"**: Ibid. **"Sometimes I commit"**: Burns. **Champman claims:** See Chapman. **"I am so"**: Anonymous, "I Feel Like I Am Trapped Inside My Head, Banging Desperately Against Its Walls," *The New York Times,* March 18, 1986, C3. **"I went to"**: Anonymous, "First Person Account: A Pit of Confusion," *Schizophrenia Bulletin* 16 (1990): 355–59. **"A policeman walking"**: A. Chekhov, "Ward No. 6," quoted in A. A. Stone and S. S. Stone, eds., *The Abnormal Personality Through Literature* (Englewood Cliffs, NJ: Prentice-Hall, 1966), p. 5. **"I got up"**: Bowers, pp. 186–87. **"Anxiety: like metal"**: Poem by Robert L. Nelson, now deceased, and published with the permission of his mother. **"During the paranoid"**: Anonymous, *"Schizophrenic Experience."* **"I felt that"**: Ibid. **"I once believed"**: R. Jameson, "Personal View," *British Medical Journal* 291 (1985): 541. **de Clerembault:** G. Remington and H. Book, "Case Report of de Clerembault Syndrome, Bipolar Affective Disorder and Response to

Lithium," *American Journal of Psychiatry* 141 (1984): 1285–88. **"telepathic force"**: Rollin, p. 132. **"I like talking"**: Chapman. **"I was sitting"**: Ibid. **"This phenomenon can"**: J. Lang, "The Other Side of Hallucinations," *American Journal of Psychiatry* 94 (1938): 1090–97. **"No doubt I"**: Poe, "The Tell-Tale Heart." **"Thus for years"**: D. P. Schreber, *Memoirs of My Nervous Illness* (1903), translated and with introduction by I. Macalpine and R. A. Hunter (London: William Dawson & Sons, 1955), p. 172. **"There was music"**: Boisen, quoted in Kaplan, p. 119. **"For about almost"**: Schreber, p. 225. **one recent study:** P. K. McGuire, G. M. S. Shah, and R. M. Murray, "Increased Blood Flow in Broca's Area During Auditory Hallucinations in Schizophrenia," *Lancet* 342 (1993): 703–06. **"auditory hallucinations"**: J. M. Cleghorn et al., "Toward a Brain Map of Auditory Hallucinations," *American Journal of Psychiatry* 149 (1992): 1062–69. **larger third ventricles:** J. Cullberg and H. Nyback, "Persistent Auditory Hallucinations Correlate with the Size of the Third Ventricle in Schizophrenic Patients," *Acta Psychiatrica Scandinavica* 86 (1992): 469–72. **born deaf:** E. M. R. Critchley, "Auditory Experiences of Deaf Schizophrenics," *Journal of the Royal Society of Medicine* 76 (1983): 542–44. **"At an early"**: Lang. **Silvano Arieti:** *Creativity: The Magic Synthesis* (New York: Harper Colophon, 1976), p. 251. **"On a few"**: Ibid. **"During the time"**: Bowers. p. 37. **"To the person"**:

Lang. **"Sometimes I did"**:
Sechehaye, pp. 87–88. **"I saw
myself"**: Coate, pp. 66–67. **"I get
shaky"**: Chapman. **"This was
equally"**: Sechehaye, p. 87. **"My
breast gives"**: Schreber, p. 207. **"81
percent"**: S. Bustamante, K. Maurer,
W. Loffler et al., "Depressive
Symptoms in the Early Course of
Schizophrenia," Abstract,
Schizophrenia Research 11 (1994):
187. **"During the first"**: J. Lang,
"The Other Side of the Affective
Aspects of Schizophrenia,"
Psychiatry 2 (1939): 195–202.
"Later, considering them":
Sechehaye, p. 35. **"I sat"**: M. Stakes,
"First Person Account: Becoming
Seaworthy," *Schizophrenia Bulletin*
11 (1985): 629. **"there has been"**: P.
Cramer, J. Bowen, and M. O'Neill,
"Schizophrenics and Social
Judgment," *British Journal of
Psychiatry* 160 (1992): 481–87.
"Half the time": McGhie and
Chapman. **"one of the"**: Chapman.
"During my first": Anonymous,
"Schizophrenic Experiences."
"Instead of wishing": E. Meyer and
L. Covi, "The Experience of
Depersonalization: A Written Report
by a Patient," *Psychiatry* 23 (1960):
215–17. **"I wish I"**: J. A. Wechsler,
In a Darkness (New York: Norton,
1972), p. 17. **"reported experienc-
ing"**: A. M. Kring, S. L. Kerr, D. A.
Smith et al., "Flat Affect in
Schizophrenia Does Not Reflect
Diminished Subjective Experience of
Emotion," *Journal of Abnormal
Psychology* 102 (1993): 507–17.
"Loneliness needs": J. K. Bouricius,
"Negative Symptoms and Emotions

in Schizophrenia," *Schizophrenia
Bulletin* 15 (1989): 201–07. **One
study found:** T. C. Manschreck et al.,
"Disturbed Voluntary Motor Activity
in Schizophrenic Disorder,"
Psychological Medicine 12 (1982):
73–84; see also M. Jones and R.
Hunter, "Abnormal Movements in
Patients with Chronic Psychotic
Illness," in G. E. Crane and R.
Gardner, *Psychotropic Drugs and
Dysfunctions of the Basal Ganglia,*
Publication No. 1938 (Washington:
U.S. Public Health Service, 1969). **In
another study:** Cutting and Dunne.
"I became": Ibid. **eye blinking:** See
J. R. Stevens, "Eye Blink and
Schizophrenia: Psychosis or Tardive
Dyskinesia," *American Journal of
Psychiatry* 135 (1978): 223–26.
"[He] stood": H. de Balzac, "Louis
Lambert" (1832), in A. A. Stone and
S. S. Stone, eds., *The Abnormal
Personality Through Literature*
(Englewood Cliffs, NJ: Prentice-Hall,
1966), pp. 63–64. **"When I am"**:
McGhie and Chapman. **"I don't
like"**: Ibid. **"I get stuck"**: McGhie
and Chapman. **"I am not"**: Ibid. **"As
the work"**: Kindwall and Kinder
(1940), quoted in C. Landis and F. A.
Mettler, *Varieties of
Psychopathological Experience* (New
York: Holt, Rinehart, and Winston,
1964), p. 530. **"The state of"**:
Sechehaye, pp. 61–62. **"to help to"**:
Chapman. **"There were two"**:
Perceval's Narrative, quoted in
Kaplan, p. 240. **Chapman believes:**
Chapman. **"My feelings about"**:
Anonymous, "Schizophrenic
Experiences." **"the only way"**:
Wagner. **Schreber:** p. 146. **"an**

enchanted loom": Quoted by O. Sacks, *The Man Who Mistook His Wife for a Hat* (New York: Summit Books, 1985), p. 140. **John Hinckley:** "Hinckley Sr. Seeks Support in Fight Against Mental Illness," *Psychiatric News,* November 16, 1984. **"self-measuring ruler":** Burns. **"Lost":** Nelson. **cited by one woman:** A. Sobin and M. N. Ozer, "Mental Disorders in Acute Encephalitis," *Journal of Mt. Sinai Hospital* 33 (1966): 73–82. **"that *strangeness*":** R. Porter, *A Social History of Madness* (New York: Weidenfeld and Nicolson, 1988), p. 9. **"Something inside":** B. Bick, "Love and Resentment," *New York Times,* March 25, 1990. **"No doubt Louis":** Balzac.

CHAPTER 3: THE DIAGNOSIS OF SCHIZOPHRENIA: VIEW FROM THE OUTSIDE

"Insanity is": Quoted in C. E. Goshen, *Documentary History of Psychiatry* (New York: Philosophical Library, 1967), p. 315. **Studies have shown:** C. S. Mellor, "First Rank Symptoms of Schizophrenia," *British Journal of Psychiatry* 117 (1970): 15–23. **patients with manic-depressive illness:** W. T. Carpenter, J. S. Strauss, and S. Muleh, "Are There Pathognomonic Symptoms in Schizophrenia?" *Archives of General Psychiatry* 28 (1973): 847–52. *DSM-IV: Diagnostic and Statistical Manual of Mental Disorders* (Washington, D.C.: American Psychiatric Association, 1994). **Rosenhan study:** D. L. Rosenhan, "On Being Sane in Insane Places," *Science* 179 (1973): 250–58; see also R. L. Spitzer, "More on Pseudoscience in Science and the Case for Psychiatric Diagnosis," *Archives of General Psychiatry* 33 (1976): 459–70. **"If I were":** S. S. Kety, "From Rationalization to Reason," *American Journal of Psychiatry* 131 (1974): 957–63. **Paranoid schizophrenia:** For a review see K. S. Kendler and K. L. Davis, "The Genetics and Biochemistry of Paranoid Schizophrenia and Other Paranoid Psychoses," *Schizophrenia Bulletin* 7 (1981): 689–709; there are other related articles in the same issue. **"positive" symptoms:** This subtyping is reviewed in an entire issue of *Schizophrenia Bulletin* (volume 11, no. 3, 1985) devoted to the subject; the articles by Drs. Crow and Andreasen are especially useful. **"are inflexible":** *Diagnostic and Statistical Manual of Mental Disorders* (Washington, D.C.: American Psychiatric Association, 1980). **Researchers in Canada:** J. Varsamis and J. D. Adamson, "Somatic Symptoms in Schizophrenia," *Canadian Psychiatric Association Journal* 21 (1976): 1–6. **gender differences:** See M. V. Seeman, "Gender Differences in Schizophrenia," *Canadian Journal of Psychiatry* 27 (1982): 107–11; J. M. Goldstein, "Gender Differences in the Course of Schizophrenia," *American Journal of Psychiatry* 145 (1988): 684–89; and S. Lewis, "Sex and Schizophrenia: Vive la Difference," *British Journal of Psychiatry* 161 (1992): 445–50.

"monster themes": A. T. Russell, L. Bett, and C. Sammons, "The Phenomenology of Schizophrenia Occurring in Childhood," *Journal of the American Academy of Child and Adolescent Psychiatry* 28 (1989): 399–407. **genetic roots:** W. H. Green, M. Padron-Gayol, A. S. Hardesty, et al., "Schizophrenia with Childhood Onset," *Journal of the American Academy of Child and Adolescent Psychiatry* 31 (1992): 968–76. **MRI scans:** R. L. Hendren, J. E. Hodde-Vargas, L. A. Vargas, et al., "Magnetic Resonance Imaging of Severely Disturbed Children—A Preliminary Study," *Journal of the American Academy of Child and Adolescent Psychiatry* 30 (1991): 466–70. **follow-up of ten:** J. G. Howells and W. R. Guirguis, "Childhood Schizophrenia 20 Years Later," *Archives of General Psychiatry* 41 (1984): 123–28. **L. Wilson:** *This Stranger, My Son* (New York: Putnam, 1968). **late-onset schizophrenia:** See M. J. Harris and D. V. Jeste, "Late-Onset Schizophrenia: An Overview," *Schizophrenia Bulletin* 14 (1988): 39–55; and G. D. Pearlson, L. Kreger, P. V. Rabins, et al., "A Chart Review Study of Late-Onset and Early-Onset Schizophrenia," *American Journal of Psychiatry* 146 (1989): 1568–74. **R. L. Taylor,** *Mind or Body: Distinguishing Psychological from Organic Disorders* (New York: McGraw-Hill, 1982). **Dr. Harold Sox:** H. C. Sox, L. M. Koran, C. H. Sox, et al., "A Medical Algorithm for Detecting Physical Disease in Psychiatric Patients," *Hospital and Community Psychiatry* 40 (1989): 1270–76. **recent German study:** B. von der Stein, W. Wittgens, W. Lemmer, et al., "Schizophrenia Mimicked by Neurological Diseases," presented at International Conference on Schizophrenia, Vancouver, July 1992.

CHAPTER 4: WHAT SCHIZOPHRENIA IS NOT

"What consoles me": J. Rewald, *Post-Impressionism: From van Gogh to Gauguin* (New York: Museum of Modern Art, 1962), p. 320. **pair of identical twins:** J. T. Dalby, D. Morgan, and M. L. Lee, "Schizophrenia and Mania in Identical Twin Brothers," *Journal of Nervous and Mental Disease* 174 (1986): 304–8. **triplets:** P. McGuffin, A. Reveley, and A. Holland, "Identical Triplets: Nonidentical Psychosis?" *British Journal of Psychiatry* 140 (1982): 1–6. **a 1994 study:** P. Wright and T. A. Fahy, "Does Schizophrenia Present as Reactive Psychosis?" Abstract. *Schizophrenia Research* 11 (1994): 181. **widely quoted study:** R. C. W. Hall, E. R. Gardner, S. K. Stickney, et al., "Physical Illness Manifesting as Psychiatric Disease," *Archives of General Psychiatry* 37 (1980): 989–95. **Koran and his colleagues:** L. M. Koran, H. C. Sox, K. I. Marton et al., "Medical Evaluation of Psychiatric Patients," *Archives of General Psychiatry* 46 (1989): 733–40. **One English study:** K. Davison, "Schizophrenia-like Psychoses Associated With Organic

Cerebral Disorders: A Review," *Psychiatric Developments* 1 (1983): 1–34. **Another English study:** E. C. Johnstone, J. F. Macmillan, and T. J. Crow, "The Occurrence of Organic Disease of Possible or Probable Aetiological Significance in a Population of 268 Cases of First Episode Schizophrenia," *Psychological Medicine* 17 (1987): 371–79. **A postmortem study:** Davison. **Viral encephalitis:** E. F. Torrey, "Functional Psychoses and Viral Encephalitis," *Integrative Psychiatry* 4 (1986): 224–36. **One study:** Davison. **One report:** A. G. Awad, "Schizophrenia and Multiple Sclerosis," *Journal of Nervous and Mental Disease* 171 (1983): 323–24. **"a common":** Davidson. **AIDS:** N. Buhrich, D. A. Cooper, and E. Freed, "HIV Infection Associated With Symptoms Indistinguishable From Functional Psychosis," *British Journal of Psychiatry* 152 (1988): 649–53. **Psychosis following childbirth:** R. A. Munoz, "Postpartum Psychosis as a Discrete Entity," *Journal of Clinical Psychiatry* 46 (1985): 182–84. **Psychosis following trauma:** H. A. Nasrallah, R. C. Fowler, L. L. Judd, "Schizophrenia-like Illness Following Head Injury," *Psychosomatics* 22 (1981): 359–61. **Infantile autism:** The best book on this subject is M. Coleman and C. Gillberg, *The Biology of the Austistic Syndromes* (New York: Praeger Publishers, 1985). An older but still useful book is B. Rimland, *Infantile Autism* (New York: Appleton-Century-Crofts, 1974). **neuropathological changes in autism:** E. R.

Ritvo, B. J. Freeman, A. B. Scheibel, et al., "Lower Purkinje Cell Count in the Cerebella of Four Autistic Subjects," *American Journal of Psychiatry* 143 (1986): 862–66. **one study:** E. F. Torrey, S. P. Hersh, and K. D. McCabe, "Early Childhood Psychosis and Bleeding During Pregnancy," *Journal of Autism and Childhood Schizophrenia* 5 (1975): 287–97. **one study has suggested:** J. L. Karlson, "Genetic Association of Giftedness and Creativity with Schizophrenia," *Hereditas* 66 (1970): 177. **creativity and schizophrenia:** See J. A. Keefe and P. A. Magaro, "Creativity and Schizophrenia: An Equivalence of Cognitive Processing," *Journal of Abnormal Psychology* 89 (1980): 390–98; and M. Dykes and A. McGhie, "A Comparative Study of Attentional Strategies of Schizophrenic and Highly Creative Normal Subjects," *British Journal of Psychiatry* 128 (1976): 50–56. **1989 book:** J. M. MacGregor, *The Discovery of the Art of the Insane* (Princeton: Princeton University Press, 1989). **"I love life":** R. Nijinsky, ed., *The Diary of Vaslav Nijinsky* (Berkeley: University of California Press, 1968), pp. 185–86. **"he could not sleep":** R. Ellmann, *James Joyce: New and Revised Edition* (New York: Oxford, 1982), p. 685. **A psychiatrist:** N. J. C. Andreasen, "James Joyce: A Portrait of the Artist as a Schizoid," *Journal of the American Medical Association* 224 (1973): 67–71. **"Joyce had":** Ellmann, p. 650. **"assailed by":** Rewald, p. 266. The other symptoms of his illness can be found on pp.

266–334. **"Oh, if I"**: B. Schiff, "Triumph and Tragedy in the Land of 'Blue Tones and Gay Colors,'" *Smithsonian* (October, 1984), p. 89.

CHAPTER 5: PROGNOSIS AND POSSIBLE COURSES

"Such a disease": Quoted in V. Norris, *Mental Illness in London* (London: Oxford University Press, 1959), p. 15. **early treatment:** R. J. Wyatt, "Early Intervention with Neuroleptics May Decrease the Long-Term Morbidity of Schizophrenia," *Schizophrenia Research* 5 (1991): 201–02. **"were considered to be"**: J. Lieberman et al., "Time Course and Biologic Correlates of Treatment Response in First-Episode Schizophrenia," *Archives of General Psychiatry* 50 (1993): 369–76. **best summary:** J. H. Stephens, "Long-term Prognosis and Follow-up in Schizophrenia," *Schizophrenia Bulletin* 4 (1978): 25–47. **"About three-fifths"**: L. Ciompi, "Catamnestic Long-term Study of the Course of Life and Aging of Schizophrenics," *Schizophrenia Bulletin* 6 (1980): 606–16. **"the current picture"**: C. M. Harding and J. S. Strauss, "The Course of Schizophrenia: An Evolving Concept" in M. Alpert, ed., *Controversies in Schizophrenia* (New York: Guilford Press, 1985), p. 347. **"The patient"**: W. Mayer-Gross, E. Slater, and M. Roth, *Clinical Psychiatry* (Baltimore: Williams & Wilkins, 1969), p. 275. **community survey in Baltimore:** M. Von Korff, G. Nestadt, A. Romanoski, et al.,

"Prevalence of Treated and Untreated *DSM-III* Schizophrenia," *Journal of Nervous and Mental Disease* 173 (1985): 577–81. **"about twice"**: P. Allebeck, "Schizophrenia: A Life-Shortening Disease," *Schizophrenia Bulletin* 15 (1989): 81–89. **"nearly a three-fold"**: D. W. Black and R. Fisher, "Mortality in DSM-IIIR Schizophrenia," *Schizophrenia Research* 7 (1992): 109–16. **"5.05 times"**: P. Corten, M. Ribourdouille, and M. Dramaix, "Premature Death Among Outpatients at a Community Mental Health Center," *Hospital and Community Psychiatry* 42 (1991): 1248–51. **double the rate:** M. J. Edlund, C. Conrad, and P. Morris, "Accidents Among Schizophrenic Outpatients," *Comprehensive Psychiatry* 30 (1989): 522–26. **Diseases:** See A. E. Harris, "Physical Disease and Schizophrenia," *Schizophrenia Bulletin* 14 (1988): 85–96; and S. Mukherjee, D. B. Schnur, and R. Reddy, "Family History of Type 2 Diabetes in Schizophrenic Patients," *Lancet* 1 (1989): 495. **prostate cancer:** P. B. Mortensen, "Neuroleptic Medication and Reduced Risk of Prostate Cancer in Schizophrenic Patients," *Acta Psychiatrica Scandinavica* 85 (1992): 390–93. **recent study in England:** M. Marshall and D. Gath, "What Happens to Homeless Mentally Ill People? Follow Up of Residents of Oxford Hostels for the Homeless," *British Medical Journal* 304 (1992): 79–80. **in Oklahoma:** J. Cannon, "Remains Identified," *Norman Transcript,* December 21, 1990, p. 2. **In Virginia:** "Face Now Has a Name,

But Slaying Baffles Va. Authorities,"
Washington Post July 13, 1988, p. C-
1.

CHAPTER 6: WHAT CAUSES SCHIZOPHRENIA?

"Something has happened": L.
Jefferson, *These Are My Sisters*
(1948), quoted in Kaplan, p. 6. **"a
lunatic is":** Voltaire, *Philosophical
Dictionary,* 1764, quoted in R. Porter,
ed., *The Faber Book of Madness*
(London: Faber and Faber, 1991), pp.
17–18. **"psychiatry and neu-
ropathology":** Griesinger, quoted in
G. Zilboorg and G. W. Henry, *A
History of Medical Psychology* (New
York: W. W. Norton, 1941), p. 436.
For recent reviews of the rapidly
increasing studies of structural
changes in schizophrenia see the fol-
lowing:
T. M. Hyde, M. F. Casanova, J. E.
Kleinman et al., "Neuroanatomical
and Neurochemical Pathology in
Schizophrenia," in A. Tasman and S.
M. Goldfinger, eds., *Review of
Psychiatry,* vol. 10 (Washington:
American Psychiatric Association
Press, 1991), pp. 7–23; K. F. Berman,
D. G. Daniel, and D. R. Weinberger,
"Schizophrenia: Brain Structure and
Function," in II. I. Kaplan and B. J.
Sadock, eds., *Comprehensive
Textbook of Psychiatry,* 6th ed.
(Baltimore: Williams and Wilkins,
1994); and M. E. Shenton, "Temporal
Lobe Structural Abnormalities in
Schizophrenia" in S. Matthysee, D.
Levy, J. Kagan et al.,
*Psychopathology: The Evolving
Science of Mental Disorder* (New

York: Cambridge University Press,
1994). **Bogerts:** B. Bogerts, E.
Meertz, and R. Schonfeldt-Bausch,
"Basal Ganglia and Limbic System
Pathology in Schizophrenia,"
Archives of General Psychiatry 42
(1985): 784–91. **PET scan studies:**
See Berman, Daniel and Weinberger,
1994. **"a broad":** J. A. Grebb, D. R.
Weinberger, and J. M. Morihisa,
"Electroencephalogram and Evoked
Potentials Studies of Schizophrenia,"
in H. A. Nasrallah and D. R.
Weinberger, eds., *The Neurology of
Schizophrenia* (Amsterdam: Elsevier,
1986), pp. 121–40. **"The fre-
quency":** L. J. Seidman,
"Schizophrenia and Brain
Dysfunction: An Integration of
Recent Neurodiagnostic Findings,"
Psychological Bulletin 94 (1983):
195–238. **1992 study:** J. Schroder, R.
Niethammer, F. J. Geider, et al.,
"Neurological Soft Signs in
Schizophrenia," *Schizophrenia
Research* 6 (1992): 25–30. **"Chronic
or process":** Seidman. **"It is impos-
sible":** T. E. Goldberg, J. M. Gold, D.
L. Braff, "Neuropsychological
Functioning and Time-Linked
Information Processing in
Schizophrenia," in A. Tasman and S.
Goldfinger, eds., *Review of
Psychiatry,* vol. 10 (Washington:
American Psychiatric Press, 1991),
pp. 60–78. **"selective, integrative":**
D. R. Roberts, "Schizophrenia and
the Brain," *Journal of
Neuropsychiatry* 5 (1963): 71–79.
"able to correlate": P. D. MacLean,
"Psychosomatic Disease and the
'Visceral Brain,'" *Psychosomatic
Medicine* 11 (1949): 338–53. **limbic**

system dysfunction: E. F. Torrey and M. R. Peterson, "Schizophrenia and the Limbic System," *Lancet* 2 (1974): 942–46. **brain tumors:** N. Malamud, "Psychiatric Disorders with Intracranial Tumors of the Limbic System," *Archives of Neurology* 17 (1967): 113–23. **Cases of encephalitis:** J. R. Brierley et al., "Subacute Encephalitis of Later Life Mainly Affecting the Limbic Areas," *Brain* 83 (1960): 357–68. **epilepsy, when it originates:** N. Malamud, "The Epileptogenic Focus in Temporal Lobe Epilepsy from the Pathological Standpoint," *Archives of Neurology* 14 (1966): 190–95; M. A. Falconer, E. A. Serafetinides, and J. A. N. Corsellis, "Etiology and Pathogenesis of Temporal Lobe Epilepsy," *Archives of Neurology* 10 (1964): 233–48. **limbic electrical activity:** R. G. Heath, *Studies in Schizophrenia: A Multidisciplinary Approach to Mind-Brain Relationships* (Cambridge: Harvard University Press, 1954); R. G. Heath, "Correlation of Electrical Recordings from Cortical and Subcortical Regions of the Brain with Abnormal Behavior in Human Subjects," *Confina Neurologia* 18 (1958): 305–15; R. R. Monroe et al., "Correlation of Rhinencephalic Electrograms with Behavior," *EEG and Clinical Neurophysiology* 9 (1957): 623–42; C. W. Sem-Jacobsen, M. C. Peterson, and J. A. Lazarte, "Intracerebral Electrographic Recordings from Psychotic Patients During Hallucinations and Agitation: Preliminary Report," *American Journal of Psychiatry* 112 (1955): 278–88; C. W. Sem-Jacobsen et al., "Electroencephalographic Rhythms from the Depths of the Parietal, Occipital, and Temporal Lobes in Man," *EEG and Clinical Neurophysiology* 8 (1956): 263–78; J. F. Kendrick and F. A. Gibbs, "Origin, Spread and Neurosurgical Treatment of the Psychomotor Type of Seizure Discharge," *Journal of Neurosurgery* 14 (1957): 270–84; J. Hanley et al., "Spectral Characteristics of EEG Activity Accompanying Deep Spiking in a Patient with Schizophrenia," *EEG and Clinical Neurophysiology* 28 (1970): 90; J. Hanley et al., "Automatic Recognition of EEG Correlates of Behavior in a Chronic Schizophrenic Patient," *American Journal of Psychiatry* 128 (1972): 1524–28. **"It is probable":** G. W. Roberts, "Schizophrenia: A Neuropathological Perspective," *British Journal of Psychiatry* 158 (1991): 8–17. **minor physical anomalies:** For a recent review see E. F. Torrey, A. E. Bowler, E. H. Taylor, et al. *Schizophrenia and Manic Depressive Disorder* (New York: Basic Books, 1994). An additional study that was published subsequent to that review is J. B. Lohr and K. Flynn, "Minor Physical Anomalies in Schizophrenia and Mood Disorders," *Schizophrenia Bulletin* 19 (1993): 551–56. **fingerprint patterns:** For a review see Torrey et al., *Schizophrenia and Manic Depressive Disorder.* **pregnancy and birth:** Ibid. **seasonality of births:** Two reviews of this rapidly expanding literature are T. N. Bradbury and G. A. Miller, "Season of Birth in Schizophrenia: A Review of Evidence, Methodology and Etiology," *Psychological Bulletin* 98 (1985): 569–94, and J. H. Boyd, A. E. Pulver, and W. Stewart, "Season of Birth: Schizophrenia and Bipolar Disorder," *Schizophrenia Bulletin* 12 (1986): 173–86. **stillbirths:** E. F. Torrey, A. E. Bowler, R. Rawlings, et al., "Seasonality of Schizophrenia and Stillbirths," *Schizophrenia Bulletin* 19 (1993): 557–62. **genes:** For good reviews see I. I. Gottesman and J. Shields, *Schizophrenia: The Epigenetic Puzzle* (New York: Cambridge University Press, 1982) and I. I. Gottesman, *Schizophrenia Genesis* (New York: W. H. Freeman, 1991). For a more skeptical view see E. F. Torrey, "Are We Overestimating the Genetic Contribution to Schizophrenia?" *Schizophrenia Bulletin* 18 (1992): 159–70. **viruses:** For a recent review of the viral theory see R. H. Yolken and E. F. Torrey, "Viruses and Serious Mental Illnesses," *Clinical Microbiology Reviews,* in press. **"a hereditary":** D. R. Weinberger, "Implications of Normal Brain Development for the Pathogenesis of Schizophrenia," *Archives of General Psychiatry* 44 (1987): 660–69. **immune system dysfunction:** See Yolken and Torrey. **nutrition:** For an early review see D. Hawkins and L. Pauling, eds., *Orthomolecular Psychiatry* (San Francisco: W. H. Freeman, 1973). **endocrine dysfunction:** For a review see I. N. Ferrier, "Endocrinology and Psychosis," *British Medical Bulletin* 43 (1987): 672–88. **rheumatoid arthritis:** For recent reviews see W. W. Eaton, C. Hayward, and R. Ram,

"Schizophrenia and Rheumatoid Arthritis: A Review," *Schizophrenia Research* 6 (1992): 181–92; and S. Vinegradov, I. I. Gottesman, H. W. Moises et al., "Negative Association Between Schizophrenia and Rheumatoid Arthritis," *Schizophrenia Bulletin* 17 (1991): 669–78. **stress:** For a recent review of this literature see S. Hirsch, P. Cramer, and J. Bowen, "The Triggering Hypothesis of the Role of Life Events in Schizophrenia," *British Journal of Psychiatry* 161 (1992) suppl. 18:84–87. **"no study found":** J. G. Rabkin, "Stressful Life Events and Schizophrenia: A Review of the Research Literature," *Psychological Bulletin* 87 (1980): 408–25. **"there is no good":** C. C. Tennant, "Stress and Schizophrenia: A Review," *Integrative Psychiatry* 3 (1985): 248–61. **"There is no evidence":** R. M. G. Norman and A. K. Malla, "Stressful Life Events and Schizophrenia," *British Journal of Psychiatry* 162 (1993): 161–66. **"In cases":** E. Bleuler, *Dementia Praecox or the Group of Schizophrenias* (New York: International Universities Press, 1950), p. 345; first published in 1911. **"I seldom see":** Letter from Sigmund Freud to Karl Abraham in E. Jones, *The Life and Work of Sigmund Freud,* vol. 2 (New York: Basic Books, 1955), p. 437. **"I do not like":** Quoted in M. Shur, *The Id and the Regulatory Principle of Mental Functioning* (London: Hogarth, 1967), p. 21. **"all mothers were":** T. Tietze, "A Study of Mothers of Schizophrenic Patients," *Psychiatry*

12 (1949): 55–65. **best-known of these studies:** P. R. A. May, *Treatment of Schizophrenia: A Comparative Study of Five Treatment Methods* (New York: Science House, 1968). **"Analysis of variance":** P. R. A. May, et al., "Schizophrenia: A Follow-up Study of the Results of Five Forms of Treatment," *Archives of General Psychiatry* 38 (1981): 776–84. **"psychotherapy alone":** L. Grinspoon, J. R. Ewalt, and R. I. Shader, *Schizophrenia: Pharmacotherapy and Psychotherapy* (Baltimore: Williams & Wilkins, 1977), p. 154. **"There is no scientific":** D. F. Klein, "Psychosocial Treatment of Schizophrenia, or Psychosocial Help for People with Schizophrenia?" *Schizophrenia Bulletin* 6 (1980): 122–30. **"outcome for patients":** J. M. Davis et al., "Important Issues in the Drug Treatment of Schizophrenia," *Schizophrenia Bulletin* 6 (1980): 70–87. **"checked the therapeutic":** I. Macalpine and R. A. Hunter, in D. P. Schreber, *Memoirs of My Nervous Illness* (1903), translation and introduction by I. Macalpine and R. A. Hunter (London: William Dawson & Sons, 1955), p. 23. **"analogous to pouring":** R. E. Drake and L. I. Sederer, "The Adverse Effects of Intensive Treatment of Chronic Schizophrenia," *Comprehensive Psychiatry* 27 (1986): 313–26. **"psychotic breaks":** S. W. Hadley and H. H. Strupp, "Contemporary Views of Negative Effects in Psychotherapy," *Archives of General Psychiatry* 33 (1976): 1291–1302. **"there is some":** *Report of the President's Commission on Mental Health* (Washington, D.C.: U.S. Government Printing Office, 1978), vol. 4, p. 1766. **"recent evidence suggests":** G. L. Klerman, "Pharmacotherapy and Psychotherapy in the Treatment of Schizophrenia" (Paper presented at the Annual Meeting of the American Psychiatric Association, San Francisco, 1980). **"To offer traditional":** T. C. Manschreck, "Current Concepts in Psychiatry: Schizophrenic Disorders," *New England Journal of Medicine* 305 (1981): 1628–32. **"strange, near-psychotic":** T. Lidz, S. Fleck, and A. R. Cornelison, *Schizophrenia and the Family* (New York: International University Press, 1965), p. 327. **"an extremely noxious":** T. Lidz, B. Parker, and A. R. Cornelison, "The Role of the Father in the Family Environment of the Schizophrenic Patient," *American Journal of Psychiatry* 113 (1956): 126–32. **"double-bind":** G. Bateson, D. D. Jackson, J. Haley, et al., "Toward a Theory of Schizophrenia," *Behavioral Science* 1 (1956): 251–64. **later essay:** G. Bateson, "The Birth of a Matrix or Double Bind and Epistemology," in M. M. Berger, ed., *Beyond the Double Bind* (New York: Brunner Mazel, 1978). **As early as 1951:** C. T. Prout and M. A. White, "A Controlled Study of Personality Relationships in Mothers of Schizophrenic Male Patients," *American Journal of Psychiatry* 107 (1951): 251–56. **subsequent studies:** See, for example, J. Block, V. Patterson, J. Block, et al., "A Study of Parents of Schizophrenic and

Neurotic Children," *Psychiatry* 21 (1958): 387–97. **"in some sense":** C. Lasch, *The Culture of Narcissism* (New York: W. W. Norton, 1979), p. 76. **"psychosis in the final":** Ibid. **"we share":** R. C. Lewontin, S. Rose, and L. J. Kamin, *Not In Our Genes* (New York: Pantheon Books, 1984), p. ix. **"An adequate":** Ibid, p. 231. **"fake disease":** T. Szasz, *Schizophrenia: The Sacred Symbol of Psychiatry* (New York: Basic Books, 1976). **"'Mental illness'":** M. Barnes and J. Berke, *Mary Barnes: Two Accounts of a Journey Through Madness* (New York: Ballantine Books, 1971), pp. 75–76. **"I was looked":** "Britain's Offbeat Psychoanalyst," *Newsweek,* November 1, 1982, p. 16.

CHAPTER 7: THE TREATMENT OF SCHIZOPHRENIA

"To lighten": Charles Dickens, "A Curious Dance Around a Curious Tree," in *Household Words,* 1852. This epigraph was borrowed from N. Andreasen, *The Broken Brain* (New York: Harper & Row, 1984). **"as a suffering":** W. J. Annitto, "Schizophrenia and Ego Psychology," *Schizophrenia Bulletin* 7 (1981): 199–200. **half of all psychiatrists:** D. J. Knesper, "Psychiatric Manpower for State Mental Hospitals," *Archives of General Psychiatry* 35 (1978): 19–24. **"What does mean":** B. J. Ennis, *Prisoners of Psychiatry* (New York: Harcourt Brace Jovanovich, 1972); for a more complete discussion of this problem see R. L. Taylor

and E. F. Torrey, "The Pseudo-regulation of American Psychiatry," *American Journal of Psychiatry* 129 (1972): 658–62. **"a man barricaded":** C. Holden, "Broader Commitment Laws Sought," *Science* 230 (1985): 1253–55. **"Public defender":** D. A. Treffert, "The Obviously Ill Patient in Need of Treatment: A Fourth Standard for Civil Commitment," *Hospital and Community Psychiatry* 36 (1985): 259–64. **"significant changes":** J. M. Kane, F. Quitkin, A. Rifkin et al., "Attitudinal Changes in Involuntarily Committed Patients Following Treatment," *Archives of General Psychiatry* 40 (1983): 374–77. **"the combination of drug":** B. Pasamanick, F. R. Scarpitti, and S. Dinitz, *Schizophrenics in the Community: An Experimental Study in the Prevention of Hospitalization* (New York: Appleton-Century-Crofts, 1967), p. ix. **The liquid form:** For a good summary of this see J. L. Geller, B. D. Gaulin, and P. J. Barreira, "A Practitioner's Guide to Use of Psychotropic Medication in Liquid Form," *Hospital and Community Psychiatry* 43 (1992): 969–71. **penicillin exerts:** J. Davis, "Maintenance Therapy and the Natural Course of Schizophrenia," *Journal of Clinical Psychiatry* 46 (1985): 18–21. **John Davis:** J. M. Davis, "Overview: Maintenance Therapy in Psychiatry: I. Schizophrenia," *American Journal of Psychiatry* 132 (1975): 1237–45. **80 percent relapsed:** N. Capstick, "Long-Term Fluphenazine Decanoate Maintenance Dosage Requirements of Chronic Schizophrenic Patients," *Acta Psychiatrica Scandinavica* 61 (1980): 256–62. **two groups of investigators:** T. Van Putten, P. R. A. May, and S. R. Marder, "Response to Antipsychotic Medication: The Doctor's and the Consumer's View," *American Journal of Psychiatry* 141 (1984): 16–19; T. P. Hogan, A. G. Awad, and M. R. Eastwood, "Early Subjective Response and Prediction of Outcome to Neuroloptic Drug Therapy in Schizophrenia," *Canadian Journal of Psychiatry* 30 (1985): 246–48. **the difference between:** "Fluphenazine Levels—Short and Long," *Biological Therapies in Psychiatry* 4 (1981): 33–34. **study reported in 1994:** S. Galderisi, A. Mucci, M. Maj et al., "QEEG Mapping Changes After a Single Dose as Predictors of Clinical Response to Haloperidol in Schizophrenia," Abstract, *Schizophrenia Research* 11 (1994): 189. **Megadose fluphenazine:** S. J. Dencker, P. Enoksson, R. Johansson, et al., "Late (4–8 Years) Outcome of Treatment with Megadoses of Fluphenazine Enanthate in Drug-Refractory Schizophrenics," *Acta Psychiatrica Scandinavica* 63 (1981): 1–12; and also S. Steiner and C. Nagy, "Follow-up Study of 281 Schizophrenic Patients Treated with High Dosage Fluphenazine Decanoate," *International Pharmacopsychiatry* 16 (1981): 184–92. **intermittent medication:** A. G. Jolley, S. R. Hirsch, E. Morrison, A. McRink, and L. Wilson, "Trial of Brief Intermittent Neuroleptic Prophylaxis for Selected

Schizophrenic Outpatients: Clinical and Social Outcomes at Two Years," *British Medical Journal* 301 (1990): 837–42. **Dr. Jeffrey Lieberman:** J. Lieberman, D. Mayerhoff, A. Loebel et al., "Biologic Indices of Heterogeneity in Schizophrenia: Relationship to Psychopathology and Treatment Outcome," *Schizophrenia Research* 4 (1991): 289–90. **for loxapine:** L. Sperry, B. Hudson, and C. H. Chan, "Loxapine Abuse," *New England Journal of Medicine* 310 (1984): 598. **"early intervention:"** R. J. Wyatt, "Neuroleptics and the Natural Course of Schizophrenia," *Schizophrenia Bulletin* 17 (1991): 325–51. **"greater duration":** A. Loebel, J. Lieberman, D. Mayerhoff et al., "Correlates of Course of Outcome in First-Episode Schizophrenia," *Schizophrenia Research* 4 (1991): 290. **"untreated psychosis":** H. A. Youssef, A. Kinsella, and J. L. Waddington, "Extreme Negative Symptoms in Schizophrenia as a Correlate of Years of Untreated Psychosis Within a Rural Irish Population," *Schizophrenia Research* 9 (1993): 142. **"The antipsychotic agents":** R. J. Baldessarini, "The Neuroleptic Antipsychotic Drugs," *Postgraduate Medicine* 65 (1979): 108–28. **One recent study:** M. P. Caligiuri, J. B. Lohr, and D. V. Jeste, "Parkinsonism in Neuroleptic-Naive Schizophrenic Patients," *American Journal of Psychiatry* 150 (1993): 1343–48. **akinesia:** For an excellent discussion of this problem see A. Rifkin, "The Risks of Long-Term Neuroleptic Treatment of Schizophrenia:

Especially Depression and Akinesia," *Acta Psychiatrica Scandinavica* Supplementum 291, 63 (1981): 129–36. **molindone is less:** H. Heikkinen, J. Outakoski, V. Merilainen et al., "Molindone and Weight Loss," letter, *Journal of Clinical Psychiatry* 54 (1993): 160–61. **"extraordinary prevalence":** T. Turner, "Rich and Mad in Victorian England," *Psychological Medicine* 19 (1989): 29–44. **under 20 percent:** V. Khot and R. J. Wyatt, "Not All That Moves Is Tardive Dyskinesia," *American Journal of Psychiatry* 148 (1991): 661–66. **tardive dyskinesia:** For a good review see V. Khot, M. F. Egan, T. M. Hyde et al., "Neuroleptics and Classic Tardive Dyskinesia," in A. E. Lang, and W. J. Weiner, eds., *Drug-Induced Movement Disorders* (Mount Kisco, N.Y.: Futura Publishing Co., 1992), pp. 121–66. **10-year follow-up:** R. Yassa and N. P. V. Nair, "A 10-Year Follow-Up Study of Tardive Dyskinesia," *Acta Psychiatrica Scandinavica* 86 (1992): 262–66. **another 10-year:** G. Gardos, D. E. Casey, J. O. Cole et al., "Ten Year Outcome of Tardive Dyskinesia," *American Journal of Psychiatry,* in press. **"Of the 10":** D. E. Casey, "Tardive Dyskinesia: Outcome With Typical and Atypical Neuroleptics," in H. Y. Meltzer and D. Nerozzi, eds., *Current Practices and Future Developments in the Pharmacotherapy of Mental Disorders,* (Amsterdam: Elsevier, 1991), pp. 49–57. **AIMS:** M. R. Munetz and S. Benjamin, "How to Examine Patients Using the Abnormal Involuntary Movement Scale," *Hospital and Community Psychiatry* 39 (1988): 1172–77. **agranulocytosis:** J. M. J. Alvir, J. A. Lieberman, A. Z. Safferman et al., "Clozapine-Induced Agranulocytosis: Incidence and Risk Factors in the United States," *New England Journal of Medicine* 329 (1993): 162–67. **average of 14 pounds:** R. Leadbetter, M. Shutty, D. Pavalonis et al., "Clozapine-Induced Weight Gain: Prevalence and Clinical Relevance," *American Journal of Psychiatry* 149 (1992): 68–72. **average of 17 pounds:** J. S. Lamberti, T. Bellnier, and S. B. Schwarzkopf, "Weight Gain Among Schizophrenic Patients Treated With Clozapine," *American Journal of Psychiatry* 149 (1992): 689–90. **As early as 1984:** B. Ekblom, K. Eriksson, and L. H. Lindstrom, "Supersensitivity Psychosis in Schizophrenic Patients After Sudden Clozapine Withdrawal," *Psychopharmacology* 83 (1984): 293–94. **only 1 of 10 patients:** P. Cavazzoni, B. D. Jones, J. Kennedy et al., "Differential Response to Clozapine and Risperiodone in a Group of Ten Schizophrenic Patients Treated Sequentially With Both Agents: A Preliminary Report." Abstract. *Schizophrenia Research* 11 (1994): 103. **Interactions of antipsychotics:** For more detailed information see E. J. Watsky and C. Salzman, "Psychotropic Drug Interactions," *Hospital and Community Psychiatry* 42 (1991): 247–56; and M. A. Rizack and C. D. M. Hillman, *The Medical Letter Handbook of Adverse Drug*

Interactions (New Rochelle, N.Y.: The Medical Letter, 1993). **"One cannot help":** G. W. Christison, D. G. Kirch, and R. J. Wyatt, "When Symptoms Persist: Choosing Among Alternative Somatic Treatments for Schizophrenia," *Schizophrenia Bulletin* 17 (1991): 217–45. **One study:** R. S. Winslow, V. Stillner, and D. J. Coons, "Prevention of Acute Dystonic Reactions in Patients Beginning High-Potency Neuroleptics," *American Journal of Psychiatry* 143 (1986): 706–10. **Lithium:** See Christison et al. 1991 and H. Y. Meltzer, "Treatment of the Neuroleptic-Nonresponsive Schizophrenic Patient," *Schizophrenia Bulletin* 18 (1992): 515–42. **Benzodiazepines:** See Christison et al. 1991 and Meltzer, 1992. **Carbamazepine:** See Christison et al. 1991 and Meltzer 1992. **A 1985 study:** J. J. Zorc, D. B. Larson, J. S. Lyons, and R. S. Beardsley, "Expenditures for Psychotropic Medications in the United States in 1985," *American Journal of Psychiatry* 148 (1991): 644–47. **paid $2.8 million:** K. Day, "In Health Care, Pay Outpaces Perception," *Washington Post,* March 31, 1993. **receiving $12.7 million:** Ibid. **only 1.1 percent:** M. Gladwell, "Review of Generic Drugs Yields 'Mixed Picture,'" *Washington Post,* November 18, 1989. **"when the onset":** W. Z. Potter and M. V. Rudorfer, "Electroconvulsive Therapy—A Modern Medical Procedure," *New England Journal of Medicine* 328 (1993): 882–83. **damage to the brain:** C. E. Coffey, R. D. Weiner, W. T. Djang et al., "Brain Anatomic Effects of Electroconvulsive Therapy," *Archives of General Psychiatry* 48 (1991): 1013–21. **gluten-free diet:** D. S. King, "Statistical Power of the Controlled Research on Wheat Gluten and Schizophrenia," *Biological Psychiatry* 20 (1985): 785–87. **given folic acid:** P. S. A. Godfrey, B. K. Toone, M. W. P. Carney et al., "Enhancement of Recovery From Psychiatric Illness by Methylfolate," *Lancet* 336 (1990): 392–97.

CHAPTER 8: THE REHABILITATION OF SCHIZOPHRENIA

"Expecting the. . .": J. Halpern, P. R. Binner, C. B. Mohr, et al., *The Illusion of Deinstitutionalization* (Denver: Denver Research Institute, 1978). **"If for example":** W. M. Mendel, *Treating Schizophrenia* (San Francisco: Jossey-Bass, 1989), p. 128. J. R. Elpers, "Dividing the Mental Health Dollar: The Ethics of Managing Scarce Resources," *Hospital and Community Psychiatry* 37 (1986): 671–72. **45 changes:** A. E. Moran, R. I. Freedman, and S. S. Sharfstein, "The Journey of Sylvia Frumkin: A Case Study for Policymakers," *Hospital and Community Psychiatry* 35 (1984): 887–93. M. A. Test, "Continuity of Care in Community Treatment," in L. I. Stein, ed., *Community Support Systems for the Long-term Patient* (San Francisco: Jossey-Bass, 1979). E. F. Torrey, "Continuous Treatment

Teams," *Hospital and Community Psychiatry* 37 (1986): 1243–47. **case manager:** See W. A. Anthony, "Managed Care: A Misnomer?" letter, *Hospital and Community Psychiatry* 44 (1993): 794–95. **Dr. Werner M. Mendel:** "Managing Dependency in a Psychiatric Patient," *Audio-Digest* 6 (1977): 16. **In one study:** G. Hogarty and S. Goldberg, "Drug and Sociotherapy in the Post-Hospital Maintenance of Schizophrenia," *Archives of General Psychiatry* 24 (1973): 54–64. **"an inability to engage":** Social Security Administration, Department of Health and Human Services, *Supplemental Security Income Regulations.* These regulations are available in all Social Security offices. **In 1991 a total:** C. Kennedy and R. W. Manderscheid, "SSDI and SSI Beneficiaries With Mental Disorders," in R. W. Manderscheid and M. A. Sonnenschein, eds., *Mental Health, United States, 1992* (Washington D.C.: U.S. Government Printing Office, 1992), p. 222. **SSI appeals process:** See J. R. Anderson, "Social Security and SSI Benefits for the Mentally Disabled," *Hospital and Community Psychiatry* 33 (1982): 295–98. **Supported housing:** See, for example, P. J. Carling, "Housing and Supports for Persons With Mental Illness: Emerging Approaches to Research and Practice," *Hospital and Community Psychiatry* 44 (1993): 439–48. **"graduated independent":** "Diabetic Lay Dead at Group Home 3 Days," *Washington Post,* April 19, 1986, p. C3. **"the police found":** "21 Ex-Mental

Patients Taken From 4 Private Homes," *The New York Times,* August 5, 1979, p. B3. **In one study:** H. R. Lamb, "Board-and-Care Home Wanderers," *Hospital and Community Psychiatry* 32 (1981): 498–500. **Fairweather Lodges:** G. W. Fairweather, ed., *The Fairweather Lodge: A Twenty-Five-Year Retrospective.* (San Francisco: Jossey-Bass, 1980). **"the presence of":** *There Goes the Neighborhood* (White Plains, NY: Community Residences Information Services Program, 1986). **6 percent:** R. J. Turner, "Jobs and Schizophrenia," *Social Policy* 8 (1977): 32–40. **"in the morning":** H. R. Lamb and Associates, *Community Survival for Long-term Patients* (San Francisco: Jossey-Bass, 1976), p. 8. **Some other countries:** B. J. Black, "Substitute Permanent Employment for the Deinstitutionalized Mentally Ill," *Journal of Rehabilitation* 43 (1977): 32–35. **highly cost-effective:** J. H. Noble, "The Benefits and Costs of Supported Employment for People With Mental Illness and With Traumatic Brain Injury in New York State," Research Foundation of the State University of New York, SUNY at Buffalo, 1991. **supported employment:** S. Trotter, K. Minkoff, K. Harrison et al., "Supported Work: An Innovative Approach to the Vocational Rehabilitation of Persons Who Are Psychiatrically Disabled," *Rehabilitation Psychology* 33 (1988): 27–36. **"I get lost":** S. E. Estroff, *Making It Crazy: An Ethnography of Psychiatric Clients in an American Community* (Berkeley: University of

California Press, 1981), p. 233. **"I just can't":** C. Smith, "Schizophrenia in the 1980's," presented at the Alberta Schizophrenia Conference, May, 1986. **social skills training:** R. P. Liberman, C. J. Wallace, G. Blackwell et al., "Innovations in Skills Training for the Seriously Mentally Ill: The UCLA Social and Independent Living Skills Modules," *Innovations and Research* 2 (1993): 43–59; C. J. Wallace, R. P. Liberman, S. J. MacKain et al., "Effectiveness and Replicability of Modules for Teaching Social and Instrumental Skills to the Seriously Mentally Ill," *American Journal of Psychiatry* 149 (1992) 654–58. **dating service:** D. J. Schemo, "A Matchmaker's Niche: Mentally Ill Couples," *New York Times,* December 14, 1992, p. A-1. **studies done at Thresholds:** J. Dincin and T. F. Witheridge, "Psychiatric Rehabilitation as a Deterrent to Recidivism," *Hospital and Community Psychiatry* 33 (1982): 645–50. **"These findings":** T. F. Witheridge and J. Dincin, "The Bridge: An Assertive Outreach Program in an Urban Setting," in L. I. Stein and M. A. Test, eds., *The Training in Community Living Model: A Decade of Experience* (San Francisco: Jossey-Bass, 1985). **26 to 53 percent:** R. P. Roca, W. R. Breakey, and P. J. Fisher, "Medical Care of Chronic Psychiatric Outpatients," *Hospital and Community Psychiatry* 38 (1987): 741–44. **"the treatment of":** L. E. Adler and J. M. Griffith, "Concurrent Medical Illness in the Schizophrenic Patient," *Schizophrenia Research* 4 (1991): 91–107. **neurobiological disorders:** E. Peschel, R. Peschel, C. W. Howe et al., *Neurobiological Disorders in Children and Adolescents* (San Francisco: Jossey-Boss, 1992). **give up custody:** R. Cohen, R. Harris, S. Gottlieb et al., "States' Use of Transfer of Custody as a Requirement for Providing Services to Emotionally Disturbed Children," *Hospital and Community Psychiatry* 42 (1991): 526–30. **Maryland sent:** M. Moran, "Initiatives Throughout Country Bring Child MH Care Home," *Psychiatric News,* March 1, 1991, p. 9. **Saskatchewan:** C. M. Smith, "From Hospital to Community," *Canadian Journal of Psychiatry* 24 (1979): 113–20. **Louisville:** B. Pasamanick, F. R. Scarpitti, and S. Dinitz, *Schizophrenics in the Community: An Experimental Study in the Prevention of Hospitalization* (New York: Appleton-Century-Crofts, 1967). **Iowa:** K. C. Buckwalter, I. L. Abraham, M. Smith et al., "Nursing Outreach to Rural Elderly People Who Are Mentally Ill," *Hospital and Community Psychiatry* 44 (1993): 821–23. **upstate New York:** G. R. Reding and B. Maguire, "Nonsegregated Acute Psychiatric Admissions to General Hospitals— Continuity of Care Within the Community Hospital," *New England Journal of Medicine* 289 (1973): 185–89. **South Carolina:** A. B. Santos, P. A. Deci, K. R. Lachance et al., "Providing Assertive Community Treatment for Severely Mentally Ill Patients in a Rural Area," *Hospital* *and Community Psychiatry* 44 (1993): 34–39. **New Hampshire:** G. M. Barton, "The Practice of Emergency Psychiatry in Rural Areas," *Hospital and Community Psychiatry* 43 (1992): 965–66. **A 1993 study:** E. F. Torrey, D. A. Bigelow, and N. Sladen-Dew, "Quality and Cost of Services for Seriously Mentally Ill Individuals in British Columbia and the United States," *Hospital and Community Psychiatry* 44 (1993): 943–50. **"an abstraction":** D. A. Bigelow, G. Brodsky, L. Stewart et al., "The Concept and Measurement of Quality of Life as a Dependent Variable in Evaluation of Mental Health Services," in W. Tash and G. Stahler, eds., *Innovative Approaches to Mental Health Evaluation* (New York: Academic Press, 1982), pp. 345–66. **"measures covering":** A. F. Lehman, "Measures of Quality of Life Among Persons With Severe and Persistent Mental Disorders," *Social Psychiatry and Psychiatric Epidemiology,* in press. **"concept of asylum":** For a good discussion of this see J. K. Wing, "The Functions of Asylum," *British Journal of Psychiatry* 157 (1990): 822–27.

CHAPTER 9: SIX MAJOR PROBLEMS

"although insanity": Anonymous, "Admissions to Hospitals for the Insane," *American Journal of Insanity* 25 (1868): 74. **80 and 90 percent:** J. B. Lohr and K. Flynn, "Smoking and Schizophrenia," *Schizophrenia Research* 8 (1992): 93–102. **10 billion packs:** Ibid. **among outpatients:** J. R. Hughes, D. K. Hatsukami, J. E. Mitchell et al., "Prevalence of Smoking Among Psychiatric Outpatients," *American Journal of Psychiatry* 143 (1986): 993–97. **recently received support:** L. A. Adler, L. D. Hoffer, A. Wiser et al., "Normalization of Auditory Physiology by Cigarette Smoking in Schizophrenic Patients," *American Journal of Psychiatry* 150 (1993): 1856–61. **smoking decreases:** D. C. Goff, D. C. Henderson, and E. Amico, "Cigarette Smoking in Schizophrenia: Relationship to Psychopathology and Medication Side Effects," *American Journal of Psychiatry* 149 (1992): 1189–94. **affect the receptors:** D. G. Kirch, A. M. Alho, and R. J. Wyatt, "Hypothesis: A Nicotine-Dopamine Interaction Linking Smoking with Parkinson's Disease and Tardive Dyskinesia," *Cellular and Molecular Neurobiology* 8 (1988): 285–91. **nicotine potentiated:** B. J. McConville, M. H. Fogelson, A. B. Norman et al., "Nicotine Potentiation of Haloperidol in Reducing Tic Frequency in Tourette's Disorder," *American Journal of Psychiatry* 148 (1991): 793–94. **incidence of akathisia:** Goff et al. 1992. **tardive dyskinesia:** Kirch et al. 1988, and Goff et al. 1992. **instant coffee:** J. I. Benson and J. J. David, "Coffee Eating in Chronic Schizophrenic Patients," *American Journal of Psychiatry* 143 (1986): 940–41. **adenosine receptors:** P. B. Lucas, D. Pickar, J. Kelsoe et al., "Effects of the Acute Administration of Caffeine in

Patients With Schizophrenia," *Biological Psychiatry* 28 (1990): 35–40. **caffeine may decrease:** S. R. Hirsch, "Precipitation of Antipsychotic Drugs in Interaction With Coffee or Tea," letter, *Lancet* 2 (1979): 1130–31. **worsening of symptoms:** Lucas et al. 1990; M. O. Zaslove, R. L. Russell, and E. Ross, "Effect of Caffeine Intake on Psychotic In-Patients," *British Journal of Psychiatry* 159 (1991): 565–67. **interfere with absorption:** F. Kulhanek, O. K. Linde, and G. Meisenberg, "Precipitation of Antipsychotic Drugs in Interaction with Coffee or Tea," letter, *Lancet* 2 (1979): 1130. **Three controlled studies:** B. DeFreitas and G. Swartz, "Effects of Caffeine in Chronic Psychiatric Patients," *American Journal of Psychiatry* 136 (1979): 1337–38; A. Koczapski, J. Paredes, C. Kogan et al., "Effects of Caffeine on Behavior of Schizophrenic Inpatients," *Schizophrenia Bulletin* 15 (1989): 339–44; K. M. Mayo, W. Falkowski, and C. A. H. Jones, "Caffeine: Use and Effects in Long-Stay Psychiatric Patients," *British Journal of Psychiatry* 162 (1993): 543–45. **47 percent abused:** D. A. Regier, M. E. Farmer, D. S. Rae et al., "Comorbidity of Mental Disorders With Alcohol and Other Drug Abuse," *Journal of American Medical Association* 264 (1990): 2511–18. **has increased significantly:** B. J. Cuffel, "Prevalence Estimates of Substance Abuse in Schizophrenia and Their Correlates," *Journal of Nervous and Mental Disease* 180 (1992): 589–92. **One recent study:** L. Dixon, G. Haas, P. Weiden et al., "Acute Effects of Drug Abuse in Schizophrenic Patients: Clinical Observations and Patients' Self-Reports," *Schizophrenia Bulletin* 16 (1990): 69–79. **rate of rehospitalization:** R. E. Drake and M. A. Wallach, "Substance Abuse Among the Chronically Mentally Ill," *Hospital and Community Psychiatry* 40 (1989): 1041–46. **remissions from alcoholism:** R. E. Drake, G. J. McHugo, and D. L. Noordsy, "Treatment of Alcoholism Among Schizophrenic Outpatients: 4-Year Outcomes," *American Journal of Psychiatry* 150 (1993): 328–29. **Disulfiram can be used:** S. J. Kingsbury and C. Salzman, "Disulfiram in the Treatment of Alcoholic Patients With Schizophrenia," *Hospital and Community Psychiatry* 41 (1990): 133–34. **73 percent of them:** J. Coverdale, J. Aruffo, and H. Grunebaum, "Developing Family Planning Services for Female Chronic Mentally Ill Outpatients," *Hospital and Community Psychiatry* 43 (1992): 475–77. **62 percent were:** J. A. Kelly, D. A. Murphy, G. R. Bahr et al., "AIDS/HIV Risk Behavior Among the Chronically Mentally Ill," *American Journal of Psychiatry* 149 (1992): 886–89. **66 percent had:** K. McKinnon, F. Cournos, H. F. L. Meyer-Bahlburg et al., "Reliability of Sexual Risk Behavior Interviews With Psychiatry Patients," *American Journal of Psychiatry* 150 (1993): 972–74. **"sexual activity was":** D. Civic, G. Walsh, and D. McBride, "Staff Perspectives on Sexual

Behavior of Patients in a State Psychiatric Hospital," *Hospital and Community Psychiatry* 44 (1993): 887–90. **"vividly described":** M. B. Rosenbaum, "Neuroleptics and Sexual Functioning," *Integrative Psychiatry* 4 (1986): 105–06. **30 to 60 percent:** G. Sullivan and D. Lukoff, "Sexual Side Effects of Antipsychotic Medication: Evaluation and Interventions," *Hospital and Community Psychiatry* 41 (1990): 1238–41. **"would routinely engage":** D. D. Gold and J. D. Justino, "'Bicycle Kickstand' Phenomenon: Prolonged Erections Associated With Antipsychotic Drugs," *Southern Medical Journal* 81 (1988): 792–94. **"the rate of children":** M. V. Seeman, M. Lang, and N. Rector, "Chronic Schizophrenia: A Risk Factor for HIV?" *Canadian Journal of Psychiatry* 35 (1990): 765–68. **31 percent of the women:** J. H. Coverdale and J. A. Aruffo, "Family Planning Needs of Female Chronic Psychiatric Outpatients," *American Journal of Psychiatry* 146 (1989): 1489–91. **"chronic psychiatric outpatients":** Coverdale and Aruffo, 1989. **guidelines have been proposed:** L. B. McCullough, J. Coverdale, T. Bayer et al., "Ethically Justified Guidelines for Family Planning Interventions to Prevent Pregnancy in Female Patients With Chronic Mental Illness," *American Journal of Obstetrics and Gynecology* 167 (1992): 19–25. **Dr. Thomas F. McNeil:** T. F. McNeil, "Obstetric Complications in Schizophrenic Parents," *Schizophrenia Research* 5 (1991):

89–101. **drugs in pregnancy:** L. L. Kerns, "Treatment of Mental Disorders in Pregnancy," *Journal of Nervous and Mental Disease* 174 (1986): 652–59. **breastfeeding:** A. Buist, T. R. Norman, and L. Dennerstein, "Breastfeeding and the Use of Psychotropic Medication: A Review," *Journal of Affective Disorders* 19 (1990): 197–206. **1.6 percent in Texas:** D. Gamino, "1 in 24 New Austin State Hospital Patients Has HIV," *Austin American-Statesman,* August 22, 1991. **5.5 percent in New York:** F. Cournos, M. Empfield, E. Horwath et al., "HIV Seroprevalence Among Patients Admitted to Two Psychiatric Hospitals," *American Journal of Psychiatry* 148 (1991): 1225–30. **3.4 percent were positive:** M. Sacks, H. Dermatis, S. Looser-Ott et al., "Seroprevalence of HIV and Risk Factors for AIDS in Psychiatric Inpatients," *Hospital and Community Psychiatry* 43 (1992): 736–37. **AIDS by shaking hands:** J. F. Aruffo, J. H. Coverdale, R. C. Chacko et al., "Knowledge About AIDS Among Women Psychiatric Outpatients," *Hospital and Community Psychiatry* 41 (1990): 326–28. **A 1993 study:** F. Cournos, K. McKinnon, H. Meyer-Bahlburg et al., "HIV Risk Activity Among Persons With Severe Mental Illness: Preliminary Findings," *Hospital and Community Psychiatry* 44 (1993): 1104–06. **In another study:** J. A. Kelley et al. 1992. **AIDS education program:** R. M. Goisman, A. B. Kent, E. C. Montgomery et al., "AIDS Education for Patients With Chronic Mental Illness," *Community*

Mental Health Journal 27 (1991): 189–97. **70 percent of patients:** P. J. Weiden, L. Dixon, A. Frances et al., "Neuroleptic Noncompliance in Schizophrenia," in C. A. Tamminga and S. C. Schulz, eds., *Advances in Neuropsychiatry and Psychopharmacology. Volume 1: Schizophrenia Research* (New York: Raven Press, 1991), pp. 285–96. **$136 million per year:** P. J. Weiden and M. Olfson, "Measuring Costs of Rehospitalization in Schizophrenia," presented at the annual meeting of the American Psychiatric Association, San Francisco, Calif., May 1993. Costs averaged for first two years. **"understanding of the disease":** E. Kraepelin, *Dementia Praecox and Paraphrenia* (Huntington, N.Y.: Robert E. Krieger Publishing Co., 1971), p. 26; first published in 1919. **81 percent of individuals:** W. T. Carpenter, J. J. Bartko, C. L. Carpenter et al., "Another View of Schizophrenia Subtypes," *Archives of General Psychiatry* 33 (1976): 508–16. **two recent studies:** X. F. Amador and D. H. Strauss, "Poor Insight in Schizophrenia," *Psychiatric Quarterly,* 64 (1993): 305–19; A. David, A. Buchanan, A. Reed et al., "The Assessment of Insight in Psychosis," *British Journal of Psychiatry* 161 (1992): 599–602. **affecting the frontal lobes:** D. A. Young, R. Davila, and H. Scher, "Unawareness of Illness and Neuropsychological Performance in Chronic Schizophrenia," *Schizophrenia Research* 10 (1993): 117–24. **medications do not improve:** J. P. McEvoy, L. J.

Apperson, P. S. Appelbaum et al., "Insight in Schizophrenia: Its Relationship to Acute Psychopathology," *Journal of Nervous and Mental Disease* 177 (1989): 43–47. **twice as high:** I. F. Lin, R. Spiga, and W. Fortsch, "Insight and Adherence to Medication in Chronic Schizophrenics," *Journal of Clinical Psychiatry* 40 (1979): 430–32. **an inverse correlation:** See Amador et al. 1991 for a review of some of these. **"Unfortunately the side":** E. Leete, "The Treatment of Schizophrenia: A Patient's Perspective," *Hospital and Community Psychiatry* 38 (1987): 486–91. **"the major finding":** P. J. Weiden, J. J. Mann, G. Haas et al., "Clinical Nonrecognition of Neuroleptic-Induced Movement Disorders: A Cautionary Study," *American Journal of Psychiatry* 144 (1987): 1148–53. **"psychiatrists misjudged":** S. E. Finn, J. M. Bailey, R. T. Schultz et al., "Subjective Utility Ratings of Neuroleptics in Treating Schizophrenia," *Psychological Medicine* 20 (1990): 843–48. **"The reluctance":** T. Van Putten, "Why Do Schizophrenic Patients Refuse To Take Their Drugs?" *Archives of General Psychiatry* 31 (1974): 67–72. **"it is still":** R. Diamond, "Drugs and the Quality of Life: The Patient's Point of View," *Journal of Clinical Psychiatry* 46 (1985): 29–35. **"Many of the mistakes":** B. Blaska, "The Myriad Medication Mistakes in Psychiatry: A Consumer's View," *Hospital and Community Psychiatry* 41 (1990): 993–98. **"I did not

want": D. Minor, quoted in A. B. Hatfield and H. P. Lefley, *Surviving Mental Illness* (New York: Guilford Press, 1993), p. 134. **found that 37 percent:** C. Clary, A. Dever, and E. Schweizer, "Psychiatric Inpatients' Knowledge of Medication at Hospital Discharge," *Hospital and Community Psychiatry* 43 (1992): 140–44. **U.S. Third Circuit:** J. L. Geller, "Rx: A Tincture of Coercion in Outpatient Treatment?" *Hospital and Community Psychiatry* 42 (1991): 1068–70, citing Brown v. Bowen, 845 F 2nd 1211 (3rd Circuit, 1988). **conditional release in Oregon:** J. D. Bloom, M. H. Williams, and D. A. Bigelow, "Monitored Conditional Release of Persons Found Not Guilty by Reason of Insanity," *American Journal of Psychiatry* 148 (1991): 444–48. **conservatorship in California:** H. R. Lamb and L. E. Weinberger, "Therapeutic Use of Conservatorship in the Treatment of Gravely Disabled Psychiatric Patients," *Hospital and Community Psychiatry* 44 (1993): 147–50. **outpatient commitment:** G. A. Fernandez and S. Nygard, "Impact of Involuntary Outpatient Commitment on the Revolving-Door Syndrome in North Carolina," *Hospital and Community Psychiatry* 41 (1990): 1001–04. **riboflavin:** S. Kapur, R. Ganguli, R. Ulrich et al., "Use of Random-Sequence Riboflavin as a Marker of Medication Compliance in Chronic Schizophrenics," *Schizophrenia Research* 6 (1992): 49–53. **isonazid:** G. A. Ellard, P. J. Jenner, and P. A. Downs, "An Evaluation of the Potential Use of Isoniazid, Acetylisoniazid and Isonicotinic Acid for Monitoring the Self-Administration of Drugs," *British Journal of Clinical Pharmacology* 10 (1980): 369–81. **"will suffer if a liberty":** R. Michels, "The Right to Refuse Psychoactive Drugs," *Hastings Center Report* 3 (1973): 8–11. **"The state must":** F. Padavan, "Focus on Mental Health," *The New York Times,* December 17, 1985, p. A27. **"reported that their":** Cited in A. B. Hatfield, *Family Education in Mental Illness* (New York: Guilford Press, 1990), p. 124. **a 1990 NAMI:** D. M. Steinwachs, J. D. Kaspar, and E. A. Skinner, "Family Perspectives on Meeting the Needs for Care of Severely Mentally Ill Relatives: A National Survey" (Arlington, Va.: National Alliance for the Mentally Ill, 1990). **"arrest and conviction":** J. Rabkin, "Criminal Behavior of Discharged Mental Patients: A Critical Appraisal of the Research," *Psychological Bulletin* 86 (1979): 1–27. **15 of 20:** D. A. Martell and P. E. Dietz, "Mentally Disordered Offenders Who Push or Attempt to Push Victims onto Subway Tracks in New York City," *Archives of General Psychiatry* 49 (1992): 472–75. **"that 27 percent":** J. Monahan, "Mental Disorder and Violent Behavior," *American Psychologist* 47 (1992), 511–21. **study by Link et al.:** B. G. Link, H. Andrews, and F. T. Cullen, "The Violent and Illegal Behavior of Mental Patients Reconsidered," *American Sociological Review* 57 (1992) 275–92. **ECA study:** J. W. Swanson, C. E. Holzer, V. K. Ganju et al., "Violence and Psychiatric

Disorder in the Community:
Evidence From the Epidemiologic
Catchment Area Surveys," *Hospital
and Community Psychiatry* 41
(1990): 761–70. **"suicide is the num-
ber":** C. B. Caldwell and I. I.
Gottesman, "Schizophrenics Kill
Themselves Too: A Review of Risk
Factors for Suicide," *Schizophrenia
Bulletin* 16 (1990): 571–89. **15 to 17
percent:** F. K. Goodwin and K. R.
Jamison, *Manic-Depressive Illness*
(New York: Oxford University Press,
1990), p. 230. **within the first ten
years:** C. P. Miles, "Conditions
Predisposing to Suicide: A Review,"
*Journal of Nervous and Mental
Disease* 164 (1977): 231–46.

CHAPTER 10: QUESTIONS
ASKED BY CONSUMERS AND
FAMILIES

"Lunacy, like the rain": *The
Philosophy of Insanity* by an inmate
of the Glasgow Royal Asylum for
Lunatics at Gartnavel, 1860. Used as
an epigraph by Albert Deutsch, *The
Shame of the States* (New York:
Harcourt, Brace and Company, 1948).
identical twins: E. F. Torrey, A. E.
Bowler, E. H. Taylor et al.,
*Schizophrenia and Manic-Depressive
Disorder* (New York: Basic Books,
1994). **"The daughter":** B. Bick,
"Love and Resentment," *New York
Times Magazine,* March 25, 1990, p.
26. **"Part of the":** J. K. Wing,
*Schizophrenia and Its Management in
the Community* (pamphlet published
by National Schizophrenic
Fellowship, 1977), pp. 28–29.
"Almost all crimes": S. Brill, "A

Dishonest Defense," *Psychology
Today,* November 1981, pp. 16–19.
"the line between": C. Holden,
"Insanity Defense Reexamined,"
Science 222 (1983): 994–95. **An
excellent description:** L. Wilson,
This Stranger, My Son (New York:
Putnam, 1968). **"We had moved":**
Ibid., p. 178. **"You know, Dad":** J.
Wechsler, N. Wechsler, and H. Karpf,
In a Darkness (New York: Norton,
1972), p. 27. **"'I read a book'":**
Wilson, *This Stranger, My Son,* pp.
123–24. **"My mother died":** M. C.,
personal communication, New York.
"Badly treated families": W. S.
Appleton, "Mistreatment of Patients'
Families by Psychiatrists," *American
Journal of Psychiatry* 131 (1974):
655–57. **"Once you have":** A. C.,
personal communication, Maryland.
"One of our": H. B. M. Murphy,
"Community Management of Rural
Mental Patients," Final Report of
USPHS Grant (Rockville, MD:
National Institute of Mental Health,
1964). **"I am haunted":** E. Leete,
"The Treatment of Schizophrenia: A
Patient's Perspective," *Hospital and
Community Psychiatry* 38 (1987):
486–91. **"There came the morning":**
J. Baum, "Mental Illness: Acceptance
Is the Key," originally published in
the *Alabama Advocate* and reprinted
in the *Utah AMI Newsletter,* Oct./Dec.
1993, p. 4. **"Well, I guess":** G. L.,
personal communication, Maryland.
Several observers have noted: W.
W. Michaux et al., *The First Year
Out: Mental Patients After
Hospitalization* (Baltimore: Johns
Hopkins Press, 1969). **"Several rela-
tives mentioned":** C. Creer and J. K.

Wing, *Schizophrenia at Home* (London: Institute of Psychiatry, 1974), p. 33. **"You've got to reach":** Laffey, p. 40. **"Recognizing that a person":** H. R. Lamb and Associates, *Community Survival for Long-term Patients* (San Francisco: Jossey-Bass, 1976), p. 7. **"A neutral":** Wing, *Schizophrenia,* p. 29. **"Superficially she *was*":** O. Sacks, *The Man Who Mistook His Wife for a Hat* (New York: Summit Books, 1985), pp. 70–74. **The best study:** M. I. Herz and C. Melville, "Relapse in Schizophrenia," *American Journal of Psychiatry* 137 (1980): 801–05. **"it is extremely":** M. Herz, "Prodromal Symptoms and Prevention of Relapse in Schizophrenia," *Journal of Clinical Psychiatry* 46 (1985): 22–25. **"In the first stage":** M. Lovejoy, "Recovery From Schizophrenia: A Personal Odyssey," *Hospital and Community Psychiatry* 35 (1984): 809–12. **"a controlled environment":** E. Leete, "How I Perceive and Manage My Illness," *Hospital and Community Psychiatry* 15 (1989): 197–99. **"recognizing when":** Leete, "The Treatment . . . " **"a seat where":** Leete, "How I . . . " **"we are more":** F. J. Frese, "Twelve Aspects of Coping for Persons With Schizophrenia," *Innovations and Research* 2 (1993): 39–46. **"Don't talk":** F. Frese, "Pointers for Person-Recovering From Mental Illness," *Newsletter of the Georgia Alliance of the Mentally Ill,* March 1992, p. 4. **"extensive help":** P. R. Breggin, "The Killing of Mental Patients," *Madness Network News Reader* (San Francisco: Glide Publications, 1974),

149–54. **"a complaint":** B. Dow, "Psychiatrist's Comments Draw Fire, But Deemed 'Free Speech,'" *American Medical News,* October 16, 1987. **"peer counselors":** C. W. McGill and C. J. Patterson, "Former Patients as Peer Counselors on Locked Psychiatric Inpatient Units," *Hospital and Community Psychiatry* 41 (1990): 1017–20. **case management aides:** P. S. Sherman and R. Porter, "Mental Health Consumers as Case Management Aides," *Hospital and Community Psychiatry* 42 (1991): 494–98. **"Look at the person":** Anonymous, personal communication, Davis, California. **"My son seemed":** A. H., personal communication, Washington, D.C. **"Patients tended to":** Wing, *Schizophrenia,* p. 27. **"I would have been":** H. R. Rollin, ed., *Coping with Schizophrenia* (London: Burnett, 1980), p. 158. **"A more realistic":** Creer and Wing, p. 71. **"One patient returned home":** Ibid., p. 22. **"One young man":** Ibid., p. 11. **"One lady said":** Ibid., p. 8. **"Leave me alone":** B. B., personal communication, New York. **"When our son was":** L. Y., personal communication, San Jose, California. **"The most remarkable lesson":** L. M., personal communication, Florida. **"I found structure":** A. H., personal communication, Washington, D.C. **"My wife will cook":** Creer and Wing, p. 30. **"The second practical":** Anonymous, personal communication, California. **"It's so annoying":** Creer and Wing, p. 10. **Respite care:** R. Geiser, L. Hoche, and J. King, "Respite Care for Mentally Ill Patients and Their

Families," *Hospital and Community Psychiatry* 39 (1988): 291–97; see also the "Respite Program Technical Assistance Guide," South Carolina AMI, Columbia, S. C. **"by teaching the patients":** I. R. H. Falloon, J. L. Boyd, C. M. McGill, et al., "Family Management in the Prevention of Exacerbations of Schizophrenia," *New England Journal of Medicine* 24 (1982): 1437–40. **"provides evidence that":** M. J. Goldstein and J. A. Doane, "Family Factors in the Onset, Course and Treatment of Schizophrenic Spectrum Disorders," *Journal of Nervous and Mental Disease* 170 (1982): 692–700. **"the parents":** D. Goleman, "Schizophrenia: Early Signs Found," *The New York Times,* December 11, 1984. **"convinced that":** R. Lanquetot, "First Person Account: On Being Daughter and Mother," *Schizophrenia Bulletin* 14 (1988): 337–41. **"and sit us":** M. Fichtner, "Children of Madness," *Miami Herald,* September 15, 1991, pp. J1–4. **Meg Livergood:** M. Blais, "Trish," *Miami Herald Sunday Magazine,* May 24, 11987, pp. 7–16. **"suddenly both":** W. Kelley, "Unmet Needs," *Journal of the California AMI* 3 (1992): 28–30. **"envious watching":** J. Mozham, "Daddy and Me: Growing Up With a Schizophrenic," *Reflections of AMI of Michigan,* May/June 1991, pp. 18–19. **"That day":** A. S. Brodoff, "First Person Account: Schizophrenia Through a Sister's Eyes—The Burden of Invisible Baggage," *Schizophrenia Bulletin* 14 (1988): 113–16. **"It's funny":** P. Aronowitz, "A Brother's Dreams," *New York Times Magazine,* January 24, 1988, p. 355. **"superkids":** C. Kauffman, H. Grunebaum, B. Cohler et al., "Superkids: Competent Children of Psychotic Mothers," *American Journal of Psychiatry* 136 (1979): 1398–1402. **"Growing up":** Lanquetot. **Moorman:** M. Moorman, *My Sister's Keeper* (New York: Norton, 1992). **"She once knew":** Mozham. **"was aware that":** Fichtner. **Julie Johnson:** J. Johnson, *Hidden Victims* (New York: Doubleday, 1988). **A 1989 study:** M. J. Edlund, C. Conrad, and P. Morris, "Accidents Among Schizophrenic Outpatients," *Comprehensive Psychiatry* 30 (1989): 522–26. **Two earlier studies:** L. E. Hollister, "Automobile Driving by Psychiatric Patients," letter, *American Journal of Psychiatry* 149 (1992): 274. See also D. O'Neill, "Driving and Psychiatric Illness," letter, *American Journal of Psychiatry* 150 (1993): 351. **In one study:** A. F. Lehman and L. S. Linn, "Crimes Against Discharged Mental Patients in Board-and-Care Homes," *American Journal of Psychiatry* 141 (1984): 271–73. **"the clergy":** D. B. Larson, A. A. Hohmann, L. G. Kessler et al., "The Couch and the Cloth: The Need for Linkage," *Hospital and Community Psychiatry* 39 (1988): 1064–69. **religious cults:** See M. Galanter, "Psychological Induction into the Large Group: Findings from a Modern Religious Sect," *American Journal of Psychiatry* 137 (1980): 1574–79; See also M. Galanter et al., "The 'Moonies': A Psychological Study of Conversion and Membership in a Contemporary Religious Sect," *American Journal of Psychiatry* 136 (1979): 165–70. For a particularly cogent analysis, see also S. V. Levine, "Role of Psychiatry in the Phenomenon of Cults," *Canadian Journal of Psychiatry* 24 (1979): 593–603; **there may be some advantages:** See S. V. Levine, "Role of Psychiatry." **"I was never":** N. Dearth, B. J. Labenski, M. E. Mott, et al., *Families Helping Families* (New York: W. W. Norton, 1986), p. 61. **"that you respond":** Frese, 1993. **lifetime risk figures:** I. I. Gottesman, "Schizophrenia and Genetic Risks" (Arlington, Va.: NAMI, 1984). See also I. I. Gottesman, *Schizophrenia Genesis: The Origins of Madness* (New York: W. H. Freeman, 1991). **28 and 29 percent:** E. Kringlen, "Adult Offspring of Two Psychotic Parents, With Special Reference to Schizophrenia," in L. C. Wynne, R. L. Cromwell, and S. Matthysse, *The Nature of Schizophrenia* (New York: John Wiley, 1978), pp. 9–24; K. Modrzewska, "The Offspring of Schizophrenic Parents in a Swedish Isolate," *Clinical Genetics* 17 (1980): 191–201. **only 28 percent:** E. F. Torrey, "Are We Overestimating the Genetic Contribution to Schizophrenia?" *Schizophrenia Bulletin* 18 (1992): 159–70.

Quoted in J. A. Talbott, ed., *The Chronic Mental Patient* (Washington: American Psychiatric Association, 1978), p. xiii. **research achievement awards:** In 1977 the National Mental Health Association (NMHA) McAlpin Research Achievement Award was given to Drs. Lyman Wynne and Margaret Singer for their work on communication among family members which may contribute to the development of schizophrenia; see *Research on Mental Health: Progress and Promise* (NMHA, Washington, D.C., 1978). **college freshmen:** O. Wahl, "Public vs. Professional Conceptions of Schizophrenia," *Journal of Community Psychology* 15 (1987): 285–91. **One poll:** C. Holden, "Giving Mental Illness Its Research Due," *Science* 232 (1986): 1084–86. **in one study:** G. Gerbner et al., "Health and Medicine on Television," *New England Journal of Medicine* 305 (1981): 901–4. **"are not falling":** M. Starin, "What Mental Illness Doesn't Destroy, the System Does," *Poughkeepsie Journal,* January 18, 1984, p. 5. **"a minority within minorities":** *Report of the President's Commission on Mental Health,* vol. 2 (Washington, D.C.: U.S. Government Printing Office, 1978), p. 362.

CHAPTER 11: HOW TO BE AN ADVOCATE

They say, "Nothing: F. Tiffany, *Life of Dorothea Lynds Dix* (Ann Arbor: Plutarch Press, 1971), p. 134. **"although audiences tended":**

INDEX

Abnormal Involuntary Movement Scale
  (AIMS), 204
abortion, 260
abstract thing, 45–46, 149, 150
acceptance of schizophrenia, 285–86
accidents, 134, 138
acetylcholine, 206
admissions to hospitals, 5, 115
  deinstitutionalization and legal
      aspects of, 24–26
  jail admissions and, 3–4
  remissions and, 130
adolescence, 299–300
adoption, 260
Adoption Assistance and Foster Care
  Act, 239
advocacy, 307, 319–31
  decreasing stigma of schizophrenia
      with, 322–25
  organizing for, 330–31
  principles of, 319–20
  research and, 325–26
affect, changes in, 30, 65–70
African Americans, schizophrenia
      among, 7–8
aftercare, 3–4
age: brain damage and, 153–55
  of onset of schizophrenia, 94, 96, 98
  as outcome predictor, 128
AIDS, 117, 259, 261–62
akathisia, 200–201, 264
akinesia, 200, 264
Akineton (biperiden), 200, 212
Alaska Youth Initiative, 240
alcohol: abuse of, 154–57, 270–71
  drug interactions with, 210
Alcoholics Anonymous (AA), 256
alcoholism, 124, 255–56

allergies, food, 162
Alliance for the Mentally Ill (AMI), 176,
  302, 326
  state contacts for, 357–61. See also
    National Alliance for the
    Mentally Ill (NAMI)
alprazolam, 215
alterations of senses, 30, 31–39
amantadine (Symmetrel), 212
ambivalence, 50
ambulatory schizophrenia, 91
American Civil Liberties Union, 26, 268
American Indians, schizophrenia among,
  7
American Psychiatric Association
  (APA), 98, 106, 176, 187, 203,
  320–21
American Schizophrenia Association,
  162
Americans with Disabilities Act, 313
amisulpriride, 209
Amish people, 7
amperozide, 209
amphetamines, 257
amygdala, 143, 151
Andreasen, Nancy C., 332
Andrews, G., langer, 285, 289, 305
Antabuse (disulfiram), 256
anticholinergics, 211, 212
antidepressants, 215, 271
antiparkinson drugs, 264
antipsychiatry groups, 292–93
antipsychotic drug treatment, 190–211
  addiction to, 197
  brain changes from, 145, 148
  childhood schizophrenia and, 98
  cognitive function impairment with,
      149–50

discovery of, 190
experimental, 208–10
families of, 190, 191
forms of administration of, 190–91
efficacy of, 192–93
emergency room administration of,
    188–89
generic forms of, 217
individual variations in doses of,
    194–96
interactions between other drugs and,
    210–11
intermittent "no dose" strategy for,
    196
length of time used, 196–97
mechanism of action of, 193
medical problems and, 238
movement changes with, 70, 71
nicotine and, 252
noncompliance and, 262–69
outcome and early treatment with,
    129–30, 197–98
possible courses of schizophrenia
    and, 131, 132, 133
potency and dose of, 191–92
pregnancy and, 213, 260–61
rehabilitation and ongoing need for,
    221
response to, 130, 194
sex differences in reactions to, 97
side effects of, 198–205, 258, 264,
    263–64
supportive psychotherapy with,
    224–25
symptom reduction with, 192, 193
symptoms of schizophrenia caused
    by, 136
types of, 191–92
apartments, 229, 231
apathy, 70, 86, 90, 193
aphasia, receptive, 41
apomorphine, 216
Appleton, William S., 282
*Approved Drugs Products With
    Therapeutic Equivalence
    Evaluations*, 217
Arieti, Silvano, 62
Armat, Virginia C., 333
Aronowitz, Paul, 306
art, reflections of schizophrenia in, 77–81
Artane (trihexyphenidyl), 200, 212
assaultive behavior, 269–70
asylum, concept of, 249–50
Ativan (lorazepam), 215
attention difficulties, 34, 36, 149

auditory stimuli: alterations of percep-
    tions of, 31, 33, 34
    hallucinations with, 58–61, 85, 99,
        113, 292
    inability to interpret and respond to,
        40–44
autism, 120–21, 238
automobiles: accidents and, 138
    driving and, 308
autonomy, 299–300, 301
awareness, heightening of, 37–38

baclofen, 216
Baldessarini, Ross J., 198
Balzac, Honoré de, 71, 82
Bark, Nigel, 19
Barnes, Mary, 34, 336
Bateson, Gregory, 169–70, 304, 336
Baum, Judith, 285
Beers, Clifford, 321
behavior changes, 30, 71–82
    limits regarding, 299
    onset of schizophrenia and, 96
    responsibility for, 277–80
belief systems, 309–11
Benadryl (diphenhydramine), 200
Benedict, Ruth, 170
Bennett, Douglas, 232
benzodiazepines, 190, 191, 207, 211,
    214–15
benztropine (Cogentin), 200, 212
Bergman, Ingmar, 48
Berke, Joseph, 172, 336
beta blockers, 216
Bethlem Hospital, London, 18
Bible, 18
Bick, Kathy, 81
Bigelow, Douglas A., 247
biperiden (Akineton), 200, 212
bipolar disorder, 106, 238. *See also*
        manic-depressive psychosis
Bipolar Disorder Treatment Outcome
        Network, 173
Birley, J. L. T., 164
birth: complications during, 154, 159
    seasonality of, 154–55, 159
blame, feelings of, 280–82, 298
Blaska, Betty, 264
Bleuler, Eugen, 43, 50, 85, 88, 123,
    165
Bleuler, Manfred, 135
blocking of thoughts, 49–50
blood tests, 101
blunting: of emotions, 90
    of sensations, 31, 38–39

board-and-care homes, 11, 229, 308
boarding houses, 229, 249
body: movement changes and, 71
    sense of self and, 64–65, 95
Bogerts, Bernhardt, 145
borderline personality disorder, 109
borderline schizophrenia, 91
Bosch, Hieronymus, 81
Boston University Center for Psychiatric
    Rehabilitation, 234, 351
Bouricius, Jean, 69
brain changes: alterations of the senses
    and, 39
    electrical abnormalities in, 147
    hallucinations and, 59, 61
    head trauma and, 119–20
    inability to interpret and respond to
        stimuli and, 40, 44
    manic-depressive psychosis and, 107
    microscopic abnormalities in,
        145–46, 155
    neurochemical abnormalities in, 146
    neurological abnormalities in, 148
    neuropsychological abnormalities in,
        149–50
    normal brain compared with, 140–42
    schizophrenia and, 75–76
    viruses and, 158–59
brain disease: children and, 238
    delusions and hallucinations seen in,
        51, 61–62
    schizophrenia as, 142–55, 292–93
brain scans, 101–2, 103, 143–44, 146–47
brain tumors, 116, 143
Breggin, Peter R., 293, 336–37
Bridge, The, 237, 245
brief psychiatric hospitalizations, 240
brief psychotic disorder, 110
Brigham, Amariah, 84
Broadway Industries, 233
Brodoff, Ami, 306
bromocriptine (Parlodel), 200, 216
Brown, G. W., 164
Burti, Lorenzo, 339–40
butyrophenones, 190, 191

Cade, John, 213
caffeine, 251, 253–54
calcium channel blockers, 216
Canada, 5, 12, 240, 241
Canadian Schizophrenia Society, 301
carbamazepine (Tegretol), 215–16
care for schizophrenia: continuity of,
    222–25, 240–41, 245
    lack of data on, 9

number of people not receiving,
    4–5
outpatient services for, 221–22, 223,
    249
overview of arrangements in, 9–12
world-wide, 5
caregivers: balancing needs of family
    members by, 286
    continuity of care and, 222–23
    death of, 315–17
    respite care and, 301–2, 328
    unwanted roles assumed in, 307
Carroll, Lewis, 170
case managers, 224
Casey, Daniel, 204
catatonia, 71, 88, 205
catatonic behavior, 71, 86, 129
causes of schizophrenia, 8, 35, 140–73
    blame among family members for,
        280–82
    brain damage and, 142–55
    deinstitutionalization and understand-
        ing of, 24
    family interactions and, 169–70, 282,
        303–4
    major theories of, 155–61
    minor theories of, 161–65
    obsolete theories of, 165–72
Center for Ethics, Medicine and Public
    Issues, 260
Center for Psychiatric Rehabilitation,
    234, 351
cerebral blood flow (CBF) studies,
    146–47
cerebral syphilis, 116
cerebrospinal fluid (CSF) tests, 102–3
Chapman, James, 50, 68, 74
Chekhov, Anton, 52–53
chemical tests, 101
childbirth, psychosis following, 118–19,
    162
childhood: autism in, 120–21
    brain damage in, 153–55
    flooding of memories from, 35
    schizophrenia in, 97–99, 121, 238–40
children:
    independence and autonomy of,
        299–300, 301
    of schizophrenic parents, 304–7, 314,
        315
    services for, 238–40, 247
chlorpromazine (Largactil, Thorazine),
    23, 190, 191, 192, 195, 202
chlorprothixene (Taractan), 191
cholecystokinin, 146, 216

chronic defect state, 135–36
Church of Scientology, 199, 203, 218, 293, 310
cigarette smoking, 251–54
cimetidine (Tagamet), 212
Ciompi, Luc, 135
civil rights, 5, 185–86, 232, 268–69
clergy, 310, 324, 349
clocapromine, 209
clonazepam (Klonopin), 215
clonidine, 201, 216
clozapine (Clozaril), 133, 191, 193, 202, 204, 205–7, 211, 216–17
clubhouses, 236–37, 242, 245, 327, 350, 353–54
CMHCs. See Community Mental Health Centers (CMHCs)
cocaine, 255
Cogentin (benztropine), 200, 212
cognitive function, 106, 149–50
colors, alterations of, 32
command hallucinations, 278
Commission on Mental Health, 168, 331
commitment process, 183–88
    confidentiality and, 312
    emergency and, 183–84
    family and, 187–88
    laws covering, 183–84, 328
    local community standards in, 186–87
    long-term consequences of, 188
    outpatient commitment and, 267–69, 329
    standard of proof in, 185–86
communication, 294–96, 302–4, 312–13
communities, resistance to housing in, 230–31
Community Mental Health Centers (CMHCs), 237, 242, 265, 327
    consumer provider programs of, 293
    deinstitutionalization and, 23, 24
    founding of, 23
    funding of, 4
    rehabilitation and ongoing need for medication and, 221, 222
Compazine (prochlorperazine), 191
Compeer programs, 236, 247, 350
compulsive behavior, 73–74, 129
computerized tomography (CT), 102, 103, 129, 143
concentration difficulties, 34, 36
concreteness, 45–47
conditional release, 267
confidentiality, 311–12
confusion, 129, 290

congregate care homes, 229
Congress, 9, 21, 22, 173, 325, 327
consent: commitment process and, 185–86
    sexual behavior and, 259
conservatorship, 267, 316
consumer groups, 292–93
consumer provider programs, 293, 352–53
continuity of care, 222–25, 240–41, 245
continuous treatment teams, 222, 223, 350, 354–56
contraception, 259–60
control: of one's behavior, 277–80
    over minds, 56–57, 85
Cooper, David, 337
coping strategies, 291–92
costs, 15–19
    calculation of, 15
    clubhouses and, 237
    comparison with other diseases for, 17
    economic benefits of research and, 17–19
    medications and, 216–18
    time frame for schizophrenia and, 16–17
    for treatment, 15–16
counseling: family and, 304
    genetic factors and, 313–15
    job skills training and, 234
    peers and, 293
    supportive therapy with, 223–25
county homes, 11
course of schizophrenia:
    rule of thirds in, 130–31
    ten-year period, 131–34
    thirty-year period, 134–37
creativity, 122–24
Creer, Clare, 287, 296
criminal behavior, 278–79, 308–9
crisis houses, 189, 228
Crow, Timothy, 90
cults, 310–11
cultural factors:
    causes of schizophrenia related to, 170–71
    delusions and, 57
    hallucinations and, 62
    psychosis and, 121–22
cyclothymic disorder, 108

daily living:
    quality of life measures in, 247–48
    structure in, 232, 298–99

surviving schizophrenia and, 291–93
Dartmouth Medical School, 241, 242
Davis, John, 192
day programs, 239, 241
death of schizophrenics, 134, 137–39
de Clerembault syndrome, 56
deinstitutionalization, 5, 21–27
    magnitude of, 23
    public awareness of hospital condi-
        tions and, 22–23
    reasons for disastrous consequences
        of, 23–25
delusions, 34, 30, 51–58
    antipsychotic drugs and, 193
    brief psychotic disorder with, 110
    communications and, 295
    cultural background and evaluation
        of, 57
    diagnosis of schizophrenia and, 86, 99
    drug psychosis with, 111
    examples of, 51–54
    lack of consistency in, 58
    noncompliance and, 265
    onset of schizophrenia and, 95, 96
    as "positive" symptom, 90, 135
    range of, 51
    reactions to, 295–96
    religious nature of, 310, 311
    sense of self and, 65
    types of, 55–57
Dencker, Sven, 195
Department of Health and Human
    Services, 227
Department of Housing and Urban
    Development, 228
Department of Justice, 330
Depo-Provera (medroxyprogesterone
    acetate), 259
depression, 66, 238, 289
    antidepressants for, 215
    borderline personality disorder with,
        109
    family history of, as outcome predic-
        tor, 127–28
    family members and, 306
    manic-depressive psychosis and,
        107
    prevalence of schizophrenia and, 6
    psychosis following childbirth and,
        118
    suicide and, 271–72
dermatoglyphics, 154
Deutsch, Albert, 23, 332–33
developmental defect theory, 160–61
Deveson, Anne, 333

dexamethasone suppression test (DST),
    103
diabetes, 138, 163, 175
diagnosis, 84–104
    auditory hallucinations and, 87–88
    brief psychotic disorder and, 110
    childhood schizophrenia and, 97–99,
        238
    definition of schizophrenia and,
        85–88
    Diagnostic and Statistical Manual of
        Mental Disorders criteria in, 86,
        92, 107
    differentiating other disorders from,
        90–94
    gender differences and, 96–97
    ideal workup in, 99–104
    late-onset schizophrenia and, 99
    medical problems and, 238
    onset and, 94–96
    schizophrenia subtypes and, 88–90
    symptoms of schizophrenia and,
        84–85, 94–96
Diagnostic and Statistical Manual of
    Mental Disorders: third revised
    edition (DSM-III-R), 86, 90, 106
    fourth edition (DSM-IV), 86, 87, 88,
        89, 92, 107
Diamond, Ronald, 264
diazepam (Valium), 200, 201, 207, 215
dibenzoxazepines, 190, 191
Dickens, Charles, 175
diet, 218
dihydroindolones, 190, 191
diphenhydramine (Benadryl), 200
disconnectedness, 44–45
dissociative disorder, 105
distribution of individuals with schizo-
    phrenia, 8–12
disulfiram (Antabuse), 256
Divine Light Mission, 310
Dix, Dorothy, 319
doctors. See physicians
dogs, 237
Domenici, Pete and Nancy, 173
dopamine, 146, 157–58, 159, 193, 206,
    209, 253
drug use:
    history taking on, 100
    problems related to, 254–57
    psychoses from, 111–15
    street drugs and, 111–12, 254–57
    violence and, 256, 257, 270–71
Dryden, John, 122
Duchamps, Marcel, 79, 81

Du Pont Corporation, 323
dystonic reaction, 199–200

Earle, Pliny, 21
eating behavior, 299
echolalia, 74
economic factors: benefits of research
    and, 17–19
    cost of schizophrenia and, 15–17
Eden Express, 234
Education Council for Foreign Medical
    Graduates (ECFMG), 178
education programs: for family mem-
    bers, 283–84, 301, 307
    listing of courses for, 351–52
electroconvulsive therapy (ECT), 108,
    167, 218
electroencephalography (EEG), 103,
    147, 152, 194, 216
Elpers, J. R., 222
embarrassment, 305
emergency commitment, 183–85
emergency room, drug administration in,
    188–89
emotions, 296–97
    blunting of, 90
    changes in, 30, 65–70
    diagnosis of schizophrenia and,
        99–100
    expressed, 302–4
    flattening of, 68–70, 86
    inappropriate, 67–68
    lack of, 69
    portrayal of, in art, 81
employment, 231–35
    availability of jobs in, 232–33, 235
    examples of good services in, 245–46
    job skills training and, 234
    sheltered workshops and, 233, 327
    stigma of schizophrenia and, 231
    supported, 234
    transitional, 233–34
endocrine dysfunction, 162–63
enhancement of sensations, 31–38
enchephalitis, 116, 152
Epidemiologic Catchment Area (ECA)
    survey, National Institute of
    Mental Health (NIMH), 4–5, 6, 7,
    9, 14, 270
epilepsy, temporal lobe, 115, 116
epinephrine, 211
erotomania, 56
estazolam, 215
estrogens, 97
evoked potential (EP) studies, 147, 152

examinations: commitment process and,
    184
    diagnostic workup with, 100–103
expectations of family members, 286–88,
    297
experimental drugs, 208–10
expressed emotion, 302–4
extended release, 267
extrapyramidal syndromes, 264
eye abnormalities, 149

Fairweather Lodges, 230, 245–46, 350
families: adult schizophrenics living
    with, 11, 231
    attitudes and behavior toward schizo-
        phrenia in, 280–88, 293–94
    balancing needs of members of, 286
    causes of schizophrenia related to
        interaction in, 169–70, 282,
        303–4
    commitment process and, 184–85,
        187–88
    communications within, 294–96,
        302–4, 313
    confidentiality and, 311–12
    death of parents and, 315–17
    delusional beliefs and, 295–96
    drug abuse and, 112, 256, 257
    eating behavior in, 299
    finding a good physician and, 176
    genetic counseling and, 313–15
    genetic theory of schizophrenia and,
        156–57
    independence and autonomy within,
        299–300, 301
    noncompliance and, 265
    noneconomic costs of schizophrenia
        to, 18
    onset of schizophrenia and, 94–95
    personality disorders among, 93
    personality traits of schizophrenics
        and, 275–77
    relapses and, 288, 302
    respite care and, 301–2, 328
    SAFE attitude in, 284–88
    siblings in, 304–7
    suicide risk and, 272–73
    support (income and housing)
        supplied by, 11, 225, 231,
        298–99
    surviving schizophrenia in, 293–302
    unwanted roles assumed in, 307
    violent behavior and, 2–3, 269–70.
    See also parents
family care homes, 11

family history, as outcome predictor, 127–28
family interaction theory of schizophrenia, 169–70, 282
family physicians, 240
family therapy, 304
Farr, William, 126
fear, 34, 66, 67, 290, 295, 306
federal programs: childhood schizophrenia and, 239
deinstitutionalization and, 24, 25
income support from, 225–28
fiction: delusional thinking examples from, 52–53
portrayal of schizophrenia in, 18–19, 82
fingerprint patterns, 154, 159
flattening of emotions, 68–70, 86
flooding of stimuli, 33–35
fluoxetine (Prozac), 211, 215
fluphenazine (Prolixin, Permitil), 191, 192, 195, 211, 216, 217, 266, 268, 311
folic acid, 218
food allergies, 162
Food and Drug Administration (FDA), 217, 259
food stamps, 228, 229
foster homes, 11, 229, 239
Fountain House, 233–34, 236, 350, 353
Frese, Frederick, 292, 313
Freud, Sigmund, 123, 166, 167–68
friendship, 235–37
suicide risk and, 272–73
supportive psychotherapy and, 223
Friendship Exchange, 236
frontal lobe, 119, 140–41, 147
Frost, Robert, 122
Frumkin, Sylvia, 15, 222
functional magnetic resonance imaging (FMR), 147
funding: advocacy for, 326
for childhood schizophrenia, 239
of Community Mental Health Centers (CMHCs), 4
economic benefits of research and levels of, 17–19
sources of, 172–73

gag reflex, 148
gamma-aminobutyric acid (GABA), 158, 253
gender differences in schizophrenia, 96–97, 127
generic drugs, 217

genetic factors, 20
antipsychotic drugs and, 194
causes of schizophrenia and, 109, 149, 156–57
childhood schizophrenia and, 98
counseling for, 313–15
manic-depressive psychosis and, 107, 109
paranoid schizophrenia and, 89
predisposition to schizophrenia related to, 157, 255
gestures, repetition of, 73–74
glutamate, 146, 253
gluten-free diet, 218
Goffman, Erving, 337, 338
Goisman, Robert M., 262
Goldstein, G., 1
Goldstein, Michael J., 303–4
Goodwill Industries, 233
Gordon, Kathleen, 305, 307
Gorman, Mike, 21
Gottesman, Irving I., 314, 333
government programs. See federal programs
state programs
grandiose delusions, 55–56, 265
grasp reflex, 148
Green, Hannah, 30, 337–38
Griesinger, Wilhelm, 142
griseofulvin, 211
Grob, Gerald, 21
group homes, 229, 230–31, 239, 309, 326
groups: family support, 301
self-help, 236, 292
substance abuse treatment with, 254–55
guanadrel, 211
guanethidine, 211
guardianship, 267, 316
guilt, feelings of, 66–67, 280–81, 282–83, 306

Hadley, S. W., 168
Haldol (haloperidol), 191, 192, 195, 211, 216, 266, 268, 311
Haley, Jay, 169
halfway houses, 11, 228, 326–27
Hall, W., 1
Halliday, Andrew, 20
hallucinations, 29–30, 50–51, 58–63, 278, 323
antipsychotic drugs and, 193
auditory, 58–61, 87–88, 113, 292
brief psychotic disorder with, 110

hallucinations, *cont.*
　diagnosis of schizophrenia and, 85,
　　86, 87–88, 99
　drug psychosis with, 111, 113
　onset of schizophrenia and, 95, 99
　as "positive" symptom, 90, 135
　range of, 51
　sense of self and, 65
　voices heard in, 59–60, 289, 292
haloperidol (Haldol), 191, 192, 195, 211,
　216, 266, 268, 311
Halpern, J., 220
Halstead-Reitan battery, 149
Harding, Courtenay, 135
Hare, Edward, 20
hashish, 111
Haslam, John, 19–20
Hatfield, Agnes B., 333
Hawkes, John, 20
Hawthorn effect, 303
head trauma, 119–20
hearing: alterations of perception in, 31,
　　33, 34
　hallucinations with, 58–61
　inability to interpret and respond in,
　　40–44
hearings, in commitment process, 185
Heath, Robert, 152
hebephrenia, 88
Henry, Jule, 171
Hershey, Lewis B., 21
Herz, Marvin, 288–89
Hinckley, John, 57, 76
hippocampus, 143, 151
Hispanic persons, schizophrenia among,
　　7
histamine, 206
history of schizophrenia, 18–21
history taking, 100
HIV, 117, 261–62
hobbies, 292
Hoffer, Abram, 162
Homebuilders program, 239
homeless persons, 1–2, 3, 5, 10, 139, 309
home visitations, 189
homosexual behavior, 168, 259
homovanillic acid (HVA), 157
hospitalization, 180–88
　benefits of, 181
　commitment process for, 183–88
　cost for treatment in, 15–16
　deinstitutionalization movement and,
　　5, 22–27
　historical overview of treatment in,
　　20–21

　length of, 183
　for manic-depressive psychosis, 108
　partial, 189–90
　prediction of outcome for, 130
　short-term, 189
hospitals (general): number of schizo-
　　phrenics in, 9
　psychiatric wards in, 9, 181
　selecting, 181–82
　types of, 181. *See also* psychiatric
　　hospitals
　state psychiatric hospitals
housing and living arrangements, 225–31
　advocacy for, 326
　community resistance to, 230–31
　examples of good services in,
　　246–47
　federal programs providing, 225–28
　independent living arrangements and,
　　11, 231
　intermittent supervision in, 229–31
　lack of, 3
　living with families, 11, 231, 298–99
　need for own room in, 298–99
　nonprofessional supervision in,
　　228–29
　overview of, 9–12
　pets and, 237
　professional supervision in, 228
Hubbard, L. Ron, 199
Huber, Gerd, 135
human immunodeficiency virus (HIV),
　　117, 261–62
humor, 284
Huntington's disease, 117
Hutterites, 7, 13
Hyland, Betty, 335
hypomania, 108
hysteria, 30
hysterical psychosis, 121–22

illusions, 58
immune defects, 161
impairment of logic, 47
inappropriate emotions, 67–68
inappropriate behaviors, 74–75
income: employment and, 231–35
　federal programs providing, 225–28
　money management and, 300–301
independence, and families, 299–300,
　　301
independent living arrangements, 11, 231
infantile autism, 120–21
infectious disease theories of schizophre-
　　nia, 158–59

influenza virus, 159
insanity defense, 278–79
insertion of thoughts, 35–36, 85
insight, 76, 263, 266
Institutes for Mental Disorders (IMDs), 189
institutions: number of schizophrenics in, 9–10. *See also* hospitals; supervised living
insulin, 163, 211
insurance, 224, 237–38, 308, 328
intelligence quotient (IQ), 106
interpretation of stimuli, difficulties with, 30, 40–45
involuntary hospitalization, 183–88
    emergency and, 183–85
    extended or conditional release from, 267
    family and, 187–88
    laws covering, 183–84, 328
    local community standards in, 186–87
    long-term consequences of, 188
    standard of proof in, 185–86
Ireland, 12, 13
Isaac, Rael Jean, 333
isoniazid, 211

Jackson, Don, 169
jails, 2, 3–4, 10
Jamieson, R., 20
Jarvis, Edward, 21
jealousy, 305
Jefferson, Lara, 140
job skills training, 234
Johns Hopkins University, 173
Johnson, Dale L., 334
Joint Commission on Accreditation of Healthcare Organizations (JCAHO), 182, 190, 330, 350
Joint Commission on Health Care Organizations, 254
journals, 348–49
Joyce, James, 123–24
Jung, Carl, 123
juvenile onset diabetes, 138

Kafka, Franz, 65
Kaleidoscope, 239
Kamin, Leon, 171
Kane, John, 188
Kelley, Wendy, 305
Kemadrin (procyclidine), 200, 212
Kennedy, John F., 23, 26
Kesey, Ken, 24, 338

Kety, Seymour, 88
Kingsley Hall, 172
Klein, Donald, 167
Klerman, Gerald, 169
Klonopin (clonazepam), 215
Kraepelin, Emil, 88, 106, 109, 123, 134, 263

laboratory examinations, 101
Laing, R. D., 172, 293, 337
Lamb, Richard, 287, 321
Lanquetot, Roxanne, 305, 306
Largactil (chlorpromazine), 23, 190, 191, 192, 195, 202
Lasch, Christopher, 170–71
latent schizophrenia, 92
late-onset schizophrenia, 99
laughter, with inappropriate behavior, 68
laws and legislation: commitment process and, 183–86, 328
    confidentiality and, 311–12
    conservatorship and guardianship and, 267, 316
    deinstitutionalization and, 24–26
    insanity defense and, 278–79
    noncompliance and, 266–68
lawyers, 5, 260, 324, 329
    commitment process and, 185 86
    deinstitutionalization and, 24–26
    employment of schizophrenics and, 232–33
    psychiatrists and, 268–69
L-dopa, 157
Leete, Esso, 36–37, 264, 285, 291, 292
Lefley, Harriet P., 333, 334
Lehman, Anthony F., 247
leisure activities, 297–98
levodopa, 211
Lewontin, R.C., 171
Liberman, Robert P., 225
Lidz, Theodore, 169, 338
Lieberman, Jeffrey, 130, 196, 198
Life (magazine), 22
limbic system, 39, 40
    in normal brain, 141
    schizophrenia and changes in, 143, 145, 151–53
literature: delusional thinking examples from, 52–53
    portrayal of schizophrenia in, 18–19, 82
lithium, 70, 108, 211, 213–14, 216, 217, 268
Livergood, Meg, 305

living arrangements. *See* housing and living arrangements
local laws, and commitment process, 186–87, 328
logic, impairment of, 47
loose associations, 45, 85, 90
lorazepam (Ativan), 215
loxapine (Loxitane), 191, 192, 195, 197, 202, 216
LSD, 111, 112
lumbar punctures, 102–3
lung cancer, 138, 253

MacDonald, Norma, 39
MacGregor, John M., 123
MacLean, Paul, 151
M'Nauhten case, 278
McNeil, Thomas F., 260
magnetic resonance imaging (MRI):
        brain damage on, 143, 147
        diagnostic workup with, 98, 99, 101–2
        as outcome predictor, 129
major tranquilizers, 190. *See also* antipsychotic drug treatment
mania, 107
manic-depressive psychosis, 6, 106–9, 124, 350
        brain damage in, 143
        causes of, 156, 160
        changes in emotions in, 67
        clinical characteristics of, 107
        differential diagnosis of, 86, 91, 108, 109
        family history, as outcome predictor, 127–28
        psychosis following childbirth and, 118
        schizophrenia compared with, 67
        treatment of, 108–9, 215
Manschreck, T. C., 169
marijuana, 111, 255, 257
Marsh, Diane T., 333–34
Martin, John Bartlow, 48
Massachusetts Commission on Lunacy, 16–17
masturbation, 166
May, Philip R. A., 167
Mead, Margaret, 170
Medicaid, 26, 228, 238, 239, 327
medical care, 237–38
        blunting of pain and, 38
        impediments to obtaining, 237–38
medical insurance, 237–38
Medical Letter, The, 113

Medicare, 26, 238, 327
medication, 211–16
        cost of, 216–18
        interactions among, 210–11
        noncompliance and, 262–69
        rehabilitation and ongoing need for, 221
        relapses and lack of, 291
        treatment team and prescription of, 179. *See also* antipsychotic medication *and specific drugs*
medroxyprogesterone acetate (Depo-Provera), 259
melatonin, 163
Mellaril (thioridazine), 191, 192, 201, 202, 211
Melvill, Charles, 288
melperone, 209
memories, flooding of, 35
memory, problems affecting, 149, 218
Mendel, Werner M., 220, 224, 334
meningioma of the temporal lobe, 116
Menninger, Karl, 338–39
menstrual cycle, 97, 118, 202
Mental Health Association, 321–22
Mental Health Law Project, 25, 268
mental health centers, 9
mental health professions: advocacy and, 328–29
        confidentiality and, 311–12
        deinstitutionalization and, 25
        diagnosis of schizophrenia and, 87
        feelings of blame for schizophrenia and, 282
        licensing of, 329
        neglect of schizophrenia by, 4
        noncompliance and, 265
        rural areas and, 240–41
        training programs for, 4, 221, 324
Mentally Ill Chemical Abuser (MICA) program, 255
mentally ill persons: homeless among, 1–2, 3, 5, 10, 139
        in jails and prisons, 2
        as providers of mental illness services, 293
mental retardation, 106, 266, 316
mesoridazine (Serentil), 191
methadone, 216
Mexican Americans, schizophrenia among, 6
MICA programs, 255
microscopic studies of brain, 145–46, 155
Middle Ages, 18–20

mild schizophrenia, 93
milieu therapy, 167
military service, 22–23
Miller, Leonard, 16
mind: delusions about control over, 56–57
    flooding of thoughts in, 35
minerals, and treatment of schizophrenia, 162
Minor, Dorothy, 265
minority groups, 57
Miró, Joan, 78, 81
mobile clinics, 241
mobile treatment team, 189
Modrow, John, 339
molindone (Moban), 191, 192, 202, 216
money management, 300–301
monoamine oxidase (MAO), 157
monoamine oxidase (MAO) inhibitors, 211, 215
mood disorder, 2
Moorman, Margaret, 307, 334
mortality rates, 137–39
Mosher, Loren R., 339–40
mothers, 305
    causes of schizophrenia related to, 166–69
    psychosis in, after childbirth, 118–19, 162. See also parents
motor vehicles: accidents and, 138
    driving and, 308
movement, changes in, 30, 70–71, 90, 203
Mozham, Jody, 305, 307
multiple sclerosis, 117
Munch, Edvard, 80, 81
Murphy, H. B. M., 284

nadolol, 216
naloxone, 216
naltrexone, 216
NAMI. See National Alliance for the Mentally Ill (NAMI)
Narcotics Anonymous (NA), 256
National Alliance for Research on Schizophrenia and Depression (NARSAD), 173, 209, 325, 350
National Alliance for the Mentally Ill (NAMI), 11, 269, 292, 310, 322, 348
    advocacy and, 307
    family support groups through, 132, 301, 307, 316–17
    listing of resources, 349–51
    research and, 173, 325

state contacts for, 357–61
National Institute of Mental Health (NIMH), 9, 16, 321–22
    Community Mental Health Centers (CMHCs) and, 24
    Epidemiologic Catchment Area (ECA) survey of, 4–5, 6, 7, 9, 14, 270
    research funding from, 172–73, 208–9, 293, 303, 326
National Institutes of Health, 159
National Mental Health Association (NMHA), 231, 322
National Mental Health Consumers' Association, 292, 349
National Stigma Clearinghouse, 324, 350
Navane (thiothixene), 191, 195, 216
"negative" symptoms, 89–90, 129, 136, 193
neologism, 47–48
neurobiological disorders (NBD), 238
neuroleptic drugs, 190. See also antipsychotic drug treatment
neuroleptic malignant syndrome, 204–5
neurological examination, 100–101, 148
neuropsychological tests, 149–50
neurotransmitters, 142, 157–58, 193
niacin, 162
nicotine, 252
Nijinsky, Vaslav, 45, 123
NIMH. See National Institute of Mental Health (NIMH)
noncompliance, 262–69
norepinephrine, 146, 206, 253
Norplant, 259
North, Carol, 334
Notkins, Abner, 159
nurse practitioners, 179, 240
nurses: home visits by, 189
    rural areas and, 240
    training of, 221
    treatment team with, 177, 179
nursing homes, 10, 329
nutrition, 162, 218

obsessive behavior, 129
obsessive-compulsive disorder, 6, 73–74, 238
Oedipus complex, 166
olanzapine, 209
olfactory hallucinations, 62, 99
ondansetron, 209
onset of schizophrenia, 94–96
    age of, 94, 96
    childhood schizophrenia and, 98

onset of schizophrenia, *cont.*
   families and, 94–95
   late-onset schizophrenia, 99
   as outcome predictor, 127, 128
   sex differences in, 96
   suddenness of, 128
Orap (pimozide), 191
orthomolecular psychiatry, 162
Osmond, Humphrey, 162
outcome: antipsychotic drugs and,
      197–98
   predictors of, 126–30
   quality of life measures and, 247–48
   ten years later, 130–34
outpatient commitment, 267–69, 329
outpatient services, 221–22, 249
   ethics of allocation of, 222
   medications and, 267–69
   psychotherapy and counseling
      through, 223

PACT (Program of Assertive Community
      Treatment), 223, 241, 245, 330,
      350, 354–56
pain: blunting of sensation of, 38
   feelings of blame for schizophrenia
      and, 282
   hallucinations of, 63
painting, reflections of schizophrenia in,
      77–81
paranoid delusions, 55, 57, 215, 265
paranoid personality disorder, 92, 93, 99
paranoid psychosis, 88
paranoid schizophrenia, 129, 301
   causes of, 168
   diagnosis of, 89–90
   hallucinations in, 62–63
parents
   childhood schizophrenia and, 239
   death of, 315–17
   feelings of blame held by, 280–82,
      298
   guilt feelings and, 280–81, 282–83.
      See also families
Parkinsonian symptoms, 204, 253
Parkinson's disease, 200
Parlodel (bromocriptine), 200, 216
paroxetine (Paxil), 215
partial hospitalization, 189–90
Pasamanick, Benjamin, 189, 240
Pathways to Promise, 310, 324, 349
patient advocates, 5
Paxil (paroxetine), 215
PCP, 111, 257
peak experiences, 37–38, 66, 309–10

peer counselors, 293
perceptual dysfunction, 31–39, 64, 85
Perceval, John, 49, 74
Permitil (fluphenazine), 191, 192, 195,
      211, 216, 217, 311
perphenazine (Trilafon), 191, 211
personality changes, and schizophrenia,
      275–77
personality disorders, 91
Peschel, Enid, 238
pestiviruses, 160
pets, 237
phenothiazines, 190, 191, 216
physical anomalies, 153–54, 159
physical examination, 100–101
physicians, 260
   board certified or board eligible, 178
   commitment process and, 184
   finding, 176–80
   noncompliance and, 264–66
   rural rehabilitation services and, 240
physician assistants, 179, 240
Picasso, Pablo, 79, 81
pimozide (Orap), 191
pineal gland, 163
Pinel, Philippe, 19, 20
pituitary gland, 162–63
Planned Life Assistance Network
      (PLAN), 316–17, 328
Poe, Edgar Allan, 31, 59
police, 324–25
polydypsia, 162
Porter, Roy, 81
Posey, Thomas, 292, 322
poisoning, hallucinations about, 62–63
"positive" symptoms, 89–90, 135, 193
positron emission tomography (PET),
      103, 146–47
precipitating events, 128–29
predictors of outcome, 126–30
predisposition to schizophrenia, 157
pregnancy:
   antipsychotic medications during,
      213, 260–61
   complications during, 154, 159
   contraception and, 259–60
prescription drug psychosis, 112–15
President's Commission on Mental
      Health, 168, 331
prevalence of schizophrenia, 6–8
   among specific groups, 7–8
   per 1,000 prevalence, 6
   possible decrease in, 14
   in urban areas, 7–8
   world-wide, 12–14

Prichard, J.C., 20
prisons, 2, 10
private psychiatric hospitals, 9, 181
prochlorperazine (Compazine), 191
procyclidine (Kemadrin), 200, 212
product test, 278–79
progestin, 259
Prolixin (fluphenazine), 191, 192, 195,
    211, 216, 217, 266, 268, 311
propranolol, 201, 216
prostate cancer, 138
Protection and Advocacy Law, 330
Prout, C. T., 170
Prozac (fluoxetine), 211, 215
pseudoneurotic schizophrenia, 91–92
psychiatric hospitals
    brief stay in, 240
    number of schizophrenics in, 9–10
    outpatient services provided by,
        221–22, 223, 249
    public awareness of conditions in,
        22–23
    readmissions to, 3–4
psychiatric nurses, 177, 179, 221
psychiatric social workers: deinstitution-
        alization and, 26
    neglect of schizophrenia by, 4
    treatment team with, 177, 179
psychiatric wards in hospitals, 9, 181
psychiatrists: antipsychotic medications
        and, 264, 264, 265
    commitment process and, 184
    deinstitutionalization and, 25
    feelings of blame for schizophrenia
        and, 282
    finding, 176–80
    groups against, 292–93
    lawyers and, 268–69
    neglect of schizophrenia by, 4
    rehabilitation and ongoing need for
        medication and, 221
    selecting a hospital and, 181–82
    suicide risk and, 273
    training of, 4, 221
psychoanalysis, 167, 169, 283, 304, 320
psychological tests, 101
psychologists: deinstitutionalization and,
        25
    neglect of schizophrenia by, 4
    training of, 221
    treatment team with, 177, 179
psychoses passionnelles, 56
psychosis: following childbirth, 118–19,
        162
    other diseases causing, 115–18

    prescription drugs and, 112–15
    street drugs and, 111–12
    suicide and, 272
    trauma and, 119–20
psychotherapy, 132
    drug therapy used with, 224–25
    outpatient psychiatric services with,
        223
    supportive, 223–24
    in treatment of schizophrenia,
        167–69, 223–25
public health nurses, 189, 240
public shelters, 2, 3, 4–5, 10, 228, 309,
        331

quality of life measures, 247–48
quarter-way houses, 228

Rabkin, J. G., 164
race, and schizophrenia, 8
raclopride, 209
Reader's Digest (magazine), 22
readmissions to hospitals, 3–4
receptive aphasia, 41
recovery rates: rule of thirds in, 130–31
    ten-year period, 131–34
    thirty-year period, 134–37
rehabilitation, 220–50
    case managers and, 224
    continuity of care in, 222–25, 240–41
    counseling and, 223–25
    employment and, 231–35
    examples of services in, 241–47
    friendship and, 235–37
    housing options and, 228–31
    income sources and, 225–28
    medical care and, 237–38
    ongoing need for hospitals as part of,
        248–50
    outpatient services for, 221–22
    quality of life measures and, 247–48
    in rural areas, 240–41
    services for children and, 238–40
relapses: families and, 288, 302
    symptoms and signs pointing toward,
        288–89
relationships: continuity of caregivers
        and, 223
    doctor-patient, 264–66
    friendship and, 235–37
    inability to interpret and respond
        appropriately and, 43–44
religious experiences, 309–11
    cults and, 310–11
    hallucinations and, 62

religious experiences, *cont.*
    peak experiences as, 37–38, 66,
        309–10
remoxipride, 209
Renaudin, E., 21
repetitious movements, 70–71, 73–74
research: advocacy for, 325–26
    economic benefits of, 17–19
    funding of, 172–73
resentment, 305
reserpine, 23, 216
respite care, 301–2, 328
response to stimuli: difficulties with, 30,
        40–50
    thought patterns in, 44–48
responsibility, and behavior, 277–80
restlessness, 200–201, 253, 264, 289
rheumatoid arthritis, 138, 163–64
Rice, Dorothy, 16
right or wrong test, 278–79
rights, and treatment, 5, 268–69
Riley, Jocelyn, 334–35
risk: genetic counseling and, 313–15
    suicide and, 271–73
risperidone, 207–8
ritanserin, 209
ritualistic behaviors, 73
Robbins, Michael, 340
role shifts in families, 307
Rollin, Henry R., 28
Rose, Steven, 171
Rosenbaum, M. B., 258
Rosenhan, David L., 87–88
Rothman, David, 21
Rousseau, Henri, 80, 81
Rubin, Theodore I., 340
rural areas, 7–8, 240–41

Sacks, Oliver, 288
safety issues, 308–9
St. Elizabeths Hospital, Washington,
        D.C., 22, 249
savoxepine, 209
schizoaffective disorder, 90–91, 118,
        129, 130, 215
schizoid personality disorder, 93, 99
schizophrenia: attempts to understand,
        77–81
    cost of, 15–19
    dimensions of disaster of, 1–5
    historical overview of, 18–22
    introduction of term, 43, 88
    lack of sympathy for, 28–30
    living and care arrangements for,
        8–12

onset of, 94–96
patients' own accounts of, 30–82
prevalence of, 6–8
stigma of, 8, 233, 235–36, 292,
        322–25
subtypes of, 88–90
schizophrenialike behavior: brief
        episodes of, 110
    diagnosis of schizophrenia and, 87
    other diseases causing, 115–18
schizophrenic character, 92
schizophreniform disorder, 87, 110
schizotypal personality disorder, 91–92,
        93
Schnider, Kurt, 85
Schreber, Daniel P., 75, 166
Scientology, 199, 203, 218, 293, 310
Scottish Rite of Freemasonry, 173
seasonality of births, 154–55, 159
Sechehaye, Marguerite, 64–65
Seidman, L. J., 148
seizures, and antipsychotic drugs, 202
self: altered sense of, 30, 63–65
    repetitive behavior and, 74
self-defense, 309
self-help groups, 236, 292
self-medication, 252, 255
semihospitals, 9–10
Serentil (mesoridazine), 191
seriously emotionally disturbed (SED)
        children, 238
serotonin, 146, 206, 207, 209, 215, 253
sertraline (Zoloft), 215
sex differences in schizophrenia, 96–97,
        99, 137
sexual behavior, 257–62
    antipsychotic drugs and, 201–2, 258,
        264
    consent issues in, 259
    contraception and, 259–60
    delusions and, 56
    hospitalization and, 258
    perceptual alterations of senses and,
        34–35
    risk of AIDS and, 261–62
    sense of self and, 65
sexually transmitted disease, 262
Shakespeare, William, 18–20
shame, feelings of, 280, 283, 305
Sheehan, Susan, 15, 222, 335
sheltered workshops, 233, 327
shelters for homeless persons, 2, 3, 4–5,
        10, 228, 309, 331
Sherrington, C.S., 75

short-term hospitalization, 189
Sibling and Adult Children Network, 307
siblings of schizophrenics, 304–7, 314,
        315, 349
side effects of medication, 198–205, 258,
        264, 263–64
sight: alterations of perception in, 31–34
        hallucinations with, 58–59, 61–62
        inability to interpret and respond in,
        41–42, 44
signs of schizophrenia: behavior seen in,
        30
        relapses and, 288–89
Six-Step programs, 256
Skills Training Modules, 225, 236, 351
sleep patterns, 96, 289
smell, hallucinations of, 62, 99
smoking, 251–54
social activities: clubhouses and,
        236–37, 242, 245, 327, 353–54
        expectations in, 297
        friendship and, 235–37
Social Security Administration, 225–27
Social Security Disability Insurance
        (SSDI), 11, 25, 226, 309, 327
social skills training, 236
social withdrawal behavior, 71–72, 90,
        96, 297
social workers, 260
        deinstitutionalization and, 25
        neglect of schizophrenia by, 4
        training of, 221
        treatment team with, 177, 179
somatization disorder, 30
Sox, Harold, 101
spectrum concept of schizophrenia, 93
speech: flattening of emotions and, 69
        word salad in, 48
Spiegel, John, 320
split personality, 105–6
spouses of schizophrenics, 304–7
standard of proof, in commitment
        process, 185–86
Stanley Foundation, 173, 209
Stanley Foundation Neurovirology
        Laboratory on Schizophrenia
        and Manic-Depressive Disorder,
        173
state departments of mental health,
        327–28
        commitment process and, 187
        deinstitutionalization and, 24
state laws: commitment process and,
        184–86, 269, 328
        confidentiality and, 311–12

conservatorship and guardianship
        and, 267, 316
        deinstitutionalization and, 25
        doctor certification by, 178
        insurance under, 328
        licensing under, 329
state programs: childhood schizophrenia
        and, 239
        examples of good services in, 242–43
        housing and income support with,
        225–26, 228
state psychiatric hospitals, 21, 181
        number of schizophrenics in, 9
        ongoing need for, 248–50
        public awareness of conditions in,
        22–23
        readmissions to, 3
        sexual activity in, 258
Stelazine (trifluoperazine), 191
Stephens, J. H., 131
stigma of schizophrenia, 8, 233, 235–36,
        292, 322–25
stillbirths, 155, 159
stimuli: alterations in perception of,
        31–39
        behavior changes and reactions to, 72
        flooding of, 33–35
        inability to interpret and respond to,
        30, 40–45
Street people, 1–2, 3, 10
stress, 164–65, 291
Strupp, H. H., 168
subclinical schizophrenia, 92
substance abuse: problems with, 254–57
        programs for, 242–43
        violence and, 256, 257, 270–71
subtypes of schizophrenia, 88–90
suicide, 271–73
supervised housing, 11, 228–31
Supplemental Security Income (SSI), 11,
        25, 225–28, 266, 300, 309, 327
supported employment, 234
support groups: family, 301
        self-help, 236, 292
        substance abuse treatment with,
        254–55
supportive psychotherapy, 223–24
Supreme Court, 185, 186, 226
survival guilt, 306
Symmetrel(amantadine), 212
symptoms of schizophrenia: behavior
        seen in, 30
        in childhood schizophrenia, 98
        delusions and hallucinations as,
        50–51

symptoms of schizophrenia, *cont.*
    diagnosis of schizophrenia and,
        84–85, 86–87, 94–96
    drug psychosis and, 112
    early, 94, 112
    effects of antipsychotic drugs on,
        136, 192, 193, 196
    onset of schizophrenia and, 94–96
    as outcome predictor, 129, 134–35
    "positive" and "negative," 89–90,
        129, 135–36, 193
    relapses and, 288–90
    responsibility for control of, 277
    subtypes of schizophrenia and, 88–89
syphilis, 116
Szasz, Thomas, 24, 171, 292, 340–41

Tagamet (cimetidine), 212
Talbott, John, 321
taractan (chlorprothixene), 191
Tarasoff decision, 311
tardive dyskinesia, 203–4, 253
taste, hallucinations of, 62–63
Taylor, Robert, 101
teams: case managers on, 224
    treatment, 177, 179, 189, 222
Tegretol (carabamazepine), 215–16
television, 41–42
temporal lobe, 61, 119, 140–41
temporal lobe epilepsy, 115, 116
Tennant, C. C., 164
Test, Mary Ann, 222
testing, in diagnostic workup, 100–101
Theodore and Vada Stanley Foundation,
        173, 209
thinking disorders: antipsychotic drugs
        and, 193
    diagnosis of schizophrenia and, 99
    drug psychosis with, 111
    onset of schizophrenia and, 95, 96
    as "positive" symptom, 90, 135. *See
        also* thought patterns
thioridazine (Mellaril), 191, 192, 201,
        202, 211
thiothixene (Navane), 191, 195, 216
thioxanthines, 190, 191
Thomas, Lewis, 155
Thorazine (chlorpromazine), 23, 190,
        191, 192, 195, 202
thought disorder, 2, 40
thought insertion, 35–36, 85
thought patterns, 44–50
    ambivalence in, 50
    behavior changes and, 71–72

blocking of thoughts in, 49–50
concreteness in, 45–47
delusions and, 54–55
disconnectedness in, 44–45
flattening of emotions and, 69
flooding in, 35–36
impairment of logic in, 47
loose associations in, 45
neologisms in, 47–48
word salad in, 48
thought withdrawal, 50, 85
Thresholds, 237, 239, 245, 351
thyroid-releasing hormone, 216
Tietze, Trude, 166–67, 341
time, perception of, 34
touch: alterations of perception of, 34
    hallucinations of, 63, 65, 85
training programs: job skills with, 225,
        234
    of mental health professionals, 4,
        221, 324
    self-defense with, 309
    social skills with, 236
tranquilizers, 190. *See also* antipsychotic
        drug treatment
transitional employment, 233–34, 245
trauma, psychosis following, 119–20
trials, and insanity defense, 278–79
treatment, 175–219
    childhood schizophrenia and, 98–99
    cost for, 15–16
    finding a doctor for, 176–80
    historical overview of, 19–22
    for manic-depressive psychosis,
        108–9
    nonphysician staff and, 179–80
    number of people not receiving, 4–5
    psychotherapy and, 167–69
    right of refusal of, 5, 268–69
    vitamins and minerals for, 162
    world-wide, 5. *See also* antipsychotic
        drug treatment
treatment teams, 177, 179, 189, 222
tremor, 200, 253
trifluoperazine (Stelazine), 191
trihexyphenidyl (Artane), 200, 212
Trilafon (perphenazine), 191, 211
Trosse, George, 19
Tuke, Harrington, 20
tumors, brain, 116, 143
Twelve-Step programs, 256

Ulysses contract, 261
Unification Church, 310

urban areas, prevalence of schizophrenia
    in, 7–8
urinalysis, 101

Valium (diazepam), 200, 201, 207, 215
valproic acid, 211, 216
van Gogh, Vincent, 77–81, 105, 123, 124
verapamil, 211, 216
Veterans Administration (VA), 236, 330,
    331
    disability payments from, 228
    hospitals run by, 9, 181, 182, 221,
        301
videotapes, 342–47
violence, 308–9
    committed against individuals with
        schizophrenia, 3
    committed by individuals with schiz-
        ophrenia, 2, 269–70
    substance abuse and, 256, 257,
        270–71
viral enchephalitis, 116
viruses, as causes of schizophrenia,
    158–60, 163
visual stimuli: alterations of perceptions
    of, 31–34
    hallucinations with, 58–59, 61–62
    inability to interpret and respond to,
        41–42, 44
vitamin B12, 218
vitamins, 162
vocational rehabilitation, 228, 233,
    245–46, 327

voices, in hallucinations, 59–60, 86, 289,
    292
Voltaire, 142

Walsh, Maryellen, 335
Ward, Mary Jane, 22
Weakland, John, 169
Wechsler, James, 69, 281, 335
Wechsler, Michael, 69, 281
weight gain, and antipsychotic drugs,
    201
Weinberger, Daniel R., 160
White, M. A., 170
Wilson, Louise, 99, 280, 281
Winerip, Michael, 228
Wing, John, 277, 287, 295, 296
withdrawal behavior, social, 71–72, 90,
    96, 297
withdrawal of thoughts, 50, 85
withdrawal symptoms, and antipsychotic
    drugs, 207
Wolfi, Adolf, 123
Woolis, Rebecca, 335
word salad, 48
workshops, sheltered, 233, 327
workup in schizophrenia diagnosis,
    99–104
World War II, 21
Wyatt, Richard, 16, 198, 203

Yolken, Robert, 160

Zoloft (sertraline), 215